A Grand Guy

A Grand Guy
The Art and Life of Terry Southern

Lee Hill

HarperCollins*Publishers*

**For
Esther and Claire Hill
and
Patty Johnson**

HarperCollins books may be purchased for educational, business, or sales promotional use. For information please write: Special Markets Department, HarperCollins Publishers Inc., 10 East 53rd Street, New York, NY 10022.

FIRST EDITION

Designed by Nancy B. Field

Library of Congress Cataloging-in-Publication Data

Hill, Lee
    A grand guy : the art and life of Terry Southern / Lee Hill. —1st ed.
      p. cm.
    ISBN 0-380-97786-9
    Includes bibliographical references and index.
    1. Southern, Terry. 2. Novelists, American—20th century—Biography. 3. Humorists, American—20th century—Biography. 4. Screenwriters—United States—Biography. 5. Satire, American—History and criticism. I. Title.
PS3569.O8 Z69 2001
813'.54—dc21
    [B]   00-063167

01 02 03 04 ❖/xxx 10 9 8 7 6 5 4 3 2 1

Contents

There are many people who appreciate the expression of sincere emotion in verse, and there is a smaller number of people who can appreciate technical excellence. But very few know when there is expression of *significant* emotion, emotion which has its life in the poem and not in the history of the poet. The emotion of art is impersonal. And the poet cannot reach this impersonality without surrendering himself wholly to the work to be done. And he is not likely to know what is to be done unless he lives in what is not merely the present, but the present moment of the past, unless he is conscious, not of what is dead, but of what is already living.

—T. S. Eliot, "Tradition and the Individual Talent"

As writers, you and I come from different worlds. You—as I understand it, correct me if I am wrong—are the pure writer who eschews any relationship between successful writing and commercial success.

I think you are trying to draw a distinction between an artist and a professional. That is the difference between a party girl and a hooker. A party girl is somebody who does it for fun, but a hooker is somebody who does it for money. I'm just talking about the distinction this way so we can limit it to this dichotomy. I'm a party girl. No, I would prefer it, and that's on record now, if you would say "party person."

—Terry Southern in an exchange with Victor Bockris, *Interview*

Prologue

For Love, Art, and a Lot of Money

Memory flash, Los Angeles, California, July 1964. Place-in-the-sun time. A convertible moves smoothly down Sunset Boulevard. The car radio seems to play Dionne Warwick's "Walk on By" and the Beach Boys' "I Get Around" constantly. The buoyant music is silenced occasionally by the latest news of the Beatles' Visigoth-like sweep through America's stadiums. Of course it's not all fun and frolic. News bulletins also mention LBJ's war on poverty and "aid" to Vietnam. Down in Georgia, a certain Lester Maddox is using ax handles to threaten black customers who enter his restaurant. However, the music and the news are just background to the two passengers in the car.

The driver, a tall urbane man with sunglasses dark as night, occasionally glances to the side. His crisp white shirt reflects the glare of the sun. In the passenger seat, Steve Schapiro, *Life* magazine photographer, meticulously frames and shoots picture after picture.

The car drives past a billboard that reads METRO-GOLDWYN-MAYER IN ASSOCIATION WITH FILMWAYS PRESENT THE LOVED ONE . . . FOR THOSE WHO *REALLY* CARE! The driver allows himself a secret smile at these words. And why not? He is, after all, adapting Evelyn Waugh's classic novel along with the noted English scribe Christopher Isherwood.

The latest subject of the Luce empire's scrutiny is a forty-year-old Texas-born writer named Terry Southern. After serving his country in

World War II, he received an English degree at Northwestern University and studied philosophy at the Sorbonne. His short stories and articles have appeared in *Harper's Bazaar,* the *Paris Review,* and *Esquire.* This courtly and reserved man of letters is also the author of *Candy,* a "dirty book" with precise comic timing. Funny, sure, but still dirty enough to get banned in *Paris, France!* It was written with a pal, Mason Hoffenberg, who is some kind of junkie poet. *Newsweek* describes their collaboration as a "Greek tragedy rewritten by Nathanael West and S.J. Perelman."

Southern is the author of two other books, *Flash and Filigree* and *The Magic Christian,* which are downright weird. *Flash* is a detective story, but the villain, a car-crazy dermatologist, never gets caught. In *The Magic Christian,* a fabulously wealthy businessman with untold millions at his disposal stages elaborate pranks to discover if it is indeed true that "every man has his price."

In its efforts to provide its readers, Mr. and Mrs. Front Porch, a full and balanced portrait of an up-and-coming author and commentator on morals, manners, and society, *Life* must ask some tough and probing questions. Is Mr. Southern a beatnik like Jack Kerouac or Allen Ginsberg? Er . . . well, he doesn't look like one. More the tall, dark silent type, especially with the monstro shades. Is he a pseudointellectual writing naughty books for the chattering classes? Hmmm. Tough call. He seems quite serious about writing. He always carries a binder or satchel full of yellow lined paper and pens. Maybe he is a communist? He worked on the script for the hit movie *Dr. Strangelove,* which put an odd spin on America's nuclear defense policy. It satirically suggested that a lone mad general could override the president's fail-safe protocol to plunge the world into all-out thermonuclear combat. Well, hey, nobody wants that. *Dr. Strangelove* got people to talk about the Cold War in a relaxed and open way, but without the gloomy last-night-on-earth confessionals à la Fred Astaire and Ava Gardner in *On the Beach.* In fact, *Dr. Strangelove* is very funny—a unique blend of slapstick and agitprop. Who would have thought the end of the world could be so exhilarating?

These are contradictions Time-Life's phalanx of editors will have to sort out as they pore over ace reporter Jane Howard's copy and Schapiro's elegantly composed snaps. This Southern guy doesn't add up. He has an attractive young wife and a cute three-year-old boy. *Life* has already taken shots of Southern and family on the bucolic grounds of his farm in Connecticut. There was even a family dog, a German shepherd. But what about the way Southern talks—just *what* part of Texas is he from?

It's a slow, seductive lilt that is the oral equivalent of mercury. There are moments when his voice eerily recalls Peter Sellers as Clare Quilty in *Lolita.* The accent is displaced—adrift between America and England. At other times, the voice evokes the measured diction of an Oxford don. Then it assumes a mock-heroic quality, especially in response to an ambiguous question. "How do I like to be addressed?" Southern might bark, followed by a sudden shift into country bumpkin mode, "Why you can call me anything you want! Just don't call me late for chow! Ho ho."

Hot off *Dr. Strangelove,* Southern is out in La-La Land to work on *The Loved One,* an irreverent adaptation of Waugh's caustic satire of Hollywood and the Denial of Death as epitomized by gaudy cemeteries like Forest Lawn. As Southern told a reporter just the other day, "I'm treating the script as I like to think Waugh would do it if he were writing today. It's an attack on smugness and the fantastic illusions of our way of life."

Unlike F. Scott Fitzgerald, Southern doesn't seem to be holding his nose as he performs what he calls "tightening and brightening." Then again, *The Loved One* is hardly typical boy-meets-girl silver screen fare. The director, Tony Richardson, is a young Brit who staged John Osborne's *Look Back in Anger* at the Royal Court Theatre. He made last year's Best Picture, *Tom Jones,* a delightful Technicolor romp, complete with New Wave jump cuts and aerial photography. *The Loved One* promises to be of more interest to the readers of *Cahiers du Cinéma* than to the lunch crowd at the Brown Derby.

Southern and Schapiro drive out to the Watts Tower—a giant piece of primitive sculpture constructed of stray bits of glass, metal, plaster, and junk by a barely literate migrant worker. They are met by Anjanette Comer, the lead actress in *The Loved One.* Schapiro takes some pictures of the two standing beneath the huge metal latticework. Southern is, to put it mildly, a bit of a flirt, but women do not seem to mind his gentle teasing and fondness for nicknames. There are rumors that he is working his way through the available female cast and crew of *The Loved One* like the proverbial wolf among a flock of sheep.

As the photo session wraps, Southern drops by the Beverly Hills Hotel, where Richardson, whom Southern likes to call "Tip-Top Tony," has arranged for dailies to be screened. It's like a cocktail party for whoever wants to unwind after a day's shooting. Feeling a little mischievous, Southern places a call to a friend in New York, Barney Rosset, editor of the *Evergreen Review* and founder of Grove Press—a kingmaker in the world of Manhattan "Quality Lit" and all-around grand guy.

Across the country, Rosset picks up the phone and hears Southern: "You'll never guess where I am. I'm sitting at the pool at the Beverly Hills Hotel with all these beautiful women."

Although surrounded by stacks of proofs, copy, sales figures, etc., Rosset indulges Southern. "Well, congratulations, Terry. Good for you. Give me a ticket, I'll come and join you."

As Southern goes into a rhapsody about bikini-clad nifties, poolside cocktails, the sunshine, and cool blue water, Rosset feels instantly transported to his friend's side. When Rosset puts the phone down, he feels glad for Terry. They had even touched on a bit of business. Could Terry arrange for Grove to publish the screenplay of *The Loved One* when it was finished? Southern said he would do what he could. Rosset felt more than a casual connection with the film. He had heard good things about it from his cousin Haskell Wexler, who was not only its cinematographer but also a coproducer. Perhaps Hollywood was changing. Maybe there was room for the kind of personal, expressive work the Europeans had been doing for decades.

Southern's wife, Carol, and his son, Nile, had just returned to Connecticut after spending the winter and spring in L.A. with him. He had seen them a few weeks ago when he had dropped in to New York for a radio show with his friends the writers Elaine Dundy and Jack Gelber to discuss the contemporary novel. The host asked Southern to tell listeners what it was like to be a success.

"Well, I'll say this. That it's grand and I am looking forward to some sort of corruption, Nathanael West–type wreck in an auto . . . a really fast automobile like a Mercedes 300 is what I am hoping for. . . . I figure if I do this picture [*The Loved One*] and one more."

Working the film scene was a lot like being behind the wheel of a fast car. You had to maintain a Zen-like control of the car. You couldn't start getting scared when the turns got too sharp. You couldn't get too focused on any one thing. You had to go with the flow.

The next day, Southern was out early on the set. He had written a sequence that was not in the novel, but that he felt was true to Waugh's intentions. The owner of the Whispering Glades cemetery hooks up with the Pentagon and NASA. He plans to convert Whispering Glades into a retirement home. The dead will be lovingly disinterred and rocketed into space.

Richardson and crew have spared no expense in re-creating the film's penultimate scene. A crowd of extras dressed as government officials, Army officers, dignitaries, and various captains of the military-industrial complex stand waiting for the launch of the first rocket with its payload—a coffin fresh from Whispering Glades. Richardson calls for silence on the set then cues camera and sound. The scene commences. Jonathan Winters bellows the countdown from a public address system: "10 . . . 9 . . . 8 . . . 7 . . . 6 . . . 5 . . . 4 . . . 3 . . . 2 . . . 1 . . . Resurrection Now!"

Richardson yells cut as the set fills with colored dry ice representing the rocket's takeoff. Southern had liked writing the scene, but seeing Richardson turn his words into reality for a few unforgettable minutes is something indescribable. It will look fabulous on the big screen and certainly something special to tell the kid when he gets back home.

1

Youngblood

Magical. Stifling.

These were the two extremes of Terry Southern's attitude toward Texas. In his final novel, *Texas Summer,* Southern described the Lone Star State as a place where contradiction reigned. "The pond was like an oasis in a desert, a Shangri-la, with an atmosphere, almost a climate, separate from its immediate surroundings. A shimmering oval of crystalline blue, fringed with weeping willows interwoven in a soft-focus double ring because of their reflection in the water, the pond resembled an exotic blue mirror, its frame intricately filigreed. But there was something else—something curiously, classically, of Texas about the scene—a quality of strange hidden contrasts, something of abrupt mystery . . . a secret celebration of nature at its most darkly persuasive: the diamondback rattler coiled in a field of bluebonnets, the scorpion beneath the yellow rose."

Southern struggled for thirty years to complete *Texas Summer.* He strived to resolve his extreme ambivalence toward his birthplace. The novel, originally called *Youngblood* (a friendly nod to the hit by his songwriting pals Jerry Leiber and Mike Stoller), reworked short stories that appeared in the 1967 anthology, *Red Dirt Marijuana and Other Tastes.* New material was slowly woven around these stories to fulfill a long-unrealized dream to write one last "hard-hitting novel." The final result, which Southern seems to have squeezed out of himself like blood from the proverbial stone, added up to just over two hundred published pages.

If Southern could never quite leave Texas in his imagination, he made damn sure actual homecomings were kept to a minimum. While Texas played a significant part in his writing, Southern had little desire to actually set foot in the state if he could help it. This love/hate relationship was hidden behind a thick mask of irony and coy reminiscence. Depending on his mood and the listener, he would either describe his youth in Alvarado and Texas as suffocating and provincial, or launch into a colorful anecdote. In 1992, when pressed by a Dallas journalist, Robert Wilonsky, Southern replied, "I love Texas . . . it's just by some unfortunate coincidence I haven't been able to get back over the years, I just haven't had the occasion."

"Growing up in Texas is probably a lot like growing up in Alberta or Saskatchewan—ideal—from a certain Huck Finn point of view. Lots of hunting and fishing, lots of baseball and football, and only a handful of grown-ups. It was also something of a cultural desert," he told me in our first interview in 1990. Variations were repeated to others over the years.

Between 1946 and 1993, Southern went back to Texas only once. In 1972, he joined the Rolling Stones on a blur of tour dates including a concert in Dallas. The tour, as immortalized in Robert Frank's notorious documentary, *Cocksucker Blues,* was largely a semiorganized bacchanal of booze and drugs. Sightseeing was not high on the agenda for any of the participants. Then, in late February 1993, an older and subdued Southern made a final visit to Dallas and Alvarado. Josh Alan Friedman, a writer and musician (and son of fellow satirist Bruce Jay Friedman), organized a reading and salute to Southern at the Dallas Museum of Art. The next day, Friedman drove Southern and Gail Gerber, his companion since 1964, to Alvarado to see if the two-story Victorian-style bungalow in which Terry had spent the first few years of his life was still standing.

"It was like *The Last Picture Show,*" recalls Gerber. "I thought his house was going to be like a mall, but when we got there it was as if time had stood still. The house was boarded up. There was just this little town square and I have pictures of Terry in what used to be the movie theater. It was moving and eerie. We drove around this little tiny village and there was a black guy playing with his kid on the other side of the tracks. There was a burial ground out back and Terry spent ages just standing there with his cane looking sort of dazed. Then he would walk ten or fifteen steps and stop, not looking at any particular grave or headstone, but just sort of standing there in some sort of daze or maybe he was collecting vibes. Who knew what he was doing! He would potter off to another portion and then he would stand there for a while. Then he got back in the car."

The writer's apparent stoicism concealed a level of pain and regret about his early years that remained an enigma to those who knew and loved him.

"I think that in order to understand Terry, you must remember he's from Texas," Carol Southern, his wife from 1956 through 1968, said. "It is the key to everything, because Texas is a strange place. I am not being pejorative, but Terry is his own person totally. He's made mistakes. He's had brilliant successes. Whatever happens to Terry, he is totally obdurate. Nobody can tell him what to do, or advise and influence him. I think this has its roots in Texas. It's a country of characters. I think the other thing he grew up with in Texas is this courtly graciousness which he has always had. A courtliness which also keeps people away."

Situated at the junction of U.S. Highways 61 and 81, Alvarado is the oldest town in Johnson County, Texas, which in spite of its proximity to Dallas has never quite managed to exceed a population of around 2,400. The town's humble origins can be traced to the winter of 1849, when a settler, William Balch, staked out a claim near an old Indian trail. By the summer of 1854, there were 100 families in the area. The focus of the town became the two-story Masonic lodge where an elementary school conducted classes. By the mid-twenties, Alvarado had an estimated 1,200 residents and more than fifty businesses. Alvarado actually grew during the Depression, helped in part by its proximity to the town of Cleburne and the urban sprawl of Dallas–Fort Worth. Farmers living in the area supported themselves on crops of cotton, wheat, corn, barley, rye, grain, fruits, and vegetables. The reddish soil could yield considerable bounty to those who worked hard.

Southern's parents were both Alvarado natives. His father, Terrence Marion Southern, born in 1894, could trace his lineage to the state's legendary founding father, Sam Houston. There was also some Cherokee blood in his family. Terrence's father was a well-regarded general practitioner. Terrence was known locally as a promising athlete who fantasized about a baseball career before enrolling in pharmacy college. Upon graduation, he returned to Alvarado and married Helen Simonds, born in 1899, the child of Irish settlers in the area. For the first few years of their marriage, they enjoyed a relatively comfortable living thanks to Terrence's role as the town's druggist. They also ran a small farm. In addition to doing the housework, Helen designed and made dresses for other women in Alvarado. A few surviving photos taken in the forties show a vibrant, good-looking, and seemingly happy couple.

Not long after their marriage, their only child, Terry Southern, was born on May 1, 1924. The birth wasn't officially recorded until the next day, creating confusion in various biographical references for the rest of Southern's life. No middle name appeared on the birth certificate.

For the first eight years of Terry's life, he was a small-town boy. The Huck Finn quality of his childhood was enhanced in no small part by there being very little for a child to do in Alvarado except make up games, help out with chores, read the funny papers, listen to the radio, and see the occasional movie. However, Terry started hunting with a small slingshot, and fishing around the age of eight. A photo of Southern from this period shows a child with thick dark brown hair sitting on a toy wagon holding a small puppy. His expression is one of happiness and delight; pure joy unmediated by the kind of irony and distance he would later become famous for.

For the first years following the crash of 1929, Terry's father's status as the town druggist provided some shelter from the full impact of a country suddenly knocked out by economic disaster. The Great Depression devastated many of the small towns and villages of West Texas. It was a gloomy time of foreclosures, dust storms, and welfare lines. Those who were lucky enough to earn enough money to support their families tried not to make a big song and dance about it.

By 1933, there were more than 15,000 people on the Dallas welfare rolls. Finding it difficult to run both a farm and a small business, the Southerns moved to the Oak Cliff area of Dallas; a protosuburb that emerged after the completion of the Dallas, Cleburne and Rio Grande railway in the early 1880s. Two entrepreneurs, Thomas Marasalis and John S. Armstrong, bought several hundred acres including the community of Hord's Ridge in 1887 and developed the area into an elite residential community.

In Oak Cliff, Southern's father worked hard to sustain an appearance of upward mobility. Like many young men of promise in the twenties, he took no small amount of strength and solace from drinking. When Southern was a small child, the drinking seemed amusing. His dad had a reputation as a jokester who liked to tie one on. He is alleged to have almost gotten shot by a neighbor sneaking back into his home after a night on the town. Southern would often relate the story of his father taking the Monkey Man from the state carnival on a drinking binge. He even refashioned this incident as a teenage prank in *Texas Summer*.

"His father was basically an alcoholic," Gerber says. "The business wasn't going well because it was the Depression and that was more of an excuse to get drunk."

In the thirties, Oak Cliff may have looked like a tranquil suburb, but the country was never very far away. On frequent visits to his grandfather's farm, Terry was encouraged to take an interest in livestock. His pets included various dogs and cats, horses, cows, geese, and chickens on the farm. Some of the more exotic pets included an armadillo and a tarantula. While there were always lots of chores on the farm, the simplicity and beauty of country life never left Southern.

During these visits his father showed Terry how to hunt. Learning how to use a gun responsibly was an essential rite of passage for a boy in Texas. Accompanying his father into the woodlands on the outskirts of Dallas, young Southern carried a .22. Deer was a popular form of game. The countless hunting trips inspired a favorite Southern anecdote that sounds so quintessentially Texan it would be heartbreaking if it weren't true.

After a deer was shot, the hunters rushed over to where the animal fell. According to Southern, as blood pumped out of the dying beast, one of the party would put a cup next to the wound to catch the flow. As the cup was passed around, one of the good ole boys would inevitably quip, "A man can get right drunk on hot deer blood."

As Terry entered his teens, his father's drinking and its effect on home life became less tolerable. On the few occasions when he discussed his family background with Gail, he would talk about his father's Saturday-night binges.

"He did tell me many times the game the father used to play. He'd demand the keys to the Cadillac and he would take off and go on a bender and his mother would worry. At one point, when Terry got old enough to figure out that this was a game, the mother would hide the keys and the father would say, 'Where are the keys?' One day, Terry had enough of the game and gave his dad the keys and said, 'Here, go.' I don't know if there was a confrontation, but it was sort of like, 'Take the Cadillac and go.'"

In spite of their mutual love and affection (Terry loved his father's stories), alcoholism would become the primary legacy that Terrence passed on to his son. But Terry's love of a good drink didn't start to take its toll until the late sixties, when money problems began to erode his confidence and good humor. Unlike his father, drinking tended to make Southern more relaxed and gregarious allowing his inner grand guy to emerge. "He felt he couldn't be the raconteur that he wanted to be unless he had a few drinks," says Gerber.

If lack of money and his father's drinking cast a pall over his childhood, on the surface, Southern was no worse for it. The move to Oak Cliff was good for his education. His third-grade report card from Winnetka Primary School shows he achieved regular As and Bs in literature and math. He seemed to mix with other children well and made friends easily. Yet Southern would remain at a slight remove from his classmates. An innate sense of life as one great rollicking narrative allowed him to see certain people and things in bold relief. School chums were turned into characters like "Big Lawrence" or "Big Herb," whose spontaneity and lack of self-consciousness were attractive to Southern.

The growing impulse to reinvent and reimagine the world around him was enhanced by Southern's quiet love of reading. His mother introduced him to Edgar Allan Poe by giving him a collection of his stories. Poe's *The Narrative of Arthur Gordon Pym,* according to Southern, "was an extraordinary turn-on for a young Western lout. Nine years old, and I was already hooked on weirdo lit. But in the best possible way, because if pot leads to cocaine, E. A. Poe surely leads to Baudelaire, Rimbaud, Lautréamont, Joyce, Kafka, Céline, Faulkner, Nathanael West, Sartre, et cetera, et cetera, ad gloriam."

In interviews, Southern recounted the story of rewriting Poe to amuse his school friends. In Poe's novel a sea voyage goes disastrously wrong, turning the surviving shipmates into cannibals. A casual reader might suggest it was difficult to push such an astonishing tale of desperation and horror any further, but young Southern was undeterred. He labored not only to re-create, but *surpass* the emotional impact of the story by writing his own version substituting characters' names with those of school friends. In one such Southern "rewrite," an unpopular teacher, one Mrs. Dinsmore, was eaten alive. He took it to school and read the story to several of his classmates. They were somewhat aghast at the tall tale and wondered aloud if their shy friend was a little loco.

Along with Poe, Southern subjected other writers including Nathaniel Hawthorne to the rewrite approach: "They never seemed to me to go quite far enough, you know, there was something a little stuffy about them, I guess they were just too subtle. I made them get really going."

As Southern entered Dallas's Sunset High School, he discovered another source of inspiration: Tijuana Bibles, bootleg versions of established comic strips with a pornographic übertext. These X-rated versions of *Blondie* and *Flash Gordon* were passed around in the schoolyard. This trash lit reinforced the feverish imaginings of a red-blooded Texas youth and led Southern to seek out other sources of stimulation.

"For a while, convinced there was more than met the eye, I tried to 'read between the lines' in the famous Nancy Drew books, search for some deep secret insinuation of erotica so powerful and pervasive as to account for the extraordinary popularity of these books, but alas, was able to garner no mileage ('JO' [jack off] wise) from this innocuous, and seemingly endless series," Southern recalled in the seventies.

For a reasonably intelligent and healthy teenager of normal urges and interests, unraveling the mysteries of womanhood went hand in hand with learning how to drive. The rituals of dating included taking one's partner to a chaperoned dance and then a ride in the country. If the weather was warm and the night sky clear, there would be a brief pit stop to admire the stars. Depending on when curfew loomed, the next challenge was seeing how far one could make out.

"The ultimate achievement—aside, of course, from puss itself—was to get 'wet-finger,' also referred to (by the most knowledgeable) as 'getting clit,'" Southern recalled. "It was almost axiomatic that, under 'normal' circumstances, to 'get wet-finger' meant that a girl's defenses would crumble as she was swept away on a tide of sheer physical excitement—and vaginal penetration would be unresisted and imminent."

This template for sexual conquest would fix itself in Southern's imagination and replay itself in his first novel, *Flash and Filigree*. The novel's heroine, nurse Babs Minter, succumbs to the persistent attentions of pharmacy student Ralph Edwards in the backseat of a car as *Wuthering Heights* plays on the drive-in screen. Edwards achieves his conquest by a series of deliberate and progressive maneuvers no doubt "researched" by the budding author while in his teens.

These and other rites of passage for many white Southerners were to a large extent achieved by guerrilla forays into the black subculture. In Dallas, the state's institutionalized racism created a countereconomy located in the "Central Tracks area."

Central Tracks near Deep Ellum (named after downtown Elm Street) was for most whites a no-man's-land where the city's railway tracks met. The area was settled by freed slaves after the Civil War. A cotton gin factory built in 1884 drew a pool of black labor that was further expanded by the arrival of a regional assembly plant for Model Ts in 1913. The Grand Temple of the Black Knights became the home for the offices of black doctors, dentists, and lawyers. An auditorium on the top floor was used for dances, meetings, and parties. A weekly black-owned newspaper, the *Dallas Express,* was also edited and published in the Grand Temple.

By the mid-twenties, Deep Ellum was a hub of retail and entertainment for blacks in Dallas. There were more than a dozen nightclubs, cafés, and domino parlors. The domino parlors were also used for backroom crap games. Blues legends like Blind Lemon Jefferson, Leadbelly, and Lightnin' Hopkins played regularly in the area.

Central Tracks became as important as Poe and other "weirdo lit" in expanding Southern's teen consciousness. Many young whites traveled to the area for the piquant barbecue and ribs, to buy 78s, check out clubs like the Blue Room where local acts such as Joe Liggins and the Honeydrippers, Lucky Millinder, and Andy Kirk and his Clouds of Joy played. It was in one of the various whorehouses in the area that Southern lost his virginity, a rite of passage shared by many of his buddies at Sunset High.

Yet Southern was not just another good old boy sowing his wild oats. He sensed that the blacks, in spite of their oppressed status and lack of opportunity, possessed a richer sense of cultural identity than the whites. In the title story of his 1967 anthology, *Red Dirt Marijuana and Other Tastes,* Southern wrote movingly of a white boy's friendship with a black farmhand called CK. Southern said CK was a composite of blacks he met as a boy and teenager. There was a farmhand at his uncle's cotton farm in Alvarado who gave Southern his first toke of a hand-rolled joint when he was around ten. Southern also recalled another CK figure who worked in a barbershop in Dallas: "This extraordinary black guy who looked like Sidney Poitier was a shoe shiner there, but he was much more than that. He was a philosopher, very well read, and he always had interesting books hanging out of his pocket."

African Americans in West Texas were second-class citizens as far as most whites were concerned. At best, they were treated as a fit and able but not very intelligent servant class. At worst, they were persecuted by the Ku Klux Klan. The Klan's reputation in Texas among middle-class whites rose and fell in direct relation to the state's economic health and shifting attitudes toward the two established parties. To many whites, it wasn't the Klan's racial politics that was the attraction, but its promises to reform local party politics, enforce Prohibition, and champion traditional morality. Klan membership across the United States reached a peak of two million members in the twenties. Infighting, a general tendency toward demagoguery, and the less than stellar IQ level of many hard-core Klan members kept the party on the extreme fringe of American politics. However, while forward-thinking white middle-class Texans disapproved of the Klan, they shared the same belief that segregation was an essential part of keeping the peace and maintaining their "special relationship with coloreds." Many local public officials and politicians in the Dallas–Fort Worth and Wichita Falls area had more than casual connections with the Klan.

Racism and the visible economic hardships of the Depression combined with his father's drinking and his mother's acquiescence were unpleasant facts of life for Southern. Culture in Dallas either meant the nouveau riche pretensions of the oil rich or the world of Sears, Roebuck, state carnivals, and evangelists on the radio. Dallas was a city where even the most prosperous and well-educated citizen was proud to be a redneck.

As a well-intentioned, thoughtful, and empathetic teenager, Southern discovered that simply being aware of prejudice was merely one tiny, perhaps insignificant step toward conquering it. The daily bus ride to and from high school was framed within that prejudice.

One day Southern got on a crowded bus coming from downtown Dallas to Oak Cliff. He could see a few empty seats at the back, but they were marked FOR COLORED. Since he was tired, Southern strode down the aisle and sat in the nearest empty seat next to a black man.

"He got very embarrassed and I said, 'No it's cool,'" said Southern, "I was that presumptuous that I thought I was the one who could control [the situation]. . . . The bus driver stopped the bus and came back and said he wasn't going on until I got up. So I said, 'Well, I'm not getting up.' So the black guy got up, so then I was really in an embarrassing situation . . . of course, I had to get up. But that sort of thing would happen early on. . . . Out of that grows an awareness of the absurdity and irrationality of [racism]."

In responding to the stifling climate of the times, Southern was generally a go-along-to-get-along kind of guy. At Sunset High, he was a popular, above-average student. He belonged to the ROTC, Stamp Club, and Biology Club. He participated in intramural sports such as football and baseball. He was also a keen amateur boxer. His bookishness did not prevent him from making a wide range of friends. They included Bill Ord (who later started the chain of Jiffy liquor stores in the Texas area), Robert Campbell, Ruck Hinson, and Louis Gillmour. It was Gillmour who introduced Southern to a concoction of grapefruit and vodka "to try to get girls drunk without them knowing it, and then slip them some Spanish fly."

After his junior year in high school, Southern hitchhiked to Los Angeles and then traveled in the opposite direction to Chicago. It was the first in a series of journeys that would take him farther from the "Texas über alles" mind-set of friends and family and closer to the cosmopolitan centers of literature, film, and art in New York, Paris, and London. Little is known of how he spent his time on the road that distant summer. However, it seems likely that the sixteen-year-old was impressed by the sheer size of Los Angeles and Chicago compared to Dallas and Alvarado. It made him "see things besides sagebrush."

Another rite of passage far less joyous than the junior year road trip: According to Carol Southern, at some point in his late teens, Terry apparently got into a fight that led to his rival's accidental death.

"It was in a bar with a marble counter. Terry slugged this guy, who fell and hit his head on the counter. The impact killed him. The parents were apparently very understanding and Terry was not blamed or charged. Terry told me so few things about his childhood and growing up that this stuck in my mind."

Other than Carol, there are no sources to verify whether this terrible accident occurred. Even in rough-and-tumble Dallas, it seems unlikely that a brawl leading to the death of another teenager would be taken lightly. Gail Gerber says the incident did not occur. Still, even taking Southern's talent for exaggeration into account, it doesn't seem to be something he would make up. Most of Southern's anecdotes were designed to provoke laughter. This story provokes only sadness. Whatever actually happened, Southern experienced a degree of violence that made him shy away from confrontation—verbal and physical—for the rest of his life.

Southern's graduation from Sunset High in June 1941 was marked by tragedy, when A.B., the brother of Bill Ord, one of Terry's best friends, was killed in a hunting accident. Southern was one of the pallbearers at the funeral. The death of A.B. reminded Southern of when he had almost drowned in a culvert used as a swimming hole a few years earlier.

In the fall, Southern briefly attended North Texas Agricultural College, but the narrow curriculum bored him. In September 1942, he transferred to Southern Methodist University in Dallas and enrolled in the premed stream. Despite its connections to the Methodist Church, SMU was an independent, nonsectarian campus that had opened on September 22, 1915, with 706 students. SMU grew steadily through the twenties and thirties and quickly built up a reputable faculty and curriculum.

One of Southern's instructors was Julien Lon Tinkle, a popular young professor of English who became one of the state's most celebrated teachers. Tinkle had graduated with a bachelor's degree from SMU in 1927 followed by a master's in 1932. He then went on to postgraduate work at the Sorbonne and Columbia University. Tinkle's wanderings beyond the Lone Star State made the Dallas native homesick. He decided to return and help build up SMU's academic reputation. From 1942 until his death in 1980 Tinkle was, in addition to his duties at SMU, the book editor and critic for the *Dallas Morning News*. He would write and edit several books, including *Thirteen Days of Glory: The Siege of the Alamo*, *The Cowboy Reader*, *The Story of Oklahoma*, and *Nobel: An Anthology of French Nobel Prize Winners*. Tinkle held memberships in the Philosophical Society of Texas and the Texas Institute of Letters. In 1960 Tinkle, as the chief book reviewer for the *Dallas Morning News*, would give a glowing review to *The Magic Christian* (perhaps thinking, without envy, of a path he himself might have taken).

Tinkle's career demonstrated to Southern that one could leave Texas. He found the professor friendly, enthusiastic, intelligent, and sympathetic. Tinkle wore his learning and cosmopolitanism lightly. It was an attitude Southern would adopt himself decades later when he taught screenwriting.

Apart from Tinkle's encouragement, premed at SMU left Southern cold: "It was very inhuman and abstract—not the friendly country doctor kind of thing. It was just chemistry and biology, without girls."

Underscoring his dissatisfaction with SMU and Dallas was Terry's dream of becoming a great writer. Throughout his teens, reading continued to grow into a strong, quiet passion. Graduating from pulp magazines like *Argosy* and *Black Mask*, Southern became enamored of the names appearing in such slicks as *Collier's*, *Esquire*, and the *Saturday Evening Post*. Novelists were the rock stars of Southern's generation. James T. Farrell, John Steinbeck, F. Scott Fitzgerald, and, number one with a bullet, Ernest Hemingway topped the charts of the young thinking-person's imagination. These writers had thrown themselves into the events of their time—war, Europe, the dust bowl, sports, high society. They turned raw experience into consciousness-shifting novels that captured and commented on the American century. Their literary success opened other doors—politics, journalism, Hollywood, globe-trotting, and the promise of fantastic sex. Being a writer was the way to escape routine, transcend family expectations, and achieve fame and wealth through one's artistry and talent. Southern, with his impulse toward reimagining his life in mythic terms, found few other occupations that suited his quietly curious temperament.

Dreams of literary glory took a distinct second place as the shock of Pearl Harbor pushed the U.S. into World War II and kick-started recruitment. Prior to 1941 isolationism and pacifism were de rigueur, but now it was America's duty to help Europe and Asia fight the fascist tyranny of Germany, Italy, and Japan. Able-bodied young men were encouraged to enlist. Southern had continued his ROTC involvement at SMU (which consisted primarily of marching drills) and was entitled to a deferment if he wished to continue his studies. However, he was deeply bored at college. In addition to patriotism and civic duty, he was driven to enlist by a yearning for the kind of life-experience war could give him.

On March 25, 1943, Southern showed up at the induction center in Dallas and enlisted in the Army. His mother gave him an inscribed Bible as a parting gift and good-luck charm. He commenced active service on April 1. Over the next two and a half years, he served in England and continental Europe with the 435th Quartermaster Platoon. Stationed in Reading, a town thirty minutes west of London, he received training as a demolitions technician.

His war experiences shaped his repulsion by and fascination with individual and societal violence, but unlike many of his contemporaries, Southern remained frustratingly tight-lipped about the war. "I want to save it for my fiction," he told me in 1993. Sadly Southern never wrote a book about World War II. Nor can any fragments of war-related fiction be found in his papers. Perhaps Southern's deep admiration for Joseph Heller's *Catch-22* and Kurt Vonnegut's *Slaughterhouse-Five* held him back. Instead *Dr. Strangelove* became Southern's antiwar "novel."

When pressed to talk about his years in the Army, Southern would reply almost like the nostalgic hero of Neil Simon's play *Biloxi Blues*. "The main effect of the war on me was the opportunity to travel. There were some tedious times and some scary times, but all the negative stuff was outweighed by the emancipating experience of seeing the world."

Most of his service was spent in Reading, with generous amounts of leave allowing him to visit London on a regular basis. After D-Day, Southern's regiment participated in the Battle of the Bulge. Like many of the soldiers in the brutal winter offensive of 1944–45, Southern spent his time trying to stay warm in flimsy campsites chipped out of the frozen soil of the Ardennes.

One of Southern's "scary times," according to Gail Gerber, included seeing a soldier in his platoon get killed: "At one point his buddy stood up in the foxhole—there was a certain fear there—and his buddy said, 'Oh no, I'm not going to die' and was beside Terry and then got blown away that minute. So that gave Terry a certain amount of pause."

According to his discharge form, he received no wounds. His good service earned him a Bronze Star, a Good Conduct Medal, and victory ribbon, as well as three overseas bars. He acquired a German infantryman's helmet. In 1956, living in Geneva with Carol, Terry bought a used Luger, which he had always longed for, and restored it. The gun floated among hispossessions for decades. One day in the mid-sixties, the playwright Arthur Kopit, who was house-sitting at Terry's Connecticut home, found the Luger in a desk. He took it out into the field for some target practice. Not thinking it was loaded, he examined the gun. Suddenly, it went off, almost blowing a hole through Kopit's skull. Apparently the gun had never been properly cleaned.

Most Americans stationed in England couldn't wait to come back home. The damp weather, mediocre food, snobbishness, and lack of the modern conveniences (what the natives called "all mod cons") that made the U.S. of A. great were alleviated only by the ardor of fair-haired English roses. However, Southern found the British fascinating. Growing up in Texas, he was sensitive to regional dialects. England, a country barely half the size of his home state, boasted countless accents, from East End cockney, with its almost scatological blurring of vowels and syllables, to the clear, elegant precision of the Home Counties (which was then the only acceptable accent for anyone in broadcasting), and the odd slow singsong of Midlands and other "up north" accents. Lurking beneath the seeming repressed English facade, Southern discovered intriguing currents of eccentricity and fantasy along with an innate love of irony, dry wit, and wordplay.

The English mass media, unlike America's commercial radio and Hollywood, used its technological resources to edify the public and raise standards of education and knowledge. As one of the bastions of English culture, BBC Radio aired talks on literature, high art, and classical music along with readings and plays. Southern discovered that regardless of class and education there was a newspaper or magazine to suit almost everyone. The working class and left could choose from the *Daily Mail* or the *Manchester Guardian.* While the middle and upper classes could enjoy fashion and society coverage in the *Tatler,* commentary in the *New Statesman* and the *Spectator,* humor in *Punch,* and a high level of journalism in the *Times* and *Daily Telegraph.* Novels, plays, and poetry were constant subjects of discussion on the radio and in magazines and newspapers. In England, Southern discovered to his relish, reading was as common as breathing.

All in all, Southern spent two years, seven months, and nine days in the Army in the European theater from October 27, 1943, through August 26, 1945. He spent a lot of his leave in London. A photograph from December

1943, shows Terry in a long army coat with a friend walking through the West End. It could be an image out of any Hollywood war movie of the period.

As he did in Texas, Southern seemed to fit in well with others, but he also discovered another group of outsiders in the Army. According to Ellen Adler, one of Southern's many close women friends, "Terry used to say he had never met a Jew before he went into the Army and then he met these Jews and he thought they were the grooviest people he'd ever met."

To Southern, the Jews were witty, intelligent, and colorful and managed to deal with the negative aspects of the era's all-pervasive anti-Semitism with dignity and humor. They wore their personalities on their sleeves and projected a blend of confidence, irony, and insight that Southern aspired to.

During his Army service, the daily influx of new influences along with the sensory overload of battle began to shape the avuncular Grand Guy persona that Southern would eventually present to the world in his novel *The Magical Christian*. Southern realized he had survived because of luck and chance. It could have been he who stood up in the foxhole and got killed. The war taught him about existentialism and the randomness of fate years before he was able to eavesdrop on Jean-Paul Sartre on the Left Bank.

Although the armed forces were still segregated as far as race was concerned, Southern met a wide range of fellow Americans in the Army. Young men in close quarters struggling with Army regulations and routine (and the barely articulated fear of death) learned to project a face to the world to protect and hide the messy confusion inside. Observing the various fronts his fellow soldiers projected, from tight-lipped silence to constant kidding, Southern was struck by the fluidity of human personality. How one spoke and behaved was very much determined by where one was at any given moment in space and time.

Terry embraced the understated elegance and irony of Evelyn Waugh and T. S. Eliot. He began to employ certain English phrases and mannerisms in his speech for ironic or humorous effect. He wasn't becoming a phony mid-Atlantic man. Something else was happening to the young Texan. He was developing a persona that simultaneously embraced and mocked a certain English way of looking at the world. It was the attitude of an independently wealthy Oxford don without the snobbishness or affectation. It was the persona of someone who felt courtesy and hospitality were all-important. One should not burden one's friends with angst, but make them feel comfortable. Gentle teasing and nicknames were encouraged.

Personal information should be conveyed through droll and amusing anecdotes, not raw and intimate confession. It was important to keep up appearances by dressing with decorum and subtlety.

These changes were the attempts by a slightly battle-scarred, but hardly embittered young man to bring another component to his development as a writer other than just sheer perseverance and ambition. Whereas American writers generally pursued some variant of naturalism, the English placed considerable importance on finding the right style to tell a story. Texans have also appreciated those who can relate tall tales, legends, and local history with the appropriate balance of gusto and modesty. The defeat at the Alamo, for example, is often retold as the quintessential story of Texan individualism. On the surface, it may seem strange for a Southern boy to gravitate to the mandarin style of English writers like Waugh, Stephen Spender, Anthony Powell, and Cyril Connolly, but the more one looks at the storytelling traditions in Terry's home state, the less wide seems the gap. By becoming an Anglophile, Southern was able to stay true to his roots and simultaneously move toward a unique, nonregional voice as a writer.

After being discharged, Southern returned to Texas and hung out with his friend Big Herb, who was now in the Dallas police. Big Herb was another CK figure, according to Southern, who was also an ardent jazz fan. Accompanying Big Herb on his rounds through Central Tracks, he witnessed a few fights and scrapes that provided the basic inspiration for the story "Razor Fight."

While it was pleasant, in a sentimental-journey kind of way, to hang out with Big Herb and some of his other high school buddies, Southern dreaded staying in Dallas.

"I think anybody with any sensitivity would not want to stay in Texas at that time. It was not just parochial, but the racism was rampant," says Carol. "Terry told me when he got back from the war . . . he said [the idea of fun] was just making 'trouble for niggers.' Terry was revolted. He didn't say he was. I think that the whole scene was repellent to him . . . the fact that he changed his accent."

By making a decision to leave Texas, Southern became part of a great state tradition. Other famous Texan emigrés would include novelist Patricia Highsmith, film director and screenwriter Robert Benton, novelist Larry McMurtry, newsman Dan Rather, choreographer Tommy Tune, film critic Rex Reed, *Star Trek* creator Gene Roddenberry, musicians and songwriters such as Janis Joplin, Kinky Friedman, Ornette Coleman, and Kris

Kristofferson, and pop artist Robert Rauschenberg. In later years, Southern would become friends with some of these fellow Texas expatriates and others like actor Rip Torn and saxophonist Bobby Keyes. Southern shared their combination of restlessness, creative energy, ambition, and an innate and specific set of talents that were as wild and distinct as Texas at its primal best. Like Southern, these other exiles sought to become cosmopolitan, but on their terms.

Studying for an English degree seemed the most convenient way for Southern to take advantage of the GI Bill and pursue a writerly vocation. In the fall of 1946, he enrolled in the Great Books program, inaugurated by the then-dean Robert Maynard Hutchins at the University of Chicago. The university was beginning to burst at the seams with young veterans. Many of them lived in barrack-style prefab dormitories erected to deal with over-crowding. The university had a solid academic reputation thanks to Hutchins's reforms, which included exams that could exempt applicants from prerequisite courses if their marks were high enough. Other writers who attended the university in the immediate postwar period included Philip Roth and George Steiner.

At the midpoint between the West and East Coasts, the gateway to the Great Plains, Chicago was a bustling metropolis with enough energy to rival Los Angeles or New York. It was also a center for jazz and the blues, the Democratic Party, two of America's finest universities, a great newspaper town. More than L.A. or New York, whose denizens acted like inhabitants of a royal principality, Chicago was urban America at full speed. Skyscrapers, crowded streets, big cars, a modern subway. In a few years, it would become the birthplace of the Compass and Second City, which helped breed a whole school of American comedy. Chicago was also the city that inspired such diverse contemporaries as Saul Bellow, Studs Terkel, and Nelson Algren. Algren, author of *The Man with the Golden Arm,* which would win the first National Book Award in 1950, would have a profound influence on Southern in the coming years.

Like many young veterans going back to school, Southern was wiser and more serious than the students who had been a little young to sign up. Fraternities with their absurd initiation rites and drinking parties seemed ridiculous, if not obscene, wastes of time. Few veterans needed to prove their manhood on campus. Southern chose instead to explore the city whenever he could afford to. For the most part, he took his studies seriously. However, his decision to transfer to Northwestern was not based solely on its academic reputation. "One day I visited the campus of Northwestern and saw all these beautiful blue-eyed blondes in their yellow convertibles, or taking the sun by the lake, and I transferred to that school pronto."

At Northwestern, Southern recalls being impressed by an English professor, Bergen Evans, and a philosophy professor, Archie Schlipp. He shared their irreverence and skepticism toward received ideas. Southern also rented an apartment with an exchange student from Calcutta, Nandan Kgal, who "turned me on to these extraordinary vindaloo dishes of eye-watering piquancy—which were too hot for most [non-Indian tastes], but delightful by Tex-Mex standards."

Southern's course work was shaped by the Great Books core curriculum, which meant an immersion in Plato, Aristotle, and other classical thinkers. Literary studies were heavily influenced by the New Criticism of the period as espoused by John Crowe Ransom. Much attention was paid to sticking strictly to the text for analysis and keeping biography out of the discussion. If Southern eventually became disenchanted with the New Criticism's prissy brand of elitism, he did embrace the idea of letting the work stand apart from its creator and the concept of art for art's sake.

Campus life at the University of Chicago and at Northwestern was largely one of quiet contemplation, an apolitical postwar idyll of literary study for its own sake. Yet Southern was not oblivious to the way the ideological climate in America was beginning to harden. He sat up at attention during one of his lectures when a professor began to explain how America's military-industrial complex established its priorities. The professor related a story about one of his colleagues in the mathematics department: "Some congressmen came to visit him at the university and asked, 'What's the stage of this research [into nuclear fission]?' 'Well,' the professor replied, 'we've come to an impasse here. Our vector mathematics can only deal with things that have a conventional relationship to space and time, which is precluded by the phenomena of the atom being split and at the same time new particles existing.' The congressmen said, 'You've got to get someone on that right away.' Heh-heh. So this guy whose research was in part militarily financed, called up his colleague at Princeton and told him what the situation was. 'Put your best man on this!' But in reality they had absolutely no idea what they were talking about or looking for."

The professor sketched out an absurd situation of professors setting up a speculative program of research to keep the government grants coming in. The professor's off-the-cuff tale of ivory tower follies reflected the very real increase in military spending on pure research fueled by Washington's growing anticommunism. As the climate of opinion began to polarize with the House Un-American Activities Committee (HUAC) hearings and Senator Joseph McCarthy's growing monopolization of public discourse, Southern's thoughts about graduate work turned to the possibilities of studying abroad.

In the spring of 1948, Southern completed his English degree at Northwestern. Chicago had many attractions, but it was not enough. His literary tastes had become increasingly European. Postwar America was entering a stultifying period of fear, anti-intellectualism, and conformity.

After considering various graduate schools. Terry decided that the real thing—art, love, truth—was abroad. Many of his heroes, notably Ernest Hemingway and F. Scott Fitzgerald, had spent time in Europe. It seemed as if a few years spent outside the country would sharpen his talent. So he applied to the Sorbonne on the GI Bill.

Passed by Congress in 1944, the GI Bill of Rights was one of the last great initiatives of President Franklin D. Roosevelt's New Deal. According to the Department of Veterans Affairs, more than twenty million beneficiaries have taken advantage of funds allowing access to an astonishing range of educational opportunities. During the late forties and early fifties, an entire generation of young veterans, from modest upbringings, would gain access to some of America's finest universities as well as institutions abroad. It was a significant political step in making America a freer and more egalitarian society.

The painter Larry Rivers, who would become one of Southern's closest friends in later years, described the impact of the GI Bill on his and Southern's generation: "The GI Bill of Rights was a World War II military award, governmental gratitude putting its money where its lip was. By offering veterans the advantage and ease of getting paid to learn, the GI Bill, like the WPA educational programs of the thirties, sent thousands of servicemen into the territory of the humanities, unintentionally creating a mass audience for artists and their efforts, and even more unintentionally producing more artists per hundred thousand civilians than ever before to seduce this mass of new lookers. It offered the possibilities of education to lower-class kids in whose hovels going to college was only possible if their parents worked their lives away for them or if they themselves worked all day long and studied at night."

Southern chose the perfect time to leave the United States. The rise of McCarthyism was creating a cultural climate of anti-intellectualism, xenophobia, and conformity. He had seen some of the professors at Northwestern suffer the Cold War chill hastened by the HUAC hearings.

By contrast, France seemed a more mature country, whose traditions enabled it to transcend the cold war tensions between the Left and Right.

Escaping American parochialism and expanding one's cultural horizons were certainly important motivations for Southern. It was easy to explain to friends. Privately, Southern probably sensed he was on the verge of reinventing himself. Growing up in Texas, the war, going to college . . . momentous events to be sure, but it seemed like a rehearsal for something bigger and better. In Paris, the proverbial City of Light itself, things would really get cooking.

2
You're Too Hip, Baby

. . . I return in my mind's eye to Paris. Paris, the dividing line. Before Paris, experience could be savored for its own immediate satisfactions. It was total. Afterwards, I became cunning, a writer, somebody with a use for everything, even intimacies.

—Mordecai Richler, "A Sense of the Ridiculous"

Those **were halcyon days** and the little-mags were cooking," Southern said with no small hint of nostalgia when recalling his formative years as a writer in Paris. "From '48 to '52, the cafés were such great places to hang out—you could smoke hash at the tables if you were fairly discreet. There was the expatriate crowd, which was more or less comprised of interesting people, creatively inclined. So we would fall out there at one of the cafés, sip Pernod until dinner, then afterwards go to a jazz club."

Southern arrived in Paris in September 1948 to study at the Sorbonne's Faculté des Lettres. There was little pressure on foreign students to actually complete a degree. Like the rest of France, the august institution was suffering from the effects of postwar austerity. The Sorbonne was quite eager to take on as many foreign students as possible and a special stream had been set up for American students called Le Cours de la Civilisation Française. Most of the students in the program would pick up only a smidgen of French and rarely socialized with non-Americans.

The specifics of Southern's program were vague: "The way it worked at the Sorbonne was you enrolled for a doctorate, chose your thesis. Mine was 'The Influence of Mallarmé on the English Novel Since 1940,' which seemed to satisfy the powers that were, and left me free to go to jazz clubs by night and the Cinémathèque by day . . . in short, the stuff of emancipation by day and by night. Theoretically, you were researching your thesis in preparation of defending it at some time in the very indefinite future. Class attendance was not required and no exams were given."

When Southern first arrived in Paris, he kept to himself. Traces of his Texas accent remained, but were hidden by his long silences and cryptic utterances. According to one of the many friends he would make in Paris, John Marquand Jr. (a.k.a. John Phillips, the son of the best-selling author of *The Late George Apley*), it was a little-known secret "that when Terry first arrived in Paris, he had been as callow as the rest of us. He had worn a necktie then, tied in a big Windsor knot, and a blue pinstripe suit with wide padded shoulders."

Southern found cheap accommodation in the Hotel Verneuil, a one-star bedsit affair run by a benevolent Corsican family, where the novelist Herbert Gold also stayed. It was close to the Sorbonne, where Southern ate many of his meals in the university's cafeteria, and the bohemian ferment of the Left Bank. Although Southern spent four years attending the Sorbonne, he never formally applied for his certificate. There was little official pressure on foreign students. Despite Southern's casualness toward his studies, he did take advantage of sitting in on various guest lectures by the likes of Jean-Paul Sartre, Albert Camus, Jean Cocteau, and Marcel Raymond, the author of *From Baudelaire to Surrealism*. The latter book, along with T. S. Eliot's *The Sacred Wood*, had a profound influence on Southern's growing preference for conceptualism over autobiography.

Southern's GI Bill allowance of seventy-five dollars a month only stretched so far. "I had to depend on getting money from my parents and on the kindness of strangers, as they say." Southern's laid-back attitude to money and work bordered on Zen-like indifference. As an only child, he was coddled by his parents. Aside from a few odd jobs, he had really known only two worlds—the Army and academe. While these experiences had matured him, they had given him little in the way of business skills. Whatever entrepreneurial zeal he possessed was directed toward his dream of becoming a great writer like Hemingway or Faulkner.

Outside the lecture halls of the Sorbonne, the earnest young veteran and college graduate quickly metamorphosed into a seasoned bohemian. The four years in Paris became a frenzy of experience. In various jazz clubs around town, Southern was able to see Charlie Parker, Bud Powell, Dizzy

Gillespie, Thelonious Monk, and Miles Davis at a time when bebop was becoming the fifties equivalent of acid rock or punk. At the Cinémathèque, run by Henri Langlois, he had access to classics of European art cinema such as Marcel Carné's *Les Enfants de Paradis,* Jean Cocteau's *Le Sang d'un Poète,* and Luis Buñuel's *L'Age d'Or.* Bebop and the European art film were influences equally important as literature on Southern's search for an aesthetic that was pure, spontaneous, and immediate.

Southern also managed to rub shoulders with Cocteau, Camus, and Sartre outside the lecture halls. The last two authors were the Lennon and McCartney of French existentialism. They could be regularly spotted "performing" at the Café Flore and other trendy bistros in the rue Saint-Germain-des-Prés. Camus represented the dashing poetic and heroic side—one could be a great philosopher and look like Bogart, too. Sartre was the enigmatic mandarin, whose intense, almost rabbinical scrutiny of the nature of language, existence, and reality was complemented by a godfatherlike skill for literary politics. Cocteau was more of a homebody, but Southern managed to get invited to his informal salon on a number of occasions.

For Southern, existentialism simply made common sense. Whether God existed or not was beside the point. Even if an Almighty Being did exist, he/she/whatever was unavailable at the best of times. One's sense of purpose shifted from moment to moment. Along with jazz, existentialism was a youthful passion that would become embedded in Southern's world-view for the rest of his life. It was a personal philosophy that had little time for self-pity, second thoughts, guilt, or regret. Southern would stick stubbornly to it until the end of his life: "I'm of the existentialist persuasion. . . . What you do is what you do. Things that you want to do and don't do don't count for anything."

Paris became a convenient base for exploring the rest of Europe. Southern would make spontaneous forays into Holland, Greece, Italy, and Spain usually with a buddy or a girlfriend for company. For Southern, the Old World was a new world, a place where one was "inescapably confronted with the dramatic contrasts of the human condition." Just looking through the window of a bus or train was revelatory: "On a trip, say from Geneva to Seville, one sees a diversity of life which could not possibly be encountered elsewhere within a comparable radius of travel. Frequent crossing of frontiers will shake one's beliefs to their very foundations."

As it did for countless other ambitious young men and women who came to the City of Light from the United States, Canada, and Britain, Paris symbolized the great adventure of the expatriate experience to Southern.

He reveled in the knowledge that he was walking in the footsteps of count-less writers from Henry James and W. Somerset Maugham to F. Scott Fitzgerald, Gertrude Stein, and Ernest Hemingway. It was the place where Baudelaire, Verlaine, and Rimbaud explored various kinds of sense-derangement without the usual moral restrictions. Here was the city where James Joyce wrote much of *Ulysses.* Here was where little magazines like *transition* and The *Transatlantic Review* were launched like Molotov cocktails at the bourgeoisie. One could still visit Sylvia Beach's bookshop, where so much of recent literary history began.

The Lost Generation of the twenties exerted an especially strong pull on Southern and his fellow expatriates. In a slightly cynical *Esquire* piece on the *Paris Review* crowd, "Looking for Hemingway," Gay Talese hinted that this new wave of expatriates were looking for a golden era that was no longer in existence. Fitzgerald was dead. Hemingway and Faulkner were now ossifying middlebrow favorites. Talese suggested that the post–World War II generation was trying to re-create an illustrious era that could never be repeated. But Talese's thesis only goes so far in defining this second "lost generation."

Hundreds of veterans came to Paris in the late forties and fifties because the GI Bill made it cheap and convenient to do so. Those that had served in the European theater were curious to experience a great culture rebuilding itself after the ravages of war. These veterans were neither lost nor cynical. Certainly many of these young men and women in their twen-ties had seen terrible things in the war, but they had not lost their essential optimism or desire for new experiences.

Many of the post–World War II expatriates were African Americans. Richard Wright, the best-selling author of *Native Son,* arrived in May 1946, seeking refuge from his sudden celebrity and persecution for his left-wing sympathies. James Baldwin moved into the Hotel Verneuil to finish his first novel, *Go Tell It on the Mountain.* Chester Himes, an ex-con turned writer, began to move away from the realist novel to create a series of books about two Harlem detectives, Coffin Ed Johnson and Grave Digger Jones. For many African Americans of ambition and talent, Europe was about as color-blind a place as they could hope for. Certainly there was discrimina-tion, as many North African blacks could attest, but it did not possess the same magnitude as in the United States. Segregated drinking fountains, racist landlords and employers, and lynchings were all too common in the land of the free. Blacks, perhaps more than their white counterparts, really did experience "emancipation" in Europe. Not only were they allowed to pursue careers in the arts without facing various institutional barriers, but they were encouraged by the enthusiasm of the French. Jazz musicians in particular thrived in the large circuit of clubs throughout France and the rest of Europe.

If Hemingway and company still cast a long shadow, Southern's generation was beginning to produce its first group of superstars. Norman Mailer, Truman Capote, and Gore Vidal had also passed through Paris in 1947 and 1948. These three writers had become the literary heroes of the postwar period with their novels, *The Naked and the Dead, Other Voices, Other Rooms,* and *Williwaw.* Their celebrity was confirmed with healthy book sales, *Life* magazine spreads, and critical raves. Although Southern would meet and become friendly with all three men in the late fifties and sixties, he probably found their media canonization distasteful. One of the first rules of the emerging hipster ethos in Paris was that popular success was incompatible with genuine artistic achievement.

Toward the end of the decade, Irwin Shaw and James Jones, authors of the best-selling war novels *The Young Lions* and *From Here to Eternity,* moved to Paris and initiated a jet-set lifestyle. Both writers threw parties and dinners where struggling young writers could mingle and eyeball the rich and famous. They were not much older than Southern and the other young expatriates, but Shaw and Jones's benevolence and generosity transformed them into father figures.

For the most part, the various social and intellectual attractions of Paris made it a congenial place to be young, broke, and unknown. As one of the primary beneficiaries of the Marshall Plan, inaugurated in 1947 by the U.S. government to aid Europe's ravaged postwar economy, France was a cheap place to live. Southern's meager funds stretched far. One could buy a simple dinner of fries, steak, and a glass or two of wine for a dollar. A private room in a hotel could be rented for fifteen dollars a month. The used bookstores and stalls yielded a bounty of easily afforded literary riches. If Parisians, with their preference for socialism of one brand or another, resented the American presence (YANKEE GO HOME would become as common a graffito as KILROY WAS HERE), they generally kept their grumbling to themselves.

The city's rich literary history and all-pervasive bohemian atmosphere made it easier for Southern to pursue his vocation. He had been writing furiously since his Army days, but chose not to show much of this material to anyone. During his first year in Paris, he tried to maintain a diary. He later told Francis Wyndham that he discarded about three novels during this period. Little is known about this material and no samples of it appear to have survived. Southern was struggling to avoid fiction that was autobiographical or regional in the manner of Hemingway and Faulkner. Instead, he was trying to learn from the modernist experiments of Joyce and Céline without descending into parody or pastiche.

When he was not quietly trying to be a writer who could be as interesting to others as he was to himself, Southern was rapidly making friends. The world of English-speaking expatriates was small enough for kindred spirits to link up fairly quickly. One of the most important of these new acquaintances was Mason Hoffenberg.

If there was a model for the hipster perfection that Southern sought, this was it. A short wiry man with slightly bulging eyes, Hoffenberg was a Beat before the term had even entered the underground, let alone the mainstream. Born in New York in 1922, he was the son of a successful businessman who owned a shoe factory. As a teenager, Hoffenberg briefly attended the same military school as Anastasio Somoza, the future dictator of Nicaragua. He knew Diane Arbus in high school. He served in the U.S. Army and was part of the forces that liberated Paris. Hoffenberg had spent the first few years after the war hanging around Greenwich Village. The San Remo bar became a regular haunt for the ur-slacker. Like Southern, he had also used the GI Bill to return to Paris. Because Hoffenberg spoke and understood French better than most expats, he was able to land a steady gig at Agence France-Presse as a copy editor.

Unlike Southern, Hoffenberg possessed a direct in-your-face attitude toward the world. Some found Hoffenberg's contrary brand of self-confidence obnoxious, but to Southern, he was the real McCoy. His worldliness was confirmed by his marriage to an attractive, upper-class French woman, Couquite, daughter of art historian Élie Faure. Hoffenberg, like several of Southern's new hipster buddies in Paris, was also in the process of developing a lifelong heroin habit. He would go off and on heroin so often that he began to give his various habits women's names, like hurricanes. William Burroughs would later say that Hoffenberg was one of those who liked the pain of withdrawal. For Maurice Girodias's Olympia Press, he wrote the "dbs" (dirty books) *Sin for Breakfast* (as Hamilton Drake) and *Until She Screams* (as Faustino Perez).

Quality Lit. Jazz. Café society. Pornography. Mainlining heroin. Hoffenberg was up for it all. He became the first of the many extreme and dynamic personalities that Southern would embrace, befriend, and try to stay loyal to throughout his life. Such relationships would lead to productive and exciting collaborations, but also to unresolved feelings of envy, resentment, betrayal, and various kinds of unhealthy psychological dependence for both parties. In the case of Hoffenberg, Southern found a buddy who shared his dark humor, flights of fancy, and willingness to go all out.

"Mason was a poet and just a very creative guy. Ultracreative. He could have been, God knows, a Nobel Prize–type poet," said Southern. Southern and Hoffenberg became inseparable. Part of the attraction was Hoffenberg's Jewishness, which Southern was endlessly fascinated by. The two also shared a love of wild, exaggerated humor often of the what-if variety. In the countless letters and postcards they exchanged through the fifties and sixties, they would address and sign off their correspondence with nicknames as varied as "David Selznick" and "Leslie."

Beneath the sarcastic quips and joking was a mutual recognition of each other's literary seriousness. They shared a voracious appetite for books, movies, jazz, various stimulants, long conversations, and women. Hoffenberg was more at ease socially. And while Hoffenberg, for Southern and many others in the expat crowd, was considered the better craftsman, it was Southern who was far more disciplined and active in realizing his potential as a writer.

Through Hoffenberg, Southern eventually met nineteen-year-old Mordecai Richler, a Jewish Canadian from Montreal. Richler had come to Paris to escape the provincialism of English Canada and the anti-Semitism of Montreal's WASP ruling class. Like Southern and Hoffenberg, Richler also had a dark and sarcastic take on life. His novels *The Apprenticeship of Duddy Kravitz* and *St. Urbain's Horseman* would successfully blend autobiography and satire. Unlike Southern and Hoffenberg, Richler proved to be more pragmatic and savvy about his career. His successes would not have the kind of cultural impact of *Candy* or *Dr. Strangelove,* but he wouldn't end up with Southern's monumental money problems or Hoffenberg's enervating addictions to drugs and booze.

Recalling Southern and Hoffenberg from the comfort of a pub near his apartment in London's chic Chelsea area more than forty years later, Richler remembers how young they all were more than anything.

"I thought Terry was very witty," recalls Richler. "I didn't know much about his actual writing then. He was interesting to be with. . . . Mason was small, lean, and wiry and had protruding eyes, while Terry was tall and had a hawklike visage. Mason always had a book in his pocket.

"Mason had a very tender, gentle side. I remember he and Couquitte had a flat in Paris they would lease. He said, he wasn't going to rent it to any fucking writer because they would always screw him. He rented it to some business people and of course got screwed on the rent anyway."

Richler was friends with another Canadian writer, Mavis Gallant, whom Southern got to know tangentially. As one of the few female writers in a community heavy on Hemingwayesque bravado, she kept to herself. In addition to making Paris her new home, she would also become one of the *New Yorker*'s favorite short story writers along with Alice Munro and John Updike.

Hoffenberg also introduced Southern and Richler to one of his San Remo drinking buddies, James Baldwin. Baldwin had left the United States because he was a triple threat—black, gay, and a writer. He seemed to be suffering from the "starving in a garret" syndrome more than most. His first year in Paris was bleak. Barely able to afford his modest rent, Baldwin didn't eat regularly and became ill. Upon recovering from the flu, he was thrown into jail for allegedly taking a bedsheet from another hotel. Southern even saw him being led off in handcuffs. After several terrifying days of desolate imprisonment, Baldwin's release was secured by a lawyer who was a friend of someone Baldwin had worked for in New York. Southern and Hoffenberg sneaked Baldwin into the Sorbonne's student cafeteria several times for a free meal. Southern also met Baldwin's great love, the Swiss artist Lucien Happersberger. The relationship would inspire much of *Giovanni's Room*.

Baldwin, Richler, Southern, and Hoffenberg were drawn quickly to the *New-Story* crowd led by David Burnett, the son of Martha Foley and Whit Burnett. Among aspiring writers, Burnett's parents were famous for creating *Story* magazine, which made it a point of publishing promising new work by young writers. Burnett hoped to create a more cutting-edge version of his parents' publication, which would tap into the headier work the younger generation was creating. Burnett and Southern also became very close. Like Hoffenberg, Burnett was a heroin addict, who somehow managed to compartmentalize his life by juggling literary enterprise and a major drug habit. He created illustrations that went along with the work in the journal he christened *New-Story* and was also an avid film buff.

New-Story's first issue appeared in March 1951. The underfunded journal managed to limp only along until 1953, but the few issues that did appear carried stories by Southern, Baldwin, Ray Bradbury, William Goyen, and Alison Lurie. Despite its brief life span, *New-Story* maintained a relatively high standard and its acceptance of two of Southern's stories quickly confirmed him as one of the expat crowd's rising stars.

In the June 1951 issue of *New-Story*, "The Automatic Gate" appeared, and eventually Southern received fifty dollars for it. In this naturalistic vignette of Parisian working-class life, Monsieur Pommard, a ticket collector in the Paris Métro on the verge of retirement, dispenses banal wisdom to a bored coworker in his twenties. The older man is obsessed with the uncivil behavior of commuters who race through the automatic gate in order to catch the trains. The story ends with a cataclysmic flourish when a pregnant woman is badly injured by the gate.

As Southern would do in the opening of his first novel, *Flash and Filigree,* the story begins with a ridiculously elaborate description of how the automatic gate works. Pommard is determined to halt, or at least slow down, those individuals disrupting his fussy notions of order and decorum. What is remarkable about the story is the deceptive quality of description. Unlike many expatriates, Southern did not stand aloof from the life of the Parisians around him. If one did not know the author was an American, "The Automatic Gate" could be a short story by Camus or perhaps an unpublished extract from Jean-Paul Sartre's *Nausea.* The grimness of Pommard's routine on the night shift is conveyed through sentences like "his uniform was shabby, and there was some dirt on the back of his hand" and "His eyes traced the track, low set between sweeps of clean concrete, all cast a sterile rose green from the overhung fluorescence." Much of the story is taken up by Pommard's almost hysterical indignation toward the commuters' seemingly moblike disregard for civil behavior. Despite Pommard's subway vigil, a horrible accident does occur because Pommard is so caught up in his role as a guardian that he has lost a significant part of his humanity.

So petty and monotonous are Pommard's monologues that it becomes easy on first reading to wonder, What the hell is the story about anyway? Southern's strange form of naturalism creates the sense of something odd and foreboding hidden on the periphery of the action. Chaos and disaster, in Southern's early stories, lurk on the margins of the routine and everyday. For a young American writer in his mid-twenties, "The Automatic Gate" is also remarkable for its unobtrusive use of French colloquialisms. Where many of Southern's contemporaries were under the sway of Hemingway, his work appears to have assimilated the existentialist viewpoint of the Europeans with little awkwardness.

In the November edition of *New-Story*, Southern contributed "The Butcher," another glimpse into the inner life of working-class Parisians. The title character, Beauvais, is a middle-aged worker in an abattoir. His son, Gerard, has been wounded in action at the front and is convalescing at home. Gerard finds it difficult to watch newsreel footage of the war. Then Gerard sees a magazine pictorial about the war and launches into a long monologue about bayoneting another man. His father listens sympathetically to the traumatic recollection. The next day at work, a coworker draws the father's attention to a local newspaper item celebrating his son's bravery in the field of action. Beauvais cuts out the article and pins it to the wall of his workstation to show to his son. The remainder of the story is taken up with a detailed description of Beauvais killing cattle entering the slaughterhouse and preparing the meat for sale. By the end of their shift, Beauvais and his coworkers stand on a floor covered with blood waiting for another worker to mop up.

The contrast between the killing on the battlefield and the more socially acceptable slaughter of animals is handled with detachment. The story is an inquiry into how various forms of violence become invisible. The violence of war may be necessary (the son understands that at the front it is either kill or be killed), but is there a connection between it and the more casual, unthinking ability to kill an animal for food? The questions are left to linger in the reader's mind to provoke and disturb. Whether they can be answered is not the point, but Southern, in a more understated way than his wild satiric novels, is already using irony to upset, provoke, and astonish his readers.

Southern also became friendly with the editors of *Zero* and *Points*. *Zero* was edited by two New Yorkers, Themoscles Hoetis and Albert Benveniste. The first issue in 1949 featured Christopher Isherwood and Kenneth Patchen. Sinbad Vail, the son of Peggy Guggenheim and Laurence Vail, started *Points* (subtitled "a Magazine for the Young Writer") in 1948. Mordecai Richler's first published short story, "Shades of Darkness," appeared in it.

The feverish literary aspirations of Southern, Hoffenberg, et al. were kept hidden by a rapidly emerging hipster cool. "Those who know, do not speak. Those who speak, do not know" became Southern and Hoffenberg's variation on Louis Armstrong's definition of jazz: "if you have to ask, you'll never know." Careerism was meant to be discreetly acted on, but never voiced. According to Southern, actually getting published was a dubious achievement.

"It was sort of an embarrassment like you had sold out or something. If it was corny enough and square enough and bourgeois enough to get accepted by some of these asshole editors, how could it be worth anything?" he recalled. "So mostly [the literary scene] was all about reading and turning people on to things you had read like Mallarmé, Malaparte, and Canetti. He was a great one. *Auto-da-fé*. And then showing people stuff you had written and then there was some things where people would read aloud, which seemed a little suspect and too social to me."

Southern was also fond of Franz Kafka and read everything by the neurasthenic Czech fabulist he could find. Kafka's diaries and letters impressed Southern as much as the novels and short stories. He shared Kafka's preference for "night-writing" and believed one's best work emerged when one was least conscious of an audience. Like Poe, Kafka had a genius for making the fantastic seem terrifyingly real. And *after all,* Southern and his café chums reasoned, wasn't this the problem with the traditional realist novel? *The concentration camp* and *the bomb* made simple naturalism seem almost obscene. In order for one's writing to have any profound meaning or impact, one had to go beyond merely mastering accepted forms and conventions, simple homage, and liberal middle-class notions of good taste and appropriate subject matter.

The hundreds of cafés and bars in Paris offered the perfect low-pressure backdrop to discuss such matters as well as the progress of various works at hand. One could sit all day nursing a drink or coffee or play pinball. The cafés were also a great place to score drugs from hashish and Benzedrine to heroin. One of Southern and Hoffenberg's regular contacts for such stimulants was a North African, Hadj, who would become one of the dedicatees of *Candy*. Southern was certainly fond of the various drugs available and experimented with most of them. Had not the great French symbolist poets Rimbaud and Verlaine championed the derangement of the senses as a way for the dedicated writer to get that visionary edge?

Southern's strong sense of self-preservation made him fear heroin. Even though he hung out with addicts constantly, and would continue to do so when married to Carol, he was deeply scared of its pull. He watched others turn on, but declined to join in. More to his liking were alcohol, cigarettes, and hashish. The latter was an especially pleasant way to alter the surroundings without any of the nasty side effects of doing too many uppers or shooting up junk. Later in the sixties, Southern would develop a dependency on Dexamyl. Dexamyl's speedlike effects gave him the seemingly limitless energy to stay up for days on end and complete screenplays. Of course, like all such drugs, long-term abuse outweighed the benefits and made Southern more susceptible to heart disease, strokes, and blood and respiratory problems.

The Old Navy, a distinctly down-market version of Le Dôme and La Coupole, was a favorite hangout for Southern, Hoffenberg, and Richler. Located on the boulevard Saint-Germain, across from the Odéon Métro station, the bar-tabac provided a mediocre, but cheap selection of coffee, beer, wine, and digestifs. A couple of battered pinball machines imported from the States before the war provided the hipster equivalent of a morning workout on a Nautilus.

Richler recalls that the general routine was to sit down at a table and gradually four or five people would gather, friends as well as strangers. The various circles—*New-Story, Zero, Points*—all overlapped. Since it was often painful to talk about work and many of them were broke, according to Richler, conversations tended to gravitate toward a running ironic commentary on what the squares were up to:

> It would be nice, it would be tidy, to say with hindsight that we were a group, knit by political anger or a literary policy or even an aesthetic revulsion for all things American, but the truth was we recognized each other by no more than a shared sense of the ridiculous. And so we passed many a languorous, pot-filled afternoon on the terrace of the Dôme or the Selecte, improvising, not unlike jazz groups, on the hot news from America, where Truman was yielding to Eisenhower. We bounced an inanity to and fro until, magnified through bizarre extension, we had disposed of it as an absurdity. We invented obscene quiz shows for television, and ad-libbed sexual outrages that could be interpolated into a John Marquand novel, a Norman Rockwell *Post* cover, or a June Allyson movie.

Patti Dryden, a New York graphics designer and illustrator who befriended Hoffenberg in the seventies and eighties, says the dynamic between Southern and his future *Candy* coauthor was very much one of an older brother tutoring a younger brother. "Mason always tried to refer to Terry as a schmuck. Like a kid brother. 'What does he know? He dresses like an idiot, blah, blah.' That was Mason being affectionate. You have to understand he was a curmudgeon and I never heard him say he loved anybody . . . it just wasn't his way. So when he was putting you down in that kind of caustic way, that was showing great affection. [Laughs] He remembered your name at least."

Another source of tension between Hoffenberg and Southern was the simple fact that Hoffenberg had access to more money. His parents sent him checks regularly and Couquitte's family helped with finances and baby-sitting. Hoffenberg was able to take off on skiing trips or run down to Spain with less hesitation than Southern.

While Hoffenberg liked to stir things up through argument and debate, Southern preferred to sit back, observe, and toss out the odd comment or one-liner. He only loosened up around those he knew well or with the aid of a few drinks. Around the same time he met Hoffenberg, Southern formed another alliance that would be less complicated and more enduring.

On an excursion to a little fishing village in the South of France, Villefranche-sur-Mer, Southern met Aram Avakian, a New Yorker of Armenian descent. "On a Sunday, about eleven in the morning, I was seated at this café near the waterfront. Behind was the village green and then the hotel. They had this French military band performing this musicale for the weekly Sunday performance. I looked around and saw this guy wearing shades with a beard walking out of the hotel towards the café where I was sitting. He walked through this whole military band formation. He looked really whacked out. He just kept coming and amazingly enough didn't manage to bump into anyone or get arrested."

Marveling at Avakian's stoned grace, Southern struck up a conversation. He discovered they were both huge jazz fans. Avakian's older brother, George, worked for Columbia Records overseeing the marketing of the international catalog of acts like Charles Aznavour and producing the likes of Miles Davis and Thelonious Monk. Aram had known Jack Kerouac at his high school, Horace Mann.

Aram and Terry became fast friends and roommates. Their interests in books, movies, and jazz complemented each other without the kind of tense one-upmanship that existed with Hoffenberg.

For someone who seemed shy and embarrassed on first meeting, Southern had a gift for making friends. He was a good listener who projected a good-humored nonjudgmental face to the various students, writers, artists, musicians, and bohemian types who made up expatriate Paris. Many of Southern's friends and casual acquaintances were the black musicians who found steady work in the clubs. He considered his conversations with them more revelatory than those he had with fellow writers.

"I don't know how to be very articulate about [my kinship with blacks] or analytical about it, but I always seemed to come away from those relationships or an evening in their company with a new and more informed outlook than I had before. I always felt I was getting a valuable education and some insights into things I might have learned eventually but was learning more quickly and more gracefully than if I had to go through the hardships myself," Southern recalled many years later.

One of Southern's jazz buddies was the saxophone player Allen Eager. He accompanied Eager on a visit to Amsterdam. Upon arrival, Eager became obsessed with scoring heroin. After some frantic investigation on Eager's part, an address of a dealer was obtained. While Southern waited back at the hotel, Eager made his rendezvous. "He comes out and gets busted and he thinks ohmigod because he's got everything on him, needles, etc., and oh, he thinks, 'this is it.' They search him and they find all this stuff, you know, the dope, and the needle and everything and they still keep looking. And it turns out that they're looking for diamonds, and so after they can't find the diamonds, they give him a good smart salute and send him on his way. So I thought, what a good drug town Amsterdam is."

Southern's firsthand observations of the jazz subculture were documented in a short story, "Thriving on a Riff," which appeared in the short-lived *Janus*, edited by Daniel Maroc. Southern reworked the story over the next few years until it became known as "You're Too Hip, Baby."

"You're Too Hip, Baby" was eventually published in the August 1963 issue of *Esquire*. Through an economical mix of character study, autobiography, and social satire, Southern constructs a subtle critique of the hipster ethos of the expatriates. That critique seems more profound and complex when one considers that Southern is ultimately questioning a worldview that he would become the embodiment of.

Bebop's spontaneity was reflected in Southern's confident and seamless ability to craft dialogue. Maintaining that spontaneity in his writing became Southern's obsession—and a value he would try to pass on to students in his screenwriting classes several decades later. He tried to avoid second-guessing his initial imaginative impulses when writing a first draft. If one allowed the idea to reach its natural conclusion, rewriting could only make it better. It was like a jazz musician who found it easier to record multiple performances in the studio than to labor over one recording.

In "You're Too Hip, Baby," Murray, an American studying at the Sorbonne, becomes friendly with Buddy Talbott, a black jazz pianist, and his wife, Jackie. To other expatriates, Murray appears in "possession of a secret knowledge." He is envied for his ability to move through disparate social scenes with a relaxed yet enigmatic charm.

As his friendship with Buddy and Jackie develops, Murray introduces them to the best and cheapest places to eat, where to score hash, art films at the Cinémathèque, galleries, and even lectures at the Sorbonne. Initially Buddy and Jackie are grateful. Murray is generous, friendly, and digs the music. They want to reciprocate in some way. When Buddy has to play a gig, Jackie and Murray stay in and listen to records. Jackie attempts to seduce Murray, but he politely waves her off. A few days later, Buddy and Murray drive out to the country for a picnic. After their meal, they lie on the ground and doze. Buddy makes an inquiring pass that Murray, as he had done with Jackie, rebuffs. More days pass. Murray spots his friends dining at an unfamiliar café and stops to say hello. After some awkward banter, Buddy asks Murray "just what have we got that interests you?" Rather unsatisfactorily, Murray replies, "I dig the scene. That's all. I dig the scene and the sounds." In response to which Buddy delivers the devastating put-down of the title.

In trying too hard to be cool and hip, Murray has run away from himself. By contrast, Buddy and Jackie know what they want—the freedom just to be. For Buddy and Jackie, Paris is a place where they can get away not only from America's racism, but also from the patronizing and ineffectual attitudes of white liberals. Murray takes the freedom of his color for granted and gropes around for something elusive and out of reach. In his noble effort to reinvent himself through the pursuit of Hip, he denies that he may be prompted by such crude motives as lust, loneliness, snobbery, and a kind of reverse racism—the idea that Buddy and Jackie must be hip simply because they are black.

"You're Too Hip, Baby" is classic Terry Southern: it astonishes the reader with a mature, concise treatment of the elusive and diffuse philosophy of Hip and blasts the smugness of those who take Hip too seriously.

Aside from drugs, cheap cafés, and great music, Paris offered a wide range of erotic possibility that the Kinsey Report only hinted at. For the average American abroad, guilt-free sex was a big plus. Unlike the down and gritty whorehouses in Central Tracks, the brothels in Paris were abundant enough to accommodate most budgets and tastes. When coeds doing their junior year abroad proved too coy, one could always get a buddy or two to get together to make an "investigative" trip to a local brothel. Southern embellished these accounts in later stories. In 1984, when asked to contribute to a salute to Kurt Vonnegut, Southern responded with a baroque reminiscence about visiting the House of Tongue, where Southern and his other *Paris Review* cronies were ministered to by lascivious and attentive nymphets.

While Southern responded to Paris's many diversions with enthusiasm, he was also productive. He wrote for a few hours every day. In addition to circulating his stories among the little magazines, he shipped off copies of his new work to publications in the States. His work found a less understanding audience there. Vance Bourjailly, for example, rejected two submissions to *Discovery* magazine, "Put Down" (which later surfaced in the *Evergreen Review*) and "Child Psychology," which is now lost. Despite these disappointments, Southern was excited by a new magazine that was being planned by George Plimpton, Peter Matthiessen, and H. L. "Doc" Humes. The three men represented the Ivy League wing of the expatriate invasion. Unlike Southern, Hoffenberg, Richler, and Baldwin, they had more money and a sense of entitlement that gave them the confidence and the chutzpah to see Paris as a blank canvas.

The *Paris Review* crowd, with which Southern would become closely identified, was just starting to form in 1952. One of the first arrivals among this privileged group was Matthiessen, who had spent his junior year at Yale in Paris and returned upon graduation in 1950. He and his stunning blond wife, Patsy Southgate, lived on the rue de Chazelles. Their apartment became an informal gathering place for other Americans in Paris. Matthiessen and Southgate were friends with "Doc" Humes, who was trying to breathe life into an ailing entertainment guide he had started called the *Paris News Post*.

"Doc" Humes was in some respects the Neal Cassady of the *Paris Review* crowd. Like Cassady, he was a charismatic center of energy, whose enthusiasm spurred more cautious souls into action. Born in Arizona, he served in the Navy during the war and then studied at MIT and Harvard. Like so many expatriates, he was putting in time at the Sorbonne while trying to be a writer. Humes was fond of taking on big projects. The *Paris News Post* was one of them.

The idea for a different type of little magazine had evolved one day over coffee at Le Dôme in Montparnasse in the spring of 1951. Humes thought a fictional component would give the *Paris News Post* a new lease on life. He offered Matthiessen the job of fiction editor, an opening that was not exactly attracting droves of overqualified applicants. Matthiessen accepted and began to put the word out that he was looking for short stories to publish.

Somehow Matthiessen came into the possession of a manuscript called "The Sun and the Still-born Stars" by Terry Southern. It was the best thing he had seen in the slush pile that was building up. He told Humes that this was the kind of story the *Post* needed to publish.

"The Sun and the Still-born Stars" was eventually published in *Paris Review* No. 4 in the winter of 1953. It begins with an understated description of the routine life of Sid Peckham, a young World War II veteran who, along with his dutiful wife, lives on a farm just outside Corpus Christi. Aside from Army service in Europe, Peckham has never left Texas. Peckham and his wife toil on their small farm without comment or complaint. On the weekends, they go to the movies. Yet the Technicolor fantasies of the big screen make little impact on their routine. They drift through their chores in zombielike silence. Finally, as if the possibilities of life can no longer be sublimated through movies, something fantastic occurs. One night a strange sea creature emerges from the kelp Sid uses to fertilize his crops. Peckham and the creature engage in a fight, which ends with Peckham being dragged into the sea. The story's coda is equally bizarre. The wife returns to the movie theater to catch the regular matinee. Has she simply gone mad and retreated into routine after her husband's bizarre death? Does she hope to see her husband on the big screen? Did she even know the difference between the routine of farm life and the dreamworld of the movies?

"The Sun and the Still-born Stars" is visionary in its simplicity. Southern describes, but never explains. The reader is left with a disturbing but poetic sense of enigma. Much less celebrated, this story is as good as Shirley Jackson's "The Lottery" in its mix of the real and the fantastic.

To Matthiessen and others in the *Paris Review* crowd, "The Sun and the Still-born Stars" was ample evidence a genuine and original talent was in their midst. It would become one of Southern's most reprinted and anthologized stories. Like much of Southern's best work, it has a deceptively naturalistic surface that belies the strange blend of nightmare and fantasy beneath. This eerie mixture owed much to Southern's childhood love of Poe. Yet the story is no mere pastiche and traces much of its vividness to Southern's experience of farm life in Texas. As with much of Southern's short fiction, an autobiographical core becomes the launching pad for an original, wondrous, and heartbreaking modern fable. Like "The Automatic Gate" and "The Butcher," the story manages to penetrate the inner life of very ordinary working-class characters without being sentimental or patronizing. It is the kind of story that makes one whistle with awe and ask, "Where does this guy get his ideas?"

Matthiessen slowly got to know Southern, whom he found "rather cryptic, with very long gaps and pauses in his utterances, attributable to ingested substances—he would sort of "lean" back into the conversation—and if he was able to link up what he said to where he had trailed off minutes before, it was always interesting and/or very funny.

"[Terry] rarely spoke of Texas (and never memorably in my hearing), which suggested there was not much in his early life that he cared to remember or had not left behind—there seemed to be something missing in his story or hidden or at least enigmatic, and this intrigued people. But certainly he mentioned Texas, since for a while I called him 'Tex' to nettle him."

Matthiessen began to take a more proactive approach as the fiction editor of the *Post*. He persuaded Humes that the listings magazine should be put out of its misery and they should begin raising funds for something new, exciting, and more relevant to their own ambitions and the community of budding scribes. Humes agreed and then sold the rights to the *Post* for six hundred dollars to a rich college girl who managed to publish one more issue. He contacted another friend, George Ames Plimpton, the son of a prominent New York lawyer, who was studying at Kings College, Cambridge. Plimpton was also searching for various forms of inspiration in Paris. It does not appear he ever needed much encouragement because a spirit of adventure and enterprise came to him naturally.

Over the next year and a half Matthiessen, Humes, and Plimpton gathered a team of supporters to discuss the editorial mandate of the new magazine with the unassuming title the *Paris Review*. One thousand dollars, a princely sum in austere postwar Paris, was scraped together to pay for the printing of the first issue. William Pène duBois, son of the painter Guy Pène duBois, already established as an award-winning author and illustrator of children's books, became the art director. He designed the *Review*'s famous helmeted bird logo.

A dingy one-room office on 8, rue Garancière was located as the base of operations. Young women from Smith and Radcliffe colleges known as "Apeteckers" for some mysterious reason, began to float in and out over the *Review*'s early years as unpaid interns, including a very young Jane Fonda. The Café de Tournon, in front of the Palais de Luxembourg, was the real headquarters of the *Review* crowd. And regardless of the weather, the likes of Thomas Guinzburg, John Train, William Pène duBois, John Marquand Jr., Jane Lougee, and other well-turned-out Ivy Leaguers could be found. They became known as a crowd that gave off—whether they intended it or not—an aura of old money and privilege. William Styron, who had recently published *Lie Down In Darkness*, wrote a letter of encouragement to the editors that was published as a kind of quasi-manifesto for the debut issue.

"I didn't have a lot to do with them, but they had a lot of money," Mordecai Richler recalls. "They used to congregate at the café on the rue de Tourneau. Richard Wright was sometimes there. And Terry."

Like Richler, Terry preferred the less chic Old Navy, but his ability to fit in with seemingly disparate social groups was rapidly becoming another characteristic of Southern's slowly evolving hipster persona. As embryonic as that persona was, many in the *Paris Review* crowd regarded Southern, Avakian, and Hoffenberg as ultracool vets on the expatriate scene. Marquand found them intimidating. Southern seemed a "silent, inscrutable presence" to Marquand often seen in an attitude of enigmatic conspiracy with Aram Avakian, who also frequented the Old Navy. At the Hotel Bar American in Pigalle one night, Southern told Marquand it was bad form to buy a girl a drink: "You ruin it for the rest of us if you pay for her beer."

Despite Southern's hauteur, Marquand became close friends with the mysterious Texan, as did Plimpton, who often ran into him at the Métro. For Plimpton, his clearest memory of Southern in Paris was the latter's anger when "The Accident," a fragment of what became Chapters 3 and 4 of *Flash and Filigree,* appeared in the first issue of the *Paris Review* in the spring of 1953.

"There's this policeman in it who looks into the window of this guy who's been speeding and says, 'don't get your shit hot.' . . . We had terrible problems with censors in those times . . . and it was shipped over to the U.S. and there was a [post office censor] on Varick Street called Mr. Dempsey who read every single word in the *Paris Review,* if you can believe it, and I had the feeling that might not get by. You can't believe how repressive the times were. We took the word out and it became the rather anemic 'don't get hot.' Terry had a fit and came around to the office, practically picketed it with signs and was furious about it in his way. According to Peter Matthiessen, he went and sulked in his room for quite a while."

Matthiessen remembers Southern dispatching a fifteen-page J'accuse concerning the edit that he wanted the *Review* to publish in the next issue. Matthiessen boiled this down to the following:

IN ERRATUM—Terry Southern is most anxious that the *Paris Review* point out the absence of two words from his story The Accident (issue one): The sentence "Don't get hot" should have read "Don't get your crap hot," an omission for which we apologize to all concerned.

Art Buchwald found the incident so amusing he mentioned the contretemps in a piece for The *New York Herald-Tribune,* but he was also forced to find a euphemism for "shit hot."

The tempest over the "editing slash censorship" of "The Accident" might have ended Southern's relationship with the *Review,* but he continued to send stories and ideas to Plimpton and Matthiessen. Southern's fifteen-page rant, was an early exercise in mock-indignation, a hobby Southern made a speciality of in letters to appreciative friends, bemused editors, and puzzled strangers in years to come. Deep down, Southern probably knew the *Review* couldn't fight every skirmish in the battle for free expression, but by making a loud hue and cry about "don't get your shit hot," he kept the *Review* from becoming too pleased with itself.

While the *Paris Review* was determined to make sure that as many people as possible read (or at least heard) of their venture through various marketing stunts (such as a flying squad of cyclists who put posters up in every arrondisement in Paris), *Merlin,* launched May 15, 1952, by Alexander Trocchi and Jane Lougee, was more defiantly avant-garde and elitist in its approach. The emphasis was on European literature that broke new boundaries in literary expression. Samuel Beckett, whose play *Waiting for Godot* would receive its Paris premiere the following year, published excerpts from his *Molloy* trilogy in *Merlin.*

Trocchi had been in Paris only a few months before *Merlin* was launched, but the charismatic Glasgow-born, Cambridge-educated six-footer quickly exerted a pull on others. Lougee was a petite American woman who resembled Audrey Hepburn. Still only in their mid-twenties, they exuded an enviable sophistication and worldliness. They promoted their brand of nihilism with unusual confidence and style. Trocchi, who could have become an influential professor at Oxford or Cambridge, embraced heroin addiction, sexual experimentation, and the then-esoteric situationist ideas of Guy Debord, the author of *The Society of the Spectacle.* For almost a decade, Trocchi mesmerized his fellow expatriates, including Southern, with his extremism (eventually the heroin and accompanying ennui would sap a constitution and energy that Southern described as "Wagnerian"). He would be forgiven flirting with other men's wives and girlfriends, never paying back loans, and a general arrogance and impatience toward those who did not recognize his "genius." Despite innumerable character flaws, Trocchi had a gift for inspiring enthusiasm in those around him.

One of those he inspired was Richard Seaver, who was one of the few expatriates with a deep love and knowledge of French language and culture. After a few drinks with Trocchi and Lougee, he came on board as a coeditor and translator for the new magazine. Trocchi also struck up a cordial relationship with Jean-Paul Sartre and ran English translations of work from Sartre's magazine, *Les Temps modernes.*

The various magazines represented different literary directions. Still the individuals behind them were all relatively new to Paris. They found kinship in the basic fact they were all English-speaking expatriates in a city indifferent to their presence.

"Terry from the start was a star," remembers Richard Seaver. "We didn't know much about Terry's background. I probably didn't see him more than half a dozen times in Paris. We used to have drinks together and talk a lot. He had already this sense of humor that he never wavered from through the course of his life. He was just a very funny guy in the way he talked and his take on life. We all thought that Terry was going to be a writer from the start. I think in a way we knew more than he did. He wasn't quite sure if he wanted to be a writer. I think he was still hoping and searching for what he wanted to be and what he had to say and finding his voice. Although when you go back and see those early pieces, his voice was already there, but he was a great raconteur.

"I didn't know him very deeply then, but he always put you in a good mood no matter what it was and very often it was not necessarily good at nine o'clock in the morning after a late night. Within half an hour of sitting down with Terry chewing the fat, you felt better, you felt 'what a pleasant half hour that was,' that guy's so full of beans, so full of life."

Merlin was supported by Maurice Girodias, part dilettante, part impresario, and in no small part, con man and hustler. Girodias's father was Jack Kahane, an Englishman who had founded Obelisk Press, which published the likes of Henry Miller, Anaïs Nin, Lawrence Durrell, D. H. Lawrence, and Frank Harris in the twenties and thirties. After the Liberation, Girodias restarted Obelisk and reissued Miller's *Tropic of Cancer* in late 1945. After severe setbacks and battles with French legal authorities, Girodias formed Olympia Press and began to oversee its operations from 13, rue Jacob. He entered into an arrangement with *Merlin* to publish book-length versions of material that appeared in the journal. Richard Seaver became Olympia's major translator and was paid between $500 and $1,000 for a manuscript. Although it should be added, as Seaver and many others under Girodias's "patronage" discovered, the money tended to come in erratic dribs and drabs, and sometimes not at all.

Southern never published anything in *Merlin,* but Trocchi and Seaver became close friends. As with Hoffenberg, Southern's friendship with Trocchi allowed him a safe vantage point from which to watch a certain strain of defiant self-destructiveness play itself out. Both Trocchi and Seaver would also deepen Southern's appreciation of such disparate European writers as Malaparte, Beckett, and de Sade. Their shared passion for iconoclastic writing would later culminate in the editing of the *Writers in Revolt* anthology in 1962.

Although generally shy and reserved when meeting new people, Southern had no shortage of girlfriends in Paris. Richler describes him as a "dashing womanizer." Tall, dark, and handsome, Southern was able to turn his shyness into a kind of mysterious reserve, a reserve that could be lifted to reveal an appealing brand of whimsy and courtliness. Women appreciated his gentle teasing, especially his habit of creating nicknames, usually abbreviations of first and last names.

Sometime during his last year in Paris, Southern settled into a relationship with Pud Gadiot. Gadiot was a tall, elegant woman, with the kind of classic beauty and natural style glimpsed only in fashion magazines. She had modeled for Irving Penn and Richard Avedon.

Southern and Gadiot traveled to Greece and Spain together. Gail Gerber says their marriage was partially one of social convenience. Being man and wife made it easier for them to share a compartment on the boat back to the U.S. This contradictory reasoning was typical of some young bohemians of the fifties caught between fading Victorian mores and the full-blown sexual revolution of the sixties. It was a time when divorce was still a source of shame and openly living together could be a hurdle in renting an apartment or getting a job. While Southern was clearly in love with Gadiot and vice versa, it seems unlikely they really knew each other as well as they should have when they married in 1953.

In late spring of 1953 Southern and Gadiot moved back to New York. The sentimental education in Paris had ended for the time being. The four years in Europe had consolidated the hip persona that his friends would come to know and love. Many of whom would never see anything other than the mask of the gentle hipster. Europe had taught Southern that his shyness, hesitation, and naïveté could be hidden behind an all-knowing silence or filtered through elaborate, amusing stories. From friends like Hoffenberg and Avakian, he learned the importance of humor as a way to put others and thus himself at ease. The warm acceptance of his short stories by the competitive Quality Lit crowd of the *Paris Review, Merlin,* and *New-Story* gave Southern the confidence to pursue his writing. Like many young writers who live outside their native land for a time, he found distance made it easier to write about America.

The emancipating influence of jazz in Paris cannot be overestimated in its impact on Southern's style. Watching Bird or Dizzy in various hot clubs du jour, Southern adapted their gift for improvisation for his literary ends. Increasingly his various stories-in-progress would begin from a basic theme and work outward. Although Southern still held the original "Lost Generation" of Hemingway and Fitzgerald in high regard, he also strove to go beyond them stylistically. Still only in his mid-twenties, Southern had a keen sense of his development as a writer. He knew that the only way to achieve success as a writer was to discover what made writing enjoyable.

Where a more self-conscious young writer might second-guess his flights of fancy, Southern followed them. "The Sun and Still-born Stars," for example, could have remained a vignette of rural life, but the introduction of a monster-man rising out of the Gulf of Mexico catapulted the story into the realm of the visionary. While he had come to Paris to follow in the footsteps of Hemingway, Faulkner, Fitzgerald, and Sherwood Anderson, Southern had discovered his own trail. He was still unknown and poor, but he had talent to burn and the stories proved it. What young writer could ask for more?

3
Flash and Filigree

After four years of expatriate freedom in Paris, the only logical destination for Southern was New York's Greenwich Village. In an America that had all but officially embraced conformity and the idea of the organization man, Greenwich Village was an underground oasis of the cool, the hip, the *engagé*, the wild, strange, and, in some cases, crazy. For Southern, who wanted to devote his energy and passion to writing, the Village combined the best aspects of both America and

Europe. There were lots of groovy new clubs, cafés, bars, galleries, and small bookstores. Rent was thirty to sixty dollars a month. African Americans, homosexuals, and women could move about with relative ease and comfort. In the words of Fred McDarrah, a longtime resident and photographer, "Greenwich Village was truly a 'village'; a small town within the large city of New York."

Upon arriving in New York in the spring of 1953, Southern and Gadiot found a cheap and cheerful walk-up apartment on Tenth Street and Sixth Avenue. Aram Avakian moved into the spare bedroom to help with the rent. Gadiot resumed her modeling career uptown. For a time, she achieved local notoriety for modeling a line of merry widow corsets with a mask on in an unusually risqué ad campaign.

Unlike Southern, Avakian found he had little patience for sitting alone in his room and writing. He was more interested in the possibilities of film. He began apprenticing with Gjon Mili, a *Life* photographer who had directed a jazz documentary. Mili was a film primitive who was full of great ideas and enthusiasm, but almost technically inept. In assisting Mili, Avakian taught himself how to use the equipment and fell in love with the Moviola editing table. Word got around quickly that Avakian had a knack for cutting film and he got a job on Edward R. Murrow's *See It Now* documentary series as an assistant editor.

With wife and buddy away during the day, Southern stayed in the apartment and devoted himself to reading and writing. John Marquand, a frequent visitor to the apartment, noted that while Gadiot was busy going to fashion shoots Southern was left "to con his soul in solitude." One of his favorite pastimes was to watch the TV with the volume turned off through the scrim of an illuminated tropical fish tank as the hi-fi played jazz.

Southern's four years in Paris consolidated his identity as a writer. The genuine admiration of peers like Alexander Trocchi, Peter Matthiessen, George Plimpton, and others for his modest published output did wonders for his self-esteem. However, their encouragement took second place to the influence of existentialism. Southern used the fierce and contrary independence of Sartre and Camus to reinforce his own ideas about writing, which could be summed up as follows: Writing was something done for its own sake—a spontaneous acting out of the imagination. Secondly, profiting from writing was a happy accident, but not something one should actively pursue.

In the Village, these purist notions would receive a further gloss as Southern embraced the emerging idea of Hip. Of course, to define Hip, as hipsters of all shapes and sizes liked to argue, was to destroy it. Still it was obvious a new attitude was emerging in the Village—a harder, more cynical version of the anarchist and bohemian ethos that had put the downtown community on the map in the twenties and thirties.

Like Paris, Greenwich Village was a hothouse of cultural ferment entering another period of exciting change. Earlier in the century, it had been the gathering place of fresh-faced, red-blooded American socialists like John Reed, Max Eastman, and Emma Goldman. Through the Depression and World War II, it remained a neighborhood where working-class Italian immigrants and downwardly mobile boho types coexisted uneasily, but coexisted nonetheless.

By 1953, the Village was, to use the parlance of the time, a crazy and happening scene. Julian Beck and Judith Malina were attracting a local following for their productions of new American and European plays at the Living Theatre. Norman Mailer and William Styron could be found dispensing advice to up-and-comers at the White Horse Tavern on Hudson Street. Bebop, which had started as a series of informal jams between Charlie Parker, Bud Powell, Kenny Clarke, Dizzy Gillespie, and Max Roach at Minton's in 1941, had now blossomed into a powerful movement. In contrast to the Big Band style of Glenn Miller and Duke Ellington, bebop was loose, unpredictable, passionate, and spontaneous. Little magazines of all descriptions were flourishing with names like *Neurotica, Kulchur,* and *Neon.* At the Cedar Tavern, 24 University Place between Eighth and Ninth streets, a new generation of painters gathered nightly to talk, argue, fight, and get drunk. Robert Rauschenberg, Willem de Kooning, Jackson Pollock, and Mark Rothko, also attracted writers such as Kerouac, Ginsberg, Gregory Corso, LeRoi Jones, and Frank O'Hara. Coffeehouses such as David's on MacDougal, Figaro on Bleecker, or the Cafe Bizarre provided a safe refuge to nurse a cup of joe, listen to the latest mad genius read his or her poetry, and chat up the seemingly endless wave of hauntingly aloof waitresses dressed in black sweaters, skirts, and tights. It was a time when every weekend promised another rent party in someone's apartment or loft.

From 1953 through 1956, Southern would float through these interlocking scenes. Where Paris had been mainly about words, Village life was more interdisciplinary. Southern met visual artists like Robert Frank, Annie Truxell, and Larry Rivers. Rivers, whose figurative style was antithetical to those of painters like Pollock and Rauschenberg, would become a close friend in the latter part of the decade. Terry continued to spend most of his time with Paris friends who had returned to the States, including

Hoffenberg, Aram Avakian, Iris Owens and Marilyn Meesky (both of whom also wrote for Girodias's Olympia house), and David Burnett. Among new Village pals were the eccentric Milton Klonsky and Boris Grgurevich, a Russian American, and his two enigmatic, vaguely sinister companions, "Cookie" and "Shadow."

The Village was also the stomping ground of many graduates of Black Mountain College. The experimental college founded in 1933 by John Rice in North Carolina achieved its peak influence in the years just after World War II before closing in 1956. In 1953, the *Black Mountain Review* was started. The journal published the early writing of Charles Olson, Robert Duncan, Robert Creeley, Gilbert Sorrentino, Louis Zukofky, and others. The Black Mountain philosophy tended toward the free-form, associative, spontaneous, and nonlinear. In addition to having an enormous impact on Canadian and American poetry in the fifties and sixties, the college inspired attendees as diverse as composer John Cage, director Arthur Penn, and Rauschenberg. By the mid-fifties, it seemed as if every second person one encountered in the Village had some connection to the college. (Even Carol Southern studied painting, pottery, and ceramics at Black Mountain one summer.)

Black Mountain College was one of many competing currents of influence that coursed through the Village in the mid-fifties. The liberating influence of bebop on many of the white veterans who gravitated to the Village cannot be overestimated. Friendships between blacks and whites—which either provoked violence, misunderstanding, or guilt in other parts of the country—evolved more naturally. The Village was also the place where the growing disenchantment with mainstream Cold War thinking—which was largely anti-intellectual, repressive, and reactionary as well as anticommunist—could be expressed openly.

During the time that Southern lived in the Village—1953 through 1956—the Beat world had yet to be circumscribed by media overkill and hype. William Burroughs, Allen Ginsberg, and Jack Kerouac were still unknown bit players who moved in and out of the real-life movie that was the Village scene. John Clellon Holmes would claim that he came up with the term "Beat" in his 1952 novel *Go.* Yet when Southern was in the Village the classic works that defined that generation—*On the Road, Howl,* and *Naked Lunch*—were still works-in-progress no different from the feverish dreams of other scene makers. The mainstream's perception of a literary underground (or any of the various Village movements) had yet to reach critical mass.

Through Mason Hoffenberg, Southern became friendly with Kerouac, Ginsberg, and Gregory Corso. Later, he would meet Burroughs in Paris at the Beat Hotel. Southern shared the same antiestablishment values as the Beats, but his own approach to writing was vastly different. He favored ideas over feelings, pure speculation over the autobiographical, and careful and deliberate rewriting over the free-form and spontaneous approach of his Beat friends. Not surprisingly, when the Beats became a media phenomenon, Southern became the "lost beat."

Like many aspiring writers, Terry was a mass of contradictory impulses and desires. On one hand, he was shy, introspective, and serious about his craft. On the other, he was also gregarious, impulsive, and playful. In social situations, the latter qualities were taking precedence to form the genial, expansive mask of a grand guy. This alter ego would reach its fullest imaginative expression a few years later when Southern began writing his second novel, *The Magic Christian*. The novel's central character, the ultrarich philanthropist and trickster, Guy Grand, would become a further extension and exploration of the expansive attitude and droll patter that Southern's friends in Paris and the Village would come to love. Eventually it became almost impossible for them to view him as anything but Guy Grand in the flesh (sans cash, alas).

The Grand Guy persona was an elaborate mask hiding a great deal of insecurity and fear, but it was a front that put people at ease, invited others to share the joke, and above all, made people relax and laugh. Everyone was always happy to spend time with Terry if they hadn't seen him in a while. In the Village, he developed a knack for appearing out of the blue as if he had a sixth sense for happenings or scenes that might prove intriguing, offbeat, or amusing. The personality traits and vocal mannerisms of friends and acquaintances would become raw material for Grand Guy Terry's real-life novel. As the persona became refined, all traces of his Texan accent were hidden by a strange mid-Atlantic mock-noblesse-oblige bearing and speech. One of Southern's Village acquaintances, the musician and composer David Amram, saw the accent as Terry's self-reflexive take on a certain kind of American Anglophilia. "Terry fancied himself as 'the subterranean Texan,'" recalls Amram, "His voice was teasing in the manner of Lord Buckley, who was influenced by West Indian entertainers, who in turn were parodying English colonials."

However, there was a strong vein of seriousness beneath the mock indignation and courtliness. In Paris, Terry had kept abreast of the American scene via the *International Herald Tribune* and lively café debates. There was much to anger and sicken one in postwar America. The last good war had produced a lot of bounty for Mr. and Mrs. Front Porch, but provincialism, conformity, and anti-intellectualism were still at the forefront of mainstream American culture. Although chinks were beginning to appear in his redneck armor, Senator Joseph McCarthy still set the reactionary tone of public discourse. The Korean War had ended in the kind of stalemate worthy of an Ionesco play. The once-vigorous Left of the thirties and forties had been shell-shocked by the blacklisting and hysteria. The intelligentsia seemed to be in retreat. The pro-Soviet utopianism of the twenties and thirties had been stripped away by news of Stalin's brutal collectivization schemes and show trials. The anticommunism at the *Partisan Review* often seemed a magic lantern show that took second place to the Bloomsbury-like domestic arrangements of Edmund Wilson, Mary McCarthy, and gang. Good taste and timidity reigned in such middlebrow churches as *Time, Life,* and the *Saturday Evening Post.*

Outside the Village, many of Southern's fellow veterans seemed intent on embracing a soulless consumerist utopia of tract housing, shopping malls, drive-ins, and dumb-dumb diversions like Milton Berle and *The Honeymooners.* Grand Central Station was a sea of gray flannel as commuters poured into work in midtown offices. Many of them were working in sales and advertising. Their youthful energies were being harnessed to the building of a brave new world of TV dinners, infrared stoves, garage door openers, tranquilizers, book clubs. It was as if Southern's generation had fought to make the world safe for homogeneity, not democracy. The complacent acceptance of a consumer culture fueled by Cold War xenophobia set Terry's teeth on edge.

In the Village, Southern found he was not alone in his distaste for America's shift from wartime idealism and energy into postwar blandness and conformity. George Avakian's most vivid memory of Terry in the mid-fifties is an image of him and his brother, Aram, hanging out with Southern and Hoffenberg in places like the Five Spot, San Remo, and Village Vanguard. The mood is one of conspiracy against the squares and a shared love for jazz, cutting-edge art and writing, and raucous conversation.

Occasionally, they acted on that sense of Us against Them. One night Terry, Hoffenberg, and Avakian became angered by McCarthy's humiliation of Secretary of Defense Stevens on the stand during the Army–McCarthy hearings and the media's response—the *New York Daily News* ran a headline MAC WHIPS ARMY. The trio went down to an Army recruiting office in the Wall Street area. They pasted the front page onto the side of the building and painted ONKLE JOE over it. Then they called up the *News* to tell them of this assault.

For Southern, Avakian, Hoffenberg, and others, New York, and especially the downtown epicenter of Greenwich Village, was becoming a twenty-four-hour combination of experimental theater, laboratory, protocommune, and all-around fun place to be. Those who met Southern in this heady milieu of cultural flux were struck by his ability to fix on something seemingly trivial in a conversation and turn it into a routine. When it came to writing, this constant flood of ideas was a bit of a hindrance. He would start a story, abandon it, and pick up something else. Then weeks, months, maybe years later, he would return to an unfinished piece and complete it. There was method in this seemingly unfocused approach. It kept Southern from becoming obsessed with perfecting one work and then becoming intimidated by the possible failure to turn a first draft into something of quality. Keeping several things in a state of constant preparation prevented Southern from getting bored. This was the case with his first novel, *Flash and Filigree,* written primarily under the influence of Henry Green.

Southern recalls becoming obsessed with Green after reading an article by Philip Toynbee in the *Partisan Review.* Toynbee called Green a "terrorist of language," a concept that must have appealed to Southern immensely.

"[Toynbee's] piece about Henry Green in the *Partisan Review* was so intriguing that I got one of his novels, *Loving,* I believe, which was the first that came to attention in the United States. I read it and was knocked out. It was so good that I immediately started reading all of his books. They seemed so extraordinary that I wrote Green a fan letter. I just wanted to express my appreciation of his work. Surprisingly enough, he wrote back. So we got into a correspondence and through that developed a curious friendship."

On the surface, Green and Southern seemed to be unlikely candidates for forming a mutual admiration society. Green, whose real name was Henry Vincent Yorke, was born far from the wilds of Texas in Tewkesbury, Gloucestershire, England, in 1905. He was born into an upper-class family who owned a beer-bottling business called Pontifex and Sons based in Birmingham. After graduating from Oxford, which he attended with the likes of Harold Acton, Anthony Powell, and Graham Greene, he married Mary Biddugh, whom he affectionately called "Dig,"in 1929. Until the early sixties, Green spent his working life as managing director of Pontifex.

Green's *Loving*, the novel that first caught Southern's attention, was published in 1945. Its subject matter is the upstairs-downstairs life of Anglo-Irish servants between the two world wars. As with all of Green's books, it is the style that immediately grabs one's attention—a kind of chiseled-down stream of consciousness akin to an all-seeing eye. Characters often speak at cross-purposes and utter nonsequiturs. Like Southern, Green was obsessed with the incongruities and misunderstandings found in daily speech. V. S. Pritchett says that Green brought a "spirit of poetry, fantasy and . . . often wild laughter" to his writing. The result is a vision of life where tragedy and comedy coexist, where human motives are murky, and even the simplest character, a semiliterate maid, for example, becomes as intriguing as the loftiest noble. Southern devoured Green's other books, including *Living* (1929), *Party Going* (1950), *Doting* (1952), *Caught* (1943), *Back* (1946), and *Concluding* (1948).

Loving's success in America led to a *Life* magazine profile, which described Green in unusually—by Time-Life standards—perceptive terms. The article argued that a Green novel is "not just a platter of realistic bare bones; it is a rich dish of human flesh and blood, fit for the most exacting cannibal. Moreover, it is subtly designed in such a way that Green himself, the creator of the dish, seems to be the one personality who has nothing to do with it. While other members of the tribe dance excitedly around the pot, the chef shyly looks the other way and pretends he has never heard of missionaries."

Southern found the novels revelatory, the literary equivalent of the burning bush in the desert. Green's balance of description, dialogue, and the handling of surrealism, social realism, and black comedy were not only unlike the American writers Southern admired, but distinct from British and European fiction of the period. Green was without a doubt sui generis.

Southern had been struggling with his various attempts at a novel prior to discovering Green. Before beginning his correspondence with Green, Southern had made a great deal of headway on *Flash and Filigree* ("Accident," a fragment from *Flash*, appeared in the *Paris Review* around the same period). However, the final tone and structure of the novel clearly indicate that Green's fiction had been absorbed into Southern's bloodstream.

Flash and Filigree is set in a vision of Los Angeles that William Burroughs later described as a place where "censure or outrage is simply irrelevant." At a chic Beverly Hills clinic, Dr. Frederick Eichner, a distinguished and urbane dermatologist, meets with a referral. The new patient, an intense well-dressed young man, one Felix Treevly (a.k.a. Ralph Edwards), describes his attempts to treat a lesion that has turned into a larger, perhaps cancerous growth. Eichner examines the young man and finds nothing but a barely visible scratch. Sensing he is part of some elaborate con, Eichner knocks the patient out as if affronted by this insult to his profession. Treevly wakes up in a nearby examining room, where one of the clinic's nurses, the beautiful Babs Minter, tends to his wound. These three characters push the plot forward by their respective attempts to cover up, manipulate, and understand a series of chaotic happenings and situations. Aside from Treevly, who is determined to deflower comely nurse Babs, the motivations behind these characters' actions are inexplicable and opaque.

However, Southern's wry vision of Los Angeles is clear and precise. Instead of the hard-boiled pessimism of Raymond Chandler, the reader is placed in a cold and cruelly elegant world. Dr. Eichner, Babs Minter, the Head Nurse, Treevly, and detective Frost (a kind of ur-Columbo) are archetypes who continually confound our expectations of how they would behave in a traditional thriller. *Flash* was dismissed by some critics as merely a series of episodes strung together, but the novel is quite tightly plotted—even though plot is the least of its concerns.

Cutting back and forth between the clinic in Beverly Hills, the flesh-pots of Sunset Boulevard and Hollywood, and the civic offices of downtown L.A., Southern subtly creates a portrait of modern Los Angeles that is ahead of its time. In the fifties, most of Southern's East Coast peers dismissed Los Angeles as a crass frontier metropolis whose only cultural legacy was the Hollywood movie. In Southern's novel, the City of Angels is an ever-shifting landscape of light and shadow where anything can and does happen. A high-speed chase down a treacherous valley road, an elaborate seduction at a drive-in, the taping of a gruesome TV game show called *What's My Disease?*, a courtroom trial whose key participants are clearly insane, etc. Murder, impersonation, lesbianism, drug dealing, and cheap thrills of all kinds are related in a calm and measured way that heightens the novel's sheer strangeness.

The only American writer who had surpassed Southern in describing Los Angeles in this satirical fashion up to that point was Nathanael West. *Flash and Filigree* deals with the same kind of fringe players as *The Day of the Locust,* but its characters are not so much souls in disarray as comic types lost in a funhouse. Southern's creation of a world akin to West's is all the more remarkable considering he had yet to spend any significant time in California except for his hitchhiking adventure as a teenager at Sunset

High. One can quite reasonably imagine Southern setting a challenge for himself by not only trying to write an homage to Green, but also to imagine himself as Green suddenly inspired to write a weird hybrid of the potboilers found in *Black Mask* or *Argosy*.

In spite of, and most likely because of, the novel's assured handling of various kinds of parody, pastiche, satire, and allegory, the book was a difficult sell for American publishers. The prose evokes the elusive quality of a shimmering mirage on a sunbaked stretch of desert highway. One can imagine an editor at Viking or Random House wondering where all the feverish shifts in action were leading. Despite the excerpt in the *Paris Review* and referrals from friends, the book kept getting rejected in New York.

In addition to his transatlantic correspondence with Green, Southern began a friendship with another literary hero, William Faulkner, who was romantically involved with another *Paris Review* acquaintance, Jean Stein, the daughter of Jules Stein, the ophthalmologist who had turned a weekend hobby booking bands into the powerhouse agency MCA. Jean met Southern in Paris while studying at the Sorbonne. She started hanging out at the *Paris Review* offices and began proofing copy and performing other editorial functions. One fateful evening, December 29, 1953, she was introduced to Faulkner, who was passing through Paris. Faulkner was working with Howard Hawks on the screenplay for *Land of the Pharaohs*. Stein and Faulkner, who was twice her age, began a romance that lasted until his death in 1962.

Of all the great American writers of the twenties and thirties, Faulkner was Southern's favorite. "Since college days and before I had regarded Faulkner as the most influential American writer of our time, and always came down vociferously on his side whenever one was obliged to choose between him and Hemingway."

Southern, who would later describe *As I Lay Dying* as a "twenty-one-gun salute to the Absurd," saw Faulkner as a sensitive and empathetic figure trying to restore humanity to a Southern culture damaged by racism and economic decline. Faulkner's experiments with language and narrative also deeply impressed Southern.

In addition to working on the Hawks film, Faulkner was traveling back and forth from his home in Mississippi to New York during the winter of 1954. He was editing *A Fable* for publication in August 1954.

Ellen Adler, a friend of Stein and Southern, says that Faulkner was like Balzac to her generation: "Everybody was dazzled to meet William Faulkner. I mean, Faulkner was more than God . . . in the fifties, Faulkner was like Balzac

. . . he was bigger than any movie star and he was remote, nobody met him and suddenly, Jean has him here. In the city and in restaurants!'"

Stein invited Southern to join Faulkner and her for dinner. Anxious about meeting his hero, Southern recalled downing a few stiff drinks with Anatole Broyard in the Village before dinner. It became one of several meetings.

"[Terry] was one of the few people that Faulkner liked to spend time with," recalls Stein. "He had respect for Terry, but not only respect. He really was fond of him. Terry, of course, has always been very courtly and there is something very Southern about him . . . they had that in common. That they were both from the South didn't hurt. He just loved to be with him.

"My strongest memory of those early years is when we would hang out sometimes with Faulkner, how much Terry respected him and loved to hear his stories. . . . They probably both had had a lot to drink, too. . . . Faulkner was very fond of him and believed in him as a writer."

Meeting Faulkner may have also prompted Terry to revisit his Texas roots via fiction. Faulkner was one of the standard-bearers, a writer who had stayed true to his art. Southern helped Jean when she interviewed Faulkner for the *Paris Review*'s Art of Fiction series. In the interview, Faulkner would maintain that a "writer needs 3 things: experience, observation, and imagination." Left unspoken was the question of what to do with these estimable qualities. For Faulkner, devotion to one's art had required reserves of quiet strength to endure misunderstanding, poverty, and self-doubt. On a spiritual level, Faulkner was superhuman. Neither Hollywood nor alcoholism had blunted his ability to write masterpieces like *The Sound and the Fury* and *As I Lay Dying*. *A Fable* was perhaps a lesser work, but no less ambitious and heartfelt than the landmark achievements of a younger man. In Faulkner, Southern could see that the writing life was as much a test of character as it was a test of one's talent.

How Southern supported himself through much of the fifties was a mystery to those who knew him. Gadiot provided the primary source of income. Occasionally a check would arrive from his parents. Terry prided himself on not taking odd jobs. In 1954, he turned thirty. Many men of his generation with no clear career prospects would have been more than a little anxious, but Terry seemed happily indifferent to his marginal economic status.

One of his rare forays into the nine-to-five during this period was a gig David Burnett got him on Martha Foley's *Best American Short Stories of*

1954. Terry received fifty dollars a week for a couple of months' work. Burnett's mother, Martha Foley, had cofounded *Story* in 1931 with her then husband, Whit Burnett. After their divorce, Foley inaugurated the yearly compendium of short stories culled from various magazines, quarterlies, and journals. Along with Whit Burnett, she helped kickstart the careers of Nelson Algren, James Thurber, Truman Capote, Joseph Heller, J. D. Salinger, James Agee, Flannery O'Connor, Philip Roth, Arthur Miller, and Sylvia Plath. Burnett and Southern helped Foley sift through the material and create a short list that eventually included stories by Ira Wolfert, B. Traven, Jean Stafford, and Ivan Gold.

It was during this period that Burnett and Southern conceived the idea of making a short film.

"David and I went for lunch on West Fourth Street across from an elementary school," Southern recalled. "We would see these children come out at recess. We got the idea that the perfect crime would be to get a box of chocolates, put cyanide inside, replace the top, and artfully put the box of candy in the schoolyard. During the recess or lunch hour, the kids would see the box and eat the chocolates. It would be a perfect crime in the Leopold and Loeb mode."

Southern and Burnett shot the film over a couple of weekends using an 8mm home movie camera. Martha Foley helped to convince her friends to allow two weirdo hipsters to use their children as the victims of poisoning. A lot of the film was taken up with the preparation of the candies. The children delighted in grimacing for the camera. But the results never added up to more than a nine-minute lark. The Kenneth Angers and Maya Derens of the world had nothing to worry about.

During Southern's first year back in America, it was becoming clear that he and Gadiot were suffering from irreconcilable differences. Southern's income was erratic at best and, in her eyes, he seemed to be more interested in making the scene than getting a steady job. Their relationship was, like so many things in Southern's private life, a puzzle.

"At one point, he described [Gadiot] as being very hysterical about something," said Carol Southern. "He did say he was responsible for keeping the apartment in order and she was the breadwinner and I don't think that worked out very well. But this is all kind of conjecture and recollection. . . . I think that she probably wanted a regular life and that was probably the source of the conflict."

By the middle of 1954, Southern and Gadiot agreed to a quick divorce. She moved to an apartment on East Thirty-sixth Street.

Although he was not one to spill his guts, Southern obviously needed a respite from the failure of his marriage. He and Hoffenberg planned a trip to Europe.

"I actually went at one point to be on a kibbutz. We went down to this ship run by a kibbutz for a couple of days of incredible work. Cleaning out the furnace of the smokestack, the worst possible work you could imagine, but it was very satisfying. It's like an ideal community, one of those Shangri-la-type concepts, and so that was great. But the next morning this guy comes in and says he's been robbed. Forty dollars was missing from his footlocker, and so everybody's freaking out saying 'we gotta get locks on the footlockers' and then half of the people say 'no no no, that would defeat the whole notion of our unity. If that person took the money, he needed it.' So there was this immediate schism, like a 50-50 split over this, and we left the ship."

Eventually, Terry got a trip on another freighter headed toward Europe in late 1954–55. He spent most of his time in Paris, where he met and hung out with David Amram. Amram was playing with various combos and had a regular gig at the Hôtel des États-Unis. Southern purchased a jazz record Amram had recorded with Bobby Jasper. One of the compositions, "The Bird of Montparnasse," was a favorite. "A groovin' gas, *mon vieux pot!*" exclaimed Southern. Southern introduced Amram to Avakian and they spent time in cafés and listening to music. "After a gig, we would go out to eat," recalls Amram. "Terry would create dramatic scenes out of what was going on around the café."

It was a relatively short trip. After a month and half, Southern was back in New York.

Along with Green and Faulkner, Nelson Algren rounded out Southern's troika of mentors. In the fall of 1955, Southern and Alston Anderson, a Paris buddy, interviewed Algren in the Village for the *Paris Review*. To many aspiring writers in the Village, Algren's life and work were inspirational. In 1949, he became the first winner of the National Book Award for his novel *The Man with the Golden Arm*, an unromantic but perceptive study of a musician struggling with heroin addiction. The Chicago-born author had developed his craft the hard way—odd jobs as salesman and carny, a stint in a Texas jail for allegedly stealing a typewriter, working for the WPA gathering stats on venereal disease, countless one-night stands, hard drinking, and living in a succession of dreary tenements. In his writing, Algren had transformed this grim quotidian experience into a series of brilliant short stories and starkly poetic novels like *Never Come Morning* and *A Walk on the Wild Side*. Algren wanted to write about American life with the intensity and depth of Dostoyevsky. To a large extent, he succeeded at this, but he had turned into a reluctant celebrity. Hollywood came knocking. Like many writers before him, Algren felt he could take the money and keep his fiction pure. When Southern and Anderson interviewed Algren, they did not see that beneath Algren's street-wise exterior was a conflicted soul struggling with an on-again, off-again relationship with Simone de Beauvoir, a bitter aftertaste from his recent screenwriting duties, and a deepening fear that he would never write fiction again. Sadly, Algren was right. Until his death, Algren's output would consist mainly of magazine articles and nonfiction books built around travel themes.

As with Faulkner and Green, Southern and Algren warmed to each other. In the introduction to the interview, Southern and Anderson write: "to talk with Algren is to have a conversation brought very quickly to that rarefied level where values are actually declared." Neither Southern nor Anderson, a Jamaican poet and jazz critic who had spent years in France and Spain, were fresh-faced rookies when it came to the life of the streets. Yet they listened to Algren's school-of-hard-knocks reminiscences of petty crime, gambling, and poverty with reverent awe. In the midst of the stories were nuggets of advice. Algren said that if you want to write a war novel you have to do it while you're in the war, otherwise it slips away. Unlike the European tradition, one became a writer in America "when there's absolutely nothing else you can do." When asked about whether his style was arrived at consciously or not, Algren said, "The only thing I've consciously tried to do was put myself in a position to hear the people I wanted to hear talk talk."

For Southern, listening to Algren was not so much instructive or inspirational as it was a validation of the direction he was heading in. Throughout his life, Southern would often tell interviewers or students that one should write from the gut like Algren. It was odd advice considering that all of Southern's heroes—Faulkner, Green, and Algren—were fastidious rewriters. In fact what Southern and his heroes do is stay with subjects and themes that engage them emotionally when logic or caution would suggest another course. Great writing thus becomes an act of faith as much as it is the result of skill and practice.

Algren and Southern stayed in touch after the interview. Algren became one of Southern's earliest and most ardent champions. In 1964, when Southern hit the big time with *Dr. Strangelove* and *Candy*, he and William Styron paid Algren a memorable visit. In later years, when he began teaching creative writing, Algren would often use Southern as an example of a great short story writer.

By mid-1954 Southern was taken on by the Curtis Brown Agency on the basis of his short stories and his novel-in-progress, *Flash and Filigree*. During his time in the Village, he accumulated rejection slips that were for the most part quite encouraging, from an astonishing range of publications: *Sight and Sound, Antioch Review, Cornell University* ("This seems to lack point"), the *London Magazine, Commentary, Esquire, Hudson Review, Kenyon Review,* the *New Yorker, Harper's,* the *Nation, Atlantic Monthly,* the *Reporter, New Directions, Ellery Queen's Mystery Magazine, Perspectives USA, Argosy, Yale Review,* the *Sewanee Review, American Vanguard, New Mexico Quarterly,* the *Story Press, Playboy, Mademoiselle, New World Writing, Cosmopolitan, New Statesman,* the *New Republic, Maclean's,* and many others.

As the wide range of these submissions indicates, Southern was, despite his laconic, indifferent demeanor, quite deliberately trying to get published in as many places as possible. Consciously or not, he wanted his audience to be as wide and varied as possible . . . he didn't want to pigeonhole himself or be pigeonholed. The submissions also indicated another quality that Southern tried to avoid broadcasting to others: his sheer industriousness. If asked point-blank, do you have any difficulty writing? Southern would reply, "Not at all." But he did feel very reluctant to talk or discuss his work.

Curtis Brown placed "The Sun and the Still-born Stars" and "The Panthers" (which was later reprinted in *Red Dirt Marijuana* as "You Gotta Leave Your Mark") in the same issue of *Harper's Bazaar*. "The Panthers" dealt with a group of aspiring juvenile delinquents who kidnap an old man and lock him in the trunk of a car. Their plans for a big ransom go wrong when the man suffocates. Due to the sheer blind impulsiveness of this crime, the police are able to arrest the culprits quickly. Southern was paid $750 for both stories.

One night in October 1955, Southern went to a party thrown by Robert and Mary Frank to celebrate Robert's Guggenheim grant. Southern approached a tall attractive woman with dark hair named Carol Kauffman, who originally hailed from Philadelphia. She had studied painting at Antioch College and was pursuing an M.A. in early childhood education.

"I had heard of Terry before," Carol said. "My then boyfriend pointed him out on the street and said, 'Terry Southern's back from Europe. He has two stories out in *Harper's Bazaar*." I had also been introduced to Terry before. He was sitting on the circle in Washington Square Park with Mason Hoffenberg, whom I'd met as a waitress at Joe's Dinette. Mason introduced me, but Terry was very cool, barely turned his head, and stared off into space as I chatted with Mason. So I was surprised when he came right up to me at the party and said, 'Hell, I believe we've met. Mason speaks very highly of you.' He made a date with me. We met at the Riviera Bar and his first words were 'Do you Know the work of Henry Green?' By the end of the evening I knew I would marry him."

As romance quickly blossomed, Carol and Terry began staying at each other's apartment regularly. Carol was surprised at the breadth of Terry's knowledge of what was going on—not just in the Village, but in the city in general. He seemed to know everyone and was up to date on the latest cutting-edge books, plays, and movies.

On December 5, 1955, Charlie Parker died at the age of thirty-five while watching television. According to a story he told Darius James in the eighties, Southern attended the funeral. There was an odd couple of days between Parker's death and his burial when the musician's body disappeared. One of Parker's widows had taken the body to a secret location. Finally after some hue and cry, the body was returned to the funeral home at five o'clock in the morning. The hearse was greeted by a lineup of horn players who began playing a dirge in the morning rain. Southern told James it was the most remarkable sound he had ever heard.

In the January 1956 issue of *Harper's Bazaar,* "The Night the Bird Blew for Doctor Warner" was published. It was a cautionary tale about Dr. Ralph Warner, an urbane musicologist attempting to write the definitive text on jazz. Dr. Warner feels the only way this can be accomplished is by becoming a hipster. Confident with his initial forays exploring the dark clubs where jazz is played, Warner tries his luck scoring some heroin. He ends up getting mugged and killed. Not only was it possible to lose one's sense of compassion if one tried too hard to be hip, it was also possible to lose one's life.

The story was further proof of Southern's ability to handle irony with unique skill. It was the kind of story that people used as an example of a writer's great promise. There was something thrillingly subversive about having such a dark fable appear in pages normally devoted to fashion and grooming.

By late spring of 1956, Terry and Carol were living in a room on Charles Street. Terry had always intended to return to Europe and asked Carol to come with him. "Of course I said yes," Carol said. "I was dying to go to Europe—I was madly in love with Terry—no way I would not go. But though I never told Terry about it, I was worried about my father's reaction. A few months later when Terry said, 'Perhaps we're to be married,' I was not only thrilled but glad that I did not have to fabricate a lot of lies."

Meanwhile, Alexander Trocchi had arrived in New York from Paris. Despite their various addictions, neither Trocchi nor Hoffenberg bothered Carol. She had met lots of junkies working at Joe's Dinette, a Village hangout where they tended to congregate. Trocchi managed to get a job with Trap Rock Corporation as a barge captain hauling huge boulders used for jetties from Poughkeepsie to Far Rockaway. The barge was an ideal place to write. Trocchi would complete *Cain's Book,* his famous novel about heroin addiction, on the barge. Trocchi was able to get Southern and others writers jobs with the company.

Terry and Carol needed money for their move to Europe, and a few months on the barge seemed to be the answer. They married on July 14, 1956, in Tupper Lake, where they were houseguests of a painter friend of Terry's, Madeline Bernard. After a few days at Tupper Lake, they came back to New York, packed their belongings, and went directly to the barge moored in Far Rockaway.

"We were barge captains, as they called themselves euphemistically, since it was a job so lowly that it was ordinarily held by guys who had been kicked out of the Longshoreman's Union, old winos and the like, being replaced now by this new breed, the dope-head writer. But it was one of those classic writer's jobs, like hotel clerk, night watchman, fire-tower guy, etc., with practically no duties ('just keep her tied up and pumped out . . .')," recalled Southern.

Carol's recollection of life on the barge was more prosaic and romantic. "There was a little cabin at the end of the barge with a tiny deck in front," she recalled. Conditions were elemental. A bucket for a john. A rain barrel for water. A primus stove to cook on. Terry fished. At night we would play scrabble by the light of the kerosene lamp. And it was lovely at dusk, sitting on the deck smoking Pall Malls, gliding along the Hudson."

Over the months of July, August, and September, Carol and Terry finetuned their plans for their European adventure. After months of letter writing, Carol had secured a job teaching nursery school for the United Nations in Geneva, Switzerland. Neither Carol nor Terry knew what to expect to find in Switzerland, but it sounded like fun.

4

Candy Christian Meets Guy Grand

What do you think the rest of life is going to be like?

What? Oh grand surely.

—Terry Southern to Elaine Dundy, 1958

Rocky seas stretched Carol and Terry's journey across the Atlantic into a twelve-day endurance test. Through Carol's father, they were able to get second-class tickets on a Norwegian freighter, but the crossing seemed to take forever.

"It was very comfortable," says Carol, "but we just got very tired of the food, a smorgasbord thing, and with eating with the captain who always got drunk. At dinner, there was just this other couple who we were sure were collaborators because they were so Teutonic. The man, a Dutchman, claimed to have done very well in the war. Soon we weren't appearing for meals at all except for dinner, and then we raided the icebox at night."

Terry and Carol arrived in Paris in late October 1956. Mason and Couquitte put them up in their apartment on rue Henri Barbusse for about six weeks until Carol's United Nations job started in the beginning of December. While still in Paris, Southern became obsessed with a 1936 Citroën convertible with a running board. It struck him as the perfect vehicle to cruise and travel the roads of Europe. He began to leave notes on the windshields of any Citroën he saw asking if the owners wanted to sell. Just before they were about to leave for Switzerland, Southern lucked out and bought a thirties model for a modest price. Driving on to Geneva, Terry and Carol discovered the Citroën was prone to frequent breakdowns. However, this did not make Terry any less enamored of the vehicle.

Their initial Geneva lodgings belonged to the École des Enfants des Nations Unies, in a sixteenth-century manor house on 46, rue Schaub. Later, the couple would move a little farther from the school to 39, rue Cramer. Carol's job would allow the newlyweds to take generous amounts of leave at Christmas, Easter, and the summer months. Aside from the savings from the barge job and whatever Southern could eke from his writing, her school wages were their primary source of income. Carol was paid $125 a month and her father sent her $50 as a stipend.

Still their apartments were spacious and centrally heated (a rarity in Europe at the time). Their modest finances did not prevent them from enjoying their newlywed years in Europe.

"We did everything we really wanted to do, but on a very tight budget," said Carol. "At least a couple of times a month, we would just get in the car and drive to France and go have dinner and it was so nice along the lake. As soon as one crossed the border, the whole atmosphere was different."

Carol thought Geneva was beautiful, but a little too perfect. She and Terry were struck by the regular number of news stories about an attempted bank heist or somebody trying to race for the border with huge stacks of currency.

Although used to wandering about the Village at all hours, Southern found Geneva a radical, but not entirely unpleasant, change of pace. Geneva, with its picturesque mountains and lake, was a town of early-to-bed-early-to-rise bankers, diplomats, and bureaucrats. There was little for Southern to do except go on long walks, sit in cafés, read the paper, and write. To his credit, and much to Carol's delight, write he did. In Geneva, Southern would not only prepare *Flash and Filigree* for publication, but he would also write *Candy, The Magic Christian,* a television play, and several short stories.

For Southern, life in Geneva was "not unlike a situation in a Kafka novel. My room was by a window overlooking the courtyard, and I would watch the children playing. They were all children of diplomats so there was this spectrum of nationalities. It was unsettling to observe that their behavior was so absolutely stereotypical: the American children were willful and bullying, and so were the Germans; the English were snobbish; the French were effete, clever, and silly; the Orientals were very bright and ultrapolite. I got so fascinated watching the children that I stopped working on anything else. I took notes on their behavior just like a child psychologist. At one point, I went to a local costume shop and bought a bunch of animal masks—lion, fox, donkey, etc., then I persuaded my wife to hang them in the children's cloakrooms. I could see which child would choose which mask. Interesting stuff. The Head Mistress, however, was a rather strict Meg Thatcher type, and she put an end to my experiments before they ever really got started."

The kind of rest and recreation Southern normally relished was sought elsewhere, but there were still things about Geneva's manic calm and order that brought a gleam to his eye. In addition to being fascinated by Carol's charges, Southern became obsessed with the garbage-disposal chute on the third floor of their apartment. In tall-tale fashion, Southern claimed to have tested the durability of this fine example of Swiss craftsmanship by throwing items like bottles, tin cans, and cutlery down the chute. According to a story he later told *Realist* editor Paul Krassner, he came up with the ultimate test of the disposal unit's might by chucking an old Royal portable typewriter down the chute. The chute made an indescribable sound of pain and Southern thought he was going to have to pay thousands of dollars in damages or find himself escorted by gendarmes to the local jail. Instead, "the machine was running again the next day, and there was a little note in the lobby that read something like, 'Residents are requested not to overload the disposal unit.' Overload! And they say the Swiss don't have a sense of humor. Anyway, it was the smugness of the machine, Paul . . . I mean you can understand how a thing like that could, well, be disturbing?'"

For Carol, these early years, from 1956 through 1959, with Terry were idyllic. This was the Southerns' "Moveable Feast" period. In spite of their erratic cash flow, the American dollar went far in Europe. With most of their basic living expenses covered by Carol's UNESCO gig, they managed to live out their own version of the Grand Tour. During Carol's vacations, they would make various forays into Paris to visit Mason and Couquitte as well as Ginsberg and Burroughs, then living at the now legendary "Beat Hotel." They would also spend time in London with Henry Green and his wife, Dig.

In early December, not long after settling in the new apartment, Southern traveled to Paris by train for a meeting with Maurice Girodias. As the publisher and editor in chief of the Olympia Press, Girodias was always eager to talk to cash-hungry writers who might pen a new "db"—dirty book—for his devoted clientele. Girodias offered Terry the equivalent of $1,000 payment for a novel he could add to his list. This pittance of an advance would be broken up in segments over the next year and a half. Southern took the train back to Geneva and hammered out an outline that Girodias received on December 10. Written in the form of a novella, the outline described the heroine as:

> A sensitive, progressive-school humanist who comes from Wisconsin to New York's lower East Side to be an art student, social worker, etc., and to find (unlike her father) "beauty in mean places." She has an especially romantic idea about "minorities" and of course gets raped by Negroes, robbed by Jews, knocked up by Puerto-Ricans, etc.— though her feeling of "being needed" sustains her for quite a while, through a devouring gauntlet of freaks, faggots, psychiatrists and aesthetic cults.

Her name was Candy.

Girodias liked what he read and scheduled the book for his spring '57 catalog. This was pure optimism on Girodias's part. Southern's initial enthusiasm for *Candy* waned, and he asked Hoffenberg if he would like to collaborate. With Southern in Geneva and Hoffenberg in Paris, the writing would proceed in fits and starts.

Carrying the lion's share of the actual writing, Southern didn't enjoy working on *Candy*. Among his many other projects was the beginning of a children's story, in the style of Oscar Wilde's "The Happy Prince," which would eventually emerge in 1977 as *The Donkey and the Darling,* a limited-edition book/objet d'art in collaboration with Larry Rivers. Southern's agent at Curtis Brown, Edith Haggard, advised him to use a pen name for *Candy* in order not to prejudice his chances of mainstream acceptance. Southern was more engaged with his other writing, particularly *The Magic Christian.*

Despite his meager offer, Girodias was the best bet in town—not just for Southern and Hoffenberg, but for the majority of expatriate scribes in the City of Light. Girodias had restructured Olympia as the publisher of "dbs," sold mainly to a mailing list of readers "looking for something for the weekend." In their gut, Hoffenberg and Southern sensed Girodias could not be trusted, but they were suckers for what Southern called his "boss charm." It was a charm that had so far seduced the likes of Vladimir Nabokov and J. P. Donleavy.

Like Paris, London became a favorite stomping ground for the couple. England was beginning a slow but gradual rise from the grimness of postwar austerity into an era of expansion and change. New figures on the literary scene such as Kingsley Amis, John Wain, Alan Sillitoe, Anthony Burgess, Muriel Spark, and Colin MacInnes were taking an impassioned, realistic look at England's postcolonial decline. The influx of "Commonwealth" writers such as V. S. Naipaul and Sam Selvon from Trinidad and Jamaica added a much-needed multicultural voice to the country's all too Anglo-Saxon makeup. The theater was moving away from the well-made plays of Terence Rattigan and Noël Coward to the angry realism of John Osborne and the absurdism of Harold Pinter. Young people in England were hungry for the same kind of excitement that their American counterparts were experiencing as rock 'n' roll introduced the whole notion of youth culture. Coffee bars were opening up all over the country. There was a small, but growing trade in import jazz and R&B recordings. Skiffle, epitomized by Lonnie Donegan's "Rock Island Line," emerged as the home-grown equivalent of Bill Haley and the Comets' "Rock Around the Clock." English art schools, once the dumping ground for adolescent misfits, were becoming hotbeds of innovation and revolution in the visual arts (not to mention countless rock groups that would take the world by storm in the sixties). The Suez Crisis of July 1956—kickstarted by Egyptian president Gamal Nasser's nationalization of the Suez Canal—embarrassed the country's upper-class establishment, but liberated a dormant middle and working class. Instead of retreating into cynicism, the country's best and brightest were taking advantage of the fact that the petrified traditions of the ruling elite were crumbling.

Mordecai Richler had decided to decamp to London from Montreal. Carol and Terry paid him and his then wife, Cathy, a visit at Christmastime. Through Richler, they were introduced to Charlie Sinclair, an East End fishmonger and hipster-in-the-making who was also a self-taught intellectual.

"Terry just adored Charlie, who had the use of an old car as part of his job. Terry called it his 'company car,'" remembers Carol. "He was a cockney who was very bright and amusing. I remember he and his wife gave us a bread knife with the word 'bread' carved into it."

While in London, Southern finally got to meet Henry Green in person at the latter's flat in upper-middle-class Belgravia. To Southern's relief and delight, they got along like a house a fire. Like Southern, Green was an essentially shy and ultrasensitive man who hid behind a mask of good cheer, hospitality, and exaggerated storytelling. Both men also liked nothing better than chatting away into the wee hours with generous amounts of port or brandy at close hand. Green had not yet succumbed to the desolate isolation of his final years and still entertained. He and Dig made sure the Southerns were introduced to such high-flying literati as Cyril Connolly, Stephen Spender, Arthur Koestler, and T. S. Eliot at various cocktail parties they hosted.

Carol found Green fascinating, but sensed the pain beneath the bonhomie and good cheer: "He was a very urbane amusing upper-class Englishman who drank too much. Very attractive. His wife, Dig, was a delightful and slightly fey aristocratic Honorable Mrs. Henry Yorke. They were both so aristocratic and exotic to Terry and me. At the same time, such amusing and open people that we both fell in love with them. I think Terry understood Henry's drinking certainly in a better way than I did and used to sit up talking with him way into the night and then put him over his shoulders and put him to bed."

After enjoying their first Christmas in Europe, the Southerns received some bad news when they returned to Geneva. On January 17, 1957, Terry's father died. Since Terry's mother had died of cancer a few years before, Southern Sr. had grown increasingly morose. He left Dallas and embarked on one last drinking binge that ended at the Royalton Hotel in Miami. According to Robert O'Bremment, the manager of the Royalton, Mr. Southern's left arm was heavily bandaged and there was a bruise on the right when he checked in. He appeared to have been drinking rather heavily. He ordered a bottle of whiskey that evening and a second one the next day. He was found in the room in the morning in a dazed condition. Police were contacted. An ambulance arrived in twenty minutes. Southern's father died forty-five minutes after arrival. The Dade County coroner said his father had died from "acute and chronic alcoholism."

According to a letter Southern received from one of his parents' friends, Mrs. L. C. Matlock, a funeral was held in Cleburn, Texas, on Monday, January 21, and the body was buried in Alvarado. A doctor who treated Terry's father a few days before his death said that Terrence appeared to have contracted a gangrene infection from a broken bottle or window in his hotel room.

The extent of Terry's grief was hard to gauge. Carol found it difficult to pry details about his family from him at the best of times and the sad lonely death of his father deepened Southern's stoicism whenever the subject was raised. Because of a lack of funds and the awareness that with the death of his father, he had no real family left in Texas, Terry decided not to return to the States for the funeral.

The desolating impact of his father's death was alleviated by some good news from Mordecai Richler. On January 17, he wrote to Southern that Andre Deutsch was considering Terry's book, *Flash and Filigree.* Deutsch had already published Richler's first novel, *The Acrobats,* and his company was known as a congenial place for relatively unknown writers to sell their wares.

Deutsch was born in 1918 in Budapest. He was educated there and in Vienna. When the Anschluss occurred, he fled to Zurich and stayed with an uncle who helped him get to London. When war broke out, he was briefly confined as an enemy alien on the Isle of Man. One of his fellow internees was a publisher and their chats sparked an interest in the gentlemanly trade. Upon his release in 1942, Deutsch worked for Nicholson and Watson and then Ernest Benn, a publisher of technical books, in sales. He used his contacts to start his first company, Allan Wingate, in 1945, but was unceremoniously ousted by members of his board. Dusting himself off from this setback, he launched Andre Deutsch Ltd. with advice from Stanley Rubinstein, a solicitor with a solid background in publishing. The company published the von Papen memoirs, the diary of one of Hitler's closest foreign policy advisers. The book was a controversial bestseller— the establishment felt Deutsch was cashing in on a morbid curiosity with the war. Deutsch used his "foreignness" to gain an edge in securing the English rights to several contemporary European writers. But it was his publication of Norman Mailer's *The Naked and the Dead* that solidified the company's status. The English may have had a xenophobic distaste for books by their continental neighbors, but they loved American writing, jazz, and movies as much as they would soon embrace rock 'n' roll. Along with his chief editor, Diana Athill, Deutsch would acquire the U.K. rights to a variety of American and Commonwealth authors including Gore Vidal, V. S. Naipaul, Margaret Atwood, and John Updike. Although he was an innovator in the stuffy Old Boys network of English publishing in the fifties, his combination of cosmopolitanism and gut instinct would eventually let him down when the multinationalization of the industry began in earnest in the late seventies.

Richler made it clear to Southern that getting a novel published by Andre Deustch was an ultraprestige gig. Still the small advances Deutsch paid out to first-time novelists would last only a month or two. Richler had been scraping by on freelance reviewing for the likes of *New Statesman* and *Encounter.* But things were looking up for hungry scribes. In various letters that winter, Richler told Southern about the lucrative opportunities for scriptwriting in British television. After several years of public debate, Parliament passed legislation in 1954 allowing private investors to bid for a handful of independent TV franchises that would be allowed to compete with the BBC. Almost overnight, there was a desperate need for actors, writers, directors, producers, and other craftspersons to provide dramatic material for fourteen new regional broadcasting companies that would now compete with the state monopoly. Sydney Newman, a producer at the Canadian Broadcasting Corporation, was recruited by London's Associated Television to create a weekly hour of live drama similar to *Playhouse 90.* Newman began to commission every available scribe in London to either adapt or write original scripts for the new show known as *Armchair Theatre.* One of Richler's first gigs, a collaboration with American screenwriter Stanley Mann, put £100 in his pocket, which was then enough to live on for several months in relative comfort.

Richler's entrée into television was assisted by his friendship with Ted Kotcheff, a recent emigré from Toronto. Kotcheff and Richler had known each other when the former was working as a stage manager for the CBC. Sydney Newman had recruited Kotcheff as a staff director on the new show. Kotcheff had flown over to London and began sharing a flat in Swiss Cottage with Richler.

The acceptance of *Flash and Filigree* was followed by a wire on March 9, 1957, from Richler saying that Andre Deutsch had accepted *The Magic Christian* based on an outline: YOU ARE NOW ENTITLED TO KNOW THE SECRET HANDSHAKE, THE STABLE CHEERS AND—SOON ENOUGH—YOU GET YR ANDRE DEUTSCH SWEATSHIRT TO WEAR.

Meanwhile, things were not going well for Henry Green at Pontifex and Sons. His drinking and diminishing interest in the business were creating a rift between him and his fellow executives. Green was feeling depressed and finding it harder to write. In the early spring of 1957, Green sent this pleading telegram to the Southerns: UTTERLY EXHAUSTED STOP CAN YOU PUT ME UP SEVEN DAYS REPLY BY TELEPHONE HENRY GREEN.

Southern got the impression Green badly needed a change of scenery and a sympathetic listener.

"I wired back 'COME AT ONCE.' During our correspondence, he said Switzerland always fascinated him because it is the one place where they inventory every stone in the country. We said you must visit, never dreaming that he would. It just seemed an appropriate thing to say when someone expresses an interest in where you live. Maybe some moment of stress in his scene in London or at his factory, Pontifex and Sons, in Leeds was behind his visit. I think he came over on a train. He spent about a week or two with us, then we decided to drive him to Paris in our Citroën."

In anticipation of Green's visit, Terry decided to repaint the study, where their guest would sleep, at the last minute. Carol didn't think that was neccesary, but Terry wanted everything to be in "tip-top shape." When Green arrived, he struck the two as being in a heightened state of emotional fragility. While Carol worked at school, Southern and Green hung out in various cafés. Green wanted to talk and Southern was an avid listener. When the subject of Green's stint as a fire warden during the Blitz came up, Southern suggested he write about it.

Grateful for the Southerns' company, Green returned to London and began lobbying various literati such as Terrence Kilmartin, literary editor of the *Observer*, about Southern's talent upon his return to London.

In addition to talking up Southern among the London literati, Green continued to act as a nonjudgmental, unthreatening role model. In his letters and conversations with Green, Southern grew to appreciate that the refinement of "a writer's style" was a delicate quest. For as soon as a writer became comfortable with his or her voice, the danger of self-indulgence and self-parody was not far around the corner. By the time Southern met Green, the latter was finding it increasingly difficult to write without the heavy burden of self-consciousness. Eventually it would become difficult for Green's friends and family to determine whether the drinking was a reaction to an increasing sense of writer's block or vice versa. As *Surviving,* the excellent collection of Green's published and unpublished shorter pieces attests, by 1958, even a short book review for the radio became excruciating to complete.

Geneva was proving to be Southern's clean, well-lighted place. In a state of almost perfect calm and solitude, he was able to read, contemplate, observe, and, most importantly, write. Several different projects occupied him at the same time. In addition to getting a good head start on *The Magic Christian,* he began to write several short stories.

One such story, "South's Summer Idyll," appeared in *Paris Review* no. 15, 1957. It dealt with a young boy playing with an air rifle on a Saturday afternoon. A small girl's pet cat gets killed in the process, but this significant detail is held back until the end of the story. It's just something that happens on a lazy weekend in Texas, when there is nothing else to do. Drawing on his childhood memories of Big Herb, the piece was a highly distilled form of autobiography. Amid the random violence and parochialism depicted by Southern, the story possessed an elusive sadness for a time and place that was increasingly alien to its author.

Terry also followed up on Richler's suggestion about writing something that was TV-friendly. He refashioned "The Panthers," with its then-popular subject of juvenile delinquency, and fired it off to Richler, who responded by saying "the half-hr is very good but needs to be expanded—too short—and also requires that the actual crime be shown (end of Act.1). Suspense, man. Shock." He suggested rewriting it for Southern. Richler would then try to sell it to the CBC in about a month's time and they could split the fee.

Meanwhile, Green had so enjoyed his spring visit with the Southerns that he began to organize a summer gathering in Spain. On April 29, 1957, he wrote to describe his plans: "After a great deal of difficulty, [Dig and I] have hired a villa 20 miles from Barcelona, Spain, from July 1st to the 31st. Of course, I have not seen it, but the Agent who appears respectable, says it will take nine people easily. It has four bedrooms, bathroom, dining room, sitting room, kitchen, garage and studio upstairs with its own terrace and 120 yards from the sea. There is a servant but that won't be much use as we have no Spanish."

Throughout May and June, Green would send further details. He and Dig were renting a villa in the coastal town of Mataró, approximately twenty kilometers north of Barcelona. He seemed rejuvenated and talked about a play and the possibility of writing about his time as a fire warden during the Blitz. His loneliness barely disguised by his courtly letters, Green repeated his invitation to the Southerns: "Come as soon in July as you can. Make us your Base but stay as much as you can. Best love to Carol."

In July 1957, the Southerns journeyed down to Green's rented villa on the east coast of Spain. Another guest, the future novelist Emma Tennant, who was engaged to Green's son, Sebastian, was fascinated by her father-in-law-to-be, but not oblivious to signs of his declining power and confidence as a writer.

Terry spent most of his time talking and drinking with Green. Carol and Tennant swam and sunbathed. The attractive Tennant brought out the flirt in Southern and Green. She confessed that she had a bit of a crush on Green Sr. Green and Southern's mutual fondness for the grotesque and surreal fascinated and repelled her.

Before arriving in Spain, Southern had written to George Plimpton about doing an Art of Fiction interview with Green for the *Paris Review*. As with so many of the classic Art of Fiction pieces (Plimpton's own interview with Hemingway comes to mind), the Q and A sessions between Green and Southern evolved into a combination of metafiction, mythmaking, and old-fashioned literary table talk. The questions and answers were sculpted by the two via letter weeks after the Spanish revels had ended. The introduction suggested the interview had been conducted at Green's Knightsbridge home one evening, but the truth was the initial work had been done in Spain with revisions and additions conducted by mail through the fall. One such letter demonstrates how much importance Green attached to the interview:

> I feel now that we ought to put this interview in a frame, I am getting more and more nervous about not having it set in something. I suggest the front porch of the Torre in Spain on that terrible road with vespas rasping by. You could do a description of this waiting for me to come out and the important thing would be that I could not bear to leave the front door for fear of the burglary that was going to happen.
>
> The last paragraph of the interview could end with my discovering that the time was 6:30 that the pubs in Knightsbridge, England, had been open for a hour and that through the pouring rain I should go off to the Spanish pub but ask you to stay on and keep guard for half an hour more until the guests come back.
>
> The last sentence might be "and at this Mr. Green drifted off into the rain as sad as a grey dead starved pigeon wet in the ash can."

Despite the spirit of mischief that informed this collaboration, the interview had a core of seriousness. Aside from talks on BBC Radio, Green detested publicity. The *Paris Review* interview became a common reference for Green scholars. Despite pieces of drollery where Green pretends to mishear the word "suttee," a reference to the Hindu custom of cremating a widow on her husband's funeral pyre, instead of "subtle" and sneaking in "cunty fingers" past Plimpton's blue pencil, the interview was, in the end, a statement of literary values.

The stay in Spain with Green was followed by a sojourn to the South of France to visit Mordecai Richler in Tourettes-sur-Loup. The medieval village in the Antibes was known for its startling views of the mountains and the sea. Southern continued to collaborate with Hoffenberg on *Candy* via post. By this stage, they had received most of their $1,000 payment from Girodias. Richler also introduced Southern to Ted Kotcheff, although Carol Southern does not recall his presence during this visit.

Kotcheff recalls Hoffenberg and Southern trying to finish up a bunch of pages so they could join a poker game. But the book was still far from done.

According to Carol Southern, Terry had grown weary of the collaboration.

"I think the idea of *Candy* initially amused Terry a lot, but he got bored with the execution. He would write longhand and I would type. He set himself a quota of two pages of typed script a day. When he would give me the longhand, sometimes it wasn't enough and he would have to write more. He really was forcing it out. That's why he asked Mason to help him finish it. Mason was involved in the inception of the idea."

Part of that weariness was due to Hoffenberg's erratic participation. Charismatic and talkative, Hoffenberg was a Roman candle of ideas, but he had little stamina for the day-in, day-out regimen of writing. Hoffenberg helped introduce characters such as Dr. Krankheit, the author of the Wilhelm Reich–like manifesto, *Masturbation Now,* who is hampered in his research by his overpossessive mother disguised as a hospital cleaning lady. Hoffenberg also supplied inspired repartee for Terry's characters, like Aunt Livia, a suburban swinger with a genius for transforming the most innocuous conversation into a minefield of innuendo and fantasy. According to Carol Southern, much of the inspiration for Candy's home life in Racine, Wisconsin, was a wild expansion and exaggeration of his encounters with Carol's father and stepmother and aunts. As the summer adventures drew to a close, Southern returned to Geneva with some more pages with the hope that *Candy* was almost finished. He had other fish to fry.

In addition to *Candy* and the interview with Green, Southern had been shopping a bunch of short stories around with varying degrees of success. In June, *Harper's Bazaar* (U.K.) rejected "The Arab and the Inspector," a mystery pastiche, saying, "the Inspector talks more like a stage Englishman than a real one." Another story, "Child Psychology," which has since disappeared from the Southern archives, was turned down by several American journals.

However, Barney Rosset bought "Put-Down," a part of *The Hipsters,* for $200, for the *Evergreen Review.* "Put-Down," like "South's Summer Idyll," transformed Southern's direct experience—the easy access to cheap marijuana in the Latin Quarter—into something disturbingly poetic. A group of jaded expatriates stoned on hashish become mesmerized by a ball of mercury pushed around the floor of their Left Bank digs. Although little more than a vignette in length, the story is packed with insinuating menace. The title speaks to the fragile sense of camaraderie that exists among those who try too hard to be cool and with it.

In November, *Esquire* bought "Sea Change" (later collected as "A Change of Style" in *Red Dirt Marijuana*) for $350. The brief story follows a Los Angeles woman of a certain age getting her hair done to appease her lover. This is not one of Southern's best stories, relying mainly on description and the awkward twist of having the woman walk in on her husband and his mistress.

Rust Hills at *Esquire* somewhat inexplicably liked "Sea Change" more than "The Road out of Axotle," a classic Southern story and in some ways his reply to Kerouac's *On the Road.* "The Road out of Axotle" was submitted to *Esquire* on September 13, 1957, and went the rounds for several years before it was published. Editors were puzzled by the story. One wondered if "this reefer-and-a-gang-of-gin story [is] really for us?"

As work on *Candy* drew to a close, Southern described his idea of bliss in an undated letter to Mason Hoffenberg: "My idea of pure sloth would be to weigh so much (say about 5,000 pounds) that one couldn't move and also to have sleeping sickness." He tells Mason that his routine consists of him getting up at 4:00 P.M., eating milk and raw eggs, reading the *Herald-Tribune,* writing, and then going to sleep with a few amytals.

Of course looking as if one were not trying too hard was all part of being a hipster. In reality, Southern was trying to apply his talents to whatever work was available. This search for extra cash led to Southern's first-ever credit writing for the screen.

Ted Kotcheff was eager to get Southern some work as a regular writer for *Armchair Theatre.* Terry suggested adapting Eugene O'Neill's *The Emperor Jones* with the view to making it reflect the continuing impasse in the American South regarding civil rights for black Americans. Southern himself said in a typically laconic fashion: "I already knew Kotcheff through Mordecai. Kotcheff said they want me to do Eugene O'Neill's *Emperor Jones.* So I did the script for that. We did it with this guy Kenneth Spencer, a lot like James Earl Jones. That was an interesting production. I got to use Billie Holiday music in the background."

Kotcheff had been hired by Dennis Vance, the executive producer of *Armchair Theatre* for the first two seasons. Most of the scripts consisted of adaptations, but the quality of that material—short stories, plays, novels, etc.—was very high. The first real show was "Tears in the Wind," broadcast on September 16, 1956, an adaptation of André Gide's *Symphonie Pastorale.*

In London Kotcheff did most of his work out of the ABC production offices on Wardour Street. Correspondence between Southern, then living at 46, rue Schaub, Geneva, and Kotcheff indicates a keen interest on the latter's part to give Southern work that would be creatively as well as financially rewarding. In a letter dated January 13, 1958, Kotcheff mentions *The*

Green Pastures and Herman Melville's *Billy Budd,* but adds, ". . . like I told you before you left, if there is anything you are interested in or excited about which you would like to adapt, or better still, if you have some ideas for an original, let me know."

Three days later, Kotcheff replied to Southern's brief reference to *The Emperor Jones.* Kotcheff had already planned to do the play, but hadn't begun work on the adaptation or hired a writer. By January 28, Southern was given a £75 commission from Kotcheff, who said, "Hope that is enough because that is the top fee they pay here." He concurred with Southern's ideas that the language needed to be "revamped and contemporized completely." Kotcheff already had very fixed ideas about the witch doctor sequence: "I've a huge crocodile idol, half crocodile, half female, surrounded by ancient totem. I've got a real witch doctor, fire-eaters and dancers. I visualize the whole thing ending up in the primeval ooze." Kotcheff, no slouch in the Quality Lit department himself, asked Southern to look up the poems "Heritage" by Countee Cullen and "I Have Known Rivers" by Langston Hughes and see if he could work them into the adaptation.

On February 3, Southern received a letter from Verity Lambert, a British film and TV producer who was then working as Kothceff's assistant. She explained the prickly question of why Southern wouldn't be getting his £75 right away: "I'm afraid the money won't actually happen until after the play has been transmitted. The money paid to you comes out of my budget and nothing is paid on the budget until after transmission."

By February 25, Southern had delivered his play and was asked by Kotcheff about the somewhat jumpy shift from Act II to Act III. Kotcheff was also worried the script was a little short and asked Southern to restore two vignettes in the jungle scenes about Jones's childhood and witnessing a lynching.

The routine for the *Armchair Theatre* broadcasts was pretty basic. Sets were constructed in Manchester and erected in Didsbury Theatre. The cast did read-throughs and basic rehearsals in London and then traveled on the 5:55 Friday train from London's Euston Station to Manchester for final studio rehearsals at Didsbury. Playwright Clive Exton, an *Armchair Theatre* regular, described the rehearsals and broadcast period as "a perpetual screaming match between Newman and Kotcheff."

In the case of *The Emperor Jones,* Kotcheff cast Harry Corbett, who appared in a number of *Armchair Theatre* episodes, as Smithers. Corbett hadn't yet been typecast as the nervous cockney dreamer in *Steptoe and Son,* the hit british comedy of the sixties that would be remodeled by

Norman Lear as *Sanford and Son.* Kenneth Spencer, a black American actor with a commanding physical and vocal presence, had made a significant impact in Vincente Minnelli's *Cabin in the Sky,* a contentious but rare Hollywood showcase for black American talent, as the General, but aside from a thankless role in the World War II melodrama *Bataan,* he found it difficult to get meaningful work in the United States. He spent most of the postwar period and the rest of his life in Europe, mainly Germany, appearing in theater, opera, and film productions. Kotcheff saw him perform in an opera in Germany and was sufficiently impressed to give him the lead.

The play was scheduled to air in February, but was pushed back to April. Kotcheff did some extra "writing" on Southern's script during the dress rehearsal, but whether this meant anything significant is debatable.

On Sunday, March 20, *The Emperor Jones* was broadcast from Manchester's Didsbury Theatre at 9:30 P.M. Southern was in Geneva.

Variety's London stringer wrote that the production was "hardly the type of program to command and hold a mass audience. At the best of times it would not be an easy-going play, but the adaptation by Terry Southern and the addition of ballet sequences to illustrate the nightmare of the haunted man hardly eased the way.

"The dramatic highlight of the production was the performance by Kenneth Spencer in the title role. A man whose stature measured up to the character, he had an authority and presence which enriched the role and gave it depth and meaning."

The reviewer generally felt that the production "strained viewers' loyalty when it entered the realm of fantasy, although that does not imply an unjust criticism of the Boscoe Holder Dancers. Their team work was fine; it just didn't fit into the scheme of things."

The English papers were much kinder. ABC's producers thought the viewing figures were quite good considering the difficulty of O'Neill. Despite the relative success of the *Jones* adaptation, considering its intimidating reputation in the theater, Kotcheff was unable to get Southern another gig on *Armchair Theatre,* although they did discuss Nathanael West's *Miss Lonelyhearts.*

In addition to Southern's screenwriting debut, March was also the month *Flash and Filigree* was published. It had taken almost almost half a decade for the book to land a publisher. Diana Athill said she took on the book "because I was crazy about it, and as far as I can remember it required no editing. . . . I do very clearly remember being amused at Henry Green's delight in the book because Terry's style was so amazingly like his own. I think Terry was a great fan of his, and may well have felt strongly enough that they were kindred spirits to risk approaching him direct."

Athill says neither *Flash and Filigree* nor *The Magic Christian* was a big earner for Andre Deutsch, but the books began to have an odd popularity among those who wanted to be on the cutting edge. Green called *Flash* the novel of the year in the *Observer*. Many of the journals of commentary such as the *Spectator* and the *Listener* commented on the debut novel favorably. The book continued to resonate through the spring and summer of 1958. Anthony Quinton in *London Magazine* singled out *Flash and Filigree* from a group of new novels such as *The Return of Ansel Gibbs* by Frederick Buechner, *Home from the Hill* by William Humphrey, a Faulkner-like drama set in smalltown Texas, and *On the Road* by Jack Kerouac: "It is a work of unclassifiable or indefinable intention, a pure literary artifice, carried out with admirable dexterity and control. . . . This is a very funny and beautifully written book, a series of acute perceptions of human peculiarity. It has no paraphrasable content, the only thing to do with it is to read. It has more in common with *Through the Looking-Glass* than with any of the other books reviewed here. It is impossible to imagine what Terry Southern will do next, but whatever it is it ought to be good."

While the English enthused over Southern's work, many American editors were still cool to Southern's approach. Roger Angell, the fiction editor at the *New Yorker* rejected "Janus" on March 5, 1958. He wrote back to Southern saying the writer was "trying to give his characters an ultra-sophisticated cast, and to make them needlessly complicated." Angell said he would like to see more work, but Southern must have been puzzled by the rejection. "Janus," which remains unpublished, is a story about a young American couple driving through Italy. Their car breaks down and the husband goes for help. Much of the story is concerned with the husband's impatience with his wife, his frustrating attempts at pidgin Italian, and a mistrust bordering on fear of the locals who come to his aid. In many ways, it was the kind of sympathetic study of grace under pressure, with discreet touches of the gothic, that the *New Yorker* loved. Perhaps the real reason for the story's rejection was that it indicated Southern was trying too hard to write a *New Yorker* story.

Despite the rejection by the big guns at the *New Yorker*, Southern could content himself with his first celebrity-type interview in the August 1958 issue of the U.K. edition of *Harper's Bazaar*. His interviewer, Elaine Dundy, was more than sympathetic. The vivacious American wife of the

Observer drama critic Kenneth Tynan was also the sister of underground filmmaker and dancer Shirley Clarke. Southern had met the Tynans at Christmastime. Tynan shared Southern's impish sense of humor. According to Kathleen Tynan's biography of her husband, Dundy and Southern had a brief affair. And while it was true that the marriage of Kenneth and Elaine was ripe material for a Kinsey case study, one also wonders where Terry and Elaine found the time or place. It seems just as likely it was an affair of the mind.

Dundy conducted the *Harper's Bazaar* interview through the mail. In the final piece, Southern appears alongside J. P. Donleavy and Don Stewart—new kids on the transatlantic scene waxing philosophic about the expatriate experience. Southern's responses to Dundy's questions are surprisingly direct and serious: "I believe I live abroad because I'm looking for isolation . . . the kind I mean that comes with an immunity to overhearing clichés, because a language you didn't hear as a child never necessarily intrudes the way it would at home, in the subway, or the drugstore. A phrase that you catch over here by chance just because you haven't heard it for the ten millionth time, is apt to seem fresh and interesting."

Southern also used the interview as an opportunity to speculate on why he was having some difficulty gaining recognition in his home country:

> I think my book [*Flash and Filigree*] was first published in England rather than America because I think most American publishers' tastes are on the level of the comic-strip. They've become just ordinary businessmen. They don't have time to read; they're too busy hustling. Consequently they never develop any personal tastes. The way they work, they examine a manuscript for awhile and then they may say, 'Oh yes, this is like *Look Homeward, Angel*' and then they look up the sales figures of *Look Homeward, Angel,* and if that's all right they'll take it. But if the manuscript happens to be just a bit original, you can save yourself the postage . . . unless it's five or six hundred pages, of course, then they're rather apt to take it, anything; they got that idea from big cars—you know, 'What's good for General Motors . . . By Cracky!' They're the first real automatons trained quite simply to spot imitations of previous imitations. But then you take a situation like in England where there's a kind of noblesse oblige to be reasonably intelligent—well, then you get a few people who, however outlandish otherwise, do have highly developed individual tastes, and so there's a chance that a manuscript will appeal directly to them, and

moreover, a chance they'll have enough security and self-respect to respond properly when it does. Would I say American publishing is behind the times? Behind the Eight-ball is what I'd say. Yes, in books and cars, we're terribly behind; we're still on a "big and hollow" kick.

By the time Dundy's article appeared, Carol and Terry were on holiday in Italy. Despite the heat and their lack of finances, they had a great time.

"We were staying in fourth-class hotels all the way. It was very, very hot," she recalls. "When we were in Crete, there was one boat every three days to Athens or Piraeus. On the day we were to leave, they notified all the hotel guests in Irákilon, except us, that the boat was not sailing because of rough seas. They didn't think any tourist would be staying in the run-down hotel we were at. We stayed in really cheap places and made our own coffee on our primus stove."

The couple also traveled to Venice and more touristy sites, such as the Tower of Pisa.

That summer, work on *Candy* was drawing to a close. Despite a growing level of mutual resentment, Hoffenberg told Southern that he was glad they had worked together:

". . . I consider it an honor to have worked with you on this job—I can't anser [*sic*] for you of course, but for me, these have been a very fruitful two years and I know I shall often look back on them as a *happy* two years come what may.

"I know we haven't always seen eye to eye on this thing, that you don't agree with some of my methods of running the hospital and so forth, but nonetheless we have stuck together on this thing, getting the job done through teamwork and—often's the time—through sheer nerve and inertia."

Candy finally appeared in October 1958 as number 64 in the Traveller's Companion Series of Olympia Press under the joint pseudonym Maxwell Kenton. Much to everyone's surprise, the Paris vice squad banned it. Girodias simply reissued it as *Lollipop* in December.

While less ambitious and formally challenging than *Lolita* or *Naked Lunch,* and less autobiographical than *The Ginger Man, Candy* was no simple "db." The blithely innocent and precocious girl-next-door of the title was a flower-child-in-waiting. Born on Valentine's Day no less, Candy Christian searches for true love and beauty in the depths of suburban Racine, Wisconsin. Like so many pilgrims, she yearns for a mentor who will guide her journey toward sweetness and light. Sadly, so many of the possible candidates seem (at least in the Matthew Arnold sense) wanting.

Her English professor, Mephesto; the Mexican gardener, Emmanuel; her boyfriend and her uncle Jack and aunt Livia are revealed as base, hypocritical, pretentious, or damaged in some way. To her credit, Candy does not condemn them for the in base lusts and desires, but strives to understand and even comfort them. Her seemingly bottomless compassion and forgiveness lead her from the Midwest to Greenwich Village to a utopian community established by the Crackers (with their hit slogan "We are the Crackers/ the Crackers are we!/ True to each Cracker as Crackers can be/ We've got to build, boys and girls, for a world of peace!/ A world of peace, a world of peace!/ without silly police!") and finally to the Himalayas, where she confronts the ultimate guru.

Candy conveys a delicious sense of fun that belies any sense of competition or animosity between the two authors. Although the characters are either fantasy figures or grotesques, they are oddly likable. Perhaps because no one in the book, except perhaps for the hunchback, ever really gets what he or she wants. The horny antagonists, from Mephesto to Aunt Livia, fail to achieve the mind-blowing sex they lust after, and poor Candy remains caught in a cycle of disbelief, shock, and astonishment with only her purist naïveté to comfort her. William Styron was only half kidding when he said *Candy* was "the stuff of heartbreak." For readers in the decade ahead, Candy's cry, "Give me your hump," could also be translated as "Candy Christian, c'est moi!"

Candy quickly became a cult hit among Paris's expatriate community, and slowly, a trickle of copies made their way to London and New York. Some of these would show up in bookstores like Frances Steloff's Gotham Book Mart in Manhattan.

Through the fall and winter of 1958–1959, Southern finished *The Magic Christian.* Carol recalls Terry laughing out loud during the writing of the novel, and he would invite her into his Geneva study to read aloud his favorite passages. Queried on the title many years later, Southern had only this enigmatic response to offer: "Titles it seems to me are made up of the most engaging words you find which correctly describe the content of the work. The words 'magic' and 'christian' are certainly two such words, and surely they describe Guy Grand to an almost uncanny degree—a billionaire who does outrageously benign and charitable things."

Southern told Paul Krassner that *The Magic Christian* essentially grew out of the question, "Wouldn't if be funny if . . . ?" The book's episodic structure alternated Grand's planning and execution of pranks with his drawing-room chats with his maiden aunts, Agnes and Esther. The pranks grow in size and intensity as the chats become more surreal in tone. Not content with teasing a hotdog vendor with a hundred-dollar bill he cannot possibly change, Grand moves on to taunting the very establishment he represents. Grand makes a pig of himself at a chic and expensive restaurant. He inserts nonsequiturs and racial slurs in one of the newspapers he owns. He uses a howitzer on a big-game hunt and enters a hungry panther in a dog show. He bribes the cast of a popular soap opera to break out of character and insult the sponsors as crass pulp merchants. But one can sense Grand getting more and more restless with these guerrilla forays that are meant to épater les bourgeois. His *pièce de résistance* becomes the building of the luxury liner the *Magic Christian*. Only the rich and powerful can afford a ticket for the maiden voyage of the state-of-the-art ship. For the first few days, the travelers revel in the ship's luxury, but then very quickly all hell breaks loose. Passengers are drugged, crew members seem to be engaged in mutiny, and the ship appears about to sink or go up in smoke. Somewhere behind the scenes, Grand shifts and alters the mood of chaos that envelops this floating torture chamber/funhouse.

As with all of his stunts, Grand must pay off a large number of people to avoid being prosecuted for his mischievious acts of subversion. The first and only voyage of the *Magic Christian* creates such a furor that Grand decides to lie low. Of course, the controversy only inspires Grand to create more insidious stunts such as the mysterious "Get Acquainted Sales" that appear and then disappear around the country.

The Magic Christian is Southern's "beat novel." Where Kerouac, Burroughs, and Ginsberg either appealed to the reader's emotions or attempted to provoke those emotions through raw (albeit carefully sculpted) imagery, Southern opted for the gentle tone of a storyteller. His targets however are the same as the Beats': Cold War America's repressive media and political culture, the public's willingness to parrot the received ideas of the status quo, the unquestioning acceptance of consumerism, the banality of middle-class notions of good taste, and the amorality of the wealthy—to name a few. Guy Grand is a Zen master of subversion unconcerned with any interpretation of why he does what he does—believing instead that the pranks and their planning already embody a critique.

Southern's relationship with the Beats was warm. He knew Ginsberg socially from his Village days. And in late 1958, he was introduced to Burroughs through Gregory Corso at the scruffy nondescript rooming house at 9, rue Gît-le-Coeur dubbed "the Beat Hotel," where the soon-to-be-famous-but-presently-broke Beats lived. Burroughs was preparing

Naked Lunch for Maurice Girodias, who was having second thoughts. Southern, along with Ginsberg and Corso, pressured Girodias to publish Burroughs's antinovel even if its titillation quotient—the homosexual couplings, hangings, weird science fiction images—was hard to deduce.

Southern had no problems with *Naked Lunch*. It was like nothing else he had ever read. However, he was less enamored with the work of Jack Kerouac. In a letter to Allen Ginsberg from Geneva, he forwarded a copy of *Flash and Filigree* and had this to say about Kerouac: ". . . [*The Subterraneans*] is certainly a much more interesting book than *On the Road*—you know? That is to say, I had the feeling with *On the Road* that it was so severely edited, butchered actually, that there was almost nothing meaningful (convincing) left. Do you happen to know anything about how, how much it changed, etc.? I felt *The Subterraneans* was unique and original in the sense that it hadn't been done before—that is to say that that particular scene hadn't been treated before, or rather so adequately. Perhaps it was more of a publisher's coup than a writer's—because the 'real value' of it seemed to me to be in the rarity of it, you know, just as a phenomenon, so to speak, in print. Anyway I would really like to know about that if you do."

In a reply, sent to Terry from the Beat Hotel, Allen Ginsberg confessed he was equally puzzled by *Flash and Filigree:* "I asked Mason then, he said it was purposely pointless, a form of wit, is that so, is that it? I was not sure, if so too Dada for me, tho perhaps inevitable if you want to destroy that form of novel, that's one way of doing it, i.e. make a speedy well-built novel with an intricate plot that at the end never ties in and closes boxlid like well made detective-Greene etc novel is supposed to—so I was confused what your intentions were—tho if one wanted to destroy novel why not invent new form of writing entirely rather than satirize old form—or perhaps I miss the point entirely?"

Henry Green remained Southern's biggest fan. Back in the summer, Green appeared on a radio show called *Recent Novels* broadcast on the BBC's Third Programme on June 20, 1958. Green artfully anticipated the critical confusion over *Flash and Filigree* by explaining, "I think it's a first novel, and there are about three books in it. Because it is a first novel it's inexperienced. But I think with any luck—and I have great faith in him—after he's written two more, I think he'll be writing more in-one-piece, as you wish."

When *Christian* came out in the spring of 1959 from Andre Deutsch,

Green wrote to Southern with more encouragement: "Although I feel it is too short and perhaps drives the same nail in with the same hammer too many times, I found it very powerful. Very funny in the bitter way I think you mean (because I don't know the US) and totally unlike anything I'd read by any countryman of yours. You have a very great distinction in every sentence, distinction in the sense that every sentence is yours and could only be yours and elevated at the same time—you will forgive me, I've just been rereading Horace Walpole's *Letters of 1753* and am using distinction and elevated."

Southern received approximately $750 for *The Magic Christian*. The reviews were positive, but even though The *Magic Christian* was the more fully realized book some were disappointed. In another roundup piece for *London Magazine,* Anthony Quinton wrote: "The whole undertaking is too directly purposive for Mr. Southern's marvelously wild talent and it is a little as if he were using a high-precision rifle with telescopic sights to shoot at a milk bottle four yards away. But even in this group of originally-conceived books it stands out for its singularity."

If the response of English critics tended toward the fussy damning-with-faint-praise side, at least there was an essential recognition that satire was a legitimate form for the novel. American publishers and editors were still looking for the big fat Great American Novel heavy on naturalism and autobiographical subtext. Coward-McCann, who would publish *Flash and Filigree* in the States in the fall of 1958, passed on *The Magic Christian.* Another U.S. publisher said, "Maybe America isn't up to satire and *Mad*-type humor in $3.50 form yet." Joe Fox, the gifted editor at Random House, did pick up the book and slated it for a spring 1960 publication.

As the English critics began to mull over *The Magic Christian* in the spring of 1959, Carol and Terry had come to a decision to return to the United States. Terry felt he was growing estranged from his source material—America the Beautiful. During the many months in Geneva, Southern had begun to daydream about becoming a gentleman farmer and he wrote to the Department of Agriculture to for pamphlets on irrigation, seeding, animal husbandry, and the like.

"While we were in Geneva, we were making plans for our future and where to live and so forth," recalls Carol. "Terry asked me about California and I burst into tears. So we decided to live in New England and so we planned this farm and got all this literature."

By the beginning of April, they were on their way. While Geneva's placid routine had obviously begun to pall, one wonders what Southern's life and work would have been like had he decided to live in Paris or London. In Paris, he might have become a bit of a jet-setter like James Jones or Irwin Shaw. In London, where Mordecai Richler stayed until the late sixties, he might have had the best of both worlds—Quality Lit and the emerging British film boom. Or maybe he could have gone the Russell Hoban route of quietly alternating between adult novels like *Riddley Walker* and children's books like *The Mouse and His Child*.

But whatever his misgivings about the new Beat phenomenon, Southern was worried he might be missing the real action. For now at least, New York was once again the red-hot center.

5
The Quality Lit Game

The big move back to the U.S. in the spring of 1959 was sobering at first. Short on cash, Carol and Terry spent almost two months in Great Neck, New York, as the houseguests of Madeline Bernard and her husband.

"She said, 'When you come back from Europe, please come and stay until you get settled.' Well, it took us a long time," Carol recalled. "Terry had no compunctions about being a houseguest for so long—I was terribly uncomfortable—but he seemed to feel he was owed this. He felt that they were lucky to have us. Mr. Bernard was not too pleased about it."

In June they moved in with John and Susen Marquand, who lived in an apartment on Eleventh Street. The Marquands spent their summers in Martha's Vineyard, giving Terry and Carol some breathing room. They immediately began looking for the farm they had daydreamed about in Geneva. Carol worried about money constantly. She was still the primary breadwinner. As Terry began to reacquaint himself with the New York literary scene, Carol got a summer job in Brooklyn. Then in the fall, she began work at the Yale Child Studies Center in New Haven. Upon the Marquands' return from holidays, the Southerns became gypsies again and lived in the various rentals around New Haven, recently vacated by "summer people."

Through John Marquand, Terry had become friendly with the pioneering bandleader Artie Shaw. Shaw had become a millionaire by the end of the forties, but grew disenchanted with the Big Band swing that made him rich. No doubt his seven marriages including Lana Turner, Ava Gardner, and Evelyn Keyes took their toll. In quasi-retirement, he began to write short stories and a novel eventually published as *I Love You, I Hate You, Drop Dead.* Like the Southerns, he was searching for a home in the country, but obviously had more income at his disposal. "[Shaw] was looking for a house and we were looking for a house," recalls Carol. "Artie said, 'I have this great real estate agent, let's all go together!' So we did and at the end of the day, the agent showed Terry and me this house and Artie said, 'I like it.' Artie put a binder on the house in order to take it off the market. Artie bought it immediately because he was able to put down the 10 percent. Mike Goldberg [the painter] said to Terry, 'You need a house for your family. Are you going to let this guy get away with this?' And Terry stood up to him. We bought the house from Artie for $23,000. We paid the down payment with my mother's inheritance and some money of our own."

The dilapidated farmhouse in East Canaan, a village in the northwestern corner of Connecticut, resided on twenty-seven acres of land. There was plenty of room for cattle to graze and a small wooded area with a pond at the edge. The Blackberry River ran along the south side of the house. On the other side was a road that connected the farm to the village, barely five minutes away.

Life in the country appealed to the Anglophile in Terry and rekindled memories of his childhood in Texas. East Canaan was located at a sufficient distance from Manhattan to allow Terry to write in peace, but close enough to maintain regular contact with editors and publishers. Buying the home also reflected Terry's jockeying between a Kafka-like embrace of the inner life and a compulsion to burn the candle at both ends in the bars, parties, and salons of the Manhattan cultural scene.

This odd impatience was also manifested by Terry's frustrations with the business of being a novelist. During his time in Geneva, the New York literary scene in the late fifties and early sixties was mutating into an ever-changing *uptown* and *downtown* scene. The *Paris Review* was now being run out of George Plimpton's Upper East Side apartment. While the Beats were gravitating to Barney Rosset's *Evergreen Review* and Grove Press in the Village.

Rosset saw the changing geography of the New York scene in somewhat conspiratorial terms.

"There was CIA and anti-CIA and I felt Terry fell between the two. He wasn't one or the other, but he was torn. He was pulled in both directions, so I forgave him. I didn't forgive a few others, but him I did. There was the sort of Peter Matthiessen–Styron syndrome and Dick Seaver and me. . . . Terry loved [the *Paris Review*], but he was somewhere floating around and Maurice Girodias was another planet that was important."

Rosset turned Grove Press and the *Evergreen Review* into a miniempire that included film distribution. Through the late fifties and sixties, Rosset would lose as much money as he would make. To some in America, he would simply be a "smut peddler," but to those interested in the best of new writing, he was a pioneer.

The child of a Chicago banker, Barney Rosset was born in 1922 and served in the Signal Corps in World War II. In 1952, he bought Grove Press for $3,000 and began acquiring the translation rights to the likes of Genet, Brecht, and Ionesco. When he published the unexpurgated edition of D. H. Lawrence's *Lady Chatterley's Lover,* he began the first of many legal battles to extend the boundaries of free expression and won a successful court battle to keep printing the book in 1959. Grove's publication of Henry Miller's *Tropic of Cancer* precipitated another costly legal battle to the tune of $250,000 before the U.S. Supreme Court ruled in Rosset's favor in 1964. Given his costly struggles with the status quo, his view of the *Paris Review* crowd as a bunch of Ivy Leaguers on permanent holiday was understandable.

It was a heady time for writers in the Big Apple. The transition from the Eisenhower years to JFK's Camelot coincided with Terry's transition from being a literary writer to something more ambitious and interdisciplinary. Thanks to distributors like William Becker's Janus Films and Dan Talbot's Thalia theater, the European art film was capturing the attention of the middle class. The philistine excesses of the McCarthy era were fading away and there appeared to be a collective unbuttoning of the collar in the American psyche. Television had gotten worse, but some of the former whiz kids of live TV drama like Sidney Lumet, Arthur Penn, and John Frankenheimer were entering Hollywood with ideas taken from the Actors Studio, *Cahiers du Cinéma,* and psychoanalysis. And instead of just poetry or paintings, the downtown galleries were staging multimedia events including screenings of films by Kenneth Anger and Jonas Mekas.

This cross-pollination of media was exciting to Terry, who tried to keep up during his forays into the big city. Like Rosset, he shared an impatience with the incestousness of some aspects of the New York publishing scene. He coined the all-purpose term—the Quality Lit Game—to express his ambivalence toward the somewhat unholy blurring of commerce, careerism, and politics with lofty literary aspirations.

"The Quality Lit Game was a term Terry used for the *New York Review of Books* crowd. He did do one or two pieces for them, but it didn't pay enough money . . . not like *Dr. Strangelove,*" said John Marquand.

Like Norman Mailer, Terry was frustrated by the limitations of the realist novels of his contemporaries. Yet Southern was not interested in writing advertisements for the self, nor did his personality allow him to seriously consider the possibility. He was more in sync with the baroque conceptualism and black comedy of such emerging talents as Joseph Heller, Kurt Vonnegut, John Barth, Harry Matthews, John Hawkes, Thomas Pynchon, and others. All these writers really had in common was that they barely knew each other.

Terry's restlessness was affecting the progress of a long semiautobiographical novel called *The Hipsters,* which he had started in Geneva. The novel began with a Southern-like character arriving in Paris to join the bohemian scene. It was intended to jump back and forth in time to trace the events that led to the character's flight from America.

"I always felt that he didn't know how to finish *The Hipsters* because it was so autobiographical," recalls Carol Southern." He got caught up in the city currents . . . he wasn't involved with film yet, but he was very interested in it. He was writing for the *Nation* and he was trying to make some money because then I got pregnant. I was not going to be able to continue to work. I just think life sort of overtook him [in the U.S.]. It's too bad that he never finished it."

Despite his reservations and quiet cynicism about the scene, Terry loved a good party. Carol joined him on his New York visits, which often included gatherings at Plimpton's East River apartment.

"Everybody was so young. George Plimpton, Peter Matthiessen, Philip Roth, Norman Podhoretz, everybody by this time was in their mid-thirties and very very lively, ambitious, and interesting. The whole culture was changing," recalls Carol. "It was a very dynamic time. The jazz scene was fabulous and the art scene was incredible. We went to a lot of openings and Leo Castelli was coming into his own. Frank O'Hara was around and Joe LeSeour and Patsy Southgate. Artists and poets like John Ashbery and Bill Berkson. Jack Youngerman [the painter] was a friend of the Seavers. There were huge parties—not only those that George gave, but also in the Hamptons. Barney Rosset had big parties."

Terry would often bring along odd and weird Village types such as Boris Grgurevich, a New Yorker of Russian descent who managed to join the Bay of Pigs assault and live to tell Southern the tale. "Boris had two friends, Cookie and Shadow," recalls Carol. "They traveled together and seemed like hoods. They were always stoned on something. Terry was fascinated by them . . . he really enjoyed their company and Boris was such a character and extremely good-looking. They were real hipsters in the true sense of the word. They were total druggies and total counterculture people. They were their *own* counterculture."

Boris, Cookie, and Shadow joined the countless athletes, call girls, junkies, and musicians who formed the lively backdrop to the main characters of the *Paris Review* salon. These included the likes of James Jones, William Styron, Norman Mailer, Philip Roth, Harold L. Humes, Jack Gelber, Sadruddin Aga Khan, Blair Fuller, the cast from *Beyond the Fringe,* Robert Silvers, Joe and Jill Fox, Peter Duchin, Jean Stein, David Amram, Jules Feiffer, and even Jackie Kennedy. Norman Mailer called it "the nearest thing we had to Bloomsbury."

At such gatherings, Southern was one of the lead actors. He was always good for a memorable quip usually accompanied by a cocked eyebrow. For example, a very young Jean Marsh (the future star and cocreator of *Upstairs, Downstairs*) was dubbed "Falling Down Jean" by Southern for her inability to remain standing after one or two drinks. On other occasions, he could be very solemn. At a party at Gore Vidal's Edgewater home on the Hudson, the author of *Myra Breckinridge* remembered: "Terry and wife [standing] on the lawn . . . a lawn that ended in the Hudson River. They were talking solemnly—I asked what of? 'What if,' said Terry, 'a child should run down the lawn and fall in the river and drown?' We agreed that this would be very depressing."

The hothouse atmosphere at these parties, combined with money worries, made Southern more conscious of the need for a semblance of career management. He bugged Curtis Brown about any opportunities to, as he often liked to say, "put some flour in the pot." One of the projects Southern considered was an offer by Peter Israel, a sympathetic editor at Putnam, about doing a biography of actor Tom Ewell, Marilyn Monroe's costar in *The Seven Year Itch.* He also approached the agencies and networks for TV work. In the latter case, a William Morris agent, Harold Franklin, responded to a query about scriptwriting by saying satire was not popular on American TV and that it would be difficult to place a writer like Southern.

In addition to reuniting with the *Paris Review* crowd, Southern began to see more of Kenneth Tynan and Elaine Dundy. Tynan had been hired by William Shawn at the *New Yorker* to become the new drama critic. And he would do this from late 1958 through 1960 until tiring of Shawn's rule that the critic discuss only Broadway fare.

"[The Tynans] were marvelous. Elaine never stopped talking and neither did Kenneth. They were very lively," recalls Carol Southern. "We went up to Harlem one night to the Savoy. There was a show and then there was an orchestra and dancing. We were the only white people there and Ken was so tall and pink faced and all these black people swarming around, it was really very funny. He looked like somebody from the UN."

Southern and Tynan loved to riff and toyed continually with collaborating on a play called *Funny Foot* based on the life of Byron. Tynan introduced Terry to Lenny Bruce during the latter's stint at the Duane Hotel in the spring of 1959. They went backstage to meet Bruce, who would become the Orson Welles of the satire boom now taking hold of the cabaret scene. Southern and Bruce clicked immediately. In Bruce, Southern recognized a kindred spirit—a comic talent who would not let categorizations limit his mode or choice of expression. As well as Bruce, Mike Nichols and Elaine May, Mort Sahl, Bob Newhart, Shelley Berman, and Woody Allen were pushing stand-up beyond the realm of the one-liner into the theater of the absurd. It was also the period when Jules Feiffer's brilliant *Village Voice* cartoon strip gained widespread popularity. The strip usually consisted of a monologue expressing one form of neurosis—political, sexual, or cultural—or all three at once.

The satire boom was still very much a New York–Chicago phenomenon as far as the rest of America was concerned. Nichols and May had made some well-received TV appearances and Lenny Bruce was an increasingly popular and well-paid club act in the big cities, but Vegas-style showbiz still dominated the substance and tenor of American comedy.

Southern's writing was becoming part of the groundswell behind the satire boom. Coward-McCann published *Flash and Filigree* in the United States in the fall of 1958. The cover art by Edward Sorel was a cubistlike collage of cars, palm trees, and hypodermic. The author photograph had been taken by Pud Gadiot several years before. American reviews were generally mixed. The consensus was that Southern's work was funny and unique, but there was uncertainty regarding the ultimate intention of his satire. Martin Levin in the *New York Times Book Review* felt Southern's characters were "Bakelite people without substance or feeling. Inevitably they leave the reader with a lingering sensation of emptiness."

When the Southerns first arrived in the U.S. the *Paris Review* ran "Grand Guy Grand," an excerpt from *The Magic Christian,* with illustrations by David Burnett. It created more excitement than *Flash and Filigree* and Southern won an in-house prize. Random House would publish the novel the following spring.

Terry submitted another fragment of *The Hipsters,* the short story

"Red Dirt Marijuana," to the *Evergreen Review*. It was published in their January/February 1960 issue. Southern received a better-than-average $250 for the piece. The story focused on the almost prosaic friendship between a young white Texan boy named Harold and CK, a black farmhand. Told mainly in dialogue form, the result was a Twain-like tale in which a child's introduction to mind-altering drugs is seen as an innocent, natural, and dare one say it, *necessary*, rite of passage.

In addition to Lenny Bruce, Southern was excited by a new play he saw in August 1959 called *The Connection* by Jack Gelber. Produced by the Living Theatre, the play re-created the world of a junkie's pad by having real addicts perform side by side with actors. Gelber, the play's author, was from the Midwest. His play grew out of several frustrated attempts to write about the Village milieu as a novel. Tynan was one of the early champions of *The Connection*, which created a sensation in New York that summer. The play won a drama prize in Paris when the Living Theatre took it on a celebrated European tour with *The Brig* by Kenneth Brown, a harrowing look at an American military prison.

Gelber recalls meeting Terry and Carol at a Christmas party thrown by the Tynans at the end of 1959. For the next three to four years, the Southerns and Gelbers would remain good friends until *Dr. Strangelove* took Terry out of the Quality Lit Game. Gelber and his wife, Carol, briefly stayed in Connecticut with the Southerns while they looked for an apartment. During the various runs of *The Connection*, Gelber would get whimsical calls from Terry suggesting "rewrites." Through Gelber, Terry was introduced to Seymour "Si" Litvinoff, a lawyer with many clients in the theater and visual arts including the French actress Delphine Seyrig. Litvinoff became Southern's lawyer and business manager until the late sixties when he shifted into film production. It was a relationship typical of the new decade when the lines between art, commerce, business, and friendship were increasingly blurred beyond definition.

When Gelber went to England and Europe to oversee various productions of *The Connection*, he maintained a lively correspondence with Terry. They tried to see each other when they were both in New York. Gelber liked Southern. As Southern would say often of his many eclectic friendships, "We shared values." What those "values" were was left unspoken, but they had much to do with the growing awareness that the sixties was going to be a decade of enormous cultural change. For his part, Gelber found Southern a delightful source of laughter whether in person or in countless letters or over the telephone. Yet beneath Terry's funny exterior,

Gelber sensed a growing internal conflict between the purist idealism of the Hipster and the material possibilities of becoming a celebrity writer.

For now, one of the ways Southern brought money in was through book reviewing. The bulk of Southern's book reviews would run in the *Nation* from 1960 through 1962. Robert Hatch, the book editor at the *Nation*, paid seventy-five dollars a review. A few others appeared in the *New York Times Book Review* for a slightly higher fee. The paltry sums must have deepened Southern's misgivings about the Quality Lit Game, but he took his assignments seriously. The book reviews allowed Southern to drop the hipster mask and by discussing the work of others articulate his aesthetics through the backdoor.

Terry's *Nation* work included reviews and commentary about Henry Miller, William Faulkner's *The Reivers*, Harry Matthews's *The Conversions*, and Peter Matthiessen's *Raditzer*. A common denominator in these reviews was Southern's preference for novels that pushed style and narrative beyond Hemingwayesque naturalism. In the December 17, 1960, issue of the *Nation*, Southern listed *The Connection* by Jack Gelber, *Clea* by Lawrence Durrell, William S. Burroughs's *Naked Lunch, Ko, or A Season of Earth* by Kenneth Koch, and *The Sot-Weed Factor* by John Barth as his year-end favorites.

"Dark Laughter in the Towers," an essay that appeared in the April 23, 1960, issue of the *Nation*, is as close to a manifesto on his own brand of satire as Southern would attempt. The piece attempts to trace the moment when the absurd began to surface in American literature when "God and Democracy folded," leaving nothing but "Laughter and Sex." Southern makes a convincing case for William Faulkner's *As I Lay Dying* as an early marker of a brand of existential fiction on par with Albert Camus's *The Stranger*. The second and final part of the essay roams more generally over works such as Nelson Algren's *Walk on the Wild Side*, Burroughs's *Naked Lunch*, J. D. Salinger's *Catcher in the Rye*, and Kingsley Amis's *Lucky Jim*. What these works share, argues Southern, is an "awareness of the absurd and candor" that is easily dismissed by those who should know better as "'novels of social criticism' and thus 'creatively impure.' This interpretation—that they are, by design, novels of protest, and further, that the protest is well founded—no doubt accounts in large measure for the work's popularity, whereas, actually the 'social criticism' aspect of it is simply incidental, an understandable by-product of the combination of sensitivity and candor. The real answer is that it is an existentialist literature."

In writing this essay, Southern indirectly sets the terms by which his novels, which were also being pigeonholed in the same way, should be discussed. The other key essay that Southern would write for the *Nation* would be "When Film Gets Good," written almost at the point when Southern was about to leave for London to work on *Dr. Strangelove.* But more on that later. Of the *New York Times* reviews, the most significant was an early rave for the work of the relatively unknown Kurt Vonnegut Jr. and his novel *Cat's Cradle.* Southern wrote, "Like the best of contemporary satire, it is work of a far more engaging and meaningful order than the melodramatic tripe which most critics seem to consider 'serious.'"

Interestingly Southern avoided writing any political commentary for the *Nation* except for a very short editorial decrying the execution of Caryl Chessman as the worst kind of nihilism. While his personal politics were very much left of center and would remain so through the rest of his life, Southern preferred to let his fiction (and later screenplays) express his political beliefs. Direct expressions of one position over another were as unnatural to Terry as frank confessions of his deepest emotions.

While moonlighting as a book reviewer, Southern became involved in an anthology provisionally entitled *Beyond the Beat* with Richard Seaver and Alexander Trocchi. (Southern also tried to get Mason, now back in Paris, involved, but nothing came of it.)

"Trocchi got a job as an editor at this small publishing house named Frederick Fell, which was a very clunky house," recalls Seaver. "Fell was a man who aspired to be a publisher, but didn't want to take any risks. That's a contradiction in terms. So Trocchi conned Fell into getting into the real publishing world. 'We'll put together this avant-garde book for you which will put you on the map! I'll guarantee it because I know what I am talking about because I have long experience in this Lit field!' So [Trocchi] called Terry and me and said, 'What we want to do is put together this anthology and we'[d] get money for ourselves and I think it will work.' We had long sessions trying to determine what we'll put in this book. There was very little common ground. We chose and settled on two or three writers and wrote to their agents. Their fees came back and they were horrendous. We had to change our whole tack. Our original plan as I remember was to do the sixties avant-garde writers, Beckett would have been in there of course . . . what we wanted to do because it was the American market was put in more Americans than Europeans."

Seaver recalls a working budget of $400–$600 for each piece to secure the rights to print an excerpt. "We shifted gears somewhat and to broaden our scope and include people in the public domain, people who were Europeans the costs were much more reasonable and some we knew. Terry wrote this letter to Candida Donadio about [getting] William Gaddis. At the point Gaddis was riding quite high because *The Recognitions* had just come out. He was very highly praised . . . we wanted a part. I think we also had a bit of the Marquis de Sade.

"It should have taken us three months to put that together, but all of us were doing other things, so it took us twice that long, but in the midst of doing the whole thing, we had probably progressed about two-thirds of the way through, Trocchi absconded.

"He got in trouble with the law and was heavily on drugs. You could really go to jail for a long, long time in those days for possessing a relatively minor dose. When he came [to the U.S.], he was a known junkie. The New York police knew he was a junkie and he lived on Fourteenth Street in a loft that was really a shambles, a junkie shambles, but Trocchi was extraordinarily smart and literate."

After Trocchi fled to England via Canada, Terry and Richard Seaver finished the project. Seaver, through his Grove Press connections, secured rights to excerpts from Beckett and Malaparte, while Southern wrote most of the introductions.

The contents of the anthology, which was finally called *Writers in Revolt,* include the Beats like Allen Ginsberg's *Howl,* the Marquis de Sade, Baudelaire and a commentary by Sartre, Artaud's "No More Masterpieces," an excerpt from Céline's *Journey to the End of the Night,* Malaparte's *The Skin,* Henry Miller, Genet's *Our Lady of the Flowers* and commentary by Sartre, William Gaddis's *The Recognitions,* Evan S. Connell Jr., Chapman Mortimer's *Young Men in Waiting,* Charles Foster, Edward Dahlberg, H. L. Mencken, the "Tra-la-la" section from Hubert Selby's *Last Exit to Brooklyn,* Burroughs's *Naked Lunch,* Ionesco, and "The End" by Samuel Beckett. The anthology was and remains as good an introduction to underground literature as any other. It certainly turned on many readers as the paperback edition became a perennial used-bookstore favorite.

Southern probably had mixed feelings about the anthology at the time. It took up a lot of his time and yielded a relatively small amount of cash. When Carol gave birth to their son, Nile, on December 29, 1960, he was delighted, but also worried. He would need to be more aggressive in finding work.

Still he persisted with the Quality Lit Game. *Nugget,* a men's magazine edited by Seymour Krim, paid $350 for a new short story, "The Face of the Arena." In this vivid tale of bullfighting, a cowardly matador sees a child run onto the ground of the arena. The matador grabs the child. Just as he does so, the bull charges and in his panic, the matador uses the child as a cape.

Much of 1961 was taken up by Southern and Hoffenberg's discussions with Peter Israel at Putnam about reissuing *Candy* as a mainstream book under their own names. These negotiations were helped by Southern changing literary agents. Sterling Lord, who was successfully managing the affairs of Jack Kerouac and other young writers, was more sympathetic to the attitudes of his clients.

"Love Is a Many Splendored," a three-part story whose abrupt scene changes anticipate *Monty Python,* appears in *The Hasty Papers.* This was a onetime publication put together by Alfred Leslie, a painter and the codirector with Robert Frank of the Beat film *Pull My Daisy.* Southern's story appeared alongside the work of Gregory Corso, James Schuyler, Frank O'Hara, Allen Ginsberg, John Ashbery, Jack Kerouac, Charles Olson, Peter Orlovsky, and others. It was a very sixties project celebrating the diversity of creative spirit in New York at the time.

In a similar spirit of generosity, Southern agreed to write a regular column for Maurice Girodias's latest venture. Girodias was starting the *Olympia Review* to compete with Barney Rosset's *Evergreen Review.* Girodias launched his first issue in December 1961.

Southern's column entitled "The Spy's Corner" got off a to a great start with a mock interview with Ernest Badhoff, the leader of the "neonada" school of painting. Badhoff describes his "strange new kind of realism" to the interviewer, a method that involves blowing up the galleries that exhibit the neonadaists' latest paintings. The burned and mangled remains of the paintings become new works. The humor of this sketch would be quickly realized by the autodestructive art of Gustav Metzger, who influenced the Who, the performance art of Chris Burdern, and even the piss paintings of Andy Warhol in the early eighties.

The next two installments of "Spy's Corner" appeared in early 1962. Both pieces were reworked for *The Realist:* "Scandale at the Dumpling Shop," a briskly effective piece of grotesquerie about toy dolls that feature "Teeny Tampons," and "The Moon-Shot," where it is revealed that one of America's latest manned space missions has taken on a certain camp approach to its noble task.

Little of this work was making Southern a lot of money. Southern was gamely exploring a number of options. He even got Richard Seaver to write a reference letter when he unsuccessfully applied to the John Simon Guggenheim Memorial Foundation for a grant.

On his excursions into Manhattan, Southern looked exactly like a big-city writer in a dark suit and tie. Yet the day-to-day routine of life on the farm in East Canaan consisted of Terry and Carol trying to live off the land. They grew vegetables, raised chickens and pigs, and even had a few cows grazing on the property. Southern also had a hunting license and would occasionally go out to hunt deer.

Meanwhile he continued to write for the *Nation* and rustle up other work. For *Glamour* magazine, he wrote an article called "The Beautiful Art of Lotte Lenya," which was intended to be a lengthy feature instead of the appreciation that was published, but Southern never showed up on time for the interview. "Razor Fight," another fragment for *The Hipsters*, appeared in *Nugget*. Rust Hills at *Esquire* had politely turned down the piece, saying, "Parts of the story seem almost like a parody of the so-called initiation story—a 'growing up' story—like (Sherwood) Anderson's 'I Want to Know Why.'"

In spite of these reservations, Rust Hills asked Southern to take over for him during the summer as an editor at *Esquire*. He would receive $125 a week for roughly two months' work. His duties were mainly to go through the slush pile and pass stories that he thought were worthy of publication. Southern would use this experience as the basis for "The Blood of a Wig." In a sense, Southern was already an unofficial employee of the magazine now entering its most vital period under the aegis of Harold Hayes.

One of the young associate editors at the magazine, David Newman, was a huge fan of Southern's *The Magic Christian* and the Olympia version of *Candy*.

"I thought I could get this guy, my hero, on the phone because I am now not only David Newman—I'm-a fan-of-your-work, but I'm an editor at *Esquire*," said Newman. "I got Terry Southern on the phone. I told him tremulously that I was a great fan and an editor at *Esquire* and we would love him to do something for the magazine and he said, 'Grand idea, Big Dave, Dave New.' He came to the magazine for lunch and we were sitting across from each other something like this. Meeting Norman Mailer, William Styron, Robert Lowell, and all this was very impressive, but meeting Terry Southern was a major event in my life because I never thought I would get to meet this guy. He had an aura to me because that [*The Magic Christian*] had been so important to me in college. We immediately hit it off."

After reading a brief news item about a baton-twirling school at Ole Miss, Newman asked Southern to go down to Oxford, Mississippi, for a few days and talk to the students. The vision of Southern, the author of *Candy,* chatting up all these fresh-faced innocent teenagers was just too irresistible for Newman.

"I thought this was so in-and-of-itself instantly satirical—the idea that only in America would you go somewhere to learn to twirl a fucking baton," said Newman. "It seemed so quintessentially America coming out of the fifties (as we were then in the early part of the sixties). Here's this guy Terry Southern and *Candy* had just been published, I don't remember the chronology, but everybody thought instantly it was just a great idea and even Terry accepted instantly. He went down to the campus and wrote 'Twirling at Ole Miss,' which is a classic and it is now one of the canonized pieces of what is now called the New Journalism."

Esquire was becoming increasingly recognized as the testing lab for a new breed of journalism that borrowed the techniques of fiction freely. Gay Talese, Jack Richardson, Garry Wills, Tom Wolfe, Norman Mailer, and others were writing about politics, race, the movies, crime, pop culture, and other subjects with an energy and style that was becoming synonymous with the excitement of the Kennedy years.

During Southern's replacement gig for Rust Hills, Newman recalls Southern walking into the office in a bit of a quandary: "He was wearing a dark blue suit and he was having lunch with somebody very important. He was really down on his luck and fairly broke at the time. Whatever that job paid at the time, it wasn't much, but he needed the job. Even though he was Terry Southern, he needed a job in addition to his writing. He came walking in and he was going to have lunch in the Berkshire House or one of those places where we were always having fancy lunches and said, 'Have you a pen with blue-black ink? I need a pen with blue-black ink instantly!' I said, 'Yeah, there must be some pen around.' He was wearing this suit which had a hole in the knee the size of a quarter. There was all this bare skin and flesh showing. He rolled up his pants legs, took the ink, and colored his knee and skin in and rolled the leg back. Unless you looked very closely, you couldn't see that it was skin, because he painted it to match the hole in his pants. So he went off to this lunch and I thought I'll never forget that in my life. I imagine that later on he probably had to scrub his knee for an hour."

Newman also vividly remembers Southern's flair for trenchant interoffice memos: "Bob Brown was Rust Hill's assistant. Bob got his bill from the Berkshire, one of those restaurants, that used monthly bills. For some reason or other, the guy who handed out the mail inadvertently put the bill on Terry's desk. Terry opened it and read it: 'Robert Brown, $234 for the month of something or other.' Terry scrawled across it, 'For the love of God, Brown, when will you settle up!' and had someone courier it over to Bob Brown's desk. Bob still has that. 'For the love of God, Brown, when will you settle up!'"

A short story containing language that *Esquire* might have problems with prompted this memo to Newman: "At that point *Esquire* was slightly puritanical about four-letter words or how explicit sex was or whatever. Terry wrote me a note, 'Do you think I should send this to Gingrich, or should I pass it on to coarse Hugh Hef?' And I have never thought of Hugh Hefner again except as coarse Hugh Hef. The thing with Terry was that he would write to you or say things that sounded like *The Magic Christian* and you would get this frisson, this wonderful thing like talking like Hemingway."

Southern's association with *Esquire* coincided with several successful submissions to the magazine. "The Road out of Axotle," one of Southern's finest short stories, finally appeared in the August 1962 issue. Rust Hills had mulled over earlier versions of the story since the mid-fifties. The story follows the strange picaresque travels of the narrator, an American hipster, and two Mexican companions. Driving through the backroads of Mexico, they come upon an array of weird sights including a town plagued by a sudden invasion of locusts and a run-down toll bridge guarded by a dope-pushing sentry. The story tapped into the wanderlust of Jack Kerouac, but was also completely lacking in that writer's sentimentality. According to Carol, Southern reconstructed anecdotes told to him by a writer named Mickey at *Sports Illustrated*. Mickey was not terribly amused to see the published result, but, says Carol, "of course, this happens to every writer. I am not even sure if Terry was aware that was *what* he was doing."

Boris Grgurevich, Southern's hipster friend, apparently had a similar reaction after reading "Recruiting for the Big Parade," which appeared in the June 1963 issue of *Esquire*. The article was culled from an interview transcript of Grgurevich's experiences as a CIA recruit for the Bay of Pigs assault. A tape recording of their original interview reveals that Southern didn't have to exaggerate much of what Grgurevich told him. With a bit of shuffling, ellipsis, and a few italics, the essential absurdity of the exercise and

Grgurevich's laconic presence, the piece was instant satire. Although the comic tone was the result of Terry's editing and emphasis, Grgurevich felt he should have been identified more fully in the piece or credited in some way as a collaborator.

Around this time, Southern scored an interview with a hot director a few years younger than himself. Stanley Kubrick, a native of the Bronx, had rapidly moved up from the ranks of cub photographer at *Look* in the early fifties to award-winning film director in 1962. He was one of a new breed of independent filmmakers using Hollywood for their own purposes. With the exception of *Spartacus,* which he took over as a favor to Kirk Douglas, and some wasted months on *One-Eyed Jacks,* Marlon Brando's ill-fated Western, Kubrick had stuck doggedly to his own trail. With his friend and business partner, James B. Harris, Kubrick had made *The Killing* and *Paths of Glory.* His latest film, a controversial adaptation of Vladimir Nabokov's *Lolita,* was just being released. Somehow Southern had wangled an interview with Kubrick at the offices of Harris-Kubrick Productions in midtown.

Jack Gelber says Southern didn't know much about Kubrick at the time. Gelber had met the young director off and on over the fifties through Shirley Clarke. While Southern had seen Kubrick's films, Gelber filled Southern in on some of the director's background. Terry did know that not long before they met, Carol Southern had once met Kubrick in a Village bar, where she was given the director's business card. A coincidence Southern found amusing.

Kubrick, by contrast, knew a bit about Southern's work through Peter Sellers. During the making of *Lolita,* the actor gave a copy of *The Magic Christian* to Kubrick, telling him it was one of his favorite books and that he gave out copies at birthdays and Christmas. Kubrick, a voracious reader, was intrigued by this, read the book, and was delighted.

When Kubrick met Southern, he was working on a new project with Peter George, the author of a novel *Red Alert,* which, as far as Southern knew, had something to do with nuclear war. However, this was not the topic of conversation during the interview, which *Esquire* hoped Southern would turn into a piece as memorable as "Twirling at Ole Miss" or "Recruiting at the Big Parade." However, the results were unsatisfying as far as big laughs went. The conversation was a fairly sedate overview of Kubrick's career to date and his filmmaking philosophy. They were hoping to follow up the interview by having Southern visit the set of his next film.

Since the *Esquire* gig often required Southern to spend the week in

Manhattan, he used Plimpton's East Side apartment as a base camp during this period. Plimpton recalls Southern as a considerate guest except for the odd bit of mischief. One visitor to the *Paris Review* salon was Jonathan Miller, then touring with *Beyond the Fringe* in New York. He found Terry "an Ariel-like figure," who was hard to pin down. Somehow Miller found himself along with a crowd of insomniacs, crouched on the floor of Plimpton's apartment while Southern screened a pornographic film. The mood was somber and the interest more anthropological than salacious. Plimpton suddenly arrived and asked for the film to be taken off his wall. "Terry in a mood of propriety picked up an index card and interposed it between the light beam and the wall so that the film was now his personal property." Miller does not remember whether or not this gesture mollified Plimpton.

The *Esquire* gig as Rust Hills's proxy ended in September, but Southern continued to spend time in the Big Apple looking for bigger fish to fry.

On November 2, 1962, a telegram arrived from London for Mr. Terry Southern c/o George Plimpton at 541 East Seventy-second Street. It read:

SUGGEST YOU ADVISE FERGUSON COLUMBIA YOU WANT ARRIVE LONDON NOVEMBER 7TH TO COVER PREPRODUCTION PHASE AND WANT ROUND TRIP TICKET WITH NO REPEAT NO ADDITIONAL WEEKS EXPENSES IF INDEED ANY HAD BEEN AGREED UPON STOP SIMULTANEOUSLY I HAVE A PROPOSITION WHICH WOULD PROF-ITABLY OCCUPY YOU IN LONDON FOR NEXT EIGHT SEEKS STOP WILL PROVIDE NECESSITIES IN LONDON WHILST YOU PONDER PROPOSAL STOP FLIGHT DETAILS SHEPFILMS MIDDLESEX AND WILL MEET YOU

It was signed LOVE STANLEY. As they say in the movies, it was the beginning of a beautiful relationship.

6

Dr. Strangelove
(or How I Learned
to Stop Worrying
and Love Hollywood)

Dark London winter mornings, and I would go over to Kubrick's place in Knightsbridge at about 5:00 A.M. We would work in the backseat of his grand old Bentley, during the long ride to Shepperton Studios . . . it was a magical time," Terry Southern wrote many years later. Despite the highs and the lows that followed his work on *Dr. Strangelove*, Southern would always recall his collaboration with Stanley Kubrick with warmth and kindness.

The magic began in the fall of 1962. Kubrick's telegram had come at just the right time. Regardless of his aura of hipster cool, Southern was a struggling thirty-eight-year-old writer with a family to support and a big house in the country to maintain. Money was tight. Since becoming pregnant and giving birth to Nile on December 29, 1960, Carol stopped teaching in order to look after their new baby. Although Southern's writing was now appearing in better-paying magazines like *Esquire,* this freelance income remained erratic. For example, when "Apartment to Exchange," a whimsical take on a meeting between Franz Kafka and Sigmund Freud appeared in the November 1962 issue of *Nugget,* he was paid $250. Ten percent of this income often went to Sterling Lord for helping to land the piece. "The Moon-Shot Scandal," a squib about the space race, was written gratis for Paul Krassner at the *Realist.* A swinging bachelor might be able to survive on that kind of cash, but not a man with a wife, kids, and mortgage. Academia seemed an unlikely refuge for Southern at this stage in his life, but cinema . . . now *that* was something.

In addition to the obvious monetary benefits of screenwriting, Southern, like so many serious writers, was in love with the movies. With the rise of the European art film and glimmers of a new American cinema, this passion was not without foundation in the early sixties. In a piece for the *Nation,* "When Film Gets Good," printed in the fall of 1962, he articulated his thoughts on literature and film: "It has become evident that it is wasteful, pointless, and in terms of art, inexcusable, to write a novel which could, or in fact should have been a film. This ought to be a first principle of creative literature and of its critical evaluation; without it the novel, in the present circumstances, has only a secondary function as art."

Southern's novels, *Flash and Filigree* and *The Magic Christian,* possessed a cinematic structure that anticipated such great films of the sixties as *Blow-Up, Jules and Jim, Bonnie and Clyde, The Graduate,* and *Belle de Jour.* It was this episodic, larger-than-life quality, a genuine surrealistic wit, and an elegant blend of naturalism and irony that appealed to Kubrick.

Last but not least, Southern was frustrated with the limitations of the novel and short story. His latest project, *The Hipsters,* drawing upon his Paris and Greenwich Village years, was losing its appeal. The kind of new writing that did appeal to Southern were works—*Naked Lunch, Cain's Book, The Alexandria Quartet, Last Exit to Brooklyn,* and *The Recognitions*—that stretched the forms and conventions of the novel. Ironically, these books also defied simple translation to the screen.

As Southern mulled over the film/literature dichotomy, Stanley Kubrick arrived in New York to meet with his partner, James B. Harris, in the summer of 1962. They were deep in preproduction for their next film, based on *Red Alert* by Peter George, a novel they had acquired for $3,000. George, a former RAF lieutenant, had written *Red Alert* to express his fears about the nuclear arms buildup. He was also active in the Campaign for Nuclear Disarmament.

Red Alert dealt with a commander of an American air base who overrides the fail-safe protocol and sends a fleet of B-52s to bomb the USSR. Despite the last-minute efforts by the American and Soviet leaders to reverse this insane act, the one-man coup escalates into a nuclear holocaust.

George said that the idea for *Red Alert* came to him during a walk with a friend. A Vulcan bomber, leaving an airfield near Bristol, was flying too low for George's comfort. "Supposing that one was carrying a bomb," wondered George to his skeptical friend, "the chap went mad and let one off."

As usual with Kubrick, the development of a rock-solid screenplay was essential. Aside from *Red Alert,* George had penned several mystery novels with titles like *Come Blonde, Come Murder* and *Final Steal.* Many appeared under pseudonyms for publishers like Harlequin, who had virtually cornered the market on dime-store romance novels. George was, to use an English colloquialism, an odd duck—a hack with pretensions. He made Jim Thompson, the pulp novelist who had worked on *The Killing* and *Paths of Glory,* look like a Nobel laureate.

George and Kubrick had started work on the *Red Alert* screenplay in London earlier in the year. Kubrick's wife, Christiane, remembers him arriving at their Kensington flat for frequent writing sessions. She recalls an intelligent, talkative, and kind man who looked much older than his forty years due to his drinking. His hands and face had the blue-veined complexion that betrayed the ravages of alcoholism. Despite his polite demeanor, he looked as if he had seen better days.

"He was like many such people totally lucid even though he was absolutely awash with liquor," said Christiane. "Because our children were small, Stanley and Peter would sort of fan out into the kitchen. George would drink a mix of whiskey and milk. I remember this impressed me. He said that the milk would keep his stomach in better order. He would then speak very lucidly, though somewhat emotionally about his past . . . stories about Ireland. I don't know how he came about those. He sort of gave me a little history about the hardship of the Irish."

James B. Harris recalls George vaguely, but does remember that he and Kubrick put together the first version of the shooting script: "After we finished *Lolita,* Stanley came across this *Red Alert* book when he was over in London and he brought it to my attention and started educating me on the thermonuclear dilemma. I started to read books like *On Thermonuclear Warfare* by Herman Kahn. So we started the development of a straight dramatic suspense story based on *Red Alert;* that's how it was treated. I was on the West Coast so I wasn't totally involved on a day-to-day basis. Peter

George came to New York and started to work on the screenplay with Stanley. I would come into town from time to time and sit in with them and bounce the ideas around and so forth. I didn't get to know Peter George that well."

George acted as Kubrick's resource person on all things military and fleshed out some of the technical nuances of nuclear defense. The United States Air Force and the State Department would not cooperate with Kubrick's production, because he would not give them script approval. Kubrick circumvented their lack of cooperation by gathering studies, academic papers, magazine articles, and books on nuclear power and the arms race to add credibility to his work-in-progress.

The early drafts of what would become *Dr. Strangelove* tried to merge this array of technical data with the need for a compelling film narrative. The initial George/Kubrick draft walked an uneasy line between the inexorable gloom of George's source novel and a broad, almost juvenile slapstick. Kubrick and George devised a cumbersome meta-satirical structure using the plot of *Red Alert* as a film within a film produced by an alien intelligence. Kubrick intended to spoof Hollywood's penchant for glitz over substance when dealing with social and political issues. Unlike Vladimir Nabokov's *Lolita*, George's 1958 novel was a straightforward, albeit socially conscious, thriller in terms of style and structure. George was too close to his material for the radical leap required to make the absurd unthinkability of nuclear holocaust seem believable, profound, and immediate. On his previous film, *Lolita*, Kubrick had Nabokov, a genius as thorough and perfectionistic as himself, to collaborate (and argue and debate) with. Peter George was no Nabokov. Kubrick knew he was gambling by choosing this subject. Stanley Kramer's *On the Beach* was the only other studio film on the subject. Despite the presence of Gregory Peck, Fred Astaire, and Ava Gardner, the earnest funereal tone of the film killed its success at the box office.

Kubrick later articulated his shift from melodrama to satire in *Films and Filming* in the summer of 1963 while editing *Dr. Strangelove*: "My idea of doing it as a nightmare comedy came when I was trying to work on it. I found that in trying to put meat on the bones and to imagine the scenes fully one had to keep leaving things out of it which were either absurd or paradoxical, in order to keep it from being funny, and these things seemed to be very real. Then I decided that the perfect tone to adopt for the film would be what I now call nightmare comedy, because it most truthfully represents the picture."

In October 1962, Kubrick told Harris that a new writer was needed.

"Stanley told me he decided to pursue certain things that we had discussed earlier. [He] kind of put them on a back burner or discarded them figuring we were onto such a good thing with a straight thriller maybe it was fool-hardy to get off a winning team. . . . But he told me that some of the thoughts that he had were that he could best present the thermonuclear dilemma in comedy form. That it was just more powerful that way—the message would still be the same—but he thought it would be much more entertaining and a better film for it. Then he started to educate me about Terry Southern who I really wasn't familiar with. He started to fill me in on *Flash and Filigree* and *The Magic Christian* and things like that. Needless to say when you start reading [Southern's work] you start realizing how tal-ented he was. So Stanley started working with Terry and that was when it was converted into a satire and the new title, *Dr. Strangelove or: How I Learned to Stop Worrying and Love the Bomb*. That's the history of that project as far as I was concerned. Then strangely enough I wound up doing as my first film as a director a picture called *The Bedford Incident* which is really the same subject matter, but I did it as a straight suspense piece."

The exact nature of the first meeting between Kubrick and Southern has become absorbed into the larger myth of the making of *Dr. Strangelove*. Southern remembers they got "into this rather heavy rap—about death, and infinity, and the origin of time—you know, that sort of thing. Meanwhile, my agent, Si Litvinoff, found out about this and a number of people wanted me to interview Kubrick. They didn't know what was hap-pening. They just heard I was going to see Stanley Kubrick and thought, 'Well, this would make a good interview.' So about three people—*Esquire,* the *Atlantic,* I think even George Plimpton—asked me about it."

In Stanley Kubrick, Terry would encounter a kindred spirit, someone who didn't just want to use film, but wanted to change it irrevocably. At thirty-six, the Bronx-born, self-educated Kubrick was part of the same gen-eration as Southern and equally keen to push the envelope of form and con-vention. As the auteur of *Paths of Glory* and *Lolita,* Kubrick was already on record decrying the lack of ambition among American filmmakers. His heroes—Orson Welles, Charlie Chaplin, Sergei Eisenstein, and Max Ophuls—were all iconoclasts. Kubrick wanted to follow their path, but he wanted to do so from a secure base of power. *Lolita* had been only a mixed success. Kubrick wanted his next film to be an event that people had to see if only because their friends were talking about it. It would be an American film as mature and complex as the finest European films, yet also as seduc-tively entertaining as the best American studio pictures.

When Kubrick's offer to work on *Dr. Strangelove* arrived, Carol Southern remembered Terry asking her if he should go. "Since we had absolutely no money, I was very keen for him to go," she recalls. "But he must have had some premonition that it would lead him into a totally different area, because there was some hesitation."

Terry left for London a few days later. Carol lost contact with Terry due to the U.S. mail strike. About three weeks later, she received a call from Terry telling her to get tickets for Nile and her to fly to London.

Kubrick knew, says Southern, that the possibility of the world going up in one big mushroom cloud of atomization was "too weird to treat in an ordinary way. So he wanted to make [*Dr. Strangelove*] a black comedy." And if there was one thing Terry was a master of, it was black comedy. Through influences like Kafka, Céline, and especially Henry Green, Southern understood that the most banal situations and statements could be charged with multiple meanings. The main characters of *Flash and Filigree* and *The Magic Christian,* Dr. Eichner and Guy Grand, were strange maguslike figures. They could be sinister, poignant, all-knowing, enigmatic, silly, or genteel by turns. Many of the characters in *Dr. Strangelove* would embody these same traits.

Kubrick's motives in hiring Terry were, in his words, "to see if some more decoration might be added to the icing on the cake." It was a somewhat disingenuous description of what became an intense merging of sensibilities. Kubrick, the bleak ironist, could meet and accommodate the black, yet oddly gentle satire of Southern. On the set, they would look like brothers (Peter Sellers and Southern, with their cocked eyebrows, hawklike noses, and wry expressions, even more so). Both favored simple black clothes. They always looked as if they were short of sleep. Terry was almost painfully shy in the mornings, but as the day wore on he would become more outgoing and playful. Kubrick, the brooding point of focus, was kept relaxed by the jokes and antics of Southern, Sellers, and other members of the cast and crew.

Upon Terry's arrival in England, George disappeared. During the "official" period of Southern's employment, November 16 to December 28, 1962, Southern and Kubrick drastically reworked George's script. Christiane Kubrick heard that George's drinking had gotten worse and that he'd had to be hospitalized for ulcers. In contrast to George, who seemed to live under a cloud of sadness, Terry, who was now a constant presence at the Kubrick household, struck Christiane as constantly cheerful and "very bohemian" in his rumpled dark suit and tie. He never seemed to eat or sleep. He didn't seem to mind the presence of the children.

"We were together a great deal," recalls Christiane, "because when you have small children, your professional life spilled over into jamming the last cold spoons of custard down a child. . . . I remember it was an immensely cold winter. Terry and Stanley would often sit in their coats in the London flat surrounded by a mixture of toddlers, all their papers, and saying 'don't touch that' to the children. They tried to flee from the family into smaller rooms."

Terry initially stayed in a hotel in Knightsbridge. Later, when Carol and Nile arrived, he would sublet Kenneth Tynan's apartment on Prince Albert Road. Then they moved into a commercial apartment across from Harrods.

What Carol Southern was able to observe of the production was an intense, fertile atmosphere of hypercreativity with Kubrick applying his all-seeing scrutiny to every aspect of the film. Carol was fascinated by Kubrick and remembers lots of conversations regarding Ken Adam, the production designer. "'Ken's doing this. Ken's doing that.' It was obvious Stanley had a very high regard for him." She found both Stanley and Christiane Kubrick warm and hospitable.

Shooting had begun in a very tentative way when Terry first arrived in London. Most of it was second unit aerial footage to be inserted into the bomber scenes. But Kubrick soon realized, to use Southern's words, "You can't do the end of the world in a conventionally dramatic way. You have to do it in some way that reflects your awareness that this is serious and important. You can't treat it in a conventional boy-meets-girl way, so it has to be a totally different treatment and black humor is the way to go. That was [Kubrick's] decision.

"The humor that attracted him in *The Magic Christian* he thought would be effective in this new approach. He would talk about the mechanics of the script in terms of making it totally credible in the fail-safe aspect and then tried to make that funny. And the way you make it funny is because the situation is absurd, you deal with it in terms of the dialogue and characters."

On January 28, 1963, principal photography began on *Dr. Strangelove*. From January to April 1963, over a fifteen-week period, Kubrick shot exteriors and interiors at Shepperton Studios and the IBM Corporation in London. Kubrick and his chauffeur would pick up Terry at 4:30 each morning and they would go over scenes in the back of the car. The writing would continue at Shepperton Studios. Terry would hand over rewritten pages from the night before, observe rehearsals, comment on scenes as they were being shot, and basically act as a kind of creative lieutenant to Kubrick's role of the Auteur as Commander General. It was a period of intense, highly stimulating collaboration.

Southern also described his collaboration with Kubrick in unintentionally revealing terms: "He's got a weird metabolism; while I'm taking Dexamyl, he's taking Seconal." Dexamyl was rapidly becoming Southern's drug of choice during the furious rewriting process. Southern pumped out dialogue and scene changes on yellow legal pads and index cards in hotel lobbies, on soundstages, and in the backseats of cars and taxis at all hours. As a big proponent of writing from the gut, Southern found that the demands of screenwriting played havoc with his metabolism. By "dexing it," he was able to keep up not just his energy, but enthusiasm.

"Terry would drink whiskey and take amphetamines," recalls Christiane Kubrick, "I didn't know this at first. I would say, 'You must eat!' not really knowing why he had no appetite. I was pushing my food. He was very nice and would say he wasn't hungry. I thought, 'My God, this man has tremendous energy. It's two o'clock in the morning and I am falling over.'

"Stanley kept saying, 'You shouldn't take those things, especially not with liquor.' Stanley being a doctor's son never took anything except maybe coffee. Still he didn't sleep very much either. No more than four hours at a time. I think as a result he lived maybe the equivalent of eighty-one years rather than seventy. Terry had his little green pills and whiskey, but he was never sloshed like Peter [George]."

Southern would remain a regular fixture on the set and guest at the Kubrick home throughout the rest of the shoot. Based on improvisations with Sellers, Southern and Kubrick would refashion the material into revised dialogue before each day's shooting. Southern found Kubrick's meticulous organization fascinating. Kubrick loved nothing more than to go into a stationery store and buy various organizational aids to assist with the production process.

"We shared the vision" is how Southern summed up his collaboration with Kubrick. If Kubrick had an intuitive grasp of the look and atmosphere he wanted *Dr. Strangelove* to have, Southern supplied the dialogue and tone to reinforce the overall mood. Although the structure of the Peter George/Kubrick draft remained the same, the film-within-a-film concept was dropped. The dialogue in the earlier drafts had strained too hard for laughs and often read like a high school parody.

In the Southern and Kubrick draft, a new standard was set for black comedy. There was a unity of time and space sustained by jumping back and forth between the Air Force base, the cockpit of the B-52 bomber, and the Pentagon War Room. The accuracy of Kubrick's research anchored the satire in a kind of hyper-realism that made the absurdity and horror mesmerizing to watch. Most important, although the characters were essentially archetypes of certain all-too-familiar figures—the hawkish generals, the bland president, the mad scientist, or the redneck Texan—the detailing of these characters by Kubrick, Southern, and Sellers gave them a specificity rare in satire.

The inexorable race toward doom in *Red Alert* remained the foundation of *Dr. Strangelove,* but rethinking the narrative in satirical terms had made the result more profound than Peter George's novel. It was the one sad note in this collaboration that George never quite came to terms with.

According to Southern, he strove to craft dialogue that emphasized the incongruity of civilized men in suits and uniforms talking about megadeaths in a casual, almost nonchalant manner: "They have all the jargon, vernacular, and vocabulary that are specific, peculiar, and particular to their skills and positions. There is something so utterly pompous about the phrases themselves, and the idea of the macho thing of the military is an absurdity in itself, that the very phrases become funny."

A classic example of this occurs when the president phones the Russian premier from the War Room to delicately inform him that nuclear bombers are headed his way. Concerned about the late hour of the call, the Russian ambassador counsels the president that the premier is "a man of the people, but he is still a man." Cupping the phone, the president asks a drunken premier to turn some music down. Then, in the voice of a soothing parent, he says, "Dimitri, you know how we always talked about the bomb . . . the bomb, Dimitri."

The dialogue that follows tugs at the viewer in two ways. The slowly mounting horror of a world on the verge of nuclear disaster is combined with laughter at the idea of two statesmen trying to maintain buddy-buddy decorum. Kubrick and Southern also refined the use of scatological or sexually charged names for the characters—"Bat" Guano, Premier Kissoff, Colonel Kilgore, etc. Perhaps the most daring name change was that of the president, Merkin Muffley—a Merkin being a wig made out of pubic hair.

The title character, who appears only in the film's third act, when nuclear holocaust seems unavoidable, was not, as many mistakenly believe, based on Henry Kissinger. In 1963, Kissinger was still a relatively unknown

Harvard foreign policy expert. Southern explained later that "[Dr. Strangelove] was modeled on a combination of the great crazy German scientists of the period and Wernher von Braun and Peter Sellers presenting [the type] as a madman."

Southern, an unrepentant Anglophile, hit it off with Sellers, the master mimic of all things American right from the beginning of production. He worked closely with the actor to find the right Texas accent for the bombardier captain.

"The financing of the film was based almost 100 percent on the notion that [Sellers] would play multiple roles," says Southern. "About a week before he was supposed to start shooting he sent a telegram saying he could not play a Texas role because it was one accent he was never able to do. Kubrick asked me to do a tape of the accent. When Sellers got to the studio, he had this tape recorder with huge, monster earphones. He looked ridiculous, but he mastered the accent in about ten minutes. Then Sellers sprained his ankle and he couldn't make the moves going up and down the ladder in the bomb bay. He was out. The doctor said you can't do it. So it was a question of replacing him, but Stanley had set such store by Sellers's acting that he said you can't replace him with just another actor. 'We got to get an authentic John Wayne (who it was originally written for) type to do it.' Wayne was approached and dismissed it immediately.

"Stanley hadn't been in the States for some time and didn't know anything about the TV programs. He wanted to know if I knew of any actors. So I said there is this big, authentic guy who plays on *Bonanza* named Dan Blocker—Big Hoss—so without seeing him, Kubrick sent off a script to his agent and got an immediate reply. 'It was too pinko' for Mr. Blocker."

Kubrick then remembered Slim Pickens from *One-Eyed Jacks,* which he almost directed for Marlon Brando.

"When Slim Pickens arrived in London, it was the first time he had ever been anywhere other than the Rodeo Circuit as a clown," said Southern." Stanley was very concerned about him being in London for the first time and asked me to meet him. I got some Wild Turkey and went down to the set with a couple of glasses to talk to Slim about the script. When he showed up, I asked him if he wanted a drink since it was only ten in the morning and Slim said, 'It's never too early for a drink.' Then I asked him if he was settled in and he said, 'It doesn't take too much to make me happy. Just a pair of loose shoes, a tight pussy, and a warm place to go to the bathroom.' One of Kubrick's assistants, a very public school type, couldn't believe his ears, but laughed along anyway."

Later, James Earl Jones dropped by to meet Pickens, whom he would be working with in the bomber sequences. Jones asked, in somewhat Shakespearean tones, how he enjoyed working with Brando on *One-Eyed Jacks.*

Pickens replied, " Well, I worked with him for six months and in that time, I never saw him do anything that wasn't all-man and all-white." Pickens didn't realize what he was saying. Jones managed to keep a straight face through this potentially explosive meeting and the two worked quite well together as shooting progressed.

Sellers's ad-libbing would add to future confusion over credit. "Sellers's improvisation was very specific," insists Southern." One scene immediately comes to mind, when Sterling Hayden goes into the bathroom, Sellers changed his lines to include 'Good idea, General, splash a bit of cold water on the back of the neck,' which is a very British thing."

Christiane Kubrick often sketched on the set and was able to observe her husband's sensitive handling of Sellers's manic genius. "Sellers would get a distinct high as his ideas became more and more fabulous and ingenious. However, he would sort of hype himself into a complete frenzy of ideas and then he couldn't reach that state again. He didn't want to do a particular take again because he felt he could never get it as good. . . . Stanley was ready with many cameras so Sellers wouldn't have to do it again. He shot a scene from every angle at once so he would have many cuts and be able to catch that one great flight of fancy. Peter was very fond of Stanley because he was willing to do this while other directors might not have prepared all those cameras for him."

Christiane remembers Sellers constantly cutting up the crew with his "Heil Hitler" salute and mimicking obscene gestures with Strangelove's mechanical hand. When the camera rolled, the crew would literally clap their hands over their mouths and almost choke trying to stifle their own laughter.

Carol Southern visited the cavernous set during the marathon shooting days that led to an elaborate pie-throwing sequence, which would be cut from the film mere weeks from release. "I don't know if this was for technical reasons, but Stanley's set was very very wide. And he didn't just bark out directions. He would sort of whisper them to his assistants. Who would then tell the person. So it was very quiet. Or he would go to talk to people quietly. And in the midst of all this quiet, people were throwing pies. It was hysterical."

The pie-throwing sequence was originally designed to end the film.

Once it became clear that the world outside the War Room was now a post-nuclear wasteland, representatives of the Army, Navy, and Air Force begin to lapse into their traditional interservice rivalry. One of the officers picks up a pie from the lavish buffet at the end of the War Room and throws it. The president is hit by accident and all hell breaks loose.

The sequence took more than a week to shoot. The pies were a mixture of dough, a generic pie filling, and shaving cream. Under the hot studio lights, this mixture eventually gave off an unpleasant stale odor.

"After a few days, the studio became very smelly," recalls Christiane. "Because of continuity, they had to leave the mess as it was. The black plastic floor of the War Room was covered with all this gunge and everybody was totally soiled. Toward the end of filming, the crew decided they were going to all throw pies at Stanley during the last take. However, Stanley had a very good scheme. He went on adding and completing shots and then telling each cast member, 'Okay, you can get cleaned up.' They were so relieved to get out of their disgusting outfits that they didn't want to throw pies at Stanley and get filthy again. So he didn't get anything thrown at him. It was very much a chessplayer's way of thinking."

"What was happening in the pie fight is that people are laughing," says Southern. "It's supposed to be deadly serious. And it was such a funny situation that people outside the periphery, including Stanley and myself, were tossing pies into the melee. And so it lost its edge. It was like a comedy scene, where everything else in the film had been played straight—except once when the Coca-Cola machine spurted in Keenan Wynn's face."

Peter Bull, who played the Russian envoy, recalls the rigors of shooting the pie-fight scene: "I know that at least 2,000 custard pies were ordered every day. Well, not custard, as a matter of fact, because they were laced with shaving cream so that they looked more like lemon-meringue pies. It was just as well that we did get fresh ones because the pastry after a day or two was as lethal as a cast-iron brick."

In addition to the genius of Kubrick and Sellers, Southern was impressed with the personalities and talents of George C. Scott, Sterling Hayden, Peter Bull, James Earl Jones, and Slim Pickens. Key members of Kubrick's crew helped maintain the level of creative excellence throughout the production. Director of photography Gilbert Taylor's glittering black-and-white imagery matched the mood of each location perfectly, from the smoky still-photo quality of the War Room scenes to the newsreel verité of the air base attack. German-born production designer, Ken Adam, reworked countless sketches

Youngblood: Terry Southern, age six
(*Courtesy of Terry Southern Estate*)

Terry Southern looking
cool, mean, and
deliberate, July 1964
(*Steve Schapiro/Courtesy
of Terry Southern Estate*)

Terry's parents, Helen Simonds and Terrence Marion
Southern, c. 1943 (*Courtesy of Terry Southern Estate*)

Copy of Terry's student ID
card, Sorbonne
(*Courtesy of Terry Southern Estate*)

Terry and Mason Hoffenberg
hanging out, early 1950s
(*Courtesy of Terry Southern Estate*)

Terry standing outside the
Sorbonne, c. 1948 (*Courtesy
of Terry Southern Estate*)

Terry in Greenwich Village apartment, mid-1950s (*Courtesy of Terry Southern Estate*)

Pud Gadiot, c. 1952 (*Courtesy of Terry Southern Estate*)

Terry smoking, 1950s (*Aram Avakian/ Courtesy of Terry Southern Estate*)

Carol and Terry, Geneva-bound with their unpredictable Citroën, 1956
(*Aram Avakian/Courtesy of Terry Southern Estate*)

Carol Southern in Geneva,
c. 1959 (*Courtesy of Terry Southern Estate*)

Andre Deutsch, Southern's
first publisher, South
Kensington, London,
November 1993 (*Lee Hill*)

Maurice Girodias, in his
New York office, 1974
(© *Gerard Malanga*)

Southern's East Canaan home
(*Lee Hill*)

Stanley Kubrick
talking with Terry,
c. 1962 (*Courtesy of
Terry Southern Estate*)

Terry and Christiane Kubrick pose for Stanley at Kubrick's Kensington
flat, Winter 1962–63 (*Photo by Stanley Kubrick © 2000 Estate of Stanley
Kubrick*)

Terry, Nile (age three) and Carol relaxing in East Canaan, summer 1964 (*Steve Schapiro/Courtesy of Terry Southern Estate*)

Terry scans the trades, July 1964 (*Steve Schapiro/ Courtesy of Terry Southern Estate*)

Terry hard at work, c. 1964 (*Courtesy of Terry Southern Estate*)

Screenwriter at large,
c. 1964 (*Courtesy of
Terry Southern Estate*)

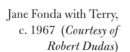

Jane Fonda with Terry,
c. 1967 (*Courtesy of
Robert Dudas*)

Filmways co-founder
John Calley (foreground)
and Terry, c. 1965
(*Courtesy of Terry
Southern Estate*)

Candy Christian look-alike
and Terry, c. 1964 (*Courtesy
of Terry Southern Estate*)

Gail Gerber, c. 1964
(*Camilla McGrath/Courtesy
of Gail Gerber*)

Having fun after the shooting of *The Queen:* Terry, Robert Brownjohn, and
Gail Gerber at far right (*Courtesy of Jerry Schatzberg*)

Terry listens to Ben Gazzara (*Steve Schapiro/Courtesy of Terry Southern Estate*)

Two grand guys: Terry Southern and Robert Brownjohn
(*Courtesy of Jerry Schatzberg*)

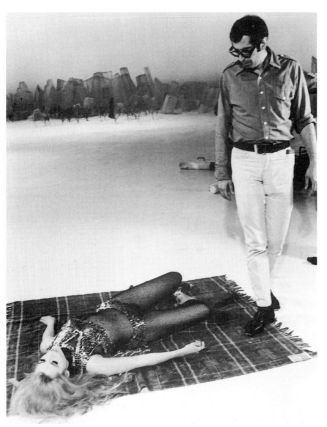

Roger Vadim and Jane
Fonda on the set of
Barbarella, Rome, 1967
(*Courtesy of British Film
Institute/Stills, Posters,
and Designs*)

Peter Fonda and Terry
confer on the New
Orleans location of *Easy
Rider,* February 1968
(*Phil Stiles/Suzan Cooper
Archive, Terry Southern
Collection*)

End of the Road director, Aram Avakian, with James Earl Jones and Stacey Keach
(*Courtesy of British Film Institute/Stills, Posters, and Designs*)

Terry with the four Beatles, May 1969
(*Courtesy of Terry Southern Estate/Suzan Cooper*)

Terry with unidentified collaborator at work in East Canaan, c. 1972
(*Courtesy of Terry Southern Estate*)

Nile and Terry with Larry Rivers looking at *Donkey and the Darling* lithographs,
c. 1972 (*Hans Namuth/Courtesy of Terry Southern Estate*)

Bianca Jagger and Terry aboard the *Lapping Tongue*, 1972
(*photographer unknown*)

Terry, Dean Stockwell,
and Harry Nilsson,
mid-eighties (*Courtesy of
Terry Southern Estate*)

Junky producer Jacques
Stern, Februrary 1976
(© *Gerard Malanga*)

William Burroughs, Dennis Hopper, and Terry confer during the beginning of *Junky* at Jacques Stern's Gramercy Park apartment (© *Gerard Malanga*)

(*Left to right*) William Burroughs, poet John Giorno, Terry, and Harry Nilsson, c. 1987 (*Courtesy of Terry Southern Estate*)

Terry at the 1988 Sundance
Film Festival (*Courtesy of
Terry Southern Estate*)

Terry and Gail Gerber shortly before his death, summer 1995
(*Andy Unangst/Courtesy of Terry Southern Estate*)

for Kubrick to come up with the technocratic nightmare of the War Room. *Dr. Strangelove* may have sounded absurd, but it looked all too real.

During the long postproduction process, Anthony Harvey, the chief editor, worked with Kubrick to establish the right pacing for the crosscutting between the War Room, air base, and bomber cockpit. While this was in the shooting script, Harvey says certain problems in continuity had to be addressed.

"It was the most stunning script I have ever read; but it just didn't work in edited film. It was too confusing—you just didn't know where you were half the time. And there was no variation of pace or buildup of tension. We found by experiment that, if we stayed for much longer on each setting, everything became clearer and clearer and interest was held much more strongly," says Harvey.

Dr. Strangelove cost $2 million to shoot, making it one of the more expensive films shot in Britain at the time. Despite these financial pressures, Kubrick's deal with Columbia pictures gave him final cut and considerable control over marketing and distribution. The film was slowly fine-tuned until the eve of its Oscar-qualifying premiere in December 1963. Kubrick spent almost eight months editing the film. One key change was the famous pie-fight ending. It would be replaced with Vera Lynn singing "We'll Meet Again" over a montage of mushroom clouds.

Near the end of his stint on *Strangelove,* Terry began canvassing for more film work. He was beginning to enjoy his new role as hot film scribe. Carol recalls him hanging out with Charles Kasher, a London producer, who made *Funeral in Berlin.* With offers of more work on the horizon, Southern decided to treat himself to a present.

"Nile, a girlfriend, and I went to Italy for about ten days to pick up an Alfa-Romeo Giulia that [Terry] had ordered, which was kind of a dream come true," said Carol. "We ordered one in white. The three of us went down on the train to pick it up from the factory."

After principal photography was completed, Carol, Nile, and Terry remained in England for a few more months. During the shoot, they became good friends with Kubrick and his family. They would visit him for dinner in his Kensington apartment. Later, Kubrick would move to a castle-like mansion with electric fences, security devices, a 35mm screening room, and state-of-the-art editing facilities. Terry envied Kubrick's combination of luxury and almost total seclusion.

"One night, somebody brought a hard-core porn film over to show to

Stanley," Southern recalled. "Very soon into the film, Kubrick got up and left. We watched some more and then stopped it. Somebody said, 'It would be great if someone were to make a movie like that under studio conditions.' We thought Kubrick would be the ideal person to direct such a movie."

These casual comments got Southern thinking about a new novel. When he came back to the States, Terry started writing the book that became *Blue Movie*. Over the years, he would send Kubrick pieces of the work-in-progress. One section elicited a laudatory telegram praising Terry for having written "the definitive blow job."

While still in England, Terry began to meet with producers about other script work. There were some discussions with John Schlesinger about a possible adaptation of Iris Murdoch's *A Severed Head*. The producers of James Bond, Cubby Broccoli and Harry Saltzman, set Terry up with Peter Yates to work on a treatment called *The Marriage Game*. Carol Southern remembered the manic quality of those meetings.

"We would have dinner at Broccoli and Saltzman's house. It was surreal, because they had this huge, elegant home with literally only a few pieces of furniture. They were in sweatshirts with their wives. They were very manic and funny, as they talked ideas. . . . They were very dynamic."

Terry spent an afternoon driving around London with the producers in their Rolls-Royce. Broccoli took particular pride in his young son's ability to point out such "historic" London landmarks as the Park Lane Hotel and various casinos. The treatment went into limbo, but the writing fees eased the Southerns' financial woes considerably.

Somehow Southern found time to write for *Queen*, the slick London monthly that documented the first glimmers of Swinging London with stories by the likes of Penelope Gilliat and photos by David Bailey and Lord Snowdon. One of the pieces was an essay on John Fowles's *The Collector*, which would become Southern's first gig as a script doctor when William Wyler began shooting the film in the spring and summer of 1964.

While the Southerns were in England, Terry's Quality Lit status was rising. The appearance of "Twirling at Ole Miss," in the February 1963 issue of *Esquire*, created a stir. Then three back-to-back issues of the magazine carried significant Southern contributions (garnering the now rising star the magazine's top dollar rate of $750). "Recruiting for the Big Parade," appeared in June, "I Am Mike Hammer," in the July literary special issue, and the short story "You're Too Hip, Baby" in August. The Mike Hammer story was a particularly droll take on the whole low-versus-high-culture debate that would become irrelevant during the sixties. The

Writers in Revolt anthology also came out that spring. Southern was now at the top of his game, working with one of the best directors in the world and getting the kind of critical attention to which Mailer, Capote, and Vidal had long been accustomed.

Southern spent this transitional period between the completion of shooting and the eventual release of *Dr. Strangelove* growing more conscious of his own celebrity. More time was spent in New York going to parties or generating heat for future projects. Whether it was restlessness or a genuine desire to have the best of both worlds, it was apparent that the traditional conventions of family life did not suit Southern's rebellious sympathies. There were rumors of women on the side, but these fissures in his marriage were invisible to Carol and, probably, to Terry as well.

John F. Kennedy's assassination on November 22, 1963, instantly changed the nature of the new decade's optimism. On the day of the tragic news, a stunned Southern conferred with an equally numb Lenny Bruce about the appropriate way to discuss the event. In the end, Bruce solemnly walked onstage and said, "Phew, Vaughn Meader," in reference to the forgotten comedian whose career consisted solely of a JFK impersonation. The assassination also forced Kubrick to tinker even more with his new film, deleting or relooping the odd line that could cause hurt to the Kennedy family or a mourning American public.

As was customary for him, Kubrick held test screenings of *Dr. Strangelove* for Columbia executives and other industry insiders in London and New York in the fall of 1963. The lack of official support from the State Department and air force had always embarrassed Columbia. Many executives found the film funny, but it was so different from their typical releases they were worried it would flop. A discreet campaign to distance Columbia from the upcoming December release was initiated. Carl Foreman's *The Victors,* a more conventional (and now almost forgotten) World War II melodrama was given full studio backing and released at the same time.

"At the time of the initial release, we were totally wiped out," said Southern. "They would tell people there were no seats for *Dr. Strangelove* at the theaters, but the film built up word of mouth."

Word of mouth quickly turned into a roar of approval and delight. As the film went into wider release in January 1964, it became an event to be celebrated either as a must-see artistic breakthrough or a shocking sign of the decline of pop culture. Both camps seemed to race to the theater to validate their preconceptions. *Time* and *Newsweek* got on the "Yes" band-wagon quickly. Bosley Crowther, the *New York Times*'s notoriously staid critic, was obviously affected by the film's hearts-and-minds satire, but ulti-mately responded with this perverse caveat: "I am troubled by the feeling, which runs all through the film, of discredit and even contempt for our whole defense establishment, up to and even including the hypothetical commander in chief." As for the film's devastating ending with the Vera Lynn soundtrack, Crowther, tongue-firmly-in-some-place-other-than-his-cheek, opined: "Somehow, to me, it isn't funny. It is malefic and sick."

January 1964 became the flash point for Terry's increasing celebrity. He had just signed a contract with Putnam to publish *Candy*. He and Mason would split the profits fifty-fifty. Of course, things would not work out as planned. A loophole in international copyright law allowed others to issue bootleg editions, which also sold wildly. The byzantine legal status of *Candy* and various royalties owing would defy the best efforts of their lawyers and agents for the rest of the decade. Hoffenberg and Southern were naturally upset about this, but the latter less so because revenue from screenwriting assignments would cushion the loss of royalties.

In addition to work on *The Collector*, Southern was approached to work on *The Loved One*, an adaptation of Evelyn Waugh's novel. The film's pro-ducers, Martin Ransohoff and John Calley, would run ads in *Variety* hyping Southern as the author of *Dr. Strangelove*. The campaign angered Kubrick and Peter George, who was still prominently credited as a cowriter.

"There was a lot of publicity about *Strangelove*," Carol Southern remembers. "Terry was interviewed by the media and was given credit for writing the script, which angered Kubrick. He didn't take sole credit, but he didn't really deny it either. He didn't say, 'No, I didn't write the script. I helped with the script.' This made Kubrick, who had worked for years on *Strangelove*, really pissed off."

Southern managed to mollify Kubrick through jokey letters, but Peter George was less easily pacified. [Terry] had been pushed to the sidelines during shooting and watched Southern become the media's literary flavor-of-the-month because of *Candy* and *Strangelove*. A lavish photo essay on Southern in *Life* prompted George to write a somewhat desperate letter downplaying Southern's participation:

Sirs: *Life* (May 8) grossly exaggerated Terry Southern's importance to *Dr. Strangelove*, referring to the "sensation Southern caused with his script." Now (August 21), *Life* implies Southern's intervention turned a serious script into an "original irreverent" satirical film. The facts, however, are that when Mr. Southern first appeared at Shepperton studio, England, the script (a satirical adaptation of my novel, *Red Alert*) was complete. Stanley Kubrick and I had been writing it for 10 months.

Southern was briefly employed (November 16–December 28, 1962) to do some additional writing with Kubrick and myself and fittingly received a screenplay credit in third place behind Mr. Kubrick and myself.

PETER GEORGE, Sussex, England.

George was not only irritated by Southern seemingly hogging credit, but his fears about nuclear war were adding to a sense of persecution and isolation. He wrote the novelization of the film's script and then began work on a sequel to *Red Alert* set in a postnuclear landscape. But the work did little to alleviate a growing sense of futility. On June 3, 1966, in his home outside London, George shot himself.

"Needless to say that in so many cases you would never suspect even when you don't know someone that well," says James Harris about George's suicide, "because you don't know what's going on in somebody's mind or what his problems might be—his deep-seated problems—which evidently he never discussed. Stanley never relayed to me any inside observations or predictions about any problems with Peter George."

"There was gossip written that Peter [George] had complained about what Stanley had done to *Red Alert* and not using his book in the way it was originally written," recalls Christiane Kubrick, "but that also was not true as far as I know because he was just very ill and he knew it. He knew he had drunk himself to death and that's why he ended his life."

Kubrick's response to the credit controversy was to take out ads, issue press releases, and patiently explain to interviewers how he had been working on the script for several years. The dispute highlighted Southern's naïveté. Eager to remain in Kubrick's good graces, he downplayed the fallout over script credit, which cast a shadow over his success with *Dr. Strangelove* and *Candy*.

"Stanley's obsession with the auteur theory—that his films are by Stanley Kubrick—overrides any other credit at all. Not just writing, but anything," said Southern. "He's like Chaplin in this regard. That's part of the reason why he rarely uses original music in his films. Having written this great bestseller *Candy*, number one for twenty-one weeks, my reputation eclipsed Stanley, so I got all the credit in places like the *New York Times* and *Life* magazine. It was just so overwhelming and one-sided, naturally he was freaking out. He would take out full-page ads saying Terry Southern has nothing to do with it. He felt [slighted] and rightly so and lashed out. It was an overnight thing. I did what I could by writing letters to the *Times*."

Although the credit dispute would irritate Kubrick for years (during the writing of *The Shining,* he told coscenarist Diane Johnson that Southern's entire contribution to *Strangelove* consisted of throwing pages out of the window of a cab once a week), the two men kept up a cordial and often warm friendship throughout the sixties. In addition to dedicating *Blue Movie* to Kubrick, Southern visited the set of *2001* several times and, most significantly, encouraged the director to adapt *A Clockwork Orange* when Kubrick's Napoleon project collapsed in 1970. Kubrick's hesitancy to share credit was later repeated in 1987 when he initially refused to offer Gustav Hasford a cowriting credit on *Full Metal Jacket,* the screen adaptation of the latter's *Short-Timers.*

Christiane Kubrick believes the tension between Kubrick and Southern has been blown out of proportion because they made good copy.

"Terry and Stanley were good friends," she says. "Terry was immensely supportive when we came to New York and had this disastrous opening of *2001: A Space Odyssey,* when everybody thought it was going to go wrong. We had this blue-rinse audience of executives who didn't understand it and walked out. There was a terrible meeting in our hotel room and Terry was saying, 'This is going to be great and just you wait and see and this is not a proper audience.' Everybody else was saying the film was impossible. The next morning it turned out people were lining up around the block. But the previous night at the hotel, we were in despair because the screening crowd had slighted it and not understood it at all, but Terry was very strong and not influenced by the mood around him. I always liked him very much for that."

Dr. Strangelove, like *Citizen Kane,* remains a landmark film around which myth, rumor, speculation, and innuendo have gathered to blur the facts of its production history. That the various principals involved—Kubrick, Southern, Peter Sellers, and Peter George—had different recollections doesn't necessarily help matters either. If there was some dispute about who made the film the success it is, there is no doubt that everyone (except George) gained immeasurably from the film's success. Sellers continued to be one of the highest-paid comic actors of the sixties and seventies. Editor Anthony Harvey went on to direct *The Lion in Winter* with Katharine Hepburn and Peter O' Toole. Production designer Ken Adam worked on other key sixties films including several in the James Bond series. Southern's fee jumped from the reported $2,000 for his work on *Dr. Strangelove* to as much as $100,000 a script thereafter. Kubrick consolidated his position as an A-list director whose need for total control would be imitated by Mike Nichols, Woody Allen, Steven Spielberg, Clint Eastwood, and others in years to come.

Without a doubt, *Dr. Strangelove* put Southern in the enviable position of being able to pick and choose screenwriting assignments. With a British Screen Guild Award, Oscar nomination, and a racy bestseller reinforcing his reputation as a hot writer, Southern was able to turn fame into cash and considerable social entrée.

Harris recalls the credit dispute philosophically: "[Stanley] had the highest regard for Terry and he felt that the third credit was the proper credit because, I suppose, of the various stages and how that thing was eventually developed. On the other hand, when I spent time with Terry he seemed to think that his contribution was . . . should have been regarded as a higher credit listing and I said, 'Well, there was so much work done on the film. The story was Peter George's, and the screenplay, and so forth.' But Terry said, 'I added the one thing that it never had and that was humor.' Needless to say, if you are doing a satire or comedy, *that* probably is the single most important additive, but I do think—being in on the development of the script from the very beginning—that the credits were just. You know, it's a hard call."

By the end of 1964, *Candy* had sold about 140,000 copies, which made it number two on the fiction list after John Le Carré's *Spy Who Came in from the Cold*. It was a good year for Quality Lit. Saul Bellow's *Herzog* came in at number three. John Lennon's *In His Own Write* and Hemingway's *Moveable Feast* managed to give the glut of Kennedy books a run for their money on the nonfiction side.

Norman Mailer, who had become an even bigger literary celebrity by this time, would see Southern occasionally at Plimpton's. It was apparent that a star was being born. *Candy* and *Strangelove* especially, says Mailer, instantly became a part of the sixties zeitgeist:

"I think, by now, [*Strangelove*] is iconographic. *Dr. Strangelove* had a huge impact. I remember seeing it and not loving it the way other people were, and I remember thinking about it and whether it was just sheer competitiveness or there was something I didn't quite like about it. In any event, it epitomized the impact it had because those years had a heady optimism. There was a feeling we were really going to take the country away from all the mediocrities that were running it—the deadhead mediocrities—so this picture sort of proved that in a way. It just gave a real spur to people: 'My God. The seventies are going to be our decade if they're making pictures like this,' and then, of course, the opposite happened in the seventies. Whatever revolutionary spirit there was in the sixties, somehow got leached out before long. Terry was very much, what could I say, his importance was directly related to that spirit of revolt in the sixties and when that spirit ended, the love that a lot of people felt for Terry began to diminish. Which was about all he needed, with all his other problems."

Those problems, or the possibility that there would be any problems, were barely perceived by Terry as he rode the wave of fame, money, acclaim, and other grand groovy things rolling in in the wake of *Dr. Strangelove* and *Candy*. Nineteen sixty-four was starting to be a very good year indeed.

7

Making It Hot
for Them

Everything went young in '64.

—Andy Warhol, *Popism*

Dr. Strangelove and *Candy* elevated Southern into an Olympian realm of glamour, money, constant motion, and excitement. There was little time to stop and think during the ride into the unknown.

In spring of 1964, Carol, Nile, and Terry went to Los Angeles for the first big Hollywood gig, to work on *The Loved One* for John Calley and Martin Ransohoff's Filmways and MGM. When the commencement of principal photography was pushed back to July, the Southerns returned to Connecticut. He was still kept busy with a rewrite on William Wyler's adaptation of John Fowles's *The Collector*.

Fowles's 1963 debut novel, a captivating mix of dense character study and psychological thriller, dealt with Frederick Clegg, a deeply shy and repressed young clerk who wins a fortune on the racing pools. The windfall allows Clegg to quit his job, buy a house in the country, and devote all his time to butterfly collecting. He becomes infatuated with Miranda, a London art student whom he stalks on his lonely forays into the city. After some planning, Clegg kidnaps Miranda and keeps her captive in an elaborate cell/studio in the cellar of his estate. Miranda quickly realizes that the usual pleas for mercy will have no effect on her obsessive captor. She slowly manipulates his almost preadolescent crush on her to lay the groundwork for an escape.

Since the novel was told alternately through Clegg's point of view and Miranda's diary entries, there were more than a few challenges in adapting it to the screen. Wyler was not crazy about the original script by Stanley Mann and John Kohn. Still they would receive official credit when the film was released in June 1965.

"I quit before the shooting began," Southern recalled. "These two American producers [Jud Kinberg and John Kohn] insisted on finding a way to save the girl. At the end of John Fowles's novel, the heroine dies of pneumonia after trying to escape in a rainstorm. Changing that didn't even seem like a possibility. It just sounded like one of those stupid ideas. I was not comfortable doing that because of my admiration for Fowles's novel. . . . Then [the producers] said, we've been thinking about it, maybe the real message is that art can triumph over an asshole like the Collector. After showing him for his complete nerd-jerk-nowhere-man creepiness, I contrived to have her escape by outwitting the Collector through her art and prevail. So I wrote a couple of scenes where [Samantha Eggar] was working with this papier-mâché sculpture in her cell. I set up a pattern of where (Terence Stamp) would open the door of this room and look in very cautiously to make sure she wasn't trying to escape, because a couple of times she tried to dart out when he opened the door. He would say, 'I want you to stand where I can see you from the other side of the room.' She created this papier-mâché likeness in such detail that it deceived him. He would open the door and look across the room and see 'her,' when she was, in fact, just behind the door. But because the sculpture was so artfully done, he fell for it. The scene was like Hitchcock. Then she locked the door behind her and him in her former cell. Years later, she would be seen having a picnic on a lovely day. 'It's so lovely here in this pastoral sylvan setting, I can understand why you like to come here,' her companion would comment. The camera would then pull away to reveal they are having a picnic just a few feet away from the cellar door. By this stage they had gone too far back to the original premise for them to use the new ending that I proposed," said Southern.

During his first phase of *Loved One* work, Filmways set up the family in a rented house in Mandelville Canyon. Then the owners had to move back in when their child became ill. For a brief period, the Southerns stayed in Martin Ransohoff's home while he was away on business, and then they moved into yet another rented house on Mulholland Drive. This hectic period lasted through August. Carol was introduced to some of Terry's new Hollywood friends, including Dennis Hopper and Brooke Hayward, Ben Gazzara and Janice Rule. The original intention during this period was for Terry, Carol, and Nile to return to Connecticut once *The Loved One* was finished. Things did not go according to plan."

"It was very disruptive and the whole period seems very disjointed. During that time, Terry took up with Gail [Gerber]," Carol Southern said. "I don't think he intended to break up the marriage. But he was having a good time and he wanted to stay in L.A. The plan was he would come back to Connecticut in October. We were planning to fix the house and do a lot of renovation and also Nile was going to nursery school. So I came back [to East Canaan]. Terry just never came back. I think John Calley, whether consciously or unconsciously, played a part in that. He wanted to keep Terry around and he was offering Terry two-to-three-week jobs that turned into four-week jobs. Finally—I don't know who it was—he was offered a Ferrari. Terry said, 'I can't turn this down.' So finally I said, 'I am coming out there.' It's was December, when Nile and I went out to L.A. He told me he had to stay. He had met Gail."

Gail Gerber was a young Canadian dancer and actress Terry had met on the MGM backlot. She had a nonspeaking part in *The Loved One* and was also in an Elvis Presley picture being shot on the adjacent soundstage.

Gail was twenty-six years old, petite, slim, and blond. She looked like Tuesday Weld, whom Terry was already enamored with. Her *blondness* struck a deep chord in Terry. Henry James's Daisy Miller had been blond. As was Daisy in *The Great Gatsby*. And of course, Candy was the *über*blond. This physical attraction by Southern gave way to a deeper appreciation of her artistic talents as they began to date.

Born in Edmonton, Alberta, in 1937, Gerber had studied music and dance as a child. She went to the National Ballet School in Montreal and studied theater as part of her core studies. She joined Les Grands Ballets Canadiens, which, along with the Royal Winnipeg Ballet, was in the vanguard of Canada's cultural scene in the fifties and sixties. She left the company after a couple of years to work on the stage and in CBC Television in Toronto. For a time she was part of a revue called *Spring Thaw* starring Don Harron, the father of *American Psycho* director Mary Harron. Like many Canadians of her generation, she moved to Los Angeles to expand her horizons. She rented a house in Benedict Canyon and began taking acting workshops with Stella Adler. When she met Southern, Gerber was a dancer on the Elvis film. There were also other very small roles in other MGM films as an extra or background player. Like many women who met Terry, Gerber found the writer charming, but his reputation and aggressiveness made her wary.

"First he invited me to lunch," recalls Gerber. "He told me very clearly that he was married and that he had a small child and all of it. I didn't know the state of the relationship. I could tell that he was making it with Margo, the makeup girl.

"There was something about the relationship [with Carol] that wasn't working and that he was living a bachelor life. He was going to work his way, sort of like Baryshnikov with the New York City Ballet, like a wolf in a sheepfold, through the entire female cast of *The Loved One* one by one."

After a few dates, Gail tried to terminate the relationship. She had been invited to a party at Jennifer Jones's, but decided not to accompany Terry in the hope she could distance herself from him. Instead Jones, in the role of matchmaker, called Gail to encourage her to attend. "She said, 'Well, Gail, you better rethink this, you know, you better come to the party and we'll talk about it.' She was playing that role. 'We'll discuss this and rethink this whole thing.' As a matter of fact, I had pretty well made a good split and she sort of wrecked it for better or worse."

Over the months of July and August, the relationship with Gail intensified. Terry clumsily tried to navigate between his loyalty to Carol and passion for Gail.

"I could always reach him during that period," recalls Carol. "He was really trying to keep both fires going. He just got caught."

Work on *The Loved One* exposed Southern to the full gamut of Hollywood's temptations. In Carol's view, *The Loved One* period allowed Terry to indulge his dark side.

"During most of our [marriage], we had practically no money. He couldn't afford liquor. We had occasional glasses of wine. We had maybe one drink at dinner. Our life was so based on home and frugality, especially in Europe. Then we came back to Canaan and building the house. We did the work ourselves, clearing the fields and planting the gardens. One winter, we just ate the food I had been able to put out in the garden. Plus venison. So [he had] that kind of discipline. He was very productive during that period. Starting with *The Magic Christian* . . . he did a lot of work for the *Nation*. He was doing his work for *Esquire*. He did very good work, but I think when the sudden money came . . . I remember one day I was ironing Terry's chinos and he said, 'Don't you understand that you never have to do that again!' It was kind of traumatic from really having practically nothing to having $3,000 a month, which was what he was paid out [in L.A.]."

After Carol and Nile returned to Connecticut, the Chateau Marmont, the legendary hotel of choice for William Faulkner and Nathanael West, was rapidly becoming Terry's second home. The Chateau was close to the active club scene that dominated Sunset Boulevard. The clientele was a mix of West Coast bohemia: musicians, singers, young actors and actresses, models, writers, and, of course, characters who seemed to have no other vocation than just making the scene.

The Chateau possessed a seductive blend of beauty, ambition, mystery, and the enigmatic buzz that made a place inspiring and energizing. The hotel management tolerated the smell of marijuana in the hallways, the parties, the comings and goings at all hours. Similarly the regulars kept such hedonistic pursuits low-key and maintained the privacy that was essential to the Chateau's appeal. *The Loved One*'s production photographer, William Claxton, already famous for his portraits of the jazz world, and his wife, Peggy Moffatt, a model who became world famous through her collaborations with the fashion designer Rudi Gernreich, were also staying at the hotel. John Calley was a frequent visitor and engaged Terry to work on other Filmways projects including *The Cincinnati Kid* and *Don't Make Waves,* a project that would ultimately be helmed by Alexander Mackendrick, the director of *Sweet Smell of Success.*

Although she was very much in love with Terry, Gail had few illusions about the man with whom she was getting involved. One night she called on him at the Beverly Hills Hotel, where he was holed up preparing a film adaptation of *Candy* for Frank Perry.

"He was writing the script and typing and laughing and he had a new bottle of B&G there and I'm ordering food, doing whatever, reading and fooling around . . . and I see the bottle and it was a third empty. I thought, 'Wow, that's interesting.' The next time I look at the bottle, it was half empty. I thought, 'It must be evaporating.' Because he's not drunk. Alcoholics when they're young don't get drunk, but they have an affinity for booze. They don't have a rejection of it like some people. So then at three-fourths empty, I thought, 'It's evaporating or it isn't evaporating, but that doesn't sound right.' Then I realized that it was going down, but yet he was not drunk. He was stone-cold sober. Typing and writing. [He had an] enormous metabolism for alcohol."

Tony Richardson, who was also a hot commodity due to the success of *Tom Jones,* wanted *The Loved One* to be as innovative as *Dr. Strangelove* in its breaking with Hollywood conventions. MGM/Filmways had given Richardson final cut, but perversely insisted on paying the Directors Guild of America scale. Richardson, in turn, perversely cast Robert Morse, an American, in the lead role of the English poet drifting through a land of

Machiavellian producers, snobbish British expatriates, and sexually baroque funeral parlor directors.

During the spring and summer of 1964, Southern, Richardson, and Christopher Isherwood transformed Waugh's novel into an all-out attack on Hollywood, consumerism, and the hypocrisies surrounding man's fear of death. Southern and Richardson's then wife, Vanessa Redgrave, visited funeral parlors as a fictitious couple for the purposes of research. William Claxton kept a photographic diary of the film's production for which Southern would write the tongue-in-cheek text. Richardson also looked to Southern for casting suggestions. Lenny Bruce was considered for a cameo as Guru Brahmin, a cynical Lonelyhearts columnist. Despite their friendship, Southern was unable to convince Bruce to join the cast. However, the gravelly-voiced Lionel Stander, a survivor of the blacklist, was a more than adequate replacement.

The Loved One would turn out to be one of the strangest films made in the sixties. It was a far blacker, if less controlled, comedy than *Dr. Strangelove*. (A young Hal Ashby worked on the rough cut of *The Loved One*, but Richardson would complete editing in London.) When the film was released in the fall of 1965, most critics viewed it with incomprehension. Promoted as the film with something to offend everyone, *The Loved One* was an acquired taste that alienated many.

Rod Steiger's portrayal of Joyboy as a lisping monster of murderous and repressed appetites was almost too painful for some viewers to stomach. Where *Dr. Strangelove* was deadpan, *The Loved One* was corrosive. John Gielgud, Jonathan Winters, and Roddy McDowall rounded out the cast. Newcomer Anjanette Comer played Morse's beautiful but prudish love interest. Liberace, Dana Andrews, Milton Berle, James Coburn, and a very young Paul Williams appeared in cameos. Haskell Wexler's black-and-white cinematography portrayed Los Angeles as a well-dressed, but bloated corpse.

Many years later, après *Monty Python/National Lampoon/Saturday Night Live, The Loved One* began to look visionary and became a cult movie. It remains a film with too many ideas for its own good. Still, if the casting of Morse is a Brechtian motif that doesn't pan out, the other eclectic performances never fail to click. Jonathan Winters is especially hilarious doubling as a fired studio exec turned gravedigger and a corporate boss with space-age designs on the funeral business. In departing from Waugh's original, Richardson, Southern, and Isherwood did not so much adapt *The Loved One* as rewrite it. The results were quite different, if equally disturbing, funny, and haunting as Waugh's novel. Unfortunately, for the purposes of marketing, Waugh was quite vocal about how much he hated the film even before shooting began.

If the reception of *The Loved One* was considerably cooler than that accorded *Dr. Strangelove,* this did not bother Southern at all. Coming off *Dr. Strangelove,* Southern was treated with awe and respect by Richardson, Calley, and Ransohoff. Richardson, who was a less assured stylist than Kubrick, often let his screenwriters set the tone for his films. Thus, the interplay between Isherwood and Southern produced an odd blend of camp and burlesque in some scenes and a sad gothicism in others. Richardson and Calley also shared Southern's belief that business and pleasure should be combined to heighten the spontaneity of the creative process. Many of the rushes were screened in the Beverly Hills Hotel with champagne and canapés laid out for the production's inner circle. Richardson would often toast cast and crew with a raised glass at the beginning of each day's shooting.

Peter Bart, then an entertainment writer for the *New York Times,* visited *The Loved One* and observed this of Southern: "[He] is another writer who stays on the set during production. It is the theory of Mr. Southern, who wrote *Dr. Strangelove,* that a script is not an unalterable document, but merely a plot outline. He not only encourages improvisation but also takes part in it himself."

The set was also visited by Jessica Mitford, whose book *The American Way of Death* had been part of Richardson's inspiration for updating *The Loved One.* She wrote an exclusive feature article on the filming for *Show* magazine. The first assembly of *The Loved One* ran five hours. A scene with Jayne Mansfield as a travel receptionist was cut out. The Whispering Glades scenes were shot at Greystone, the estate built by Edward Laurence Doheny II, which would later become the home of the American Film Institute.

One of the first people outside the production to see *The Loved One* was Barney Rosset, whose cousin Haskell Wexler was one of the coproducers. Rosset wanted to publish the script of the film, but Terry had already made a deal with Random House to create a pictorial souvenir of the film's making. The result, *The Log Book of the Making of The Loved One,* was one of the more bizarre tie-ins in movie marketing history. Its chief strength was William Claxton's photos, which captured the production's infectious spirit of mischief. Many of the stills showed Southern looking like a perfect icon of cool in his sunglasses, T-shirt, and chinos. Southern's text was amusing, but shed little light on the actual difficulties of getting *The Loved*

One made. Unlike his *Esquire* pieces, the Grand Guy persona was too much in the way of the subject.

One of the most terrifying scenes in *The Loved One* is Aimee's introduction to Mr. Joyboy's mother. Played by the all too convincingly obese Aylene Gibbons (who managed to get a few bit parts in TV shows like *Ironside* and *It Takes a Thief*), Aimee's distaste turns to terror as she watches Mom flick the channel changer in search of her favorite Taylor Ice Cream commercial. As the meal begins:

JOYBOY (happily)

You should have helped yourself, Aimee—we don't stand on ceremony around here. (Beams at Mom.) Right, Mom?

At the words "we don't stand on ceremony", Mom tears into the pig like a savage, holding it as though it were a slice of melon. Aimee watches in sickened fascination. Ghandi pecks wildly at the pig, screeching "There is no death! There is no death!" Aimee seems on the verge of swooning, tears her gaze away from Mom, and looks down at her own plate, which is piled with a mound of stew. She quickly averts her gaze, looking now at Joyboy—who is shoveling stew into his mouth with gusto. There seems no escape; she turns her eyes toward the wall, is confronted by the TV screen showing a man eating a turkey leg with wild-eyed zeal.

As *The Loved One* completed shooting in the fall of 1964, Southern began work on *The Cincinnati Kid,* a gritty look at high stakes poker set in the Depression starring Steve McQueen. Shot on MGM's Culver City soundstage with additional location work in New Orleans, the Filmways production had script problems. The source novel by Richard Jessup was heavy on atmosphere and character, but short on the kind of A-to-Z plotting that producers are comfortable with. Ransohoff said he and Calley had gone through several scripts: "[Paddy] Chayefsky started it, then George Good wrote on it. . . . Then we had Ring Lardner [Jr.], Terry Southern. I think there were four or five really good writers before we finally got that script down to where it went to. And even then two top writers, Lardner and Terry Southern, shared screen credit. . . . I had $300,000 in that script."

Then of course there was the little matter about the film's original director, Sam Peckinpah. Peckinpah was shooting scenes he wasn't supposed to shoot. Some say they were unauthorized nude scenes. Others say he was shooting in black and white. Ransohoff and Calley decided to fire Peckinpah about a week into principal photography. The hell raising director would not make another film until 1969's *The Wild Bunch*. His replacement was the Canadian-born director, Norman Jewison, mainly known for producing television variety shows like *The Judy Garland Show*. His four films as director up to that point were unremarkable. Jewison was eager to work on something with some depth to it. He was determined to make *The Cincinnati Kid* that film.

Jewison and Southern got along well. During one difficult setup, Southern, ever so helpful, came up to Jewison and whispered, "Think Mavor Moore!" Moore, a legend in Canadian theater in the late fifties and sixties, had been one of Jewison's mentors. The out-of-nowhere reference sent Jewison into a fit of hysterical laughter and he wasn't able to restore his composure for at least half an hour.

In addition to Claxton, Southern was also becoming fast friends with Rip Torn. The character actor was a fellow Texan. Torn had a reputation for being difficult, but what this really meant was that he took his acting very seriously. He had little time for the superficial backslapping of the typical movie set, but Southern's lack of pretension and antic humor won him over. They would become close friends until the end of Southern's life.

The Cincinnati Kid and *The Loved One* were released in the fall of 1965. Unlike the latter, *Kid* was a commercial success. The film can be seen as an accidental allegory of Southern's future struggles with success and artistic purity. In the film, the Kid played by McQueen plays poker for kicks and just enough money to get by. He is persuaded by his buddy Karl Malden, who is under pressure from Torn's character, to set up a big game. As the match begins, the kid discovers the game is fixed, unbeknownst to his chief opponent, played by Edward G. Robinson. Thus his loyalties become complicated. Should he help his friend? Should he stay true to his gift for championship poker? Should he take the money and run? The kid eventually decides to take the high road, but he loses anyway. Although he still has his pride, he has lost his girlfriend, played by Tuesday Weld, as a result of having a quick affair with the Ann-Margret character. In real life, Southern would be faced with similar conflicts about mixing art with commerce as his screenwriting took him further away from the values of Faulkner, Algren, and Henry Green.

In the evenings and weekends, Southern and Gail went to parties and clubs to soak up Los Angeles's social scene. In addition to Torn and Claxton, Southern became friends with actors like George Segal, Richard Benjamin, James Coburn, Peter Fonda, and Dennis Hopper.

Hopper had lost a lot of acting work after fighting with Henry Hathaway on a Western. He still got the occasional bit of television work, but he was spending most of his downtime investing in pop art and developing a sideline in photography. Many of his subjects included the new artists emerging in California such as Bruce Conner, Ed Ruscha, and Wallace Berman. Hopper introduced Southern to a young London gallery owner, Eton-educated Robert Fraser, who would become a close friend in the mid-sixties. Fraser and Hopper would later collaborate on "Los Angeles Now," a group showing of new California art, at the former's Mayfair gallery.

Some old associates, like John Marquand, found it sad, ironic, and inevitable that Terry was now going Hollywood in a big way. The Quality Lit Game was in distinct second place to Terry's new life in the film world.

"Artie Shaw thought Terry was great," says John Marquand. "When Terry began to make it with *Dr. Strangelove* and there was the money and the wife was sort of left behind and he began to pick up babes, Artie said, 'That's the story of my whole generation. I saw it happen again and again.' [The affair with Gail] broke up the marriage with Carol. Gail was referred to sardonically by Carol and my first wife, Susan, as Miss Beach Ball because he had apparently met her on the beach.

"I remember Terry once sitting around Paris and saying F. Scott Fitzgerald was a sellout and then seven years later, who was a sellout? He was doing *Dr. Strangelove*. None of us had ever gotten to do that."

Despite a small degree of envy and resentment over Terry's somewhat patronizing attitude toward his (Marquand's) New England roots, Marquand understood that his friend was becoming a part of the sixties in a way others from the *Paris Review* salon would never be. *Dr. Strangelove* not only gave Southern an entrée into the international film world and the high-roller lifestyle, it brought him into contact with an emerging generation of actors, producers, filmmakers, painters, musicians, and writers who wanted to merge different media, break down barriers, and test the limits. In public, Southern would be tight-lipped about such artistic aspirations or make fun of them through deadpan tomfoolery, but beneath the hipster persona, he understood that film was the perfect medium for the sixties. To him, it was the only way one could capture the energy and the chaos that now permeated life in America.

Southern's acclaim and achievement as a natural screenwriter did not come without a price. His marriage to Carol would not survive his relationship with Gail. Carol and Nile moved out of the house in East Canaan. Mutual friends took sides. Terry became spiritually, as well geographically, isolated from the New York literary establishment. Over time he would discover not everyone in the film business was as cool as Richardson, Kubrick, or John Calley. There was an emptiness to the film community that could deaden the mind at times. Yet Terry had no choice really. Henry Green had told him that a writer must seek out new forms of communication. Making the decision to go to London and work on *Dr. Strangelove* had started Terry's own search. Now he was too far down the road to find his way back even if he wanted to.

Little of this change appeared to disturb Terry. He was obdurate about the quality of his new life. He was working on a bigger canvas, deeply in love, living the real-life movie called the sixties, and making it hot for them.

Throughout 1965 and 1966, Terry and Gail seemed to be everywhere. When not in Los Angeles, they hung out in Malibu, where there were lots of weekend parties, brunches, and barbecues hosted by the likes of Jane Fonda and Roger Vadim, or maybe a producer type like Dominick Dunne. In New York, the couple would often stay at the Chelsea Hotel, another cool scene like the Chateau Marmont, where one might bump into the likes of William Burroughs, Joni Mitchell, Leonard Cohen, or Arthur C. Clarke. Eventually Terry and Gail decided to rent an apartment on West Twenty-fifth Street as a kind of base camp during this gypsy period. Terry was writing everywhere—in airplanes, hotel lobbies, restaurants. Sometimes he would come into Si Litvinoff's office on West Fifty-fifth Street and work with a secretary.

Meanwhile the farm in Connecticut was dormant much of the time. When the movie money came in, Carol supervised the renovations alone. The kitchen was remodeled with Spanish tiles. One of the big rooms was converted into a recreation area where eventually (but, sadly, without Carol and Nile), Terry would listen to jazz, Lenny Bruce, or some of the new pop music by Bob Dylan or the Beatles.

Contact with Carol and Nile had become increasingly erratic since he began living and traveling with Gail. For a while, not knowing how long the relationship would endure, Gail would gently persuade Terry to reconcile with Carol, if only for his son's sake. It was a difficult period. Terry was conflicted about his relationship with Gail. He still loved Carol and was nostalgic for the life they shared in Europe and East Canaan. Yet he was also deeply in love with Gail, his passion for her tied up with the possibilities of the sixties and the giddy rush of his new fame and fortune. "Terry was terribly conflicted and he did try to reconcile," says Carol, "but his desire to be with Gail was stronger."

Almost all of Southern's activity now revolved around one film project or another. The odd Quality Lit pieces grew few and far between. A review of *Naked Lunch* for the *Washington Post Book World* was followed months later by a feature on his new best friends, Dennis Hopper and his lovely wife, Brooke Hayward, for *Vogue*. The logbook for *The Loved One* was published to a puzzled response along with the film that prompted it. There were also the sketches and parodies for Paul Krassner at the *Realist*.

On the screenplay front, Southern was juggling an adaptation of *Candy*, a Western treatment called *Something Else*, and the first of several drafts of a *Magic Christian* script. Peter Sellers was underwriting the last gig through his Brookfield Productions. Then there was the early work on *Blue Movie*, which Southern was privately hoping Kubrick would direct.

Southern did lots of interviews in this period. Because of *Candy* and *Strangelove*, he was now seen as a hip commentator on the times. The *London Evening Standard*'s film critic, Alexander Walker, was all ears when Southern described the premise of *Blue Movie*.

"A film about love can be an aesthetic experience, but at what point does it become an erotic one? Can a pornographic novel be an artistic success?" he asked Alexander rhetorically.

Alexander asked Southern if there were any limits to freedom of expression: "That's what people have assumed, that there must be limits. But that assumption seems to be being disproved over and over again. We're only at the start of exploring the relations between the aesthetic and the erotic. There's only one rule I know. 'You won't make it unless you go flat out.'"

The media attention encouraged Southern to indulge his philosophical side. Plimpton asked Maggie Paley, a writer and *Paris Review* associate, to interview Southern for the Art of Fiction series. They did the bulk of the interview at the Russian Tea Room, where Terry was becoming a regular.

He often met friends there and picked up the bill for lavish meals. Southern had a bit of a crush on Paley (as was the case with many of his friendships with women) and felt relaxed enough in her company to talk seriously about screenwriting. The Grand Guy volume was on low.

During the interview, which sadly was unpublished, Southern was at great pains to explain why he thought movies were now more important than novels. "The only excuse for writing a novel is if it can't be done as a movie" is a recurring refrain in the interview. He says his primary motivation for seeing his new novel, *Blue Movie,* through to the end is that he has never seen "a good dirty movie." The erotic, Southern believes, remains a formidable barrier to filmmakers because it is so subjective.

When Paley asked whether success will change Terry Southern, the writer became circumspect.

"As for my 'outlook,' I would certainly welcome a change there, because it is basically one of extreme discomfort. I'm afraid, however, that God would have to show his hand, in a more dramatic way than 'money and fame' before that could happen. . . . No, the important thing is to keep in touch with the youth of whatever culture you're in. When you lose them, you can forget it. When they're no longer surprised or astonished or engaged by what you say, the ball game is over. If they find it repulsive, or outlandish or disgusting, that's all right, or if they love it, that's all right, but if they just shrug it off, it's time to retire. Well, you could still write for a living if you wanted to, but it would be uncomfortable if you had any relationship to the work other than that."

I n early 1966, Terry flew to London, where he began work with Joseph McGrath on what was intended to be a timely parody of the James Bond craze. McGrath, a cheerful Scot who worked with Richard Lester on *The Running Jumping and Standing Still Film,* was best known for directing Peter Cook and Dudley Moore's British TV show, *Not Only . . . But Also.*

Charles Feldman, the legendary superagent of Hollywood's golden years, owned the rights to *Casino Royale,* the only Ian Fleming property not owned by Cubby Broccoli and Harry Saltzman. Feldman had a smash hit the previous year with *What's New, Pussycat?* and planned to use one of its stars, Woody Allen, in the role of Bond's younger brother, Jimmy, a meek pretender to 007's mantle. Feldman was a producer who could never leave a good idea alone. *What's New, Pussycat?* became a hit in spite of cast changes and heavy rewrites of Allen's original screenplay, but this approach would backfire on *Casino Royale*. It was to have been McGrath's feature film debut, but Feldman hired, fired, and then rehired him along with four other directors—Robert Parrish, Val Guest, John Huston, and Ken Hughes. The results were edited together to form a quasi-psychedelic burlesque. Other writers, credited and uncredited, included Allen, Huston, Wolf Mankowitz, Michael Sayers, Frank Buxton, Joseph Heller, Ben Hecht, Mickey Rose, and Billy Wilder.

Casino Royale production took up almost all of 1966. Feldman had crews and sets working off and on soundstages all over London. Terry didn't seem to mind the delays. It was another scene and there was lots of raw material he could work into *Blue Movie*.

"I received a call from Gareth Wigan, a famous British agent, who was representing me at the time," Southern recalled. "He had this call from Peter Sellers saying he wanted me to write some dialogue for him on this movie. Wigan said, 'I think you can ask whatever you want because the producer, Charles Feldman, wants to make it a blockbuster.' There was a lot of heavy weight on that movie because of Orson Welles and Woody Allen. However, Woody Allen and Peter were such enemies on that film that I didn't really associate with anyone but Peter. An extraordinary thing happened. Because Woody Allen was having such a bad time on the picture, his agent came over to the Dorchester Hotel to speak to him. When he came into the lobby, he was dead sure he spotted his client Woody Allen at the newsstand reading a paper. The agent came over and said, 'Hey, Woody, we're gonna fix that fucking Sellers and he'll be off this picture.' But it was actually Peter Sellers he was talking to. Sellers immediately realized that it was a case of mistaken identity and of course went right along with it and apparently gave a masterful impersonation of Woody Allen. He used to repeat this imitation with the grimace and glasses. The agent kept ranting for three or four minutes how Sellers should be fired and some specific things like 'I've seen his contract and I know how much he's getting, blah, blah, blah,' and then he split. Peter was so irate (later he was amused) that he walked straight out the door and flew home to Geneva and announced he was taking a few days' holiday. So this multimillion-dollar movie came to an abrupt halt. It was an incredible situation costing thousands a day. They tried to shoot around Peter in his big confrontation scene with Orson Welles in the casino. Welles was furious. They didn't even have all the actors in the master shot, just some stand-ins, and each day they would shoot around whichever star didn't show up."

Southern concentrated on polishing Peter Sellers's dialogue. He claimed to have earned about $25,000 for the work: "I was staying at the Dorchester during *Casino Royale.* I stayed at a number of hotels. Writing on a contract for a major studio you get the very best. I would go back and forth on these over-the-Pole flights, where you would go from L.A. to London. I wrote a lot during those flights."

Southern accepted the revolving door of cast changes, new directors, production delays, and other writers with amusement. Like many key players on the film, he was kept on full pay much of the time with very little to do. But in London in the mid-sixties, having too much free time and a pocketful of per diem money was a guaranteed ticket to a grand time.

During his frequent visits to London, Southern had gotten to see a lot of Robert Fraser, whose Duke Street art gallery was the showcase for breaking the work of American pop artists such as Jim Dine, Roy Lichtenstein, Andy Warhol, and Larry Rivers into the European market. Work by cutting-edge British artists such as Bridget Riley, Colin Self, Richard Hamilton, and Peter Blake was also on view. Terry loved the new developments in painting, sculpture, and multimedia. "I think pop artists are doing for art what I'm doing in literature," he told *Life* magazine only a few years before.

The Fraser gallery became the center of a free-floating "salon" that Terry and Gail took an active part in. Surrounding Fraser was an eclectic group that included photographer Michael Cooper, the Rolling Stones and Beatles (and various camp followers), the collector and decorator Christopher Gibbs, model/actress Anita Pallenberg, and singer Marianne Faithfull. Donald Cammell, the charismatic painter-turned-filmmaker, was often around the Fraser circle with his companion, Deborah Dixon, a beautiful model from Texas. Donald's brother, David, was a successful producer of commercials in a company he ran with Hugh Hudson (who later directed *Chariots of Fire*). Another partner in the company, Robert Brownjohn, was a New Jersey native best known for his art direction (he had shot the title sequence for *Goldfinger*). Sandy Lieberson was an up and coming American agent with the London office of Creative Management Associates (CMA) working closely with Peter Sellers, Richard Harris, and Lindsay Anderson. Others on the periphery of the Robert Fraser crowd included the cinematographer Nicolas Roeg, the painter Francis Bacon, and William Burroughs, now living in London. Harvey Orkin, Lieberson's boss at CMA, was another American expatriate. Orkin was renowned for his no-nonsense wit and became a regular on a talk show hosted by David Frost called *Not Just a Programme More a Way of Life.*

It was a pretty fast crowd for the time. The Stones were seen as a kind of antichrist version of the Beatles, and the British media played up the contrast. In reality, the two groups were close friends and shared the same nascent interests in mind-expanding drugs, pop art, movies, and experience for its own sake. The older members of the crowd liked the energy and unpredictability of the gatherings in Mayfair and Chelsea.

Gail Gerber recalls the frenzied pace of the Fraser social scene at that time: "I'd never seen people party like that; it was just party, party, party . . . it was exhausting and I wasn't used to staying up that late. It was very intriguing. The Stones were the come-uppers and angry young men."

"I knew about Robert Fraser's gallery because friends of mine like Claes Oldenburg, Jim Dine, Larry Rivers, and others would show there," Southern recalled. "[Fraser] was an extraordinary guy. Kenneth Tynan lived on Mount Street near the gallery. He used to take me to a lot of places like that. Fraser's gallery became very common knowledge in the industry. One day, Tynan said I had to see this friend of his, Colin Self, who had done this extraordinary piece of sculpture which was like the *Strangelove* plane. They wanted me to pose with it at Fraser's gallery. That was my first actual trip there. While I was there, Michael Cooper, the photographer who took some pictures, said, 'You must come over for drinks. Mick and Keith are going to be there.' Robert used to have this very active salon at his flat. So I went over and got to know them in a very short time. Christopher Gibbs, the antique dealer and production designer for *Performance,* was part of the crowd at Robert Fraser's. Then there was Tara Browne, who was killed in the car crash John Lennon wrote about in 'A Day in the Life.' It was through him that I knew Christopher. Sandy Lieberson, who was an agent who optioned *Flash and Filigree* and produced *Performance,* was there a fair bit. He was involved with the American film industry in London."

Southern bought Self's missile sculpture, but it became lost in transit to New York.

In addition to the openings, Fraser and company threw parties and dinners throughout the West End. There were film nights at Fraser's Mount Street apartment, where Marianne Faithfull vividly recalls seeing *The Blood of a Poet,* the Jean Cocteau classic. There was dancing at the new discos like the Ad-Lib or Bag O'Bones. There was friendly chatter and limitless book browsing at Barry Miles and John Dunbar's Indica bookshop, where, if one were lucky, one's purchases might be gift-wrapped in paper designed by Paul McCartney. The wine flowed freely. Marijuana smoke filled the air and tabs of Owsley acid were dropped like proverbial pennies from heaven. In addition to head turners like Faithfull and Pallenberg, there were the likes of Donya Luna, a model who was the Naomi Campbell of her time. On more subdued nights, Southern might take in a game of poker with Ted Kotcheff and Mordecai Richler.

Through Fraser, Southern and Gerber became especially close to Michael Cooper. The photographer had a studio at 4 Chelsea Manor, Flood Street, where he shot various assignments for New York and London fashion magazines. Cooper carried his Nikon with him constantly. His real subject was the "family" of friends he shared with Southern and Fraser. Even the camera-weary Stones and Beatles allowed Cooper to take informal snapshots of them. Cooper was also interested in film and was constantly "talking" story with Lieberson and Southern.

Cooper, Southern recalls, persuaded Fraser "to install a 45 rpm record player under the dashboard of his car—a removable Italian device that would absorb the bumps and cobbles of Old Smoke without skipping a note."

Cooper, Southern, Fraser, and company would drive through the streets of London listening to the Beatles, the Who, or the Kinks at full blast while racing toward a chic bistro or to catch jazz at Ronnie Scott's in Soho. Or sometimes they would pop by to say hello to Paul McCartney, who was then living with Jane Asher and her parents.

Through Robert Fraser's gallery and the Swinging London scene that surrounded him, Southern found himself at another red-hot center.

"It was really a meeting place for everybody from every background and walk of life," says Sandy Lieberson. "Who turned up that was unexpected? To be honest with you, you expected everybody from Muhammad Ali to you name it. It was that sort of feeling in London at the time. I don't know why. Everybody converged on London at that time. I had it before in Rome in the early sixties. So I was lucky enough to get it in two places."

Everybody was drawn to Southern by his Grand Guy persona, but Lieberson recognized there was a downside.

"He was not interested in business at all. He never had enough money. He was always short of money no matter how much he was getting paid. Probably part of the problem came down to his lack of interest in the business side of it. Terry loved to have a good time. He loved to be around people. He was quite lonely and didn't like to be alone. He seemed to really love being the center of attention, being the center of the group, the crowd. He loved talking and storytelling. . . . He would talk about the quality of the drugs. Who was fucking who. Oh yeah. He loved it. He was a great gossip."

"In England, a veritable renaissance occurred—The Beatles, Stones and the dress—people were beginning to recognize London as a creative mecca, such as post-war Paris had been. London was the center of the universe for a two-to-three year period. In every era, there is a place for artists to go—London was that place in the 60s," Southern later wrote in *Blinds and Shutters*, a 1989 book of the photography of Cooper, who died in 1973.

Anita Pallenberg saw the social circle that surrounded Fraser as a natural extension of his personality. The German-Italian model was then dating the Stones' guitarist, Brian Jones.

"He was just very open to new influences and very avant-garde," Pallenberg recalls. "[Robert] liked us to put this effect together. There was another friend of ours, Christopher Gibbs, and he had a house down on 100 Cheyne Walk and we used to have get-togethers there as well. We always went out for dinner together and we were all very jaded and arrogant and put up these big scenes. After that we used to go to the Ad-Lib or the Speakeasy, these clubs that no longer exist. So it's all very hazy to remember, but it was all very exciting."

"Terry was definitely everywhere and everybody worshiped him at the time," Pallenberg adds. She was somewhat intimidated by the writer, who was naturally fascinated by her femme-fatale aura. Terry nicknamed Pallenberg "Neat" and would send her little notes teasing her about her broken English.

Drug use played an important role in cementing the unity of the group says Pallenberg. She admits they had tremendous naïveté about the long-term ramifications of using harder drugs like cocaine and heroin so freely. "I think we had one thing in common and that was drugs, and in the early days it was experimenting. It wasn't like being a drug user and losing control and being a junkie. William Burroughs was our hero and he sometimes came to Robert Fraser's as well. We kind of thought that the rest of England and London wasn't into it. We thought we were pioneers [laughs] . . . we were using it together and we smoked hash. I don't want you to think there was this high intellectual thing about it."

Pallenberg believes Southern was always just a little detached from the group. "Well, Terry was fascinated by them and they were fascinated by him and Michael Cooper was there a lot. He was very close to Terry and I was. I think it was more like mutual admiration and then obviously when we were high it was more gossipy and there were stories and that kind of thing. That's really quite social. I never felt that the scene really had an impact on Terry, or what kind of impact it had on him. He seemed to be above it [the rock world]."

Even reclusive filmmakers like Stanley Kubrick and Michelangelo Antonioni broke with habits and checked out the scene. Antonioni dug the atmosphere so much he shot the epic morning-after party scene from *Blow-Up* at one of the group's apartment's on Chelsea's Cheyne Walk.

Yet for all the superficial decadence (the hangover wouldn't start to kick in until after the infamous Stones drug busts of June 1967), there was an air of tremendous excitement and energy. The cultural artifacts of the era speak for themselves: the Beatles produced a trilogy of classic albums, *Rubber Soul, Revolver,* and *Sgt. Pepper;* the Stones countered with *Aftermath, Between the Buttons,* and *Their Satanic Majesties Request.* Newer groups like the Kinks, the Who, the Small Faces, the Yardbirds, Pretty Things, and Pink Floyd would move away from R&B covers to writing strikingly original songs. Fraser's gallery openings (and those of his rival Paul Kasmin) introduced Peter Blake, David Hockney, R. B. Kitaj, Allen Jones, Richard Hamilton, and other new artists to the British public. Even the furniture was interesting, as anyone who visited any of the homes Gibbs designed could attest. The success of the James Bond series and the "kitchen sink" films like *Room at the Top* and *Saturday Night and Sunday Morning* led to an enormous investment by the American studios in England's modest film industry. All the major studios in Los Angeles opened large operations in London. Kubrick was shooting *2001* at Shepperton and François Truffaut was making *Fahrenheit 451* at Pinewood. Blacklist refugee Joseph Losey revitalized his career with *The Servant* and *Accident.* Roman Polanski was attracting attention for psychological thrillers like *Cul-de-Sac* and *Repulsion.* Michael Caine became a star as *Alfie* and Harry Palmer.

Although he was almost a generation older (and had seen real suffering in World War II), Southern did not recoil at the occasionally glib love and peace sloganeering of younger people he met in London. In turn, his association with *Dr. Strangelove,* arguably the hippest, most political film up to that time, *Candy,* and *The Magic Christian* made Southern everyone's favorite uncle. The London scene was more about fun in the form of recreational drugs and music than politics. Lieberson recalls few if any political conversations. Instead there was a boundless optimism about the future. "We now know there are no limits," Terry would roar . . . he was half joking, but he was also dead serious.

As the spring of 1966 rolled around, Terry and Gail attended the Cannes Film Festival. Andy Warhol and Gerard Malanga were also there, to show *Chelsea Girls*. Malanga and Southern would stay in touch and become neighbors in New England in later years. One of the films Terry caught was *Ride in the Whirlwind,* which was being toted around by a barely employed actor/writer named Jack Nicholson, whom Terry and Gail knew from the Malibu get-togethers of Fonda and Vadim. Kathleen Tynan remembers bumping into Southern there a great deal. Kenneth wanted to get Terry to help him with a revue he was planning that would deal with the sexual revolution. It would be a collection of sketches featuring the contributions of Sam Shepard, Beckett, Pinter, and others. Southern was keen to oblige and said as soon as he had time he would write something.

Southern never did get around to sending Tynan a skit for what became *Oh! Calcutta!* Nor did anything come of an intriguing approach by Jean-Luc Godard to assist him with a treatment called *A Certain French Girl.* Southern was a big fan of the French *nouvelle vague.* He would later cite the *ménage à trois* scene in Godard's 1980 *Every Man for Himself* as one of his favorite examples of on-screen eroticism.

Back in London, Southern continued to put in time on *Casino Royale* as well as work on *The Magic Christian* adaptation for Sellers. Sandy Lieberson was trying to move from being an agent to producing. He optioned *Flash and Filigree,* which became an on-again/off-again property. Lieberson had hoped to land Robert Mitchum as Dr. Eichner, but the project never took off.

Last, but not least in terms of cinematic potential, was *Candy*. Frank and Eleanor Perry, the husband-and-wife team behind *David and Lisa,* convinced David Picker at United Artists to give them development money to option *Candy*. This process was complicated by the increasingly bitter estrangement between Terry and his old Paris buddy and collaborator, Mason Hoffenberg. Mason's talents as a writer had proven to be conceptual at best and heroin became the dominating force in his life. Drifting from one friend's home to another, Hoffenberg was not only an unrepentant junkie, but a professional freeloader. Many of Terry's friends, such as Jean Stein, disliked him. Terry, no doubt sensing this, kept Hoffenberg at a distance. Hoffenberg also felt Terry had sold him out for Hollywood success, a claim that barely held water given the fact that half of the *Candy* movie money automatically went to Hoffenberg or to his most recent address.

Hoffenberg's perversity also made it difficult to mount a united front in the battles over lost monies and pirated editions as the copyright war over *Candy* the book grew as mazelike as a Borges story.

Candy and Hoffenberg were, at their worst, annoyances. Terry and the film world were dancing till dawn cheek to cheek. Si Litvinoff, who remained Terry's lawyer and business manager, advised him that one way to avoid the inevitable tax penalties that the sudden influx of big money would bring was to become a producer himself. It was practical advice, but acting on it would end up leaving Terry more impoverished than he ever was in the fifties.

Michael Cooper lent Southern a copy of Anthony Burgess's *A Clockwork Orange*. The two began to talk up the book as a possible film project to star the Rolling Stones as a gang of "droogs" raping and pillaging in near-future England. One film version of the book had been shot—*Vinyl*—a Factory quickie loosely scripted and directed by Ronald Tavel and Andy Warhol. *Vinyl* consisted of a series of vignettes that looked like a continuous aborted gang rape of whichever Warhol groupie was available the day of filming. Given the nature of *Vinyl*'s production, it wasn't difficult for Southern through Si Litvinoff to option the book for a bargain basement $1,000 against a final price of $10,000. David Puttnam and Lieberson helped to set up a development deal at Paramount. The studio underwrote a draft written by Southern and Cooper.

When David Hemmings was briefly considered as Alex, the Stones and Cooper became upset and Mick once more went back to the top of a very short casting list. Getting the film off the ground was increasingly problematic. The attentions of the Stones ebbed and flowed, given the demands of recording, touring, and having fun. Potential directors like Richard Lester balked at the violence and the difficulties of translating Nadsat—the nearly incomprehensible dialect of the book's narrator—to the screen. Ted Kotcheff, who had just directed a sequel to *Room at the Top,* became the director of choice. But then the Lord Chamberlain, the chief censor of film and theater in Britain, sent back the script unread with a note: "I know this book and there is no way you can make a movie of it. It deals with youthful incitement to authority which is illegal." Paramount put the project into turnaround.

During the downtime on *Casino Royale,* Southern was asked by John Calley to help him and Martin Ransohoff on a troubled London production called *Eye of the Devil.* Based on an obscure novel called *Day of the Arrow* by Philip Loraine, it was a gothic thriller about the wife of a French nobleman trying to prevent a strange religious cult from killing her husband. It starred David Niven as the patriarch Philippe de Montfaucon, and David Hemmings, just coming off the shoot of *Blow-Up*. Rounding out the cast were such British film stalwarts as Emyln Williams, Flora Robson, and Donald Pleasance, one of Southern's favorite character actors.

It was a "tightening and brightening job" for a picture that had been shut down in 1965 with Kim Novak in a role taken over by Deborah Kerr. The original director was Michael Anderson. He was replaced by J. Lee Thompson (who directed the original *Cape Fear* with Robert Mitchum and Gregory Peck). Sharon Tate was also in the film. Ransohoff and Calley had invested a lot of energy in trying to save this troubled project. On paper, it resembled the kind of potboiler that could be transformed into an elegant horror film, but it lacked the kind of charge that even a similar disaster of the time, Joseph Losey's *Secret Ceremony,* possessed.

In the summer of 1966, Southern returned to the States. He had just enough time to drop in on friends in New York before going out to the coast to do some more work for Filmways on a Tony Curtis comedy, *Don't Make Waves,* based on a novel by Ira Levin. Curtis played a go-west-young-man bachelor who becomes mixed up with a variety of California hedonists, health nuts, and zanies. Alexander Mackendrick, best known for his Ealing comedies and *Sweet Smell of Success,* was the director, but he had little love for this overheated comedy. Most of Southern's work was involved in writing dialogue that could then be looped into the film. When asked about the film years later, Southern could recall only the grim death of a stuntman involved in a skydiving scene. The stuntman became entangled in his parachute and drowned after landing in the water. One macabre detail stuck with him—the fact that a camera in the stuntman's crash helmet filmed the fatal accident. *Don't Make Waves* was best remembered for its surreal finale when Tony Curtis wakes up in a beach house that is about to slide off its hillside perch into the sea.

Returning to New York, Southern began work in earnest on *Blue Movie*. He also became involved in an odd theatrical venture called *Pardon Me, Sir, but Is My Eye Hurting Your Elbow?* The revue included contributions by Gregory Corso, Southern, Jack Richardson, Arthur Kopit, Philip Roth, Allen Ginsberg, and Bruce Jay Friedman. Southern's contribution was a sketch called "Peaches and Plums," a study of teen sexuality that covered the same territory as *Candy*. The sketches were later collected in a book with illustrations by *Mad* magazine's Mort Drucker. Bruce Jay Friedman recalled a publicity launch for the revue: "I think the producer was Si Litvinoff, when it was going to be a film. They took a picture of all the authors: Jack Richardson, Arthur Kopit, Jack Gelber, maybe Terry— I'm not sure, but there was one guy I didn't recognize. I was pissed off about it, such was my arrogance. 'Who the fuck is this guy and why is he in this picture with all these literary immortals!' Well, it turned out it was Francis Coppola. He was a writer and he had a piece in there. He was the asshole I didn't recognize."

Just as Robert Fraser's gallery was becoming the in place to be seen in London, a little Italian restaurant on Manhattan's Upper East Side was attaining a similar status. Opened by Elaine Kaufman in 1963, Elaine's became a club for the decade's up-and-coming writers. By the seventies, it was attracting movie stars, business types, fashion models, producers, and other glitterati, but Kaufman remained loyal to the early group that put the restaurant on New York's cultural map. Before Woody Allen became a regular, the hierarchy was very simple. Those who had published got first dibs on the best tables and those who hadn't paid their tab were, if it wasn't too crowded, allowed to pull up an extra chair. The perpetual regulars at the time included Jack Richardson, Arthur Kopit, David Newman, Peter Maas, Gay Talese, Harry Joe "Coco" Browne Jr., Harold Hayes, Willie Morris, Jerry Leiber, Mike Stoller, Frank Conroy, Lewis Lapham, and George Plimpton. It wasn't an A-crowd or a B-crowd. It was a scene unto itself with a growing list of special guest appearances by icons like Muhammad Ali, Warren Beatty, Michael Caine, or Shirley Maclaine.

"I started going to Elaine's as soon as it was open," David Newman recalled warmly. "Elaine's used to be a narrow corridor. One room. It used to be just a long hallway. The thing is, Elaine—and we would all credit her many times over in print, various tributes, and anniversaries—in those years, which were the lean years for most of us, just carried us. My wife and I ran a tab at Elaine's for over a year. We were there every week and every now and then you would say, 'Gee, I feel terrible.' You would tip the waiter and never pay for the bill, but we knew she was keeping a record. But Elaine would always say, 'Someday, I've got plenty of confidence in you, when your ship comes in, you'll square off with me.' And it wasn't just me, it was me, and Jack and Bob Brown [*Esquire* editor] and twenty other people . . . who lived through years when Elaine said, 'You can pay when you can pay me.' The wonderful thing was that we all did. I remember that the year my ship came in around the time of *Bonnie and Clyde,* I suddenly had this huge tax bill—I settled up a little up front—but my accountant said to me, 'Who the fuck is this Elaine! Your income is going to her.' Terry used to be part of the Elaine's gang. He went, all the *Esquire* editors went, all the playwrights, and Terry was as a regular there as much as anybody."

Newman says the big attraction of Elaine's was that it was like having "a dinner party without having to make a dinner party. We would say, 'Let's have dinner with all our friends' and then we would say, 'Let's go to Elaine's, there's bound to be eight of them there.' Table Four was the writer's table. You would just go in with no reservation. You would squeeze two more chairs in and sit around with ten guys and girls. Deals were made, marriages . . . ended, and clandestine affairs went on. Elaine's was home. It was like being in a private club."

Bruce Jay Friedman was another of the founding patrons of Elaine's. For him and other writers coping with the pressures of work, the restaurant was a clean, well-lighted place.

"Jack Richardson had a play running and I admired him tremendously. He took me up [to Elaine's] and suddenly I had a place to go where I knew there would always be a table where I could sit with a sort of modest party going on. When I got separated and divorced, I went there a lot. I still make it a first stop whenever I go into Manhattan. Terry was a player, one of the people who would show up. . . . Careerwise [the mid-sixties] were a good period, but with great personal sadness. That was one thing that made it tolerable. That place. It saved my life. Elaine being a great friend. You always knew that any hour of the day or night—well, any hour of the night, there was this one table where there would be a scene. If there weren't writers assembled already, some would drift in and it would be comfortable. It was a club for writers initially until slowly film-business people and other unsavory types came in."

Given the heavy literary contingent, the talk was of projects and specifically money and deals. There was also chatter about politics, local, national, and global (from a defiantly New York point of view). Civilians (or those just wanting a meal) were often irritated by Elaine Kaufman's enigmatic reservations policy. Many a hardened veteran of haughty maître d's found their match in Kaufman, who exiled with one expression while simultaneously bidding a hearty welcome with another.

Terry also hung out at O'Neal's. Patrick O'Neal, the dashing Irish American actor of *How to Seduce an American Wife* and *The Kremlin Letter,* and his brother co-owned this Upper West Side version of Elaine's just off Columbus Circle. Meanwhile, downtown in the Village, Mickey Ruskin was starting Max's Kansas City, a dive for the most part, with the exception of its legendary back room. In the back room, bathed in warm bloodred light, café society met the demimonde. Warhol's Factory crowd made the place a popular hangout.

"Edie Sedgwick would always come around at one point in the evening. About two or three o'clock in the morning. The place would get tremendously electric with anticipation. . . . Although Warhol was ultragay, he was always surrounded by beautiful women," Southern recalled.

Business and pleasure were inseparable now. Terry quickly became accustomed to the perks of working in the movie business. In the blur of movement from one groovy scene to the next, Gail recalls a moment that epitomizes the carefree ease (thanks to the largesse of his big studio employers) with which they traveled. "We were going from L.A. to London, and we got on the plane and I didn't really have any cash on me," says Gerber. "So I said, 'Terry, do you have any money?' He said, 'No, why?' 'Well, I don't have any money, do you have any money?' 'No, about $1.25.' 'Well, how do we get to the hotel from the airport without any money?' 'Oh, there'll be a car there.' He just took off from L.A. pre-credit-card time knowing there would be a car at the other end and without five dollars in his pocket. Then we ended up in London and sure enough there was a car there."

Gerber's acting aspirations took a distinct second place to Southern's work. Eventually she would start teaching at a private girls' school near East Canaan and work for the Actors Studio to preserve her own identity, but during these go-go years, she seemed happy just to join the ride.

As 1966 drew to a close, it became apparent that the youth culture fueled by the Beatles, the Rolling Stones, and Bob Dylan was undergoing a significant change. Various strands—the folk movement, the Students for a Democratic Society, the growing antiwar and civil rights movements, the new priests and prophets of LSD like Ken Kesey and Timothy Leary— were moving toward a brief synthesis that became known as the counterculture. The counterculture would include a core of individuals as disparate as Leary, Dr. Spock, Abbie Hoffman, Alan Watts, Herbert Marcuse, Allen Ginsberg, Tom Hayden, Martin Luther King Jr., Eldridge Cleaver, Betty Friedan, Germaine Greer, and many others actively involved in articulating and promoting educational reform, drug experimentation, sexual liberation, freedom of expression, human rights, and radical political change from social democracy to Marxist-Leninism, Maoism, and anarchy. Universities and colleges around the world became receptive focal points for this ferment. Surrounding this growing center of activism was a more apolitical and detached majority. For this group, mainly in their teens and twenties, the counterculture was expressed in long hair, informal clothes, recreational drug use usually in the form of marijuana, and rock music. For the larger group, the agenda of social change was probably only icing on the cake of sex, drugs, and rock 'n' roll. Yet together these parts of the counterculture formed a formidable alternative to entrenched systems of governance, authority, taste, and behavior.

Like so many of the leaders and innovators of the unruly beast that was the sixties counterculture, Southern was older and more experienced than many of the young people he came into increasing contact with. Although he did not talk about it, his war experience, coupled with boyhood memories of racism, made Southern keenly aware that one could not passively accept violence, injustice, or intolerance as givens. One could effect change through example, and by embracing new ideas and staying curious. While Southern was making a lot of money and having a lot of fun, he wanted his work to have relevance to the sixties landscape. If he wasn't exactly sure how he could contribute, he would do his best to keep an open mind.

"I think this is a golden age for creative work of any kind," Southern told *Newsweek*. "The people who go all out will make it. We've only scratched the surface of our Freudian heritage. We are undertaking an exploration of the mind and we're making some interesting discoveries. We have discovered the value of not being prejudiced. The assumption has always been that there have been limits. But we now know there are no limits."

Such pronouncements were rare from Southern. He preferred to express his seriousness through his writing. To many of the new friends he met in this period, there was always something a little opaque about Terry's motivations. Arthur Kopit, whose off-Broadway hit *Oh Dad, Poor Dad, Mamma's Hung You in the Closet and I'm Feelin' So Sad,* led to some strange screenwriting assignments, maintained a jokey relationship with Southern in the hectic years of the mid-sixties. While Kopit enjoyed his friend's humor, he felt he never really got close to Southern.

"Terry created the enigmatic Grand Guy and he saw himself as being safe if he played this role. Maybe there was a kind of safety in this invented character, in this way of talking. He was the only person I knew who talked in quotation marks. He could say, 'Good morning, eh, Art?' and you thought, 'Well, yes, it's a good morning. . . . I haven't thought of good morning in quite that way.' So he would put quotes around everything. 'Know what I mean? Chuckle, chuckle. Seen any good shows lately, Art?' He would see somebody else and he would have a quip. He was a quipster and it was delightful, but I don't know if it took its toll on him. He was such a charismatic and strong figure and a brilliant writer, but I don't know the degree to which he was trapped by this kind of manner that he had. Beneath the brilliance, the cleverness, the imagination, there was a hiding of some sort . . . a real shyness. He invented himself in some way. I don't know whether that trapped him finally."

While working on a script for Otto Preminger in early 1967, Kopit came up with the idea of a Terry Southern–like prank to play on his friend.

"There wasn't much to do because the film wasn't going anywhere. I would go to the office and hang out and make phone calls and talk to Preminger, who was between projects. It was kind of a lazy time. Preminger sort of knew the film was never going to get done and I sort of knew it wasn't going to get done. I was being paid by the week, so I would just come in and call friends and have chats with Otto about other projects and about his painting. I now was pretty good at imitating Otto's voice and at one point I recorded Otto calling me from one room to another, saying, 'Kopit, Vy aren't you verking? You should be verking. I know you're in your office and you're pretending to be verk, but you're not verking. Tell me the truth?' . . . So then I started calling Terry and just putting on Otto's voice and saying, 'I know you're not verking. Why aren't you verking? Vot ist going on?' And Terry so loved that because everybody could recognize Preminger's voice. At first, Terry was freaked out. He thought this was really weird, Otto Preminger calling him and saying, 'Why aren't you working?' And of course, Terry wasn't working. . . . That was a pretty safe bet."

During the winter of 1966–67, Southern was beginning work on *Barbarella,* based on Jean-Claude Forest's sexy science fiction comic strip, for Roger Vadim. The film version of *Candy* was now passing into the hands of Christian Marquand. Southern's script was still attached to the project and he hoped to be a coproducer. He also did some writing on a new television version of *The Desperate Hours* for Ted Kotcheff and talk show host/producer David Susskind. The hostage drama that was first made popular by Humphrey Bogart as an escaped fugitive terrorizing a suburban family was a little stodgy, so Southern and Kotcheff tried to update it, with mixed results. Their mutual friend George Segal played the bad guy as a kind of criminal hipster and Yvette Mimieux was the wife who creates the sexual tension. When Kotcheff began working on another TV play for Susskind, a version of John Steinbeck's *Of Mice and Men,* Southern arranged for Andy Warhol, of all people, to sit in on the shoot.

In February, Warhol joined Southern, Larry Rivers, and Edie Sedgwick to judge a beauty pageant of female impersonators at Town Hall. Si Litvinoff and Lewis Allen coproduced a Frank Simon documentary of the event later released as *The Queen.* "I had to go pick Edie up because she was so doped up. We just got the documentary together in about two weeks and gathered everybody we knew," Allen recalled. "Edie burned up her apartment smoking or something and was living down in the Chelsea Hotel. I waited interminably for her . . . she could scarcely move. There was a good deal of footage of Terry interviewing all the 'girls' in the show that's not in the movie."

On June 1, 1967, the Beatles released *Sgt. Pepper's Lonely Hearts Club Band* in England. The following day it was released in the United States and Canada. For the rest of the summer, no other cultural artifact, let alone record album, seemed more important to discuss. In addition to the psychedelic beauty of the music, everyone was fascinated by the elaborate cover featuring the Beatles flanked by a crowd of cult figures dead and living. In the cover's upper left-hand corner surrounded by Lenny Bruce, Francis Bacon, Tony Curtis, and Dylan Thomas, was a certain Terry Southern wearing his favorite shades and looking a bit like Marcello Mastroianni in *La Dolce Vita.* The album cover was designed by Peter Blake and photographed by Michael Cooper on March 30. The famous faces on the cover were chosen by the Beatles with recommendations by Blake, Cooper, and Fraser. Ringo gave the thumbs-up to Southern.

Southern had just put out his own "album," *Red Dirt Marijuana and Other Tastes.* The anthology had been in development for several years. Joe Fox at Random House had encouraged Terry to put a collection together back in the early sixties, but it ended up being placed at the New American Library. Like *Sgt. Pepper,* the cover of the anthology was striking. It featured a photograph taken by Robert Dudas of Jane Fonda embracing Southern, who looks toward the camera (or reader) with a half smile and slightly cocked eyebrow.

With the exception of a few smaller pieces and unpublished work, *Red Dirt Marijuana* assembled all of his critically acclaimed fiction and nonfiction since his Paris days. "The Butcher" and "The Automatic Gate" from the now defunct *New-Story* appeared alongside "I Am Mike Hammer" and "The Road out of Axotle" from *Esquire.* Like an expertly compiled greatest-hits album, the anthology played to Southern's many strengths as a stylist, journalist, satirist, short story writer, and commentator. The back cover featured blurbs from Nelson Algren, Lenny Bruce, Norman Mailer, and Gore Vidal (not known for dispensing raves easily), who called Southern "the most profoundly witty writer of our generation."

But which generation did Vidal mean? As the summer of 1967 began, Southern's World War II generation and the somewhat younger fifties crowd were now being supplanted by baby boomers in their teens and early twenties. There was now a word—hippie—for the young people with long hair, colorful flowing clothes, and beatific smiles who seemed to be everywhere, walking city streets, hanging out in parks, and traveling the highways that summer. Unlike the hipsters and the beatniks, hippies were not *cool* so much as *warm*. They were always smiling, digging things, and expressing love of one kind or another. San Francisco, with its Haight-Ashbury district, was pushing London out of first place as the world's grooviest city. Bands like the Grateful Dead, Jefferson Airplane, and Moby Grape were creating a blend of hard-edged rock that paid improvisational nods to jazz, folk, and the blues. The hippies liked to gather en masse for happenings or be-ins where marijuana was smoked openly, music was played all day and night, and everyone was encouraged to "to do their own thing," which often meant getting laid or getting stoned or variations thereof. Yet even if the hippies seemed to spend a lot of time doing nothing, beneath their blissed-out expressions, one could detect the fervent belief that something revelatory, liberating, and consciousness-expanding was just around the corner.

For Southern, the summer of 1967 was an emotional peak. *Red Dirt* was getting strong reviews from critics who had him pigeonholed as just a madcap humorist. The movie work was rolling in and he was meeting the movers and shakers of the decade. And to top things off, he was considered, thanks to the Fab Four, one of those movers and shakers.

Southern and Gerber took some time off during the summer and rented a house in Southampton. It was a summer filled with music, wine, food, and passionate discussion. In addition to hanging out with Larry Rivers, Southern saw a lot of Bruce Jay Friedman and his sons, Josh Alan, Drew, and Kip. Friedman was also generating a lot of heat due to the success of his play *Scuba Duba,* about a man whose wife runs off with a black man. Friedman's most vivid memory of the summer was of Southern dropping by his house with two gifts. One was a Lenny Bruce album featuring the classic routine "Frank Dell at the Palladium," about a Vegas comic who lands a prestige gig at the London theater only to bomb because of his inappropriate jokes about Dunkirk and the like. The other gift was *Sgt. Pepper.*

"'Frank Dell at the Palladium' remains to this day my favorite nineteen minutes of anything. Just extraordinary. I always use it as an example of what I find funny," said Friedman. "*Sgt. Pepper's Lonely Hearts Club Band* opened up a whole world. . . . I had written my first play, *Scuba Duba,* and I was rewriting it and casting it and I was very swept up in the theater. He in turn was pushing film. Both of us had begun as prose writers or whatever and he was strongly suggesting that theater was a waste of time and unreal and that movies were good. And we argued literally, neither one giving ground, for long hours into the night and these were close to being hostile arguments. I remember him saying, 'How can you take a medium seriously when you are in the audience and you can see people spitting?' And he would just spit into the surf. And I would say, 'It's a live transaction between you in the audience and the actors and that makes it real and immediate, whereas in film, it's removed and on the screen,' and on and on into the night with that particular argument. "

Unlike Southern, Friedman still believed in the possibilities of Quality Lit. Movies, especially American movies, were "nothing for a serious man to be doing. Now, of course, I would kill to get a screenplay job. I thought what you did, even the theater was a little meretricious . . . serious people wrote novels, serious people lived in the shadow of Hemingway, Fitzgerald, and Faulkner, and I was self-conscious about doing a play. And he was totally sold, one of the early people in, dare I say, 'our crowd' of the people I knew, who took movies seriously. There are only two I know of. The other is David Newman, who is a pure screenwriter, and then Terry."

Despite their difference of views, Friedman and Southern respected each other's work. Southern even asked Friedman about the possibility of turning *Scuba Duba* into a film.

"At one time, he was in the picture as someone to adapt *Scuba Duba.* He was the right choice actually. I was not the key figure here nor did I care particularly. I just really wanted to make a film sale. I never really believed in . . . in other words, the play existed exactly the way I wanted it onstage. Whatever happened to it after that, it's always been my attitude, just had nothing to do with me. If they made a movie, fine, if they didn't, I had my play. Now I am wrong. I have had some films and my son, Drew, would remind me, 'Dad, kids who see this won't know that you've written any-thing else.' So I've been wrong.

"There is no question that Terry's work spoke to me. In a nutshell, it was screamingly funny, always outrageous, and he always pushed the edge of the envelope, it seemed to me. And that spoke to me. And also the thing that's lost in all of that is his books were very hot, you know, *Candy* was and even *Blue Movie,* later on, which was my favorite. They were very, very hot. Forget about erotic. They were hot! So there was that. That's a trick. I've never been able to write about sex. In fact, I wouldn't know how. I like it, but I've never been able to write about it. He was absolutely magnificent in hitting that right note."

The only dark note in the summer had been the arrest of Mick Jagger and Keith Richards on highly dubious drug charges. Robert Fraser had also been arrested after the police raided a country gathering at Richards's Redlands home outside London on June 28. The two Stones were released after an appeal ruled the charges were made in error. Unlike Jagger and Richards, Fraser was not so lucky and lost an appeal for possession of twenty-four heroin tablets. He was given a six-month sentence When he was released in 1968, Fraser's ebullient devil-may-care attitude was shaken. His gallery, which had never been known for its rock-steady finances, went out of business. He continued to deal in art with mixed success until dying from AIDS in 1986.

From 1964 to 1967, Southern had seen very little of Nile. In 1968 Terry returned to New York to live, and Nile recalls Terry popping up at his mother's New York apartment as he played with neighborhood kids. "Hello, son," said Terry tentatively. Nile realized this was his mysterious father and reserve turned to excitement as Terry's visits accelerated into drop-ins at the office (stockpiled with boxes of Cracker Jack and other candies), expensive presents like a fully functioning minicar, and excursions to the country. Gail even taught Nile how to ski as he became older.

As a father, Terry maintained his support payments and was always warm, kind, and encouraging to his son. But he wasn't much of a disciplinarian. Since work and play were inextricably tied together for his father, Nile would find it difficult to accept the same harsh realities Terry avoided as he grew older. And Terry continued to relate to his work as a purist. Seeing it not as a series of career moves, but as new ways to express himself. While the money was a potent influence, Terry never managed it effectively.

According to Carol, Terry continued to hint that his relationship with Gail was only temporary. A part of him seemed to have difficulty comprehending that the success of the last few years and the glamorous lifestyle that went with it had changed things forever.

"I waited for him for a long time," Carol said. "We had Nile and 'the place' and memories of a relationship that had been very romantic and intense. Four or five times over those years he did come back, but never more than a few days, and it was always very painful. He wanted to come back, but he was very tied to Gail and there was something in that relationship that was very strong for him. Addictive almost. After he left, he kept a kind of imaginary relationship in his head . . . he always idealized our life together. Finally, I realized that his talk of coming back was just that and would never materialize. But he was just such a persuader. It took me a long time to get used to the changes."

Facing such difficult decisions was beyond Southern at the best of times. And for now, as the Summer of Love raged on, he felt it was too negative and counterproductive to dwell on such matters.

8

An Easy Rider at the End of the Road

I want to forget the sixties, not remember them. I look on that period as one of bad karma for me. I want to start from now.

—Anita Pallenberg, quoted in *Blinds and Shutters*

As the *Sgt. Pepper* summer blossomed, Southern continued to play hard and work hard. Dino De Laurentiis, with the endorsement of Jane Fonda and Roger Vadim, hired him to fly to Rome and work on the rewrites for *Barbarella*. Principal photography would lumber on through the summer and fall of 1967. It was the biggest Italian-French coproduction in some time, with a secured distribution deal through Paramount.

Terry was familiar with the Jean-Claude Forest comic strip through the *Evergreen Review*, which ran an English translation. Forest, a veteran French illustrator and cartoonist, had created *Barbarella* for his own amusement and eventually sold the strip to the Paris-based *V* magazine in 1962. *Barbarella* combined Brigitte Bardot's pinup sexiness with imagery that mixed *Flash Gordon,* the Marquis de Sade, and *Vogue.* The plots were also a study in inspired incongruity—the *Perils of Pauline* as written by Michel Foucault or Simone de Beauvoir. The strip became an instant hit in France and Belgium, leading to a best-selling book. Thanks to English fans like Barney Rosset and Robert Fraser, the strip became a cult fave in

England and the United States. And what was *Barbarella,* after all, but *Candy* in space?

As an example of big-budget international filmmaking, *Barbarella* was a *Casino Royale*-size headache for De Laurentiis. Like *Dr. Strangelove,* Southern's script doctoring on Vadim's epic would prompt endless speculation over what he did or didn't contribute to the final result. In addition to Southern, the credits listed almost half a dozen other names. A team of Italian and French writers, including Jean-Claude Forest, had already labored on the initial drafts that got the production the green light. Tudor Gates, an English scribe known chiefly for his work on Hammer horror films, supplied some of the English translation. Then there was Charles Griffith, an alumni of Roger Corman, friend of Fonda and Vadim, and the *other* American writer on the film; in the end he would not receive an on-screen credit. According to Carol Southern, Terry did more than touch up *Barbarella* and apparently completed a draft that had a fairy-tale quality, little of which ended up in the final film.

When preproduction began in earnest in April 1967, Southern flew to Rome, where he worked for a few days in a hotel near the Spanish Steps. Southern would return to Rome in the fall to supply deadpan throwaways like "A lot of dramatic scenes begin with screaming" that could be dubbed in at the last minute. Southern was already friendly with Jane Fonda and Roger Vadim through his regular attendance at Sunday brunches thrown at their Malibu home.

"The strain was with Dino De Laurentiis," recalled Southern. "He was just the flamboyant businessman. His idea of good cinema was to give money back on the cost of the picture before even going into production. He doesn't even make any pretense about the quality or the aesthetic."

The *Barbarella* gig was yet another opportunity to mix business and pleasure. It was another over-the-top megaproduction with complex special effects, giant sets, and weird costumes. John Phillip Law played the Bird Man. Veteran New York stage actor Milo O'Shea was the evil Duran Duran. Anita Pallenberg had been recommended to Vadim as a natural for the role of the Black Queen and she was given a screen test in Rome.

"The fact that Terry was writing was flattering," Pallenberg recalls. "It was Vadim who gave me the screen test, but I always felt very grateful to Terry for supporting the choice. *Dr. Strangelove* has always been one of my favorite movies. I remember when we were doing *Barbarella,* it was all very complicated because we were filming very slowly. I don't know if it was due to De Laurentiis, Vadim, or Terry—it was one of the three—but the script pages weren't always ready. Sometimes Terry used to send the script by telegram and one time it was this one line—'You're a dead duck'—and he wrote my lines as well. So it was kind of funny in that way. Then again, when *Candy* was made, I got a role in that as well. So I felt really a part of his work. Like he was my protector."

Pallenberg's involvement led to a mini-reunion of the Robert Fraser gang. Keith Richards, Mick Jagger, and Marianne Faithfull visited her on the set in April. In her memoir, Faithfull recalls Christian Marquand, Southern, and Living Theatre founders, Julian Beck and Judith Malina (who were touring Europe and avoiding the IRS, which had shut down their operations in New York), adding to the Dionysian atmosphere surrounding the film. Southern teased Pallenberg about her Method-like approach to the role of the Black Queen: "Ah, by my troth, here comes the Black Queen! Rats scurry across polished marble floors, and little snakes hiss at her baleful entrance."

In September, "Blood of a Wig," the last story in *Red Dirt Marijuana,* was published in the October *Evergreen Review.* Inspired by his stint at *Esquire,* the story ranked among Southern's best in spite of (perhaps because of) its odd structure. A memoir and meditation, it begins in a low-key, matter-of-fact fashion with the hipster narrator describing his efforts to endure the banality of a nine-to-five gig at an *Esquire* wanna-be run by a managing editor who is more a crass Jerry Springer type than an urbane and thoughtful Harold Hayes. Taking a small nugget of personal experience as a jumping-off point for fantasy was now a major part of the Southern approach. Where the *Esquire* gig was, for the most part, a pleasant way to pick up a steady paycheck, in "The Blood of a Wig," the incident is transformed into a strange psychedelic escapade. Looking for a new high, the narrator gets a lead on "red-split," a hallucinogen synthesized from the blood of a schizophrenic Chinese poet, Chin Lee. The specifics of the drug experience are barely detailed by the narrator except to say: "Sense-derangementwise, it was unlike acid in that it was not a question of the 'Essential I' having new insights, but of becoming a different person entirely. So that in a way there was nothing very scary about [the drug], just extremely weird, and as it turned out, somewhat mischievous."

However, the drug's influence on the writer's efforts to complete a tedious assignment are immediate. Southern then appropriates Paul Krassner's controversial "Parts Left Out of the Manchester Book" sketch, which almost led to the *Realist* getting shut down in 1965. Krassner's scandalous vision of LBJ humping JFK's head wound aboard Air Force One is pitched by the narrator to his boss, who reacts with disgust. According to Krassner, Rosset and company at *Evergreen* had to clear the story with him first to ensure the "appropriation" was homage and not plagiarism.

The Krassner reference is the least satisfying part of "Blood of a Wig," which doesn't so much end as slowly fade out as its narrator ruminates on insights he has gained into "Viet Nam, Cassius Clay, Chessman, the Rosenbergs and all sorts of things" thanks to "red-split." "Blood of a Wig" would be Southern's last published short story for some time. It signals an increasing shift away from the "clean deliberate prose" so admired by Norman Mailer to a looser, more colloquial style that reached its peak in *Blue Movie*. Although "Blood of a Wig" is still a richly told comic fable that ranks alongside Southern's finest work as a short story writer, one detects a level of impatience in its construction.

In October 1967, toward the end of his stint in Rome, Southern, accompanied by Gail, visited Peter Fonda in the French village of Roscoff. As *Barbarella*'s seemingly endless production began to wind down, Vadim had started to shoot "Metzengerstein," an episode of the anthology film *Spirits of the Dead* (Louis Malle and Federico Fellini directed the other two episodes). Vadim, with his yen for erotic frisson, had decided to cast Jane and Peter as brother and sister characters to raise the incest subtext an extra notch. As was with many cinematic endeavors of this Mad Hatter period, a hectic shooting schedule did not get in the way of sightseeing, fine dining, and getting quietly, but determinedly wrecked. During one of many such confabs, Peter told Southern about an idea he had for a movie.

Before coming to France, Peter had been promoting *The Trip,* directed by Roger Corman for American International Pictures, at Showrama, a convention of North American exhibitors, in Toronto. He had gotten the idea for a modern Western while relaxing in his hotel room on September 27, 1967. Not surprisingly, Fonda had been smoking dope at the time. In his pleasant haze, the iconographic beauty of a publicity still of him and Bruce Dern standing in front of motorcycle bikes from another Corman film, *The Wild Angels,* began to mesmerize him. Gradually his musing coalesced into a high-concept epiphany. Let's make a modern Western with two hip guys on bikes instead of old movie stars on horses!

Upon his return from Toronto, Fonda called Dennis Hopper and described his idea for a different kind of biker film. Hopper needed something to enthuse about. His marriage to Brooke Hayward was floundering. He had a not entirely undeserved reputation for drinking and drug taking combined with on-the-set histrionics. Through his interest in photography and collecting art, Hopper was becoming intrigued by directing (Corman had let him shoot second unit footage for *The Trip*) and was considering becoming an acting coach.

Fonda's pitch for his hybrid biker Western, initially dubbed *The Loners* or *Mardi Gras* before Southern came on board, captivated Hopper. Without really knowing why, Hopper understood Fonda's idea was a way to break out of their respective career doldrums. During a series of manic planning sessions where the two men paced up and down Fonda's tennis court, they idealistically divided duties. They would both star. Fonda would produce and Hopper would direct. Hopper's brother-in-law and a childhood friend of Fonda, Bill Hayward, came on board as coproducer. Pando Productions was formed to create an air of seriousness as they went ahead in the search for financing. Fonda also says he and Hopper approached Torn before meeting Terry in France.

Southern's response to Fonda's new project was enthusiastic: "That's a great story. I'm your man." Fonda was apprehensive about hiring Southern as his screenwriter. His mid-sixties fee was now $100,000 per script (although nobody could figure out what the hell Southern was doing with the money). But Terry said he would agree to work for scale, roughly $350 per week, in order to lend Hopper and Fonda's independent production the legitimacy of a name screenwriter. There was also well-intentioned but vaguely defined talk of Terry sharing in the film's profits.

Although the impetus for *Easy Rider* came from Peter, he admitted in his 1998 memoir, *Don't Tell Dad*, that: "Terry was certainly doing more than just putting an idea into script form. The first thing he did when we began working was give the story a proper title. He explained to me what 'easy rider' meant. Perfect. This was going to be a humdinger. Terry fucking Southern! He'd come to Roscoff straight from Rome and a screening of *Barbarella* to help with the final editing stages and now he was drawn into the possibilities of our little low-budget motion picture."

By late November, Fonda, Hopper, and Southern began meeting at Litvinoff's West Fifty-fifth Street office in New York for regular story conferences. The conferences would spill over in the evening to Southern's town house on East Thirty-sixth Street. Fonda would crash in the spare bedroom on the third floor. Hopper and Fonda would talk animatedly while Southern made occasional comments and made notes on his favorite yellow legal pad. These handwritten pages were given to a secretary to type up. According to Southern, Hopper and Fonda's idea for a movie was still embryonic:

"The first notion was that it be these barnstorming cars, stunt driver cars, where they do flips and things, but that just seemed too unnecessarily complicated. So we just settled for the straight score of dope, selling it and leaving the rat race. We forgot about the daredevil drivers, which is a commonplace thing. It was going to be this troupe who play a few dates and places and eventually get fed up with that and make this score. Finally, we forwent any pretense of them doing anything else than buying cocaine. We didn't specify that it was cocaine, but that's what it would be. They go to New Orleans to sell it. Then once they got their money, they ride to coastal Florida or someplace like Key West where they could buy a boat cheap, not in New Orleans, because it would be too expensive."

Fonda and Hopper related the concept to Southern *verbally* during the story meetings. Their conversations became the basis for the initial treatment and screenplay Southern *wrote* through December and April of 1967–68. The script, which went through two drafts, contained vividly detailed camera directions and lots of dialogue. In the final film, the dialogue would be pared down and several episodes abandoned or left on the cutting-room floor, but the visual strategy, the backstory and narrative, remained the same as it was in Southern's script.

Two stunt riders, Billy and Wyatt a.k.a. Captain America (to be played by Hopper and Fonda, respectively) buy cocaine in Mexico and sell it for a profit to a big dealer in Los Angeles. With their big score hidden in Wyatt's gas tank, the two travel through the southern United States from Los Angeles toward Key West. During their ill-defined journey, they encounter a startling contrast of groups representing America at the end of the sixties—ranchers, rednecks, commune dwellers, etc. In a nondescript Texas town, they are briefly jailed for riding in on the end of a civic parade. In the cell next door, they meet George Hanson, a good ole boy turned ACLU lawyer who is recovering from one of his regular drinking binges. Hanson joins Billy and Wyatt on their trip so he can visit a mythic New Orleans brothel, Madame Tinkertoy's, but Hanson is killed when the trio's campsite is ambushed by a group of locals. Arriving in New Orleans, Billy and Wyatt drop in at Madame Tinkertoy's out of respect for Hanson. They hire two prostitutes and take in the Mardi Gras bacchanal. The four take an LSD tab that was given to Wyatt at the commune. Their acid trip culminates in a terrifying series of hallucinations in a cemetery. In the script's final scene, Wyatt and Billy are back on the road traveling faster toward their dream in Key West. Two men in a pickup drive by. Intending only to scare the two "longhairs," their shotgun blast accidentally hits Billy and he crashes. As Wyatt rides back to assist his fallen comrade, the pickup circles back. Wyatt is also gunned down. The gasoline tank on his bike explodes and both script and film end with:

> LONG SHOT from above as the old pickup truck turns around again and drives down the desolate highway leaving in the ditch, the two bodies and the wounded chrome bike, which as distance lengthens, continues to burn with a small bright glow.

According to Fonda, the story sessions in New York were a manic and volatile hothouse of brainstorming. Hopper and Southern had the idea of going to a whorehouse in honor of Hanson's dying wishes, says Fonda. Michael Cooper was there, says Fonda, when a now legendary "missing tape" of Fonda and Hopper talking out the entire story was made. Southern came up with the ending in which the two bikers are gunned down by two good ole boys in a pickup. The tape was transcribed by a secretary, says Fonda, and edited to a twenty-one-page treatment. This treatment and the now lost tape were used to secure financing.

Southern says one of the secretaries at the Fifty-fifth Street office was also a devotee of UFOs. She apparently entertained Hopper, Fonda and Southern with her fervent belief in flying saucers and secret bases in Mexico. Southern worked some of her conversation into George Hanson's famous campfire speech. Hopper says the UFO soliloquy by Hanson came out of his readings of a book by George Adamski.

The script, however, was still unfinished in January 1968, when Fonda and Bill Hayward took the treatment and a tape to a series of meetings in Los Angeles. One stop in Fonda's search for a production deal was Samuel Arkoff at AIP, which had financed most of his biker flicks. Arkoff, a strong believer in low overhead and short-term gains, passed. A few days later, Fonda met up with Bob Rafelson and Bert Schneider, whose Raybert company had created *The Monkees* TV show. Raybert agreed to a $360,000 budget in exchange for a third of the film's profits. Columbia, where Schneider had important connections through his father, Abe, and brother, Stanley, would distribute the film on a pickup basis. Schneider and Rafelson advanced Pando (Hayward and Fonda's company) $40,000 to complete preproduction.

As *Easy Rider* gathered momentum, the film version of *Candy* had started shooting at Rome's Incom Studios in December 1967. The baton had been passed from Frank Perry to French actor and Marlon Brando pal

Christian Marquand, best known to North Americans for supporting roles
in *The Longest Day* and *Flight of the Phoenix*. Southern was friendly with
Marquand and initially gave his blessing to the actor's efforts to put Candy
Christian on the big screen. Marquand had directed one film, *Les Grands
Chemins,* in 1962, but the new backer, ABC Pictures, came on board
mainly because of Brando agreeing to star. Brando's involvement consoli-
dated the participation of James Coburn, Richard Burton, Ringo Starr,
Sugar Ray Robinson, and Walter Matthau in well-paying cameos. Southern
had originally hoped either Hayley Mills or Jane Fonda would play Candy,
but under the rationale that the auteur knows best, Marquand decided Ewa
Aulin, a recent Miss Sweden, would give the role a more universal appeal.
It was at this stage that Southern parted ways with Marquand.

Marquand then brought in Buck Henry, who had just completed *The
Graduate* with Mike Nichols, to write a new adaptation. Henry, who would
get to know Southern on a casual but friendly basis in later years, described
the shoot as follows: "I didn't know anything about Terry's screenplay of
Candy although I think I heard he'd written one. I never talked to Terry
about it although I heard he didn't think very highly of the film. But then,
neither did I. Marquand was a friend of mine and has remained so through
the years. . . . I was still writing the screenplay while he was shooting. In
spite of the result, a good time was had by all."

The seventeen-year-old Aulin was blond, beautiful, and generally
naive, but she could not act. Her halting English did little to disguise her
modest acting talent. Aulin found the *Candy* shoot a harrowing initiation
into the seedier aspects of big-time moviemaking. Brando and other cast
and crew members took turns propositioning her. After *Candy,* she
appeared in Bud Yorkin's *Start the Revolution Without Me* opposite Gene
Wilder and Donald Sutherland and then it was a few Z-grade Italian horror
films and obscurity.

Candy was released to almost universally bad reviews in December
1968. *Time* compared Henry's screenplay to "scrawlings on a cave wall."
Many of the reviews seized upon the film's shortcomings as an opportunity
to take potshots at the source material. The novel's daring episodic simplicity was seen as a demonstration of its shallowness rather than an example of
big-budget filmmaking at its most reckless and wasteful. Southern's
attempts to distance himself from the film were only partially successful.
Middlebrow tastemakers like Richard Corliss would cite *Candy* and the
forthcoming *Magic Christian* film as examples that Southern's satire was
now becoming old-hat.

In defense of the movie, one could at least argue that it wasn't boring. With its garish sets and multiple cameos, the film unfolded like a series of car accidents viewed in slow motion. Richard Burton is amusing as the pompous Professor Mephesto. James Coburn seems genuinely crazed wielding a giant hypodermic. Anita Pallenberg looks life-threatening as a leather-clad nurse. And for fans of Brando in autodestruct mode, Brando's embarrassing turn as a libidinous guru is one for the record books. Like Michael Sarne's equally weird and awful adaptation of Gore Vidal's *Myra Breckinridge, Candy* keeps one watching in stunned disbelief at good people making bad film. If Southern and Hoffenberg's novel was an artful burlesque of liberal and conservative assumptions about sex, the movie was a kind of "so bad it's good" case study of the worst pretensions of the European art film and the crass greed of a studio system in decline.

The writing of *Easy Rider* was energized by the decade's shift from the Summer of Love's blissed-out optimism to 1968's raging nihilism. The Tet offensive gave greater weight to the growing sense that the U.S. government was fighting a war in Vietnam it didn't understand. Lyndon Johnson's dream of a Great Society that would reinvent the New Deal for the country's inner cities failed to achieve bipartisan support. More left-leaning, antiwar Democrats were finding it harder to accept LBJ's blueprints for a welfare state in the face of the escalation in military spending. In France, clashes between the government and various student-worker coalitions culminated in strikes, sit-ins, and ugly rioting. In Czechoslovakia, the Prague Spring that brought a human face to communism was about to end as the Soviets authorized a police action. It was a year in which mainstream and countercultural notions of order seemed on the verge of meltdown.

The world seemed to be going mad. Robert Kennedy and Martin Luther King Jr. were assassinated, their deaths provoking despair among whites and outbursts of understandable fury among blacks. Each day seemed to bring new magazine, newspaper, and television images of fires, barricades, fighting, protests, shouting, and so many angry, contorted faces. Two of the most popular songs of the year, "Hey Jude" by the Beatles and "Those Were the Days" by Mary Hopkin, tried to counter the black days with evocations of communal joy and nostalgia.

In the February issue of *Ramparts,* Southern signed a petition protesting the Vietnam War and announced his refusal to pay taxes. It was a well-intentioned act of protest, but the sad reality was that Southern had not been paying taxes since he started making crazy money in Hollywood. His lawyer and business manager, Si Litvinoff, tried to advise him, but it was an uphill struggle working with a client who believed money was meant to be spent.

"When money came in I would take care of bills with his approval, but he was on a short leash . . . [unless] there were some expenses he needed [to pay for]. When he came back from *Dr. Strangelove* he took me and Peter Duchin, who had taken him out before, to the Russian Tea Room. I'll never forget it. He said to the waiter, 'I want that chicken where you shoot the needle through it!'—which is chicken Kiev. And he turned to us and said, 'From now it's first class all the way, first class all the way!' . . . Terry could spend but he was on a short leash with me in terms of the cash he was given; he managed to spend it, but not crazily."

Carol Southern remembers things differently and wishes Litvinoff had been more diligent. Although they were separated, Terry was generous with financial support for his estranged wife and son. As Terry's expectations of the high life rose and his spending increased exponentially, Carol was becoming frantic about whether enough money was being set aside for tax purposes. "I remember bursting into tears on the telephone with Si and saying, 'You've got to do this or there's going to be terrible trouble.' It just goes to show that recognizing something is wrong doesn't mean you can prevent it from happening." Carol believes Litvinoff was too impressed by the movie business and she recalls him playing down her fears by saying, "The guy's never had a chance to enjoy himself. For God's sake, let the guy live a little!"

"I was so worried about this that I persuaded Terry to change accountants," recalls Carol. "Because [songwriter] Jerry Leiber always had money I thought maybe he should use Leiber's accountant. This was as big a mistake as using Si. This accountant was a very straight arrow and he filed these taxes for 1966–67, but there was no money to pay. So he filed the returns without a check. And Si later said he would have made a deal with the government if I hadn't done that. So I compounded the problem. . . . And that started Terry's terrible financial problems."

Despite Carol's concern and Litvinoff's advice, which had served clients like Jack Gelber well, Southern continued spending money as if he *were* Guy Grand. He often carried a thick roll of bills in his pocket. Its presence prompted Southern to sudden sprees of largesse such as picking up the check in the Russian Tea Room for ten people or giving various friends and acquaintances "loans" (a word synonymous with "gift" in the Southern lexicon). He gambled a lot and often lost. He acted like someone anointed by Hollywood with a special kind of grace instead of just another scribe whose status was determined by commercial considerations rather than aesthetic ones.

The year 1968 was when the cash flow began to slow down. The IRS cloud would descend on Terry three times: first in 1968, then in the eighties, and finally in 1992, when the IRS placed a lien on his *Dr. Strangelove* and *Easy Rider* residuals. It took the better part of the seventies to pay off the first tax bill. The second was settled in 1988 with an offer of compromise. The final lien was removed after Southern's death in 1995.

Whereas *Barbarella* had been a big-money gig, *Easy Rider* was strictly Indiesville. Neither Fonda, Hopper, Rafelson, Schneider, nor Southern had a clue the little film they were preparing would become a phenomenon. According to Gail Gerber, Terry was paid a mere $3,900 for his work on *Easy Rider.* He would receive residuals (usually fifty to one hundred dollars a year) from film rentals and TV screenings of the film, but nothing compared with the money he would have gained from even a single profit point in the film.

After Fonda had secured the deal with Raybert, he returned to New York to finish the script with Terry. Fonda and Hopper's relationship was growing more tense and fractured. As the director, Hopper believed the film would be written in the process of filming the road trip. In preparation, he and Paul Lewis, the film's production manager, took off for a two-week location scouting trip in late January/early February.

Back in New York, Hopper turned up at a restaurant where Fonda, Southern, and Rip Torn were gathered. Torn had been the first choice to play George Hanson. The actor was lukewarm about the film because he found Hopper too much of a loose cannon, and two upcoming theater projects, a James Baldwin play and Jack Gelber's controversial *The Cuban Thing,* were probably going to interfere with his availability. When Hopper began to rant about the Southern rednecks he encountered on his trip, Torn, a Texan like Southern, began to politely disagree. This further enraged Hopper and the two got into an argument that almost reached the point of a fistfight. Things eventually cooled down, but Hopper's flare-up convinced Torn to withdraw his involvement. Since no contracts had been signed and the project was still far from being cast, there appeared to be no hard feelings.

Like amateurs prepping a community-theater play, Hopper, Fonda, and company stumbled through the finer points of hiring cast and crew, drawing up contracts, securing locations, and nailing down the script. Many mistakes were made, but the team was rewriting the template for independent feature film production in the process. One of the most famous mishaps occurred when Fonda got the dates for Mardi Gras mixed up, thinking he had a month to spare.

As a result, Fonda, Hopper, Southern, and an ad hoc crew hastily convened in an airport hotel parking lot in New Orleans on February 23. It was a wet and cold morning that began unpromisingly with Fonda and Hopper yelling at each other. Somehow over the next six days, several hours of cinema verité footage of Billy and Wyatt wandering through Mardi Gras was shot. Hopper and Paul Lewis were angry at Fonda and Southern, claiming they had written only three pages of script. Whether this was true or not at the time, it was a moot point. Judging from the paper trail, only three pages were needed—backstory and additional dialogue for the cemetery sequence—since the bulk of the New Orleans footage was essentially second unit work that would eventually be accompanied by a wild track of street noises and music.

Despite Hopper and Lewis's claims, Southern did supply the following guidelines for the acid trip sequence:

> Ghost figures of parades in off colors through multiple optical illusions. Dark areas of umbrellas. In tearing the clinging objects of clothing from her body, MARY finds new freedom from light that bursts from wrought-iron crosses. In the light BILLY and LILA become more piglike in their orgasm and mannerisms. They wallow in the mire and in open tombs. WYATT saints himself by revealing his mother's death and the tears and the begging for forgiveness and his hate for her having left him in such an early stage of his development. The same time he sits talking to a giant tombed statue of Miss Liberty. He asks to hold her hand. He rocks MARY, still fully clothed, in his black leathers. She, nude, her white body standing out firmly. She tries to remember her rosary, the confessional, from years and years before. She believes she is conceiving the Son of God. She stretches nude as raindrops fall and tear the rounded prism. She reaches forward, hands stretching to the sky. The tears fall and hit her stomach and blur her as if in an impressionistic dream.

Hopper claims that he went off to write his script of *Easy Rider* when the New Orleans segment was wrapped. But when the production reconvened in Los Angeles, where the drug buy and the commune scenes were staged in Topanga Canyon, cinematographer Laszlo Kovacs clearly remembers it was a Terry Southern script they were given by Hopper.

"We had a very specifically written script by Terry Southern, Dennis Hopper, and Peter Fonda. All the scenes were carefully followed, especially the dialogue sequences after the Jack Nicholson character joins them. It wasn't just a bunch of stoned guys sitting around a campfire improvising that."

To add to the increasingly *Rashomon*-like proceedings, Fonda would assert that Southern withdrew as coproducer because he couldn't afford to stay on for $350 a week plus expenses and deal with Hopper. (Given that Southern's next project was another indie, the equally low-budget *End of the Road*, this explanation seems a tad pat.) However, Fonda does remember returning to New York after the New Orleans shoot to finish the script with Terry. In his memoir, Fonda states that Hopper's claim that he wrote the script stems from the time when Hopper dictated a portion of "treatment" into a tape recorder. Fonda also says Hopper had the idea of Billy and Captain America at a drive-in watching their own credits. Terry took credit for creating the George Hanson character.

"The idea of meeting a kind of a straight guy, which turned out to be the Jack Nicholson role, was totally up to me," Southern recalled. "I thought of this Faulkner character, Gavin Stevens, who was the lawyer in this small town. He had been a Rhodes scholar at Oxford and Heidelberg, and had come back to this little town to do whatever he could there. So I sort of automatically gave the George Hanson character a similar sympathetic aura. I wrote the part for Rip Torn, who I thought would be ideal for it. When shooting began, we went to New Orleans and Rip was going to come, but he couldn't get out of this stage commitment."

Hopper claimed Hanson was inspired by a drinking buddy, Jack Sterritt, who later directed Fonda in *Race with the Devil* and had attended the University of Texas.

During March and April of 1968, Southern and Fonda finished working on the script. Fonda became increasingly preoccupied with production details, which would include some studio and backlot work in Los Angeles and Topanga Canyon for the brothel and commune scenes, then location work along the Colorado River to Needles, California; Kingman and Flagstaff, Arizona; Taos, New Mexico; and Wichita Falls, Texas. The famous roadside café scene in which Billy, Captain America, and Hanson encounter hostile locals was shot in Morganza, Louisiana, with *real* hostile locals.

As his work on the script came to a close, Southern grew worried that Fonda and Hopper would discard much of the dialogue for portentous silences and monosyllables. In a letter to Fonda dated April 24, Southern criticized Fonda for the "dumb-bell dialogue" that he had introduced into the brothel scene. "I am certain that you will remember that probably the worst scene in *The Trip* was the 'merry-go-round' scene where Dennis ran off at the mouth, trying to explain things to the audience, instead of to the person he was talking to . . . whereas one of the very best scenes in the movie was the one in which he was talking exclusively to the other character, i.e., the scene in which you come back to his pad, and he questioned you saying: 'Man, I can't tell if you are still high or if you're putting me on.'"

But as Southern grew increasingly detached from *Easy Rider,* Fonda and Hopper continued to pare the dialogue down. It was a decision that worked against the characters that Fonda and Hopper were trying to embody. The character that the audience warms up to the most is George Hanson, who doesn't stop talking during his brief twenty minutes in the film.

Jack Nicholson would turn out to be the script's (and hence Southern's) greatest ally. After Torn moved on, Bruce Dern was considered for the part. Burt Schneider persuaded Hopper and Fonda to cast Nicholson instead. The former lifeguard from Neptune, New Jersey, had worked as an office boy in the MGM cartoon department and studied acting under Jeff Corey in the late fifties and early sixties. Nicholson had spent much of the sixties in minor roles in such films as *The Raven* and *Ensign Pulver,* but seemed to be having more luck as a scriptwriter with work on *Ride in the Whirlwind, The Trip,* and *Head.* By the age of thirty-two, his future as an actor was not encouraging. His only A-list role, as a flower child opposite Barbra Streisand in Vincente Minnelli's *On a Clear Day, You Can See Forever,* was strictly paint-by-numbers stuff.

Hopper was reluctant to cast Nicholson because he couldn't picture him as Hanson, but Schneider's gut instincts prevailed. When Nicholson arrived in Texas to film his scenes, he knew his lines and carried the script protectively. Nicholson understood George Hanson was *Easy Rider*'s conscience. The conviction he brought to the part energized the film. Nicholson was also funny and easy to be around—a considerable advantage on a film set that was fraught with constant bickering between Hopper and Fonda.

Southern's extensive work and input were played down by Hopper and Fonda after *Easy Rider*'s release in favor of the more exotic notion that the screenplay was largely improvised. Neither man, however, disputed that Southern came up with the title, a gritty colloquialism for a man who lives off the earnings of a whore. The title was a stroke of genius: simple, imagistic, and elusive. It reinforced the basic pitch of two bikers "on the road" but also underscored the idea that America had become lazy and materialistic in its pursuit of money at all costs. Terry's work on the script of *Easy Rider* was embarked on in a very sixties spirit of idealism and cooperation. Through a combination of naïveté and indifference on his part, and insecurity and ego on Hopper and Fonda's, Southern's work would become reduced to footnote status. Although he was involved with the project practically from the beginning and through the beginning of production, Terry found himself almost erased from the film's history by two men he considered friends. *Easy Rider* became the gig that launched a thousand bad vibes.

As *Easy Rider* began shooting in earnest, Southern kept busy with a variety of projects. In addition to completing the novel *Blue Movie,* he and Larry Rivers began talking about a collaboration called *The Donkey and the Darling* for lithographer Tanya Grossman and her specialized press, Universal Art Limited Editions. *The Donkey and the Darling* was a children's story that Southern had been playing around with since his days in Geneva.

Southern was also working on the final drafts of *The Magic Christian* screen adaptation for Peter Sellers. And as if this weren't enough, he and Aram Avakian were meeting regularly about *The End of the Road,* an adaptation of the John Barth novel. Max L. Raab, a garment manufacturer in Greenwich Village and friend of Si Litvinoff, had raised a modest half-million dollars to independently produce the film. It was during this busy summer period that Terry decided to grow a beard and eschew the clean-shaven jacket-and-tie urban hipster look of his generation. He began to wear a silver chain with a peace symbol and jeans with a matching jacket.

As *End of the Road* began to gear up for a late summer shoot, Terry was approached by *Esquire* to cover the Chicago Democratic Convention along with William Burroughs, Jean Genet (a last-minute substitute for Samuel Beckett), and John Sack. It didn't take a psychic to intuit that the convention was going to be an event of some historical significance. After the King and Robert Kennedy assassinations, racial tensions were literally aflame in America's inner cities. Lyndon Johnson had decided not to run for a second term, leaving the Democrats to decide between Hubert Humphrey and Eugene McCarthy, whose liberal pieties and good intentions seemed beside the point in an increasingly fragmented and disillusioned political climate.

Many Americans were finding the rise of baby-boomer counterculture about as comforting as a constantly mutating virus. Richard Nixon, the candidate who wouldn't die, along with his running mate, Spiro Agnew, was getting raves from the Silent Majority for his law-and-order platform. Before the convention started, the United States had resumed a bombing campaign in Vietnam.

Southern flew to Chicago with Gail during the weekend of August 26–28. He would be paid $1,250 and expenses. At the Sheraton Hotel, he met up with his fellow correspondents and Richard Seaver, who was acting as Genet's translator. Michael Cooper was on hand to take photos. This group would offer their impressions of the convention that many pundits anticipated would be an epic standoff between police, hippies, Yippies, and middle-of-the-road liberals. John Berendt, an *Esquire* editor who later achieved bestsellerdom with *Midnight in the Garden of Good and Evil,* accompanied this motley crew as a kind of chaperon. For Southern, the assignment would become his last venture into the New Journalism he had helped to pioneer.

"Going there wasn't our idea. The magazine may have known something," recalled Southern in 1993. "We had no idea it would be that dangerous. I got hit on the head and back a couple of times. You have no idea how wild the police were. They were just totally out of control. I mean, it was a *police* riot, that's what it was."

On Saturday, August 24, Southern joined Allen Ginsberg and William Burroughs at a massive gathering at Grant Park. A lot of the time he was hunkered down in the bar of the Chicago Sheraton riffing on the crazy scene beyond the glass and getting drunk. Southern called Genet "Jean-Jacques Genet." Genet called him "Folamour," the French word for *Strangelove.* Despite the dark mood in the streets, there was a convivial school-outing spirit among the *Esquire* team, which went out to the airport to see the arrival of Eugene McCarthy on Sunday, August 25.

On Monday evening, a group of 3,000 or more young people, some claiming to be members of the Youth International Party or Yippie movement founded that year by Abbie Hoffman and Jerry Rubin, refused to leave Grant Park at closing time. Southern and his *Esquire* team joined the group marching on police barricades. At approximately 12:30, the police charged on the marchers with tear gas and clubs. This led to chaos, with crowds fleeing into Clark Street, where they encountered police more than ready to use their clubs. In fleeing the scene with Genet, Berendt and Seaver knocked on a door and took refuge with a University of Chicago student working on a dissertation about Genet. On Monday morning, at a protest hosted by Ed Sanders, Southern, Burroughs, Ginsberg, and Genet read statements condemning the police riot. An afternoon march at Grant Park led to another round of police violence.

Michael Cooper took a famous picture of Burroughs, Southern, and Ginsberg walking along a bridge into Grant Park. Ginsberg recalled the event as follows: "Burroughs on my right looking young and lighting up a cigarette, Terry and I practically arm to arm. I've got a little shoulder bag and to my left there's Genet and behind him a monitor for the peace march. A barefoot kid, probably a nature boy, walks behind. David Dellinger had asked for a peaceable march and for those who wanted a violent thing to separate out and go somewhere else. I think I had lost my voice chanting earlier through tear gas. The night before, the Chicago police had tear-gassed the cross which a group of priests had raised in Lincoln Park. My own speech had been a sort of croaked 'ohm,' prefaced by some remarks explaining the use of the mantra. My intention was to unite and co-ordinate everybody's attention and calm everyone down. So I was probably talking to Terry Southern about the importance of keeping calm and not escalating the anxiety and violence. Jean Genet is probably thinking about the blue pants of the soldiers or the police, and Burroughs is probably considering which riot sounds on his tape recorder would recreate psychic conditions for further escalation of hysteria."

The convention was one of many ideological turning points in 1968, in which no one—liberal, pacifist, radical, law-and-order patriot—came out looking good. Twenty percent of registered Democrats deserted the party following the debacle. While the Yippies had captured the media spotlight, their two founders, Hoffman and Rubin, would become embroiled in a long, protracted trial along with Dellinger, Tom Hayden, Bobby Seale, Rennie Davis, John Froines, and Lee Weiner.

Southern's piece on the convention, "Groovin' in Chi," was delivered promptly. It would be his last contribution to *Esquire*. Describing himself as "the anchor man," Southern seems at a rare loss to find the right tone for the piece. On one hand, he accurately describes the police reaction to the young protesters in Grant Park as "a phenomenon somewhat unexpected, which we were to observe consistently throughout the days of violence— that rage seemed to engender rage; the bloodier and the more brutal the cops were, the more their fury increased." Yet the truncated nicknames, such as Big Dave for Dellinger, and the reference to Ginsberg as "that loony fruit" reduce much of Southern's outrage to mere slapstick. The carefully

modulated irony of "Twirling at Ole Miss" is absent. Instead, Southern
seems to be struggling between turning his observations into a routine and
recording his sense of ineffectiveness. Toward the end, he describes himself
sitting with William Styron and John Marquand in the hotel bar aware that
"there was a certain undeniable decadence in the way we sat there, drinks
in hand, watching the kids in the street getting wiped out." More of that
candid self-examination would have made "Groovin' in Chi" another classic Southern piece.

To be fair, none of the other *Esquire* pieces had the immediacy of the
live TV news footage. Genet's "Member of the Assembly" eventually sank
into a murk of obscurantism. Burroughs's "The Coming of the Purple
Better One" was a cut-up that made use of Robert Ardrey's theories of animal and human violence. The conceit was intriguing, but shed little light
on the long-term implications of the convention. John Sack's "In a Pig's
Eye" attempted to understand why the police reacted with such hostility
toward the crowds (many of whom were registered convention delegates).
The piece was written from a Chicagoan's point of view after numerous
interviews with police, but lacked a sense of direction. *Esquire*'s convention
team looked great in pictures and on the cover of the magazine, but their
respective accounts were far from definitive. As commentary, Norman
Mailer's *Miami and the Siege of Chicago* was more rigorous in its inquiry
into the growing schism between left and right, mainstream and counterculture, while Haskell Wexler's dazzling film *Medium Cool* used a mix of
fiction and documentary footage of the rioting in an almost visionary way to
capture the surrealistic tension between competing visions of America.

The agony of a country tearing itself apart, which Southern witnessed
at the Democratic Convention in Chicago, became an explicit part of
End of the Road when it began principal photography in September and
October of 1968. Whereas his *Esquire* piece rambled, *End of the Road* was
cold and unrelenting in its analysis of crisis and disillusionment.

Adapted from John Barth's first novel, published in 1958, Southern
and Avakian's film is faithful to the book's distanced narrative. Jacob
Horner (Stacy Keach), a recent graduate of Johns Hopkins, is found in a
state of catatonia on a rail station platform by Doctor D (James Earl Jones),
who takes him to his Remobilization Farm, a combination mental hospital,
commune, and experimental lab, where Esalen meets *A Clockwork Orange*.
In his examination room, Doctor D bombards Horner with a variety of

stimuli, from shouting abuse to role-playing and flashing slides of sex, pop art, and Vietnam. The doctor also introduces Horner to the other patients, a motley crew of psychopaths, obsessives, and fetishists. These unorthodox methods shake Horner back to something resembling consciousness. In order to complete his recovery, Horner is instructed to get a normal job and avoid personal and political engagement, and finds work at a small college teaching prescriptive English grammar. He becomes friends with a senior professor, Joe Morgan (Harris Yulin) and his wife, Rennie (Dorothy Tristan). Joe is a narcissistic tyrant who humiliates and starves Rennie of real affection and friendship. In response, Horner, as if preprogrammed, embarks on an affair with Rennie. When she becomes pregnant, she decides she doesn't want to have the baby or leave her husband. Horner, with little conviction, arranges an abortion performed by Doctor D, who accidentally kills Rennie on the operating table and is reduced to the same catatonic immobility that Horner was lost in at the beginning of the film. All the characters, not just the aimless Horner, find there are indeed limits to the politics of self.

End of the Road, more than *Easy Rider,* was one of the few truly independent feature films of the sixties. Avakian, a talented editor (*The Miracle Worker, You're a Big Boy Now*), had directed only *Lad: a Dog* and a small part of *Paper Lion.* These experiences convinced him that playing by the rules was doing little for his directorial career. Southern was looking for more creative control over his scripts. They optioned Barth's novel and began refashioning an earlier treatment by Dennis McGuire. Max Raab raised the meager half-million-dollar budget. A distribution agreement was worked out with Allied Artists.

Shooting started in an abandoned button factory in Great Barrington, Massachusetts, and the surrounding countryside in the fall of 1968. Southern and Avakian pooled their contacts and assembled an unbelievably talented cast and crew. Gordon Willis, late the legendary cinematographer behind *The Godfather* films, *Annie Hall,* and *All the President's Men,* made his debut on the film. He was selected after Avakian and Southern saw a showreel of his work lensing commercials. Willis's assistant, Michael Chapman, later shot *Taxi Driver* and *Raging Bull.* Fueled by the bitter passions of the times, Southern and Avakian encouraged cast and crew to collaborate and improvise.

Avakian's wife, aspiring actress Dorothy Tristan, was not the first choice for the part of Rennie. Southern lobbied for someone like Tuesday Weld.

"During the writing of it, they all hung out in the house. . . . I, of course, was the cook and cleaner. I had no part in it. I was studying acting by then. I wanted to be in the film, but they would talk about the casting in front of me, which was very difficult for me," said Tristan. "I would be sitting there washing the dishes and feeding them. I was intimidated by those guys. Anyway, I finally was given the role. I was standing right in front of their faces, but they wanted a name and my opinion was that Terry and those other guys, not Aram because he wasn't like that, wanted somebody whose pants they could get in. That's been my experience with a lot of filmmakers including any of the stars. When they are choosing scripts, who they want to go to bed with has a lot to do with their choices. Who's available? Who will allow herself to be taken to bed?"

While Tristan found her first film role difficult to adjust to, she later realized that the working environment's freedom and spirit of intense collaboration was the exception not the rule. Max Raab was a hands-off producer who simply wanted to help his friends get a film made. She did think Southern and Aram were spending too much time working the political ferment of the year into the script.

"I felt that this was a mistake. I think that the novel was enough. I did not think that the political [slant] was needed. But of course, that was going on at the time. Aram and Terry were very politically minded, so that was the direction it took. And I think that was to a large degree the film's downfall and led to the X rating it got. I think it was not only the abortion [scene], but the political aspect. Nobody was stepping out that far at that time."

The film's marital theme placed a strain on Avakian and Tristan's marriage. While they managed to keep their disagreements to a minimum, it was sometimes difficult for Avakian, as director, and Southern, as writer and coproducer, to control their actors. "There was one thing I didn't like and neither did Aram, and that was the relationship between Stacy and Harris," said Tristan. "They were very good friends, but as sometimes happens between actors, they formed an alliance and decided what they were going to do. Which was difficult because Aram was very strong minded. Terry was also very strong-minded and he also gave line readings, which didn't really work. Terry was on the set a lot. Normally that wouldn't work between a writer and director, but Aram and Terry's relationship was so good and close that there was no conflict. However, the actors often went to Terry for information about the characters. Naturally they would go to the writer if the writer is there. But it's annoying nonetheless when the director is standing right there. I felt he had no place doing it. There is a difference between writing a novel and hearing those voices in your head and hearing the actors speak. It's almost forbidden to give line readings, frankly. He did it and he was so well respected that the actors would not [object], but I felt it was detrimental to particular performances."

During the shoot, Keach was also playing Falstaff for Joseph Papp's N.Y. Shakespeare Festival in the evenings. After a day's shooting in Great Barrington, he would don his makeup in a station wagon en route to Manhattan. After the performance, he would drive back and catch a few hours' sleep. Keach thought Southern's writing was "terrific" but felt "Aram Avakian, our director, had his own agenda, and I don't think anybody ever knew what it was. What finally ended up on the screen is simply not the movie we shot. Some of it was way ahead of its time, and some of it is brilliant. But it's not the story we were trying to tell. *End of the Road,* which was supposed to explode on the American scene like another *Graduate,* instead was withheld for two years. When it finally did come out, it received an X rating because of the abortion scene. Women fainted, it was so graphic. Aram would not listen to anyone who spoke in such mundane terms as 'This scene is unwatchable.'"

Avakian described the scene to Keach as "symbolic of the abortion of America." It was one of the first scenes that Keach and Tristan filmed. Tristan had injured her left arm learning to ride a horse for a montage sequence. When she managed to complete the harrowing abortion scene without indicating there was anything wrong with her arm, any reservations about her ability to play Rennie were cast aside.

Southern's input on *End of the Road* would be superseded by Avakian once the film wrapped. The director spent almost a year tinkering with the film before its New York release in January 1970. The cuts were very self-conscious, heightening the framing and chiaroscuro lighting of Gordon Willis. As the musical consultant, George Avakian spent a great deal of time gathering sound effects as well as music to add to the aural assault that Keach's character experiences in Doctor's examination room.

A few month's before *End of the Road*'s release, *Life* magazine ran a favorable cover story which Tristan believes irritated the New York critics.

"There was this seven-page rave on the film. It was very hard for the film because the critics did not like that. It was like 'are you going tell me what is good and what isn't?' And it had a negative effect on them, plus there was plenty to get your teeth into as far as political content, aside from the abortion. To a large degree, the political content was more aggravating to people than the abortion sequence. Although that's what everybody talked about."

Barth's novel was informed by the apolitical conformity of fifties college life when McCarthyism kept liberal academics in a state of paranoid silence and retreat. By contrast, Avakian and Southern underscore Horner's nervous breakdown with images of the social and political meltdown of 1968. A hypnotic opening montage of still photos and newsreel footage presented a sideshow of postwar history, culminating in the assassination of Robert Kennedy and Martin Luther King, riots and protests, the resurgence of law and order Republicans like Nixon and Agnew, and of course, the Vietnam War. Horner's catatonia is a direct response to the madness of LBJ's Great Society. Whereas the doctor's race was not significant in the novel, the film's casting of James Earl Jones is central to Avakian and Southern's adaptation. Jones's interpretation of D's therapy of shock acts as a counterpoint to the ineffectual liberalism of the white characters.

Southern and Avakian also found a corollary to Barth's arch, self-referential prose. The editing combines scenes of seamless, flowing cuts with others that are disassociative and allusive. The dialogue is simultaneously banal and charged with menace and foreboding.

"We tried to give the film a full-on sixties flavor—student unrest and so on—which seemed inherent in the book . A very good book, and, I like to believe, a most faithful adaptation, with a little something extra in the form of Doctor D's theories," Southern said.

Upon release, *End of the Road* was met with either indifference or incomprehension. In a typical review, Molly Haskell wrote, "The apocalyptic vision is an excuse for blackwashing moral distinctions." Judith Crist dismissed it as tasteless and superficial. With no hot young stars (but fine actors) or groovy rock score (but Bach, Billie Holiday, and Teo Macero), *Road* was a film that fell between the cracks of youth culture, the New Hollywood, and the traditional art-house audience.

In his memoir, *Once Upon a Time,* John Barth dismissed the adaptation as "vulgar," but actually the film extends the ideas of his novel. It pushes the book's nihilism further and stresses the links between the personal and political. The result is a raw cry over the death of sixties idealism filmed in a year when this anguish was starkly felt by millions around the world. Like *Two-Lane Blacktop* and *Performance, End of the Road* is an elegy for a decade that we are still coming to terms with.

End of the Road was forgotten, but it has built up a small cult reputation thanks to video. Nicolas Roeg, who probably appreciated Avakian's fragmented mise-en-scène, paid homage to the film in *The Man Who Fell to Earth*. When Thomas Newton watches his bank of multiple TV sets, one of them shows James Earl Jones taunting Stacy Keach.

Written and shot in 1968, *End of the Road* is a great lost film of the period. Dismissed by critics during its brief New York run in January 1970, *End of the Road* was burdened with an X rating because of its explicit abortion sequence. Allied Artists, the film's distributor, didn't go to bat for it, and as a result, the film never got the kind of promotion *Easy Rider* and *Midnight Cowboy* enjoyed. Perhaps it wouldn't have helped much anyway, since *End of the Road* is an uncompromising study of alienation and political despair. Avakian came closer to emulating the Brechtian outrage of Jean-Luc Godard than any other American director of the time, surpassing in many respects the work of Stanley Kubrick and Arthur Penn.

End of the Road is a tattered signpost pointing to a road not taken by American cinema. The New Hollywood of the late sixties and early seventies, like most new waves, promised more than it could deliver. As great as the work of Coppola, Scorsese, and Spielberg was in the seventies, their politics were often safely couched in genre or technical display. If *Road* had been even a modest success, Avakian might have joined Robert Altman or John Cassavetes in creating a more rigorous brand of new American cinema.

Southern's work on *End of the Road* overlapped with the completion of a workable shooting script for *The Magic Christian*. As a result, he wasn't able to keep an eye on the *Christian* script as preproduction went into high gear. Since 1965, Southern had written several drafts for Sellers that were used to raise money. Commonwealth United, a relatively new American/British production company, was financing *The Magic Christian's* $15 million budget as part of a slate of films that would make them a minimajor like United Artists. (The company's president, Bernie Cornfeld, was implicated in a financial scandal shortly after the film's release and spent four years in a Swiss prison.) Sellers had convinced Joseph McGrath, who had since made two small comedies, to forget the rancor of *Casino Royale*, and to direct the big-screen version of a book they both loved.

Between 1965 and November 1968, Southern had worked on a dozen different versions of the script. Additional writing went on with McGrath when the director came on board the summer before filming. Somewhere along the line Southern had agreed to the idea that Guy Grand be accompanied by an adopted son to play on the generation-gap theme that was all the rage in sixties mass media. Sellers thought it would be good to get one of the Beatles to play the son. Initially John Lennon was approached, says McGrath, but his relationship with Yoko Ono eventually precluded a long-term film commitment. Ringo Starr, who apparently decided to ignore the terrible reviews of *Candy,* was more than eager to take Lennon's place as Youngman Grand. McGrath and Southern also approached Stanley Kubrick about playing a director not unlike himself who decides to take a bribe. While the reclusive director passed on the rare opportunity to do a Hitchcock in somebody else's film, others were more than willing to sign on, including Yul Brynner, Laurence Harvey, Roman Polanski, Raquel Welch, Christopher Lee, Wilfrid Hyde-White, and Spike Milligan.

Sellers's love and admiration for *The Magic Christian* did not prevent the impetuous actor from tinkering with the script while his favorite writer was distracted by *End of the Road.* In the interim between delivering a final draft and principal photography, Sellers, who was prone to sudden bouts of insecurity, decided to have Southern and McGrath's draft rewritten by Graham Chapman and John Cleese, a talented Oxford-educated acting/writing team who were establishing a name for themselves through work on British TV programs like *The Frost Report* and *Doctor in the House.* According to Cleese: "The Terry Southern script had been through thirteen drafts by the time it got to us. We read one that contained the most elegant and verbose stage directions I have ever come across in my life, but quite hopeless dialogue, I'm afraid. . . .Graham and I managed to put this script into shape in three or four weeks until we got it the point where they were able to raise money on it, at which point Terry Southern arrived and was laid to rest in a nest of bourbon crates."

In addition to his low opinion of Southern's work on the film, Cleese described McGrath as a "a very nice man who had no idea of comedy structure and [the film] finished up as series of celebrity walk-ons."

"I always remember John Cleese saying after reading the opening of Terry's *Magic Christian* script, 'Hah, I mean who wrote this, this is rubbish, why does it have to say there is an ormolu clock on the mantel shelf? This attention to detail is ridiculous. Who needs this!'" recalled McGrath. "Well, that's just silly. Terry wrote an ormolu clock because he wanted to get across it's Guy Grand and the man is rich and you don't just cut to any clock."

The soon-to-be founding members of *Monty Python's Flying Circus* would also act in *The Magic Christian* film. Chapman would play an easily bought rowing coach in the Cambridge-Oxford regatta scene. Cleese played an auctioneer at Sotheby's. Southern hated this scene as Cleese wrote it. He argued that defacing a Rembrandt had nothing to do with his concept of Guy Grand as a deflater of middle-class pretensions. Intriguingly one of the other scenes Cleese and Chapman wrote for the film, which was cut, was "The Mouse Problem," a mock TV exposé depicting men wanting to be mice in the same context as closet homosexuals. According to Cleese, the scene was cut because Sellers's milkman didn't like the sketch. It was later used in the premiere season of *Monty Python*.

The *Magic Christian* began shooting on February 2, 1969, and ran through May 2. Filming took place on all three stages of Twickenham Film Studios as well as various locations in and around London. Ringo began work on the film just after completing the *Let It Be* documentary/album with his fellow Beatles. Southern and Gerber arrived a week later. They stayed in the Whitehouse Hotel near Regent's Park.

Both McGrath and Southern found Sellers fun to work with, but were wary of his mood swings. "Working with [Sellers] was like working with two people," said Southern. "He was an ultratalented person who was one of the fastest improvisers ever. He could add to and enrich a scene or character tremendously beyond what was written. On the other hand, he could take it too far and detract from the quality of humor when it was his own. He was too complicated because he was so insecure. If he had reached the saturation point with the particular innovations he was making and you said, 'Yeah, I don't think we should go any further with this,' he would take it very personally as though you were putting him down as a friend. He thought you were withdrawing your affection from him or whatever he felt was there. Then he would just get more and more into [the improvisations], which would represent something excruciatingly personal, which was a lot more important than the movie or any of the aesthetics involved. It was tough because it was a constant balancing act."

McGrath believed one of the problems was that Sellers did not know how to play Guy Grand:

"There's a sequence right at the beginning of the film on the train where Guy Grand talks to his Board, introduces his son to them and then throws them all off the train. We did some camera tests and stuff with extras and Peter. Peter wanted to play the scene and get the character. He did one camera test as Groucho Marx, which was wonderful, and then he lost his courage and did it the way he did it. He was always very keen to go on rewriting until he felt this is wonderful and then he would work on top of a wonderful script. He would never go in loose. He always wanted to know exactly what to do and then he would deviate, but he would know that he had to go back [to the script]. It's very funny. He did another sequence where he had to go through a room full of priceless objects, ceramics and stuff. And he said, 'The thing is if I go through that room and we close the door, one of them could fall over and that would be funny. What I should try and do is go through the room as quickly as possible so that it looks as though I'm going to knock everything down. But I don't knock anything down and then when I close the door still nothing falls down.' And I said, 'Yeah, that's very funny, do you want to walk it and try it?' Then he said, 'Wait a minute,' and he closed his eyes and we're all standing there, the film crew and everything. He stood there for about a minute, opened his eyes and pointed to his forehead, and said, 'Oh, I wish you could have been with me in there. It was wonderful. Let's just do it now. It can never be as good.' That sums him up."

In contrast, McGrath appreciated Southern's nonthreatening way of offering advice and suggestions. He says Southern saw the tone of the adaptation as symbolic of the end of the sixties. "Terry said, 'We've really got to show a period. This is what's happening to us at this time. Our kids will never believe us.' Because you could literally do anything. 'You want to direct a movie? Go ahead and direct a movie.'"

McGrath and Southern began discussing a follow-up project, *The Last Days of Dutch Schultz*. William Burroughs, who was living in a flat near Piccadilly Circus, was fascinated by the gangster's life and a transcript of his dying words. With Southern's encouragment, he began working on a screenplay.

"My wife and I, Terry, Burroughs, and Alexander Trocchi met at Burroughs's flat in St. James's to talk about Dutch Schultz and getting the rights," recalls McGrath. "Burroughs said okay, let's meet up and talk about it. So we went up to Burroughs's place and met Alex Trocchi, who was a novelist of the fifties, but he was from Glasgow, an Italian Glaswegian. I was thinking, 'I'm going to meet Alex Trocchi and Burroughs, this is really great.' We got up there and Trocchi just spent about an hour or two talking to me about Glasgow. Burroughs was talking to Terry and my wife [Peta Button, an assistant art director on *The Magic Christian*] was there. I realized that we were sitting around an orgone box in this flat. He had chairs, but there was this orgone box. Burroughs had brought a few bottles of whiskey and we were just drinking whiskey neat and talking and we never got anywhere with Dutch Schultz. *Not anywhere.* That was the end of that evening and time went on and Terry said, 'I think . . . Hilly Elkins, a stage producer . . . eventually got the rights,' but Burroughs had said that he wanted Terry and me to do it, but we could never get the rights from this guy. So Burroughs was telling us one thing, but on another level, the guy who had the rights wouldn't give them to us. They disappeared. Eventually the movie was made. Somebody bought the rights and the movie was made in some warehouse in Covent Garden, and it has never been shown. Pity, too."

Gerber recalls that the various actors doing cameos in *The Magic Christian* seemed to revel in the chance to poke fun at their images. During the *Hamlet* striptease, Laurence Harvey kept pestering McGrath to do one more take so he could push the scene a little further. Yul Brynner appeared in drag singing "Mad About the Boy" to Roman Polanski. The next day he kept his wife and chauffeur waiting outside the screening room so he could watch his dailies several times.

On May 4, Peter Sellers threw a wrap party for *The Magic Christian* at Les Ambassadeurs, a London casino. All four Beatles showed up for the event and Southern got his picture taken with the group. In addition to Starr, the Beatle connection was strengthened by the involvement of Paul McCartney. He produced the original music recorded by Badfinger and wrote the theme song, "Come and Get It." The single was released several months before the film's release and became a hit.

One crucial scene remained to be shot: the arrival of the *Magic Christian* superliner in New York City. The sequence would culminate with Guy Grand erecting his offal-filled vat of money at the base of the Statue of Liberty. Much to McGrath's surprise, the U.S. National Parks Service agreed to the use of the location. According to Southern, Gail suggested it would be great to travel to the location by the *Queen Elizabeth II*. Thus, McGrath, Starr, Sellers, and Southern found themselves sailing to New York in luxury style at roughly $10,000 a head (on the studio's dime).

"So we all went on this fantastic cruise and crossing," Southern remembers. "Peter Sellers had just discovered hashish and was absolutely enthralled. He couldn't get enough of it. It was very strong stuff. Before we left, I'd introduced him to this Arabic pusher, who had given Peter some hash oil, which is the essence of hash. A very thick oil. Peter put drops of it with an eyedropper on tobacco and smoked the tobacco, or if he had cannabis, he would drop the oil on that and smoke it. It was just dynamite, like opium. So the whole trip was spent in a kind of dream state. Instead of eating in the ordinary first-class place, they had this special dining room. It was beyond first class. It was called the Empire Room. It was a small dining room with about six tables in it. That was another $2,000 right there."

When they arrived in New York, Sellers found out the producers did not want to pay for the New York shoot. An angry series of telexes flew back and forth across the Atlantic. The scene was eventually shot on June 23–26 near the newly built National Theatre on London's South Bank. During the lull, Starr invited Southern, Gerber, McGrath, and Button to join him in the Bahamas for a weeklong holiday. They were all guests of a Greek millionaire, Luna Nicastro. For Southern and Gerber, the Bahamian idyll would be one of the last revels of the decade.

As **Terry and Gail** made their way back to Connecticut from the fun times of *The Magic Christian* shoot, *Easy Rider* was near completion. When filming wrapped in late June 1968, Hopper assembled a three-hour rough cut. That length proved unworkable to Fonda, Bert Schneider, and a growing collective of "auteurs" that also included Henry Jaglom, Jack Nicholson, and the official editor, Donn Cambern. They all took turns pruning and cutting the film down to a more commerically palatable ninety-minute running time.

Many of the cuts were long balletic shots of the bikers on the highway. Other cuts included the initial setup of the coke score on Sunset Boulevard, a longer title sequence with billboards providing ironic commentary, ten additional minutes of the volatile roadside café scene, more dialogue in Madame Tinkertoy's, and extended versions of all the campfire scenes.

Hopper was livid when he saw the new version. "You've ruined my movie," he told them. Fonda, Schneider, and the others persuaded Hopper that they were maximizing the film's potential. Some of Hopper's visual ideas, which he would take to the limit in *The Last Movie,* were simply wrongheaded. Hopper wanted the Mexican opening screened upside down. Southern persuaded him that this Brechtian device would alienate not just the straights in the industry but the hip, young audience they wanted to see the film.

Hopper was able to ditch a proposed score by Crosby, Stills and Nash and use the songs laid down for the rough cuts. The music of Steppenwolf, the Byrds, the Band, Holy Modal Rounders, Jimi Hendrix, Electric Flag, and others underscored the film's broad appeal to the counterculture.

Throughout 1968, Hopper and Fonda screened the film for friends and associates. Mike Nichols and Michelangelo Antonioni were early champions. The film was invited to the Cannes Film Festival as the official American selection. Southern was originally going to be the sole screen-writer credited, but during postproduction he was asked by Hopper and Fonda if he would agree to share credit. Against the advice of the Writers Guild of America, who had won the right to strictly limit directors angling for such credit, Southern agreed. His naive rationale was that a three-way credit accurately reflected the collaborative spirit behind the venture. He also felt it would make it easier for them to produce future projects.

When *Easy Rider* was unveiled at the Cannes Film Festival on May 13, 1969, the ending was greeted with silence and then loud and vigorous applause. While the Palme d'Or went to Lindsay Anderson's *If . . .* , a poetic allegory of late sixties rebellion, Hopper was given the Camera d'Or for Best New Director. When the film went into major release, it proved to be a runaway hit and the fourth-highest-grossing picture of 1969, raking in more than $19 million that year and grossing more than $50 million by the end of the eighties. By contrast, number five, Twentieth Century-Fox's big-budget musical, *Hello, Dolly!,* had cost $26.4 million and grossed only $15.2 million. Columbia executives, who were previously embarrassed by *Easy Rider,* were now scrambling to imitate this model for box office suc-cess. The film would receive two Academy Award nominations: for Best Supporting Actor (Jack Nicholson) and Best Original Screenplay.

As *Easy Rider* began to gross its millions at the box office, Southern turned his attention to finishing *Blue Movie* and his mounting problems with the IRS. Businesswise, Southern was beginning to find himself in what Vietnam vets might call "a world of shit."

On the surface, the seventies appeared to be a continuation of the good years. As 1970 began *The Magic Christian* and *End of the Road* entered theaters almost simultaneously. *Road*'s X rating combined with the mis-leading *Life* magazine hype led to almost universally hostile reviews. Allied Artists cut back the release schedule. Although George Avakian says the film did quite well in the few theaters it played in New York and Los Angeles.

The Magic Christian received its world premiere on February 12, 1970, in New York. Roger Greenspun in the *New York Times* praised its "gentle throwaway virtuosity," but he was in a minority. Pauline Kael in the *New Yorker* dismissed the film with a few lines of vitriol. *Christian* was a modest success, but the collapse of its backer made it difficult for it to achieve momentum outside New York and Los Angeles.

Southern would later dismiss the film as a vulgarization of his novel.

Yet he was as intimately involved with its production as a screenwriter could hope to be. He had certainly enjoyed working on the movie and with McGrath. True, the adaptation lacked the comic precision of *Dr. Strangelove,* but many of the set pieces, especially the climactic voyage, were marvelously staged. Southern could take comfort in the film's cult status. In the nineties, the comedy writer and performer Paul Merton called it "one of the few British films with an epic sensibility" and even hosted a retrospective screening at London's National Film Theatre.

Southern retreated to California for a while to work on a script with William Claxton. The photographer wanted to break into films with an independent production. Claxton optioned *Trixie,* a novel by Wallace Graves, about a black high school dropout who is taken under the wing of two college professors. Through a series of experiments, they try to see how quickly they can raise Trixie's educational level. The script, which was also known as *Electric Dreams,* was set against the backdrop of the Watts riots.

In the fall of 1970, *Blue Movie* was published. Stylistically it was a departure for Southern. There was a raw edge to the description and dialogue that accentuated the coarseness of the cynical film world of the novel. Boris Adrian, a critically acclaimed director with box office clout, is wooed by B-movie producer Sid Krassman to make *The Faces of Love,* which will be an erotic film with all the production values A-list talent can buy. In Barnum & Bailey style, Krassman has arranged for the film to be shot in Liechtenstein, which will not only double as the location, but turns out to be the only place where Adrian's masterpiece can be seen.

Once Southern briskly establishes this premise, he spends the remainder of the novel exploiting the comic possibilties of Adrian's bargain with the devil. Despite the film's explicit subject matter, the same problems that plague a traditional Hollywood production occur. The director and producer must reassure a neurotic starlet, Angela Sterling. On-screen sexual encounters become off screen ones. Drugs and alcohol are consumed to cope with the boredom and isolation of location filming. Arcane technical problems need to be resolved. The book's plot is driven by Adrian's struggle to create, in collaboration with Tony Sanders, "the hot-shot writer from New York," unique and original variations of the sex act. As the film wraps, the negative is seized by a special Vatican commando team to prevent such sacrilege from being unleashed on the masses.

In addition to its ribald dialogue, *Blue Movie* features several of Southern's most inspired crazies. Sid Krassman is a vulgar, sex-obsessed movie producer par excellence. His engaging brand of sleaziness is surpassed only by Teeny Marie, a birdlike seventy-eight-pound body double whose stock in trade is her dazzling white teeth and perfectly shaped mouth. Like Krassman, Marie is a whirling dervish of lust and greed. In addition to the all-American Angela Sterling, there is her costar, Arabella, a worldy veteran of the European art film. Arabella manages to seduce both her director and costar during the making of *The Faces of Love.* Boris Adrian is perhaps the strangest creature in this showbiz menagerie. His motives for making the film are murky. Adrian doesn't need the money, but he is also tired of his career. *The Faces of Love* is an aesthetic challenge, to be sure, but Adrian's genius is quickly revealed to be a higher form of self-delusion.

The book's publication was hampered by the *New York Times*'s refusal to run ads for it. Reviews were decidely lukewarm. There was a consensus that Southern was simply recycling *Candy* in a different guise. David Dempsey in the *New York Times* conceded that the Hollywood vernacular rendered by Southern was funny, but concluded, "This is one of the longest peep shows ever made, and the dullest. It is pornography without Portnoy."

But Michael Wood in the *New York Review of Books* not only gave the novel a positive review, he also provided one of the few rigorous looks at how Southern's style had evolved: "[his] language here is no longer ironic or mocking. It is comic, rich and fluent, full of jargon and gags, but it is a language of its own, not a series of echoes."

Wood zeroed in on *Blue Movie*'s tragic theme: "The point is not that you can't make a truthful and beautiful movie about the most intimate moments in sex—but that making such a movie would be an inhuman activity, which it becomes in this book: a clinical cruelty under the alibi of art."

Unfortunately for Southern, Wood's insightful review didn't appear until March of 1971. Upon *Blue Movie*'s immediate release, there was a sense that Southern was not keeping pace with the decade he seemed to so embody. As was the case with 1968, 1969 and 1970 were dark years for America. The election of Richard Nixon led to the emergence of the Silent Majority and a backlash against the counterculture. The Woodstock Festival's celebratory mood was overshadowed by the Manson murders, which shocked many in the Hollywood circles Southern moved in. He and Gail had met Sharon Tate a number of times with Polanski in London and L.A. The Stones' Altamont concert, with its Hell's Angels, beatings, and a fatal stabbing, revealed a desperate, selfish side of the counterculture, while the escalation of the Vietnam War led to increasingly militant protests on

American streets and campuses. And here, some argued, was the great satirist Terry Southern simply writing about sex yet again.

George Plimpton sometimes thought of his *Paris Review* friend as a painter whose work is briefly in vogue and then forgotten as the times change.

"I remember I was told Mrs. Bennett Cerf threw *Blue Movie* in the fireplace when she read it. They never really got behind it that much and it came out when permissiveness was very much in vogue, so it didn't have the impact it should have. There was some wonderful stuff in it. I thought that book was going to really do well. It was the time of *Behind the Green Door* and all that. If it came out a year or two earlier it might have worked."

Southern's mind was not really on the zeitgeist when the IRS began to squeeze him for back taxes. "Terry made a tremendous amount of money," said Carol Southern. "As it tapered off, the IRS came around. I remember because I didn't have any money then—I guess Nile was about ten—I spent the summer in Maine in [painter] Neil Welliver's extra cabin. It had no electricity or running water. I thought it would be a good sort of camping experience. The IRS came down this dirt road looking for me. I said you have to be joking. They weren't joking. It took a long time to settle."

Somehow, despite the steady big-time script assignments over the last seven years, Southern was broke. What little money he had was being siphoned off by the IRS. He could barely keep up the mortgage payments on the house and he was worried about Carol and Nile. In desperation, Southern looked to his friends. On December 5, 1970, he found himself in the humiliating position of asking Dennis Hopper for a point in *Easy Rider*.

"I am aware that there may be a difference in our notions of who contributed what to the film (memory flash highly selective in these cases), but the other day I was looking through a copy of the original 55th street script that we did together, and was amazed at the amount and strength of the material which went from there intact to silver-screen.

"Please consider it, Den—I'm in very bad trouble."

9
From Green to Amber

f a writer is sensitive about his work being treated like Moe, Curly, and Larry working over the Sistine Chapel with a crowbar, then he would do well to avoid screenwriting altogether," Southern explained to a panel in New York in the early seventies. However, he added sagely, if one was truly in love with the magic of the lens, "the wise thing, of course, is to become a filmmaker. Simply insist on being in charge of your material—don't give it up. In the end, they [Hollywood] must relent—because without a story, without a script, without the creative element . . . there is no film possible."

When asked if this was what Southern intended to do, he replied without hesitation, "Yes, it's the only way to protect the work."

If the postboom years of Southern's movie career were distinguished by any one theme it was his spectacular failure to achieve either control over a project or win success for even the most cash-starved independent filmmaker. Southern's "sensitivity" would become slowly bludgeoned by neglect and indifference in the seventies, a decade that should have led to at least one or two more achievements on the order of *Dr. Strangelove* and *Easy Rider*. It is tempting to argue that Southern was too dangerous for Hollywood, but then so was the early work of Martin Scorsese, Francis Coppola, Brian De Palma, Terence Malick, and all the other young turks who gained an industry foothold thanks to *Easy Rider*'s success. Although the Hollywood New Wave began to show signs of ebbing around 1975, films as quirky and subversive as *The Godfather* and *The Godfather: Part II, Beyond the Valley of the Dolls, M*A*S*H, Little Big Man, Deliverance,*

Five Easy Pieces, Badlands, Mean Streets, Harold and Maude, The Hospital, The Heartbreak Kid, Blazing Saddles, and *Sleeper* were green-lighted and achieved wide distribution. Many of these films were satires or parodies or at least employed different strains of irony. Several maverick independent filmmakers—John Cassavetes, John Waters, Henry Jaglom, John Carpenter, and David Lynch, to name a few—emerged or began working in this period. The influence of foreign films on the look and sound of American *mainstream* studio filmmaking was also reaching its zenith. Colleges and universities were offering various courses and degree programs. Film societies and repertory cinemas kept *Dr. Strangelove, The Loved One, Barbarella, Candy,* and *The Magic Christian* in constant view. To compound the irony of Southern's post-1970 decline was the fact that he had helped create *Easy Rider,* the very film that gave so much momentum to the Hollywood New Wave and encouraged the filmmakers who would ride it to success and fame.

The seventies should have been a continuation of the Terry Southern boom that started in 1964. Instead, as the new decade began, Southern entered a frustrating and puzzling twenty-five-year stretch of grand projects, fascinating possibilities, and dead ends. The great mystery surrounding Southern's postsixties career is why he had such difficulty getting work into production. There are no simple answers, but various contradictory theories that shed light on Southern's sudden fall from the A-list have been proposed. Some say it was because of Terry's fondness for drinking and recreational drugs, but this does not seem to have adversely affected the hard-living New Hollywood crowd. Almost everyone in that gang was experimenting with cocaine and nobody batted an eye at an exec or director rolling a joint. Some pointed to a "graylisting" of Southern because of his left-wing political activism, but he still got commissions. Still others argue that his brand of satire had fallen out of fashion, but the vibrancy of American and international film culture in the seventies had room for all kinds of sensibilities.

Southern's lousy business sense was a big part of the problem—forgetting to sign urgent papers forwarded by his agent or lawyer, spending and lending money at a jaw-dropping rate, and generally not caring what was a good career move and what wasn't. As a collaborator, Southern became increasingly associated with extreme personalities and marginal figures that gave studio execs pause. He also clung perversely to a bohemian ethos formed in the cafés of Paris that held that one should never try too hard to achieve success. Of course, the irony was that Southern had achieved success beyond his dreams and had no idea how to cope with it.

The grand good times of the sixties were ending. Southern was finding it harder to mix business with pleasure. The projects he now embarked on were tainted by the kind of plain dumb bad luck that gives new meaning to the term "development hell."

For starters, the IRS was now aggressively pursuing taxes owed since 1966. By late 1970, the taxman garnished Terry and Gail with a vengeance. When friends like Ellen Adler came to visit them in East Canaan, it was obvious that the Hollywood gravy train had run out. Beneath Terry's expansive greetings and Gail's gracious hospitality, there was sadness, uncertainty, and desperation. Terry, the perennial fringe player, had briefly been in sync with the zeitgeist, but the tax problems had derailed his confidence. Career management wasn't his forte at the best of times, but the pressure from the IRS to pay up stymied him.

"[Terry] didn't know how to take care of himself. He didn't know how to have a home and . . . he was like an orphan," Adler remembers. "I went up there once and it was like seeing people in an orphanage. . . . I think when you really get poor it really becomes impossible to see after things. The trees were falling and apple trees were on the ground. The grass was long. And I said to Terry, 'What is this *The Cherry Orchard,* for God's sake?' Then, you couldn't get hold of him. You had to call some bar in Canaan and he was dogged by that and poverty, but he didn't talk about that."

As a struggling student and writer in Paris, Southern had kept body and soul together by borrowing from friends. Now, as a celebrity in decline, he responded in much the same way to the financial stress. He asked friends about jobs and wondered if so-and-so wouldn't mind advancing a thou or so? Few turned Terry down. After all, they reasoned, as friends went, he gave great value. Nobody ever felt bad after a few hours spent riffing with Terry Southern.

These were humbling times. Many of the friends whom Terry used to hang with in the Village or on the Left Bank were now financially secure. They had managed to transform their various pursuits into careers.

"There was this 'embourgoisement' and this turning of everybody into people of enormous wealth," Adler continues. "I don't know how that happens. Larry [Rivers] got very wealthy. [Terry] used to joke about Larry all the time. . . . He would say, 'Larry took me to the safe to look at his money.' But all of his friends and even Carol got substantially wealthy . . . everybody husbanded the money and took care. Terry was like this counterbohemian who is still twenty years old. He had tremendously fancy tastes. He would go out and order the best brandy . . . he loved the idea of very fine things and cars."

Adler tried to help out by renting Southern her station wagon, but he neglected to take over the insurance. "I got word that I had lost my license for a year and I really got mad at [Terry]. He didn't know how to cope with somebody mad at him. He didn't know what to do. Of course, he sent all kinds of presents, all kinds of letters, but he needed the station wagon above all. He put money into it. It was something or other. It was a loan, so I got mad at him. Then not having seen him . . . he used to come [to Adler's Manhattan home] and he and Gail would sleep on my couch quite often."

During 1971, Southern's writing revolved around projects like *God Is Love, DJ,* based on Norman Mailer's *Why Are We in Vietnam?,* *Hand-Painted Hearts,* based on a story by Thomas Baum, a not-too-promising young-kids-in-the-publishing-world script, and *Drift* with Tony Goodstone. All of these projects were highly speculative and the collaborators were not exactly household names. Goodstone, for example, was primarily known as the author of a book on the history of the pulp magazines. Southern was making a couple of thousand on each job at the most.

DJ was at least a paying pig. Mailer had granted the option on his novel to an English documentary filmmaker Dick Fontaine, who had filmed his mayoralty campaign and march on the Pentagon, for a dollar. Fontaine raised some seed money to hire and pay Southern; he had written a draft and showed it to Southern, who was curious.

"Terry was drinking a lot at the time," recalls Fontaine, who wasn't crazy about Southern's script—although it did begin promisingly with a mock-Western shoot-out between the narrator and an Indian.

Mailer's novel was an update of William Faulkner's *The Bear* put through a Burroughsian blender of scatological language. Working out his father-son relationship on a corporate hunt in Alaska, DJ, the Holden-Caulfield-on-acid narrator, can't help but see the excursion as a metaphor for the racial, political, and generational meltdown of the sixties. *DJ* was the kind of seemingly unfilmable project that appealed to Terry. There was a lot of latitude for exploring ribald dialogue and extreme situations.

Fontaine's documentary work was moving away from the cinema verité style of Richard Leacock and D. A. Pennebaker toward the kind of film essay Godard and Chris Marker were known for. Fontaine had just made a film in this style called *Double Pisces* in London, which opened at the New York Film Festival in September 1970. Terry's buddy Robert Brownjohn (who would die from to much high living in 1970) appeared as a Grand

Guy figure visiting a slaughterhouse with Amanda Lear, the future Roxy Music cover girl. Later in the film, Fontaine wards off a bailiff hoping to collect alimony from his ex-wife and then visits his mother in the Home Counties. The film concludes with Fontaine loading up a Sten gun on the roof of his boarding school in a none too discreet homage to *If . . .* by Lindsay Anderson. Fontaine had started making the film with a cooperative, but took over the reins when their constant indecision and bickering became tiresome. As a document of the disenchantment with the elusive promise of the sixties, *Double Pisces* remains fascinating. Presumably, Fontaine would have injected a similar tone of fragmentation and self-reflexiveness if the Mailer adaptation had gotten off the ground. Despite Fontaine's persistent search for funding, there were no takers.

God Is Love was a Buñuel-like treatment focusing on Maria, a peasant woman in her thirties who discovers she has miraculous powers when she makes love. Through her "ministrations," she is able to cure the sick, the crippled, etc. No one remembers who prompted Southern to turn out the treatment.

In a desperate gesture to get back on the A-list, Southern dashed off a note to Stanley Kubrick, who was editing *A Clockwork Orange* in England. That was a project he knew he should have been working on. After all, he brought the book to Big Stan's attention when MGM decided not to back the director's costly Napoleon project, but there was no point harboring a grudge. Kubrick's response—that he was open to any ideas Terry might have—was friendly but noncommittal.

The post-*Strangelove* relationship between Kubrick and Southern was fertile ground for rumors. There were those who believed that Kubrick was angry at having to share profit participation in *A Clockwork Orange* with Si Litvinoff and Max Raab. These Southern associates had bought the rights to Burgess's novel in 1966, forcing Kubrick to cut them in on the profits. Southern believed Kubrick thought he had let Litvinoff and Raab steal the director's lead. The other theory was that Kubrick continued to bear a grudge against his *Strangelove* collaborator for receiving all the credit for the script. A less sensational and more plausible reason why the director and writer didn't work together was that Kubrick hated to repeat himself. Like an Olympic athlete, Kubrick wanted to surpass the achievements of the previous film. In striving to make each film a radical departure from the last, Kubrick constantly sought out new collaborators.

"With each new film, you sort of marry new people. Stanley is often accused of having done this to a fault," said Christiane Kubrick. "He did it no more or no less than than anybody else. . . . Stanley always said, 'With each new film I get a real education. It's like another college I can attend.' He would read up on subjects and buy books and hang out with a new gang. He was not being malicious when he dived into another pool. That was just his process."

As with Stanley Kubrick, if Southern felt that Hopper had let him down over *Easy Rider,* he didn't let it show. During 1970, Hopper, Fonda, and Jack Nicholson rode a wave of publicity and acclaim. In interviews, they diminished the importance of the screenplay and highlighted the importance of improvisation as a key to the success of the film. Neither Hopper nor Fonda seemed eager to share their unexpected *Easy Rider* profits with the man whose participation helped seal their deal with Columbia. Aside from a letter to the *New York Times* in June 1970 regarding Nicholson's alleged improvisation of the UFO speech, Southern was publicly silent about getting the shaft creditwise. To the puzzlement of more business-savvy friends, Southern remained friendly with Hopper and Fonda.

Fonda and Hopper followed up their *Easy Rider* success with two solo efforts: *The Hired Hand,* a neo-Western heavy on atmosphere but short on narrative drive; and the appropriately titled *The Last Movie.* Underwritten by Universal, *The Last Movie* began as a promising script by Stewart Stern, the screenwriter behind *Rebel Without a Cause,* but ended up as a fascinating mess of improvisation and sub-Brechtian ideas about breaking the fourth wall between the viewer and the screen. On location in the Andes, with a cast and crew with little to do except party, Hopper had tossed out Stern's script in search of his own elusive vision.

To everyone's surprise, *The Last Movie* won the Golden Lion at the Venice Film Festival. Universal loathed the film and gave it a token New York release. Eventually Hopper bought the film back in order to screen it to more appreciative audiences at film festivals and cinémathèques. *The Last Movie* did succeed in capturing the kind of exhaustion and rootlessness that began to typify the late sixties and early seventies. However, it ultimately lacked the discipline, ambition, and formal rigor of films like *Two-Lane Blacktop, Performance,* or even *Easy Rider.*

Southern and Hopper met up in New York in the fall of 1970 shortly after *The Last Movie* wrapped. Fred McDarrah took a picture of the two looking shaggy but amiable in the jeans and long-hair look that was all the rage in the New Hollywood. It was a look that didn't suit either of the men very well. Southern had a drink in his hand.

As the IRS began garnishing Southern's income, he retreated closer to home. During the summer months, it had become the custom for Terry and Gail to visit friends in the Hamptons. During one of countless visits to Larry Rivers's home in Southampton, a curious script called *It's the Little Things That Count* began to evolve. Its flippant title disguised its seriousness; it was a straightforward study of how the rumor of child abuse affects the reputation of a painter and his son in a small town. It went no further than a treatment.

In December 1971 Stanley Kubrick's *A Clockwork Orange* was released in New York. It was endlessly compared and contrasted with Sam Peckinpah's contemporary look at violence in an English village, *Straw Dogs,* released the same month. Kubrick had written the shooting script himself and encouraged the cast, especially Malcolm McDowell, to embellish their roles through improvisation. The film employed an episodic structure. It divided audiences upon its release. *Time*'s Jay Cocks hailed Kubrick as America's "most audacious filmmaker" but felt *A Clockwork Orange,* in spite of its wit and irony, lacked "a sense of grief or of rage, and finally a portion of humanity." Pauline Kael called both Kubrick and Peckinpah's films fascist. The controversy over violence simply boosted the film's box office. It received several Oscar nominations including one for Best Picture.

A Clockwork Orange's success was a mixed blessing for Kubrick. The good news was that the film cemented the beginning of a very fruitful and open-ended arrangement with Warner Bros. that would last until his death. However, the film inspired a few copycat crimes in England and public outrage over concerns of violence. Sensitive to possible threats to his family, Kubrick withdrew the film from distribution in the U.K. (The Kubrick estate finally gave the go-ahead for Warners to reissue the film in England in March 2000 just over a year after his death.) The other major fly in the ointment was that a significant portion of the film's profits was now going to Si Litvinoff and Max Raab.

The year 1972 began with Southern's official divorce from Carol. One of the nastier effects of Terry's tax problems was that the IRS seized a recent inheritance from her father. After considerable hard work, she began to move up from the ranks of reader and became an editor at Crown Publishers. She married *Newsday* film critic Alexander Keneas, who later died of cancer. Eventually Carol became a publishing executive and was able to buy a weekend house on Long Island. While Carol raised Nile, Southern continued to visit or had Nile stay with him in Connecticut on weekends. Despite his stubborn refusal to manage his finances more responsibly, he continued to make sure that Nile was well cared for. Some of his book royalties went into a fund for Nile's education.

Despite his growing reputation for hell-raising, Southern was concerned not only about his son's material welfare, but about his cultural development. He would tell Nile that the best job in the world was that of a film director, and to prove this began making Super-8 films with Nile.

"We started to make these great—now I would call them hallucinogeneric—films," recalls Nile. "These cross-genre films. Terry talks about making an 'A-Dult Western,' a horror Western art film. He had me playing Lar, Larry Rivers, I knew that as a name, and I was a portrait painter. There was this character called Mr. Weird. It was called *Night of Terror, Day of Weird*. I did the titles. We had made this drum spit that would be the rolling three-dimensional credits. I made this papier-mâché distorted head and it would say Monstro Films Limited. And I would film that with this weird lighting. There would be these scenes of a portrait painter who is painting someone weird who is wearing a mask. Mr. Weird, who is played by my dad, is very agitated all the time. "During these playful shoots," Nile continues, "Terry would quote Peter Sellers and say, 'The way into the character is the voice.' Even though the films were all silent. He's a tremendous actor on-screen. He really is fantastic on-screen. Even though these were silent films, he uses the Voice like Peter Sellers used to say. . . . He would do these mannerisms as Mr. Weird or whoever he was. We had found this crude portrait of someone wearing a suit at a tag sale and picked it up. Cut to a cue card: 'Say, you've been at it for quite a long time. Just what kind of painter are you anyway?' I look at the work and I look at him and I say, 'Well, nonrepresentational!' and he comes over and looks at the painting and does a double take. He's wearing a mask and takes out this huge knife and stabs the painting, which bleeds all over the place like a Tarkovsky film. We had this great slow-motion Kodachrome red paint [and] he was blasting it with this baster. And he does this great pratfall where he is running in the snow, looking back and running, falling on his face, and then keeps getting up to run."

Back in 1965, over borscht at the Russian Tea Room, Maggie Paley had asked Terry what book he would most like to film. Without hesitation, he said *Naked Lunch*.

Since 1969, two friends of William Burroughs had been a in a flurry of activity about adapting *Naked Lunch*. Antony Balch, a London film distributor and underground filmmaker, would direct and Brion Gysin would write and design the film. At the end of the day, their efforts amounted to little more than a pile of intriguing four-color storyboards, the kind of thing that would make a wonderful coffee-table book. Then Chuck Barris, the mercurial producer of such TV shows as *The Dating Game*, took out an option on *Naked Lunch* and sent Southern and Burroughs first-class plane tickets to talk story at his Bel-Air mansion. The two literary outlaws were picked up by a chauffeur-driven Daimler at the airport and taken to their audience with Barris.

"Barris was just all-out insanity," says Burroughs's longtime assistant, James Grauerholz. "The story is that he said, 'I finally read the book last night. Can you take out the sex and drugs?' Terry and Bill looked at each other and said, 'We'll try.'"

At their next meeting with Barris a few days later, they discovered their patron had called off the project. They were ushered out of Barris's offices and told to find their own way home. The two men walked to a nearby friend's house and called a taxi. The cab was so small that Burroughs had to sit on Southern's lap.

That same spring, a promising A-list project came Southern's way. Jerry Schatzberg's second film as director, *Panic in Needle Park*, starring Al Pacino, had generated considerable buzz at Cannes. Twentieth Century-Fox asked him what he would like to do next. With a development deal in hand, he hired Southern, whom he knew socially when he co-owned a discotheque in the late sixties.

"Nathanael West was one of my favorites," remembers Schatzberg. "I had read all his stuff. The people at Fox didn't know who [West was]. They just knew *Panic* was getting good reviews and they wanted to do something with me. So I suggested *A Cool Million* and they said, 'Oh yeah, anything.' The book was tied up. I think Columbia had the rights to it. My agent had to get the rights through Columbia and we started to work on it with Martin Bregman as the producer. I told him I wanted Terry to write this and our agents talked and all that and Terry came in. I think we worked for about a week. He drank all my liquor and we didn't get very much done. So I told him that he would come at this time, at this hour, and we would write this thing together. And that just worked very good . . . he was brilliant with dialogue. And we had a lot of fun."

Timothy Bottoms was discussed as Lemuel Pitkin, the young hopeful, trying to pursue the Horatio Alger dream in an America where everyone is

on the make. Faye Dunaway was considered as well. Donald Pleasance and
Sally Struthers were other names who came up as possible casting choices.
Schatzberg and Southern attempted to work in allusions to Nixon and
Watergate. Schatzberg enjoyed the process of working hands-on with
Southern, but he was surprised at how much pushing Southern needed.

"I think he was just insecure like all artists are. We used to eat, drink,
talk, joke, laugh, and fart and whatever would go. Then his girlfriend
would come by to pick him up and they'd sit here and finish the rest of my
liquor. I just put a stop to it. I love having fun, but we were getting paid to
[write this]."

Schatzberg was pleased with the script, but the results got tied up in
Twentieth Century-Fox's bureaucracy.

"They read the script. . . . [Richard] Zanuck may have said, 'Yes, let
[Schatzberg] do a script, do a film,' and then the guy who read the script
didn't understand it. That's usually what happens. Our agents tried to keep
it happening, but I guess it was a little bit too bizarre for them. Probably
now, in the last ten years, somebody like Terry Gilliam could do it. With
different kind of money. I could probably do it [now] with some European
money. . . . But it's still a good idea. I remember I talked to Terry about it
once. It's still an interesting screenplay. I guess the screenplay is still ours. . . .
Anytime in this business when you can give them some good name or project they go 'yeah, yeah.' Then they read the script and close the door. It's a
bizarre business and it's still the same."

Merlin, yet another promising screenplay from this period, was written
for a producer who hoped to get Mick Jagger to play the lead of an
Arthurian knight who is close to the magician. Southern remained close to
the Stones, especially Keith Richards, but Jagger's commitment to a film
project was always a tentative proposition. Still, Terry's friendship with the
world's greatest rock 'n' roll band gave him a ringside seat at one of the
biggest media events of the summer of 1972.

Southern accompanied the Rolling Stones on their first U.S. tour since
the disastrous December 5, 1969, Altamont concert. He was covering the
tour for the *Saturday Review* along with Richard Ellman from *Esquire* and
Truman Capote for *Rolling Stone* (Capote never turned in his copy). In
addition to the roadies, groupies, and prestigious scribes, the Stones were
followed by a shifting cast of café society types such as Lee Radziwill and
her then boyfriend, photographer Peter Beard; Atlantic Records head
Ahmet Ertegun; Andy Warhol; and Mick's estranged wife, Bianca.

Documenting this intriguing collision of sense and sensibility was Beat photographer and filmmaker, Robert Frank. Working with a two-man crew, Frank shadowed the Stones and Company to compile the official documentary of the tour, provisionally entitled *Cocksucker Blues,* the title of a song Jagger had written to fulfill the Stones' contract with Decca Records. Gluttons for punishment, the Stones had commissioned Frank to document the tour cinema verité fashion. *Gimme Shelter* should have been a warning. In the Maysles Brothers film, Mick and Keith hardly come off as Albert Schweitzer types as they stare blandly at chaos and murder in the Moviola footage of Altamont. Somehow Frank had gained the Stones's confidence with his landmark black-and-white album cover design for the newly released double-album set, *Exile on Main Street.*

The tour became notorious for a level of excess monumental even by the Stones' jaded standards. Frank would detail that excess with fly-on-the-wall exactitude in his documentary. While much of the film is standard handheld, grainy rock-doc shtick—the monotony of life on the road, the interchangeable towns, the freakish adoration of American boomers—the ways in which a group of musicians could insulate themselves from the rigors of touring had never been photographed so clinically and without apology. Drugs of all kinds are used and displayed openly, from the reasonably innocuous booze and reefer to cocaine and heroin. Roadies grope seemingly compliant women like grapes on a withered vine. Their chauvinistic behavior culminates in a notorious midair gang bang on the Stones' touring plane (with Mick and Keith providing impromptu musical accompaniment). As the rich and famous drop by to chat backstage, they are greeted with varying degrees of ennui. *Cocksucker Blues* is a film about people seeing how close they can skirt despair and death and still survive.

In a cameo that he would later prefer to forget, Southern looks remarkably disheveled in jeans, matching jacket, and turtleneck. His beard is scruffy and his glasses look like the kind of cheap frames that need to be taped. It is a jarring contrast to the cool, elegant hipster in sunglasses staring from the cover of *Sgt. Pepper.* Joking backstage, Southern is filmed snorting cocaine and then saying, "If you had a million dollars a week to spend on coke, you could probably develop a habit."

As fascinating as *Cocksucker Blues* remains, when the Stones viewed it months later in the cold light of a London screening room, they unanimously agreed to shelve the film. Frank fought the decision. A compromise was arrived at. The film could be shown only with Frank in attendance in a highly structured context such as a museum. However, the Stones' decision would not halt a healthy bootleg trade in the film.

During the tour Southern befriended Peter Beard, who was supposed to be taking pictures to accompany Truman Capote's piece. Beard's combination of nihilism and gung-ho preppiness intrigued Southern.

Terry started to get excited about a possible film inspired by Beard's elegiac book on elephant hunting in Kenya, *The End of the Game*.

"Peter immediately showed me these notes for a screenplay based on his experiences in the Congo with wildlife conservation and poaching, where this entire population of elephants died off," recalled Southern. "He wanted to have a movie exploring this mismanagement . . . [with a character called] Major Thomson, this asshole British park warden and his wife and their relationship."

The End of the Game turned into a project that the two would tinker with until Southern's death. Countless directors were discussed and approached, including Nicolas Roeg. Beard even toyed with the idea of directing the script himself.

"When we first started talking, we were flying to San Francisco and there was this terrible storm," Southern recalled. "It was so severe that we had to make a wide approach to San Francisco airport, so we flew right over the Golden Gate Bridge. When we crowded around the window to look down at the bridge, we saw these buildings. . . . Truman Capote said, 'Well, that's probably the most horrible prison there is. That's San Quentin.' Keith said, 'What a gas it would be to play a gig there.' And Capote, who was ultragay, replied, 'Well, they would love it, and they would certainly love you and MICK! They would just devour Mick.' So Keith spoke to Mick about it and Mick asked Truman and me to go check it out. So we did that. The prison was a horrific situation . . . talk about stress and density . . . they had a record number of stabbings . . . in the end, basically the warden said yes, but the security people said it was [too difficult to arrange]. And there wasn't enough insurance to stage the gig."

The tour was exhausting. Terry was almost kicked off it by Peter Rudge, the tour manager, who was worried about another Altamont-type scandal. Returning to New York, Beard and Southern were greeted at JFK by Lee Radziwill.

"I had a car parked in the long-term lot at JFK. It was a blue '65 Mustang convertible," said Southern. "I was going to stay at Larry Rivers's in Southampton. We got to the airport and Lee Radziwill met us. She had no car. We told her we had made arrangements to go to Southampton. She said that's okay, she had something to do in New York, but that she would come out and pick us up. So we went to Larry Rivers's place. The next day

I got a call from Peter, who said, 'Listen, Lee Radziwill is in love with your car. She'll give you anything if she can buy it!'"

Instead of taking money for the car, Southern decided to lend it to Radziwill.

"The next thing I knew she was driving around with Jackie . . . did you ever see *Grey Gardens*? Well, they were working on that film and I didn't have the heart to reclaim the car, which they had for about two weeks. Larry had a car. So that was part of my early history with Peter Beard."

Terry's piece on the tour, "Riding the Lapping Tongue," appeared in the August 12, 1972, edition of the *Saturday Review*. The perpetually ailing journal of middlebrow liberalism was an unusual venue for one of Southern's now infrequent forays into journalism. "Riding the Lapping Tongue" was an uncertain mix of styles. Screenplay-type directions broke up various digressions on a feminist protest, a newspaper spoof describing Capote's attempts to hold the Stones ransom, Jagger's "extraordinary potential for acting," and quick collagelike descriptions of the activity on the tour plane, backstage shenanigans, and the music itself. There were flashes of the target-specific irony of "I Am Mike Hammer" and "Twirling at Ole Miss," but generally the piece was a disappointment. Southern seemed to be trying too hard to be with it. Instead of him, it was Robert Greenfield, a *Rolling Stone* freelancer who replaced the couldn't-care-less Capote, delivered the definitive account of the tour in a series of articles that were collected in his book *STP: Travels with the Rolling Stones Across America*. Greenfield managed to be sympathetic to the Stones' fishbowl existence, but also detached enough to analyze how the rebels of the sixties were becoming increasingly alienated by money and power from the counterculture they helped inspire—counterculture, Greenfield also recognized, that was beginning to show visible signs of the same decadence.

Sometime during that frenzied summer, Southern found time to do a bit of agitprop for George McGovern's campaign. At a rally in Easthampton, he cowrote a playlet that featured Taylor Mead. Josh Alan Friedman, then in his midteens, attended the rally with his father, Bruce Jay, and recalls seeing Southern's bizarre arrival.

"He really looked like a lunatic that night. His hair was disheveled. It was the height of the hippie-antiwar era and Terry amongst even the hippest people was really underground. He had Taylor Mead on one side, he had some porn star with him, some blond porn star—some tall woman who looked wiped out. They put on a sketch he had written at this performance hall. Tom Paxton played. It was a little anti–Nixon, anti–Vietnam war rally to raise money for McGovern, that kind of thing. It didn't really make sense to me. I remember Taylor Mead kept falling down in the middle of the sketch and yet it didn't matter somehow. I was asking my parents, 'Who is this disgraceful man who can't seem to recite dialogue without falling down?' I guess they just patted me on the head: 'It's all part of the show. Don't worry about it.' I remember being amazed at Taylor Mead, a guy who could be so drunk and was literally falling down as he was reciting lines."

Southern's skit, "Nixon: No Tit and Ass Man," did not exactly rank with Bertolt Brecht in its concerted attack on a corrupt political establishment. McGovern's campaign was troubled by the resignation of his running mate, Thomas Eagleton, and a general perception that he was too "pink." Although disillusionment with Vietnam was at its peak and the Watergate scandal was gaining momentum, Richard Nixon was eventually reelected.

The summer revels provided a welcome distraction from the very real cash flow problems that were making life along the Blackberry River desperate. Gail was helping to pay the mortgage by continuing to teach dance at a private girls' school. Her dreams of becoming an actress were now subsumed by her efforts to maintain a clean, well-lighted place where Terry could write.

Southern's Quality Lit reputation was still good enough for Tom Wolfe and A. W. Johnson to include "Twirling at Ole Miss" as one of the forerunners of gonzo in their anthology, *The New Journalism*. The other writers in the anthology, from contemporaries like Gay Talese and Norman Mailer to relatively new kids like Joan Didion, Michael Herr, and Hunter S. Thompson, had taken the possibilities of the diffuse genre and extended them to the limit. Like Southern, these were all writers who had grown dissatisfied with the traditional novel and short story, but it was journalism and not the cinema that had reinvigorated them. Southern might have been better off following their lead, as the cinema was proving to be a rather fickle and temperamental mistress.

Southern was entering his "I can't even get arrested" phase. With the tax problems, child support, and projects increasingly stalled in development hell, a gig as a lecturer at New York University for $1,000 per semester was nothing to sniff at. Beginning in the fall 1972 through the spring 1974, Southern taught screenwriting. His students included the future film comedy director Amy Heckerling and writers like Steven Aronson (the coauthor of the celebrated true crime book *Savage Grace*) and Lee Server, who would write about subjects as varied as pulp fiction and Asian cinema.

Southern's search for extra cash led to some humbling scenes. Tony Hendra, one of the editors at *National Lampoon,* recalls him walking into the magazine's offices offering to write anything for $100 a shot. Hendra and other *Lampoon* editors like Michael O'Donoghue felt bad for the man who was something of an icon to them.

Southern's first *Lampoon* contribution, "Hard-Corpse Pornography," appeared in the November 1972 issue. It showed that Southern's ability to shock was not lost. The piece was written in the form of a letter dashed off to Michael O'Donoghue, relating Southern's shocked discovery of an organization of Vietnam veterans involved in a clandestine practice called "gook rimming." This extreme metaphor for a war that tested the limits of absurdity and obscenity was a perfect example of form merging with content. It also pointed out that Southern's most effortless and enjoyable writing was now being done in the form of letters to friends. As wonderful as these letters were to receive, some wished Southern would apply his energies to more substantial work.

Southern's other *Lampoon* contributions were not as effective. A "collaboration" with William Burroughs, "Strange Sex We Have Known," was hyped on the front cover but was essentially two unrelated squibs grafted together by the subject of bizarre sex. "Puritan Porn" and "The Dawn of Corn-Hole" were the kind of labored dirty jokes that Nelson Lyon would come to dread when he became Southern's writing partner in the eighties. Aside from "Hard-Corpse Pornography," Southern's work for the *Lampoon* was unmemorable. Clearly the pressures of keeping the taxman at bay, diminishing fortunes, and sheer survival were stretching Terry's bullshit detector to the limit.

A mere year or two after the publication of *Blue Movie,* the kind of erotic cinema Southern believed was beyond Hollywood began to connect with the barely articulated needs of the Me Generation. Radley Metzger had started Audubon Films to mesh soft-core imagery with a European art-film style. Russ Meyer was breaking out of the exploitation circuit with films like *Faster, Pussycat! Kill! Kill!* In Baltimore, John Waters was mounting his assault on the middle class with *Pink Flamingos. Deep Throat* and *Behind the Green Door* brought hard-core to the suburbs. Then there was Marlon Brando giving Maria Schneider a bit more than the Method in *Last Tango in Paris.*

Along with Gore Vidal, William Burroughs, and Sylvia Miles, Southern served as a jury member at the 1972 New York Erotic Film Festival; a compilation film was later released. Southern met Nelson Lyon, the director of one of the entries, *The Telephone Book,* a dark satire about obscene phone calls. The two would become close friends and collaborators in the eighties.

The commercial success and media attention surrounding these disparate films briefly opened the door to the notion that anything was possible in commercial cinema. Certainly Southern thought so. As he enthused to Michael Perkins at *Screw,* ". . . we're getting into a golden age of filmmaking with videotape. There'll be no censorship or sponsor problems. It will be the era of the home-made dirty movie. Imagine the enormous impact that will have."

These were prophetic words. Video would indeed have an enormous impact . . . on the coffers of the major studios and the adult film industry concentrated in the San Fernando Valley. Its emancipating effect on American culture would remain minimal.

Still the early seventies seemed ripe for mind-expanding forays into the erotic. At least that was the idea behind *Fourplay,* an ambitious anthology film pitched by Carl Gurevich in the winter of 1973. Drawing upon a mysterious source of capital (eventually $700,000), the neophyte producer hired a group of writers—Jack Richardson, Bruce Jay Friedman, Dan Greenburg, and Southern—to write four half-hour original scripts exploring sexuality in our time, or something to that effect. John G. Avildsen, the director of *Joe,* which starred Peter Boyle as a right-wing construction worker turned vigilante, agreed to direct one of the episodes. This creative team, rounded out by coproducer Amy Ephron, then Greenburg's sister-in-law, began preproduction.

As documented in an amusing *Playboy* article by Dan Greenberg, Southern's contribution was a piece called "Twice on Top." In imagery and tone, it resembled something from Luis Buñuel's *Discreet Charm of the Bourgeoisie* or *Phantom of Liberty* period. Rip Torn had agreed to play the part of a judge who sentences a woman to be executed because of her failure to climax. Gurevich and Southern eventually fell out over the latter's apparent failure to deliver. According to Amy Ephron, Southern had written two scripts—one called "Slippery when Wet," about a group of swingers at a Long Island house and "Twice on Top." Gurevich asked for a rewrite and Southern apparently merged part of "Slippery" into "Twice on Top." He also tried to convince Gurevich to get William Claxton to direct his segment. Gurevich dubbed Southern a hustler, "a Bobby Riggs of the literary world," using his $10,000 script fee to run up restaurant and hotel bills instead of sitting down to write.

Foreplay, as the film was finally known, stumbled into a few theaters in 1975 sans Southern's involvement. Most of the film was structured around Avildsen's contribution, "Inaugural Ball," written by David Odell, in which the president's daughter is kidnapped. The ransom consists of forcing the president and first lady to have sex on national television. Zero Mostel played the leader of the free world.

In the midst of teaching and gigs like *Foreplay*, Southern began work on his first novel since *Blue Movie, Double Date*. Southern wrote a treatment to get an advance from Dell and fleshed out the book as a possible screenplay. Both dealt with the elaborate efforts of Jimmy Wilson, a trendy young stockbroker, to date two women, Pamela and Vickie, at the same time. He does this by pretending to have a twin brother, Rod, a laid-back, longhaired swinger. Jimmy's ruse becomes more complicated to sustain when the women demand more of Jimmy and his fictional brother. *Double Date* would explore the moral as well as sexual implications of Jimmy's con:

> [Jimmy] is now, in effect, *screwing four different girls at the same time*. It is a grand ego-trip for him, and his highly buoyant spirits reflect his sense of triumph.
>
> Gradually though he becomes vaguely disturbed by the realization that *both girls have betrayed him*—Pam by making it with "Rod," and Vickie by making it with "Jimmy." As Jimmy, he quizzes Vickie about *her* feelings for "Rod," and as Rod, he quizzes Vickie about *her* feelings for "Jimmy." Both girls, of course, firmly deny any interest beyond mere friendship, and that due to the fact that "he is, after all, your *brother*." Yet, as Jimmy, he knows that "Rod" has been clandestinely screwing Pamela; and as Rod, he knows that "Jimmy" has been clandestinely screwing Vickie.
>
> On the other hand, from the girls' point of view:
> (1) Pamela knows that Rod is screwing both her *and* Vickie.
> (2) Vickie knows that Jimmy is screwing both her *and* Pamela.
> (3) Pamela does *not* know that Jimmy is also screwing Vickie.
> (4) Vickie does *not* know that Rod is also screwing Pamela.
> (5) And neither girl, of course, suspects that Jimmy and Rod are the same person.

Southern selected an Arthur Miller quote as an epigraph for his novel-in-progress: "There is no power on Earth that can break the grip of a man with his hands on his own throat."

Double Date excited sufficient anticipation that Jann Wenner wrote to

Southern on June 20 and July 16 asking to see excerpts. Wenner was hoping to boost the sales of *Rolling Stone* with a peek at a counterculture hero's latest salvo at establishment mores. Given the prominence Hunter S. Thompson achieved through *Rolling Stone,* Southern's lack of response seemed puzzling. Southern eventually stopped working on *Double Date,* much to Dell's displeasure. The material that survives is sketchy but tantalizing. *Double Date* foreshadowed David Cronenberg's masterful 1988 film *Dead Ringers,* where twin gynecologists pretend to be the same man in order to share the bed of a movie-star patient. Distracted by money problems and the allure of another *Strangelove* lurking around the corner, Southern lacked the commitment and focus to take the premise to the limit.

During the summer of 1973, Southern exchanged a series of letters with Kubrick. In one he broached the issue of whether there was anything Kubrick was mad at Southern for. Kubrick replied: "Have no concern about yours truly being against his true friend. I have nothing but great fondness and respect for you, and wish that there was something we could do together."

In another letter, Southern asks Kubrick about permission to use of his *Blue Movie* points (which Southern and Kubrick jointly owned in a complicated deal) to keep the IRS at bay. All Kubrick could really do was not stand in Southern's way if and when a movie deal became possible.

These pressures were not made any easier to endure when Southern read an article by Sam Merrill called "Mason Hoffenberg Gets in a Few Licks" in the October 1973 issue of *Playboy.*

Hoffenberg was currently living in Woodstock, New York, hanging out with the Band's Richard Manuel and doing very little except drinking. He had managed to kick heroin after entering a methadone program. The interview was conducted in a bar where Hoffenberg downed eight vodka martinis without looking any the worse for it. The bulk of the article simply recorded Hoffenberg's acerbic comments on his situation. However, the sarcastic asides about Jack Kerouac and Henry Miller eventually drifted over to a foul-tempered assault on his more celebrated *Candy* collaborator. Among the gibes were such black pearls of bitterness as "Terry screwed me," "I'm the guy who turned him onto everything in Paris," and "Terry is a good rewriter and he writes some funny shit himself but he always grabs top billing."

The last comment Southern found particularly hurtful. It was an accusation that had haunted him in his work on *Dr. Strangelove* and *Easy Rider.* Now here was Mason, whom he had stood loyally by in their dispute with

Girodias, dismissing him as a hack, square, and drunk. Instead of dismissing Mason's comments as typically grumpy Masonisms, Southern vowed he would sue. In a lawsuit he filed against Mason and *Playboy,* he would allege that Mason's characterization of him as an alcoholic had cost him some valuable screenwriting jobs.

As understandable as Southern's sense of betrayal was, Mason was right. Southern was an alcoholic, albeit a functioning one. He drank at various times of the day to buoy his spirits or hide his shyness. It was the cause of bitter arguments between him and Gail, who often had to drag him back to the car when he fell asleep after a heavy evening at Elaine's or some other funky bistro. Southern was in no danger of ending up a skid-row bum, but he drank too much for his own good. Still, coming from a major junkie like Hoffenberg, the "alcoholic" tag stung.

At Christmastime, Southern heard that Henry Green had died on December 13, 1973, in London. They had been out of touch since 1960. Green, who hadn't written anything since that time, had ensconced himself in his Belgravia flat to get down to some heavy drinking and frantic inactivity. His last days were one long dying sigh.

Southern had successfully transcended Green's influence in his novels after *Flash and Filigree,* but his infatuation with film would probably have puzzled Green. Green recognized that Southern shared his precious and fragile gift for shaping language and narrative. While Southern might have been better off dedicating himself to expanding the limits of the novel, he was too restless and curious to let the shyness he shared with Green mutate into isolation and alienation. Still Southern was paying a price for the choices he had made in leaving Quality Lit for the film world. As Southern threw himself into screenplays and treatments over which he had less and less control or emotional involvement, an odd kind of creative laziness was reinforced. Southern was becoming less and less choosy about what he wrote. As 1973 came to a close, Hoffenberg's bitterness and Green's lonely death cast a long shadow.

Blue Movie became the next project that seemed to hold the most potential for getting the green light. Southern had somehow convinced Mike Nichols and Warner Bros. to film the novel, in his words, "as a full-on erection-and-penetration movie using big-name stars." John Calley, who as production chief at Warner Bros. had green-lighted such difficult projects as Kubrick's *A Clockwork Orange* and John Boorman's *Deliverance,* hired Terry to write an adaptation especially for Nichols. Southern flew out to L.A. and began working on the script at the Chateau Marmont.

"As soon as I had this news and was convinced that it was for real, I started immediately, without even getting into a contract, and working and doing it," recalled Southern. "We did eventually have a script, but the deals didn't go through. That was as close to a movie ever being made as I ever experienced and had ever heard of. There didn't seem to be any possible deal-breaking element. It was just a total freak thing."

Southern completed a promising first draft, but *Blue Movie* fell apart over a dispute over points between Nichols/Calley/Warners and Ringo Starr, who had the option on the novel. A key stumbling block was that Nichols wanted to retain control over the distribution of points so that he could use them in negotiating with actors—an understandable strategy given the desire to make the adaptation as faithful in its explicitness to the book as possible.

In a letter to Calley dated April 16, 1975, Southern writes: "It is really too grotesquely absurd that what could be a fantastic and innovative ('the porn to end all porn') film not be made because of point considerations. After all, if a film makes, as this one could, 200 million what difference does it make if you've got one per cent or two-and-a-half per cent. . . . The main point, John, is this—your instinct, hip savvy, and general know-how told you the TIME WAS RIPE. Well, it is, and it does not depend on Nichols. What about Stanley? Or Coppola?"

As both Southern's novel and adaptation demonstrate, *Blue Movie* remains one of the great dream projects of film history. Conceived at a time when mainstream and "adult" filmmakers were looking over the fence at each other with Oscars and dollar signs in their eyes, under Nichols's direction, the results could have rivaled *Dr. Strangelove* as a satiric land-mark. But as *Blue Movie*'s auteur character tells his crew, perhaps some things are beyond the magic of the lens:

"I wish I were able to to give each of you a finished script today—but, since I am not, I'll tell you a little about the film. It's called 'Act of Love,' and that is what it's about—the physical act of love under various circum-stances. I want to do something which has never, so far as I know, been done before—namely, to portray lovemaking as the beautiful thing that it is—not something sordid, or furtive, or ludicrously grotesque . . . but exquisitely beautiful. You understand we're not talking about pornography here, we're talking about the aesthetically erotic . . . the act of love. . . .You see . . . it may not be possible . . . it may be that there is something so inherently personal about love-making that no cinematic portrayal of it can ever be shared by a theatre audience—an audience of strangers . . . each self-consciously aware of other's presence. (Shrugs.) That's what we shall find out. One thing is certain—we can make a film that is immeasurably more successful in that respect than any film ever made."

Southern had devoted most of 1974 and 1975 to working with Ringo Starr and Kubrick to get the appropriate clearances on *Blue Movie*. Southern and Kubrick had a respective sixty/forty split in the novel and on possible options and film sales in the Starr/Warners/ Nichols deal. A lot of Terry's early script work before Warners came on board had been done for a modest couple of thousand dollars doled out by Ringo's lawyer.

John Calley felt bad about the collapse of *Blue Movie*. He had always admired "You're Too Hip, Baby" and asked Southern to work on a script provisionally titled *The Paris Musician's Story*.

"[Calley] had the idea of a screenplay set in Paris dealing with those characters," said Southern. "It did get as far as an outline, which I was paid for, but nothing further was pursued. When *Blue Movie* fell through, that was really the end of our relationship."

During the ups and downs of the *Blue Movie* project, "Fixing up Ert," a new short story, appeared in the September 1974 issue of *Oui* magazine. Inspired by an anecdote related to Southern by John Calley, the story was the first of a series of "con game" stories that Southern turned out occasionally from mid-1970 through 1985. Part tall tale, part barroom joke, the story's flimsy source of inspiration was redeemed only by Southern's mix of the ribald and genteel. A young stockbroker convinces Ertegun, a hated rival, to drop off some papers at the home of an important client, Duchess Marleton, a Park Avenue matron with an obsession for cleanliness. Ertegun has been told that if he shows up at her apartment and defecates on her carpet when she leaves the room, he will be rewarded with fellatio and other sexual delights. The story's payoff depends entirely on the reader's willingness to believe that Ertegun is such a horny fool that he will do anything to get laid, including losing a valuable client. "Fixing Up Ert" was sadly the only kind of Quality Lit Southern appeared to have the patience to see through.

Strange and more dubious projects came over the transom. One dark and stormy night, a six-foot-plus Norwegian director, Ingmar Ejve, showed up at East Canaan like Mark Twain's mysterious stranger and asked

Southern to adapt *The Hunters of Karin Hall,* an obscure novel by Carl-Henning Wijkmark.

Karin Hall was Hermann Goering's country estate during the thirties and forties, where the German Luftwaffe commander and invited guests indulged in elaborate feasts, sex orgies, and hunting treks. In the novel, a Swedish athlete is recruited by the British to spy on Goering and finds himself caught up in a series of power plays within the Nazi Party. Full of baroque touches, Terry's *Karin Hall* screenplay features this bizarre moment after a wild boar hunt reaches its gory denouement:

WOLKENSCHATZ begins rolling up Goering's sleeve to give him
an injection, notices the two hares tied to his belt.

WOLKENSCHATZ
Ah, a splendid brace of Hungarian hares! Good shooting, Your
Excellency!

GOERING (dourly)
Hmm, I think I got a Beater as well.

WOLKENSCHATZ (shocked)
Oh no!

GOERING
Be thankful it wasn't the British Ambassador!
(Impatiently) Will you hurry?
Wolkenschatz has the syringe prepared, but looks around anxiously.

GOERING (demands)
Now what, in God's great name?

WOLKENSCHATZ (at a loss)
I've nothing to tie off the vein with, Your Excellency.

GOERING (disgusted)
Oh for God's sake! Use your head, will you?
(He looks around.)

WOLKENSCHATZ
A boot-lace perhaps?
Goering's eye falls on a two-foot length of boar's intestine lying

nearby. He seizes it, ties it around his bare arm above the elbow, holding one end of it (classic 'Man With Golden Arm' style) in his teeth.

> GOERING (muttering between clenched teeth)
> Ingenuity! Where do you think the German people would be today without it? Hit me, Colonel, hit me!
> Wolkenschatz deftly makes the injection.

Arlene Donovan at ICM was handling Terry's film work at the time. Another of her clients was David Newman. He read *The Hunters of Karin Hall* but wasn't crazy about it: "Actually I was in the middle of my Nazi period, which a number of us went through. Bruce Friedman is another one. It started with the Albert Speer book, where we became Nazi freaks and read every book about Hitler, Goering, and Goebbels for about three years. We're still trying to figure out the reason why all these Jewish writers suddenly became fascinated with the Nazis. I have a lot of theories about it but I knew all about that period and I knew it well. I knew that Karin Hall was where they used to dress up in forest green Robin Hood outfits with bows and arrows, hunt deer or boar and blow hunting horns. Herman Goering and his Nazi crowd. I thought, 'Ohmigod, Terry Southern and that subject, this is going to be the greatest script since *Strangelove*.' And I thought, 'This is so great, I can't wait, this is going to be so wonderful,' and I called Arlene and said Terry asked if you could get a copy of that screenplay to me and she said 'yes' and I heard something in her voice that was very reticent.

"[*Karin Hall*] was like Terry parodying Terry instead of being genuinely outrageous. It was strange, whatever it was. Since then I have read scripts of lesser quality and they've been made. Probably if I got a chance to read it again, I would like it a lot more. I remember having this sinking feeling of 'Oh, what's happened here?' because this is not the level of work for Terry. I knew there was no way in the world that I could call anybody I knew and say, 'Here's this movie you've gotta make,' because I really didn't believe that it was. Consequently, I might have mentioned it to somebody, but I didn't come on strong about it to anybody. So I always felt bad about that. I felt bad that I didn't like it more and I felt bad that I couldn't do anything about it."

Since Southern was the only known element in the *Karin Hall* package, the Norweigan producers were unable to attract additional backing.

Then Ted Kotcheff approached Terry about working on a Watergate script. Kotcheff was finishing work on *Fun with Dick and Jane,* a comedy starring Jane Fonda and George Segal as an unemployed suburban couple who turn to bank robbing. Southern did some uncredited rewriting on the film's problematic ending. Warners felt confident that *Fun with Dick and Jane* was going to be a hit (which it was) and gave Kotcheff development money to hire Southern to write *A Piece of Bloody Cake.*

"*A Piece of Bloody Cake* was ahead of its time," recalled Kotcheff. "I thought *All the President's Men* was a decent piece of work, but it concentrated on the newspaper reporters. This script was about the actual people involved in the break-in like Gordon Liddy and the guy who thought he was James Bond. It was about how these sociopaths suck otherwise normal people into their crazy power fantasies. For example, Liddy wanted to stock this houseboat with call girls and film Democrats being fucked on camera. There was also a scene where these White House plumbers stage hippies having sex on the American flag and plan to insert this footage into antiwar films."

A Piece of Bloody Cake is a remarkably sedate piece of writing. The absurdity of the Watergate conspiracy emerges slowly as the script cross-cuts between the growing reservations of a clean-cut FBI family man assigned to the Nixon team and the black security guard who will stumble upon the break-in. If the film had been made, it would have made an appropriate companion piece to Francis Coppola's *The Conversation.*

Kotcheff was unable to get the script approved. Southern mailed a copy to Kubrick, who once again responded with a friendly and noncommittal "read with interest and pleasure and will advise."

Still things were looking up. The time spent with Kotcheff in Los Angeles had brought in enough money for Southern to forge ahead. Terry secured a prestigious commission from CBS to write a script for *The American Parade,* a series of historical teleplays designed to commemorate America's Bicentennial. CBS gave the producers an unusual amount of freedom. William Claxton ended up directing Terry's contribution, *Stop Thief!,* starring another friend, Rip Torn, as Boss Tweed. It was aired on August 21, 1975. Reviews were lukewarm applauding the series' good intentions, but with little enthusiasm. Americans may have been proud of their history, but they preferred not to watch it on network television, thank you. *Stop Thief!* would be Southern's only on-screen credit in the seventies.

That same summer, Southern went out to visit Torn in New Mexico on the set of Nicolas Roeg's *The Man Who Fell to Earth.* Si Litvinoff and Max

Raab were the producers of the film. Terry decided to take Nile, now fourteen, along. It was a chance to meet one of his heroes, David Bowie. Nile recalls a strange interlude visiting Bowie at his motel, where it was obvious that the rock star's relationship with costar Candy Clark went beyond simply rehearsing lines together. During a couple of days off, Terry, Rip, and Nile went on a classic hunting and fishing trip in the country. It was the kind of outing Terry felt every boy should have with his father.

According to David Cammell, who was an associate producer on the film, Southern raised a few eyebrows by taking off on the trip with a car belonging to the production. Southern was getting his expenses covered by Litvinoff and Raab with the hope that he would write a magazine piece about the making of the film. Instead, Roeg decided to film Southern playing himself in a scene where the media gather as Thomas Newton, the Bowie character, is about to embark on a space mission. The scene was cut out of the initial theatrical release and then later restored when a "director's cut" was issued on video and laser disc in the mid-nineties.

For the rest of the fall and winter, Southern stuck pretty close to home in Connecticut. He worked on a couple of highly speculative projects including a teleplay called *On the Loose,* with William Claxton and Michael Parks. Southern had known the cult actor, who became famous for his role in the TV series *Then Came Bronson,* since his Filmways days. Parks enjoyed Southern's company immensely, but he was unable to pay Terry more than a nominal fee for the work he did. Southern tried not to complain when these funds did not appear as expected. Although as a tense answering-machine message from the period suggests, Southern's patience and generosity barely disguised his desperate need for cash. He was still living beyond his means and the house in Canaan was a constant drain on his resources.

Some more pin money came his way when Earl McGrath, then the Rolling Stones' manager, arranged for Southern to accompany photographer Annie Leibowitz on the group's Black and Blue tour. A coffee-table book with Southern's text was the plan. In sharp contrast to 1972, this tour was quite sedate. Jagger had become more involved in the detailed planning of the tour and there was little room for the kind of twenty-four-hour partying of yore. The tour was notable for its elaborate set designed around the lapping-tongue logo of Rolling Stones Records. At a key moment during concerts, a giant air-filled phallus would billow up from the stage and confetti burst out over the group and audience. This type of gimmicky Vegas-style showmanship would dominate live concerts of the late seventies. The coffee-table book did not emerge until 1978, but Southern kept the Stones camp amused with a parody tabloid paper called *The Record World*.

After the Stones tour, Southern and Gail again retreated to the Hamptons to visit Larry Rivers. Another script idea was discussed. Yet again, it focused on one of Rivers's obsessions, sex. Southern wrote a treatment called *Johnny Stud,* which referred to one of two inflatable dolls that a fashionable couple "uses" for amusement.

As the decade passed the halfway mark, the Southern scorecard was looking bare. *A Cool Million, Blue Movie,* and *A Piece of Bloody Cake* were bright prospects that never quite gelled. The other work—the occasional magazine piece, the teaching, and spec work with friends—brought in some extra cash. Southern was doing his best to stay positive and keep busy. He didn't stop to notice that he was turning invisible.

10
Junky

Good writers have so much (dare I say 'beauty and excitement'?) to come back to that they are likely not to stray far afield for any great length of time," Southern wrote in an unpublished essay about drugs and the writer. He added that heroin was the exception to this theory. The effect of the seductive opiate "is to reduce everything to a single glow, where it is no longer a question of doing or becoming—one is. A difficult package for anyone to resist. Almost no one kicks a major junk habit; only super-artists, whose work is even stronger than the drug itself: Burroughs and Miles Davis are rather obvious examples. Mere mortals, however, beware."

If these cautionary words were in Terry's mind when he embarked on the ill-fated adaptation of William Burroughs's first novel, *Junky,* one can only guess. The project surfaced at a time when, rightly or wrongly, a perception of Southern as a "druggie" or "hippie" had dramatically slowed down his influence and power in the Hollywood creative community. There was considerable hypocrisy in this kind of labeling. Hollywood was awash in cocaine by the end of the seventies. It was the decade's drug of choice. When its presence at informal meetings and parties was as ubiquitous as a lunchtime martini was in the fifties, the question of who had a problem with blow was moot.

Nonetheless Southern's druggie image, regardless of its validity, did not help his stature in the ever-shifting pecking order of Hollywood. In the substance-abuse department, Dexamyl was Terry's real crutch. The amphetamine was a popular diet pill in the fifties that gained popularity because it didn't lead to the horrific downers of other forms of speed. As Southern began juggling screenplays and script-doctoring assignments, the need to "dex it" became more neccesary. The drug gave him the psychological and physical support he needed to complete huge chunks of writing in a short time and still have energy left for some rest and recreation. Combined with Terry's drinking, Dexamyl had a damaging effect on his constitution. He gained and lost weight radically throughout the seventies. Unlike *Paris Review* colleagues like Peter Matthiessen and George Plimpton, who were more physically active, Southern did not take care of himself. Photographs from the decade show dramatic changes in Southern's appearance. Sometimes he looked bloated and heavy. Then after a few weeks at his East Canaan dacha, he would emerge fresh-faced and energetic again. But the years were taking a heavier toll on him than they should have.

For the first half of the seventies, Southern had endured the IRS, the still-birth of *Blue Movie,* and an almost complete estrangement from Quality Lit. The oppressiveness of career and money problems had been compounded by Richard Nixon, Watergate, inflation, the seemingly endless Vietnam conflict, and then its dispiriting conclusion with the fall of Saigon. These events had sapped much of Southern's sixties optimism. However, the election of Jimmy Carter in the fall of 1976 gave Southern hope. There were also some fascinating signs of cultural revolution as punk, disco, and reggae surfaced in the clubs. He had been to CBGB a couple of times and dug the scene. He was especially fond of Debbie Harry, the peroxided lead singer of Blondie.

Southern's financial pressures and doubts about his screenwriting career had been lightened by a Washington lawyer, Richard Ben-Veniste, who obtained some of Terry's files through the Freedom of Information Act. The files Ben-Veniste was able to get released were not as voluminous as some suspected. In early 1965, the FBI had Terry under surveillance because of *Candy* and *Dr. Strangelove.* An informant had led the FBI to believe that Southern was in possession of a cache of pornographic films and other material. Further investigation (which mainly involved watching who visited Terry in East Canaan) led to this vague filing:

> With reference to the pornographic library of films which SOUTHERN allegedly has in his possession, it is not known to this office whether it is a local violation in Connecticut to display films to "guests" and it is therefore left to the discretion of the Bureau as to whether such information should be made available, strictly on a confidential basis, to a local law enforcement agency covering SOUTHERN's place of residence.

The rest of the FBI's watch on Southern consisted of monitoring the vigorous sales of *Candy* in Hartford despite the efforts of the vice squad to get distributors to remove copies from bookstores and newsstands. Carol Southern was also described as a "'beatnick' [*sic*], in that, she is sloppy and extremely dirty." As Terry recalled it, the times she was probably spotted were when she was working in the garden or surrounding grounds and wore appropriate clothing for such work.

As with much of the FBI's surveillance of writers, the reports revealed little more than bureaucratic stupidity and overkill. The FBI appears to have lost interest in Southern very quickly. Still the released reports were not pleasant reading for Southern or Gerber. They had felt terrorized by their treatment by the IRS. In 1972, Andy Warhol and Robert Rauschenberg had been audited not long after their public endorsement of the McGovern campaign. The two artists were able to pay what they owed and continue with their work, but the effect was chilling. Things were starting to improve a little bit for Terry. Through his lawyer, Peter Herbst, he had negotiated an offer of compromise with the IRS.

As the Carter administration entered the White House, Southern began to get sucked into a new Hollywood pipe dream appropriately called *Junky*. It was a project that had the potential to be a New Hollywood classic like *Easy Rider* or the recently released *One Flew Over the Cuckoo's Nest*. It would be a chance to bring the dark vision of his grand good friend Bill Burroughs to the screen.

Jacques Stern, an old Beat Hotel friend of Burroughs with connections to the Rothschild family, was now living in New York. A childhood bout with polio had left him wheelchair-bound. His lawyer, Joe Bianco, had helped him form an offshore entity, Automatique Ltd., to develop film projects. Burroughs and Stern had an odd love-hate relationship in which old slights hadn't quite been forgotten. Nonetheless, Burroughs was grateful when Stern decided to produce *Junky*. Of all Burroughs's novels, it had the most obvious appeal as a commercial film venture. Published in 1951 as a cheapie Ace paperback under the pseudonym Bill Lee, *Junky* remains a fascinating first-person account of heroin addiction in the forties. It was the book that gave Burroughs the confidence to become a writer and pursue the groundbreaking vision of *Naked Lunch*.

Under the terms of Stern's option of *Junky*, Burroughs was to receive a $20,000 advance up front. Southern was taken on as screenwriter and Dennis Hopper would act and direct in the proposed film. They, too, received $20,000. The film's total budget was estimated at $1.7 million and

Stern and Bianco had reserved hotel suites to conduct presales meetings at
the Cannes Film Festival in May.

On March 3, 1977, Burroughs, Southern, and Hopper received their
checks at a party organized at Jean Stein's Central Park West apartment to
celebrate. Gerard Malanga took a picture of the group.

"It was kind of vague why all this was happening," recalled Malanga.
"Here's Dennis Hopper, here's Terry, here's Bill. Something must have
happened because it didn't get off the ground. That's always a big mystery.
[Stern] was kind of a wiry guy like Steve Buscemi. Really thin with the hair
dangling down the side. That day I think I took one photo of Jacques in the
wheelchair on the side. . . . I don't know why but I always associated
Jacques Stern's name with drugs."

A press release issued on March 14, 1977, by Abracadabra Productions
(a rather unfortunate name given the eventual poof-and-it's-gone nature of
Stern's completion guarantee for *Junky*) and Automatique Ltd. optimisti-
cally stated that filming would commence on July 15 with principal locations in New York and Mexico City.

On paper, the *Junky* team didn't look entirely crazy. Hopper arranged
for Paul Lewis to sign on as a line producer on spec. In addition to working
as the production manager for *Easy Rider,* Lewis had worked with Peter
Bogdanovich and Brian De Palma. Hopper and Southern's mutual friend
Jean Stein also lent her moral support and name to *Junky*. Paul Wasserman
agreed to handle public relations.

Ted Morgan in his biography of Burroughs described the *Junky* project as a yearlong orgy of drugs, booze, and reckless spending. True,
Hopper, then in the throes of his own addictions, was not in the best shape
to command a feature film. He was, to his credit, trying to use work as a
way of coping with his demons. He had just returned from the Philippines,
where he had completed a role as a war photographer in *Apocalypse Now,*
when the *Junky* project began to percolate. James Grauerholz, Burroughs's
companion and secretary, remembers Hopper saying that his feelings were
really hurt because Brando wouldn't act opposite him in front of the camera. Most of his scenes with Brando were played to the air.

High-strung and agitated, Hopper was hoping *Junky* would put him
back in the director's chair after the debacle of *The Last Movie.* Burroughs
was still getting used to New York life. He was living in the Bunker, a former
YMCA locker room converted into a Bowery apartment. His assistant,
James Grauerholz, helped to reorganize his business affairs. Both
Grauerholz and Burroughs were hoping a feature film might generate

income and interest in Burroughs's books. Southern obviously needed the money, but he was also excited about working with a kindred spirit and great friend. If any screenwriter understood the underground milieu that had shaped Burroughs, it was Terry.

March and April were dominated by a flurry of activity surrounding the script. Terry and Gail moved into room 320 of the Gramercy Park Hotel to be close to Stern's apartment at 11 Gramercy Park South. They were able to look out on the private garden and watch Stern glide over from his apartment in his motorized wheelchair. As one might imagine, Stern's Strangelovian appearance was a source of quiet amusement to Southern.

"Stern was trained as a physicist," said Southern. "He would doodle these mathematics equations. He would get mad at Burroughs and claim that Burroughs prevented him from winning the Nobel Prize by telling people that Stern was on junk. I would ask Stern, 'What is your first language? French?' 'No, my first language is mathematics!' Burroughs would say to Stern, 'Go on, show Terry your stuff,' and Stern would write out these long, beautiful intricate equations. Stern was a complete decadent drug user. He had paralysis from polio, which left him wheelchair-bound, and he lived in Gramercy Park . . . he had this hypodermic-type device taped to his wrist. All he had to do was tap this device and he would get a jolt of speedballs made from heroin and cocaine. We would see him coming out of his brownstone town house zooming around in the wheelchair. He was ultra-lucid. He had these two girls, one black and one white, both wearing short miniskirts, who were his assistants. One was a philosophy student. They were just sort of gofers and when called upon would perform certain unnatural acts for Stern."

Southern would spent the day writing the script based on the meetings, which would lead to parties or dinners. It was another business-mixed-with-pleasure scenario that Southern thrived on. He carried a small tape recorder around to record the free-flowing discussions. On one tape is recorded a very drunk dinner where Hopper, Southern, and Burroughs try to remember Jean Cocteau's advice to the young poet. "Étonne-moi!" croaks Burroughs. Hopper says, "Astonish me, man." Terry begins to recite the quote in a Chill Wills–type accent.

Once again, Southern was the man in the room with the pen and paper. His genial demeanor and laid-back working methods gave the mistaken impression he wasn't doing anything. Stern's erratic behavior was also making Burroughs and Grauerholz nervous.

"I remember one time Jacques Stern was on a cocaine rampage and said that he was going to get Samuel Beckett to play William," recalls Grauerholz. "Or to play somebody, I don't know who. Then [Jacques] picked up the phone and supposedly reached Beckett and demanded that he take this part. I just remember one side of the conversation. He could have been talking to the dry cleaner downstairs. But he screamed at [the phone] and hung up."

Another observer of the *Junky* story sessions was Victor Bockris, then a contributor to magazines like *Interview* and *High Times*. Bockris was spending a great deal of time playing Boswell to Burroughs's Johnson with plans to turn the table talk into a book. He felt that Hopper saw *Junky* in less than collaborative terms.

"I think that Burroughs had a lot of trouble with Hopper in that situation because in the script conference Hopper would be so coked up that he would just talk for hours and hours and not listen to anything Burroughs had to say. Bill would say, 'Now listen to me and shut up!' Which is rare for Burroughs, and they did listen to him. There was a certain amount of annoyance with Hopper. [Ted] Morgan may have picked up on that and misinterpreted it and thought it may have had to do with Terry . . . . a lot of people were left blaming each other for why [*Junky*] fell apart. I'm sure it had something to do with Jacques Stern.

"The whole thing from the beginning was a combination of really nutty people who needed someone really together—a practical overseer for the project. Jacques Stern couldn't be that person, so the whole thing broke down. It was a drag, because it was a very good idea."

Increasingly it became apparent in the story meetings that Hopper wanted to set *Junky* in the present. Burroughs and Grauerholz believed the original 1940s setting would be less familiar, and thus more fascinating, to viewers. Stern had his own bizarre vision of *Junky*—another treatment called *The Creation of Adam*, a freewheeling look at the history of narcotics enforcement in America, whose specifics changed on a daily basis. Southern kept writing pages that stayed close to the book, but would occasionally throw in the odd idea by the others.

On April 30, a series of meetings hosted by Joe Bianco was held to break some bad news. Stern, as it turned out, had been heavily dependent on a group of West German partners—Abracadabra Productions—who were now pulling out of *Junky*. Although Stern was rumored to be worth around $14 million, most of these assets were tied up in offshore accounts or inaccessible tax shelters.

Bianco's announcement deepened a growing divide between the principal players. The only thing that held them together was that they all wanted to make a film of *Junky*—except Stern, who still held the option. In a weird sort of Machiavellian way, it looked as if *Junky* was an elaborate attempt for Stern to get back at Burroughs. Why? No one was sure. Despite his wealth, Stern had never really succeeded at being anything other than a rich addict. Burroughs, a pauper by comparison, had become influential and famous by staying true to his literary vocation. Well, that was one theory. Grauerholz said Stern would often bring up the allegation that Burroughs had stolen from his top dresser drawer years ago at the Beat Hotel.

On the morning of May 9, Stern called Burroughs and Grauerholz at their hotel. In a long rant, he claimed that he had copyrighted his *Creation of Adam* script in 1975, that he did not want Burroughs to do any writing on *Junky,* that he and Hopper would write the script, which would take place in the seventies with Burroughs playing himself in the latter part of the film. Stern claimed to have talked to Bob Dylan, who expressed interest in the part of Roy, a fellow addict in the book. If this manic call had a purpose it was to show Burroughs who was the creative boss. And if Burroughs and Grauerholz didn't like Stern's new plans for the film, he still had the option. "You can call it off if you want to, I'll pay the guarantees . . . but it'll be a long wait!" On this dramatic flourish, Stern hung up.

Stern's intransigence left Southern in limbo. He recognized that Stern was a loose cannon, but he felt an allegiance to Hopper as well as to Burroughs. For his part, Hopper was starting work on a draft of his own. Instead of playing an active role, Southern attempted to sit things out. The day after Stern's call, Burroughs and Grauerholz met Southern and Hopper for an emergency meeting at the latter's apartment. Grauerholz recalls expressing a hope that Dennis would concede that *Junky* "did not allow for an auteur director, and agree than any script submitted should be unanimously endorsed by Southern, Burroughs, and Hopper. I also pointed out that there should probably be some official recognition of the fact that Burroughs, as well as Hopper, [was] participating in the actual writing of the script—and not Southern alone, as in the original understanding."

Grauerholz felt Hopper was not amenable to the spirit of the kind of collaboration needed to make *Junky* fly. "He appears, for instance, to have concluded that the only acceptable and most dramatic ending for the story would be for William Lee to shoot his wife in the head, accidentally. I will leave it to you to imagine what William's view of this idea would be."

As Stern's lawyer, Joe Bianco was in the thankless role of picking up the pieces after the latest of his employer's tantrums. He attempted to reassure Burroughs and Grauerholz that Stern's phone call was due to ill health and added, "I have never known Jacques to find a paltry two million dollars or so an obstacle."

However, a memo received the same day from Stern referred to the production as *The Creation of Adam,* further deepening the sense that the project was on a rocky voyage. Stern was sounding more like the mad captain at the wheel who was going to drown them all.

On May 15, Southern attended the funeral of James Jones with Hopper, Walter Hopps, and Jean Stein. After the funeral, Southern brought Hopper over to Ellen Adler's, where a somber reception was in progress. Adler asked Southern and Hopper to leave not long after they arrived. Hopper, whose behavior was growing increasingly confrontational, was arguing with guests and using profane language in a situation where many children were present. For Southern, who prided himself on his courtly manners, being kicked out of a funeral reception was embarrassing in the extreme.

It was becoming clearer and clearer that *Junky* was a mess. The Cannes Film Festival, which was to have been the launching pad for *Junky,* was in full swing without anyone from the production attending. Southern received a call from Stern simply stating, "Gone to Geneva. Dennis in charge till I get back." If the project had any hope of getting made, alternative backing would have to be sought.

Despite all the uncertainty and personality conflicts, Southern delivered a first draft of *Junky* on May 25, 1977. At 101 pages, it mirrored the book's laconic style faithfully. Southern managed to stick closely to the book without using too much narration. His adaptation shifted quickly from New York, where Bill Lee, Burroughs's alter ego, is involved in the petty dealing of Army Syrettes to support his heroin habit. Eventually Lee is arrested for trafficking and goes into detox at the Lexington rehab facility. After his release, he goes to New Orleans and then to Mexico for a while. Lee's attempts to kick are foiled by narcotics officers who want him to become an informant. Lee avoids this only by staying on the run and leaving the country. As in the book, he embarks on a search for Yage, "a kick" that will bring enlightenment as well as a new high.

Southern wove in a motif from *Naked Lunch* wherein Bill Lee stumbles into the Past Time Bar. Here his past and present converge—old cronies greet him, police officers and doctors reveal the corrupt faces behind the masks of officialdom, and most poignantly, Mary, a junkie who is dying from a bone disease, continues to look for tricks. The script ends with "the Mooch" entering the bar and shooting Lee. The images that pass before Bill Lee's dying consciousness are the subway trains that he used to travel in search of easy marks.

For the most part, Southern's draft is spare and economical. There is the occasional episode written to appease Stern. For example, while Lee is given a tour of the Lexington facility, the script jumps from the forties to the present. Suddenly, this scene becomes a film within a film being screened on a video monitor by Dr. Miller. This is followed by a surreal sequence where Dr. Miller monitors an experiment where an alligator pumped with heroin is being monitored for withdrawal symptoms.

Upon the delivery of this draft, Southern and Hopper had a meeting with François de Menil in the hope that the latter's oil-rich family would take on the costs of development. Some form of "wildcat independent financing" was now needed, argued Grauerholz. Terry suggested approaching Lewis Allen, the producer of *Lord of the Flies* and *Fahrenheit 451* and various New York theater productions.

As Stern's behavior became increasingly unpredictable and with the first draft still awaiting feedback, Southern checked out of the Gramercy Park Hotel on June 1. Southern would later say that *Junky* failed because Stern lacked the background to attract and secure Hollywood's attention: "It turns out that Dennis wasn't that interested in making it and Jacques Stern didn't have enough money to produce the film, but he had enough money to option the book and finance a screenplay. . . . He would get mad at Burroughs. He claims that Burroughs prevented him from winning the Nobel Prize by telling people that Stern was on junk. If Jacques Stern had taken it more seriously as a real project instead of as a way to work out his relationship with Bill, it might have worked. . . . 'Is that why you spoiled my chances for the Prize!' There was an atmosphere of ultraparanoia between Jacques and Bill."

James Grauerholz tallied up the work done to that point. From what he could determine Dennis hadn't written anything in any traditional sense. Jacques made lots of notes, including the mishmash that was *The Creation of Adam*. Terry's final script was a combination of working drafts followed by notes from Jacques, Hopper, Burroughs, and Grauerholz. One of Terry's drafts opened with a hydrogen bomb cross-fading into an extreme close-up of a hypodermic needle filling with blood. A team of temporary secretaries and stenographers racked up a lot of time keeping track of all the paper.

"The whole thing was really a Jacques Stern production as in not a movie production, but a scene," Grauerholz recalled wearily. He began working on a draft called *Bill Lee*. "As often happens when a project fails, the second-string players who really had their hearts in the project all along will walk up to bat and try to play the game, but it never works out. William wasn't supposed to [write] anything, but be in on the whole deal. Terry wrote several drafts. William wrote like a number of twenty to thirty pages of summary which Terry used. Terry's drafts, as I recall, borrowed liberally from *Naked Lunch*.

"One thing that comes to mind is that Dennis wanted to, if memory serves, put the thing in present time. I was always deeply opposed to this. I always thought that the beauty of the story was [that] it happened in the forties and that the character was William. None of them knew William well enough to write anything for him, including Terry. Terry had known him for years and they were very, very chummy, but as far knowing William as a human being well enough to put words in his mouth in a scene that would have verisimilitude, they did not."

Ironically, at the very point when *Junky* was beginning to look like a lost cause, the media, especially the rock press, began to run brief news flashes about the project. Rumors floated about that Patti Smith, Miles Davis, and Lou Reed were planning to contribute to the soundtrack. Jack Nicholson might do a turn (Grauerholz does recall that Patti Smith was interested in playing the part of Mary, the only significant female role in the book and film). Penguin reissued the novel with a new introduction by Allen Ginsberg, giving the impression to the outside world that the project had a good chance of being made. *Time* magazine reported that Southern was also helping Hopper with his autobiography and that Hopper had just gotten his portrait done by Andy Warhol.

Southern remembers one of the more amusing casting ideas. "The first scene [of Southern's draft] deals with this guy who is coming to sell a package of Army Syrettes, 3cc ampules of morphine that are in medical kits for soldiers on the front, so that if you get wounded, you can shoot one of these up. That was one of the things was sold in trafficking at the time. Bill suggested we use Herbert Huncke, one of the guys he knew who actually sold this stuff at the time. So we located Huncke and asked him and he said, 'I don't think this part would be good for my reputation. I don't need that kind of exposure!' Burroughs would say to Herbert, 'But you could use the heat!'"

s Southern began to look for a way to discreetly extricate himself from *Junky*, the Non-Movie, *The Donkey and the Darling*, a limited edition children's book started in 1968 with Larry Rivers, was finally published by Tanya Grossman's Universal Art Editions. Not so much a book as an elaborate objet d'art, *The Donkey and the Darling* consisted of a series of handsome lithographs combining calligraphic-style text with Rivers's striking illustrations. Each page of the story was signed by Southern and Rivers. The entire book was housed in a beautiful wooden green lacquered box roughly the size of a small cedar chest. When one opened the box lid, one could look into a mirror imprinted with the title of the book. Only thirty-five copies were made.

The book was a beautiful thing to behold, but an artistic dead end for Southern the writer. A section of *The Donkey and the Darling* apppeared in *Wonders*, Jonathan Cott's 1980 anthology of children's literature by people who didn't normally write for children. However, the more logical destination for the work, a trade edition, never materialized. It was a shame because the story was unlike anything Southern produced before or afterward. It was an exercise in style and narrative that Henry Green would have relished.

The Donkey and the Darling is set in Sillicreechie, a kind of Winnie-the-Pooh fantasy land of cuddly animals. They coexist in various stages of harmony but fear the Bad Witch. The story focuses on the trials and tribulations of Baby Grey, a kitten, as she tries to find a friend among such disparate characters as Mouse, Good Toad, Bad Baker, Blue Fairy, and Real Painter. Southern takes delight in coming up with outlandish, almost iconic names for the inhabitants. On one level, the story is kind of a pop-art experiment in merging word with image. Rivers's lithographs take this premise to the limit. Yet the text itself can be read simply as a playful excursion into myth as this excerpt demonstrates:

> Thick Toad was so fat he could hardly see. He would just loll about in Crystal Pond for hours on end, soaking up the water and getting more thick and thick. One time he just sat in the water all night, and by morning he was so swollen he could not get out of the crystal pond.
>
> Miss Mouse came to the pond bright and early each morning to wash her face; she could not bear Thick Toad, and she would not even speak to him he was always so fat and wet. The truth was that this Miss Mouse did not even like the water, but she would put a drop on her pointy-face each morning because she was so proper.

It was as far removed from the heroin-is-not-a-kick-it-is-a-way-of-life world of *Junky* as one could get.

Southern's interest in *Junky* was waning. He had found himself a new writing partner, Joe Loguidice, the owner of a Chicago art gallery and occasional business adviser to Abbie Hoffman. Loguidice had written a script called *Tough City* about a tour bus that takes customers through the worst New York has to offer. Southern read the script over and suggested they collaborate. Loguidice was still getting his feet wet as a writer, but he had a lot of experience setting up meetings and making cold calls. They began a series of field trips to Los Angeles to pitch *Tough City* and flesh it out.

Meanwhile, *Junky* was in limbo. On behalf of Burroughs, Grauerholz began to look for other backers and work on his *Bill Lee* draft more seriously. Stern's *Junky* option was still in effect for the rest of the year, but Stern was doing nothing to keep things moving. Joe Bianco was still trying to impose some order on the project in spite of his client's manic behavior. Hopper wasn't actively working on the project, but was asking for $5,000 to waive his participation as director for four months and to compensate Paul Lewis. It was obvious that the community spirit of a few months back was fading away.

Grauerholz considered the possibility of buying back *Junky* for $30,000, a portion of what Stern had thrown into the project. There was also talk with Joe Bianco about approaching other actors—like Jeff Bridges. Martin Scorsese, Steven Spielberg, Nicolas Roeg, Sydney Pollack, Terence Malick, John Milius, John Schlesinger, Milos Forman, and Kubrick were some of the big-name directors that were thrown around. Both men sensed they were clutching at straws. Grauerholz also wrote to Rudy Wurlitzer, the screenwriter behind *Two-Lane Blacktop* and *Pat Garrett and Billy the Kid*, to feel him out about possibly writing a new draft. Wurlitzer politely declined, citing other commitments.

In July, as Southern's house was assessed by Raymond and Pierre Real Estate at $52,000, Grauerholz received $7,500 from Stern to keep *Junky* alive. However, dealing with Stern's mood changes remained as big an obstacle as the lack of production funding. In a letter to Burroughs, then teaching at the University of Colorado in Boulder, Grauerholz described how Stern alienated a William Morris agent who had the idea of bringing Brian De Palma on board with Kris Kristofferson as the lead. Suspicions arose about Southern's loyalty to Burroughs and *Junky*. Grauerholz had heard a rumor that Southern was in L.A. shopping a radically revised version of *Junky* around: "What it *means* Bill, this trip of Terry's, what it *means* is that he doesn't give a *shit* about your wishes—the wishes he so often claimed he would abide, [by], and here he is out in L.A. on an expense account from Jacques, $2,000 in his pocket from Jacques for 'work on recent drafts' . . . and he's waltzing around Hollywood handing out copies of this mad, offensive script without having made *the slightest attempt* to have your opinion of it, or even my opinion."

In another letter, dated August 11, 1977, Grauerholz tells Burroughs about tracking Southern down at the Sunset Marquis in Los Angeles, where Southern and Loguidice were working on *Tough City*. After playing phone tag with Terry, he got through to Gail: "I can't escape the strong feeling that Terry is avoiding me, that my message of over [a] half-hour ago was in fact received and that is why Gail was answering, that for some reasons there is something going on they don't want me to know about."

Grauerholz continued to keep Burroughs apprised of other developments over the summer. There was some vague interest at Paramount, where Michael Eisner was also considering Hunter S. Thompson's *Fear and Loathing in Las Vegas*. By the end of September, Grauerholz completed *Bill Lee*, his version of *Junky,* and mailed it to Burroughs. Southern had moved on. By February 1978, *Junky* reverted to Burroughs. As Stern retreated into his Gramercy Park apartment, his friendship with Burroughs was now damaged beyond repair. In 1979–80, Wim Wenders expressed some interest in *Junky*. In the late nineties, Steve Buscemi, the talented character actor who had directed the critically acclaimed *Tree's Lounge*, took another option on *Junky*. He seemed to have as good a chance as anyone else to get this ill-fated project off the ground.

Reflecting back on *Junky*'s brief promise and then equally swift disintegration, Grauerholz had this to say about the illusory nature of star power and the vagaries of film financing:

"You get this prostitution factor that just never appealed to me. I could never see chasing celebrities for their fame, their money, cocaine, or anything else. I always felt that if you have a good idea, regardless of the famous people involved, the idea is to make a great piece. I have this profile of being a skillful handler of William's reputation and all this, but my preoccupation has always been with the various books that were going to be submitted for publication, or the records, readings, whatever. They should be good. It should be professional and of a very high standard of care. To see these people falling all over each other being idiots, I could see we were never getting anywhere. The *Junky* movie project wasn't a Hollywood project. It was a rich guy with money footing the bill for a lot of drug-addled insanity and delusions."

Tough City attracted a bit of development money and a nibble from *All in the Family* producer Norman Lear, but didn't go anywhere. Southern began writing *With Extreme Prejudice* with James Coburn and a London-based company called Artiofilm. It was a prescient thriller about a plot to kill the pope. Southern spent a lot of time with Coburn at the actor's home talking story. As with *Junky,* he taped some of the writing sessions. Coburn loved to describe the atmosphere of papal intrigue and the clothes the characters wore. Jazz played constantly in the background. There were the occasional breaks to ingest substances of one form or another. Southern would receive approximately $10,000 in installments for his work.

In the spring, with little fanfare, *The Rolling Stones on Tour—A Log Book*—was published. It consisted of Annie Leibowitz's exhaustive pictures of the 1976 tour. Southern's text was amusing and occasionally informative. The book sold reasonably well to music fans, but added little luster to Southern's name in Quality Lit circles. Southern fans, who did not live in the incestuous orbit of café society, could be forgiven for wondering out loud, "What the hell is this guy doing?" Southern seemed oblivious to the fact that all the energy devoted to yet another unfilmed screenplay was draining his talent.

What, for example, was someone as talented at novel writing and the short story doing churning out a screen outline for another version of "The Most Dangerous Game?" It was a story so stale that one of the more recent versions had been a forgettable made-for-TV movie. It was a far cry from *Dr. Strangelove* and *Easy Rider.*

Southern kept his counterculture credentials intact with work on *Haven Can Wait,* a play cowritten with Loguidice for an August 23, 1978, benefit to raise legal funds for Abbie Hoffman. Jon Voight, Allen Ginsberg, Dave Dellinger, Ron Kovic, Kinky Friedman, Ossie Davis, Odetta, Rennie Davis, Anne Waldman, Ramsey Clark, Michael O'Donoghue, Paul Krassner, Bobby Seale, Taylor Mead, and Rip Torn were among the star-studded cast that appeared before what Loguidice described as an "absolutely out of their minds rock 'n' roll crowd." Hoffman, who was still on the run, made a virtual appearance through film and videotape. *Haven Can Wait* was the kind of unwieldy gargantuan *son et lumière* display that energized Southern. The play was an absurdist treatment of Hoffman's life and struggles, including this strange re-creation of the Chicago Seven Conspiracy Trial:

SCENE:
THE HAVENLY COURTROOM OF JUSTICE
JULIAN 'J.O.' JULIAN.

The Judge fixes the Prosecutor with a fomrulative gaze.
JUDGE: Has the sexual-witness arrived?
PROSECUTOR: No, I regret to say the eminent Dr. Benway has not
yet arrived. The Prosecutor, however, is prepared to offer at this time
a series of anecdotes which may well—
JUDGE (*impatiently interrupting*): Anecdotes?
PROSECUTOR: Yes, your honor, anecdotes which may prove to be
germane or analogous, to the issues at hand—These anecdotes being
rendered in the format of the so-called 'Polish Joke.' With the Court's
permission?
JUDGE (*nodding sagely*): Proceed.
*The Prosecutor assumes the easy and expansive manner of the
professional raconteur.*
PROSECUTOR: Well, there were these two Polock [*sic*] fag hair-
dressers, and—.
COUNSEL (*rising*): Objection . . . Your honor, I submit that 'Polish
Jokes' are not an acceptable substitute for testimony and evidence in a
court of law. If the Prosecution has no witness to call at this time, the
Defense will do so.
JUDGE (*after peering eccentrically at the Counsel, looks to the
Prosecutor*): Any objection, John?
PROSECUTOR (*shrugs, chuckles*): Beats fucking mud.
COURT REPORTER (*being one of the boys*): Yer fucking A!
JUDGE: Give 'em enough rope, eh Jack! (*Wags a finger
mischievously.*) Yer a shrewd one, ye are, Jack Mitchell!
PROSECUTOR: Ay, and that's what they be payin' me for now, isn't it?
*They exchange BROAD CONSPIRATORIAL WINKS, and the Judge faces the
Counsel.*
JUDGE: All right, Mr. Constable, bring on your next weirdie.
COUNSEL: Your honor, the Defense wishes to call to the stand at this
time our distinguished poet laureate, Mr. Allen Ginsberg.
*APPLAUSE. The Judge raps vigorously for silence, eyes Counsel
narrowly.*
JUDGE (*his expression changing to one of sly shrewdness*): 'Poet-
deviate'? Did you say 'poet-deviate,' Mr. Kunstler?
COUNSEL (*with emphasis*): I said, 'poet laureate,' your honor, and I
must take the most serious exception to your uncalled for—

JUDGE (*interrupting furiously*): Just one minute, Mr. William
Counselor! Are you trying to tell the court that this witness—this
Jehovah's Witness is not, in actual fact, a self-avowed PREVERT?!?
COUNSEL (*cooly*): Your honor, I would suggest to you that the sex-life
of the witness is not relevant to the substance of his testimony.
JUDGE (*menacingly*): And I would suggest to you, Mr. William A.
Kunstler, that you are on the verge of being in contempt.
COUNSEL (*bewildered*): In contempt, your honor?
PROSECUTOR (*chuckling with good-natured drunken joviality*):
That's a little town just outside of Scranton, P.A. (*continues
chuckling, starts coughing, has a nip.*)
*His laughter is joined by that of the Judge, and the weird chortle of the
Reporter.*

For a time, Southern briefly toiled on a treatment for a script about
pyramid power called *Dawn of the God Kings.* Then, in September 1978,
Joel Freeman, a producer of films like *Trouble Man,* commissioned
Southern to adapt Harry Crews's novel *The Car,* relating the life of a carnival worker who has the ability to eat automobiles whole. The project
seemed an ideal marriage of two darkly comic sensibilities. Southern's
adaptation faithfully captured the flavor of Crews's bizarre allegory about
America's love affair with the automobile. Of course, as always, the problem seemed to be getting the project past the development stage.

In the fall, Southern was one of many shadowy contributors, along
with Michael Arlen, Carl Bernstein, Nora Ephron, and Frances Fitzgerald,
to *Not the New York Times.* It was a parody issued during the 1978 newspaper strike, which began August 9 and lasted until the late fall. Tony
Hendra, George Plimpton, and other Elaine's regulars assembled the lark
at Plimpton's East River apartment on the pool table.

Southern also surfaced at the Nova Convention in New York, an eclec-
tic gathering that brought together Brian Eno, Patti Smith, Merce
Cunningham, John Giorno and others to pay homage to William
Burroughs and his influence on art and culture. The event ran from
November 30 through December 2 at a series of venues around New York
University. Aside from a nonappearance by Keith Richards, whose connec-
tion to Burroughs was tangential anyway, the convention was a hit of sorts.
Southern introduced Burroughs, who was entering an exciting phase of his
career, revolving around charismatic readings.

Burroughs read carefully selected excerpts from his work behind an
old wooden desk as a doctor delivering a diagnosis of some awful terminal

disease. Earlier during the convention, Southern read a fragment of his autobiographical novel dealing with his Texas boyhood, now called *Youngblood*. Howard Brookner, a young filmmaker, filmed the proceedings for what would turn out to be a long documentary project on Burroughs, which was finally released in 1983.

The event culminated in a lively party at Mickey Ruskin's new restaurant at One University Place. It was one of the last high-profile public appearances by Southern. As he balanced Victor Bockris's girlfriend, Marcia Resnick, on one knee and a glass in the other, he was still the life of the party. His Grand Guy persona continuing to serve him well in what was not his most fertile period.

11

Grossing Out

I've had a long friendship with Terry, I like his work, think he's funny; he's a mess, but he's also marvelous. He's a picture of the human condition. If there's a median where you're OK, and one side is heading toward being awful and the other toward possibly being beautiful and poetic, he's somewhere between the median and the bottom. He eats too much, he drinks too much; at the same time he's so funny and strangely polite and gentle.

—**Larry Rivers**

As the seventies ended, Southern still dreamed of another big Hollywood score. It was a form of addiction as debilitating in its way as heroin or alcohol. Peter Sellers, the absurdly talented and possibly mad actor who had worked on *Dr. Strangelove* with Southern, shared this addiction.

Sellers was able to maintain his habit thanks to the profits from the highly successful *Pink Panther* series. Yet the actor was weary of playing Inspector Clouseau and his relationship with writer/director Blake Edwards was so acrimonious they often communicated only through assistants on the set. Audiences loved watching Sellers as Clouseau don an endless array of silly disguises, engage in judo with his manservant, Cato, and drive Herbert Lom as Inspector Dreyfus to the brink of madness. The latest installment, *The Revenge of the Pink Panther*, released in the summer of 1978, proved to be one of the most popular films of the year, along with the John Travolta musical *Grease* and Warren Beatty's *Heaven Can Wait*. The *Pink Panther* money allowed Sellers to sustain eccentric obsessions with astrology and the afterlife as well as maintain a hideaway in Gstaad, Switzerland. The revenue also made up for such embarrassing flops as *There's a Girl in My Soup*, *Where Does It Hurt?*, and *Murder by Death*. However, as batty as many of his career decisions were, Sellers was sufficiently self-aware to know that he was capable of performances that would stand the test of time. *The Ladykillers*, *I'm All Right Jack*, *Lolita*, and *Dr. Strangelove* remained perennials on late-night TV, repertory cinemas, and retrospectives.

Like many stars, Sellers tried to exert more control over his work by optioning and developing screenplays. In the early seventies, he became obsessed with Jerzy Kosinski's 1971 novel *Being There*, the story of Chauncey Gardiner, who spends his entire life as a rich man's gardener cut off from the outside world except for television. When his patron dies, this blank slate of a human being wanders into the Washington beltway. His innocuous meanderings are mistaken for political wisdom and he becomes the friend and adviser of a dying presidential kingmaker.

Kosinski's fable had a powerful resonance with Sellers, who often felt as if he lacked a clear sense of self and only felt truly alive when impersonating others. Sellers hired a number of writers to adapt *Being There*, with little success. Eventually Sellers and producer Andrew Braunsberg hired Kosinski himself to write a screenplay. Hal Ashby, the quintessential seventies director of *The Last Detail* and *Shampoo*, came on board. The package attracted Shirley Maclaine, Jack Warden, and Melvyn Douglas. Lorimar, the successful producers of the TV show *The Waltons*, had just started a film division and agreed to underwrite principal photography. The cast went before cameras in the fall and winter of 1978–79. United Artists released the film in late 1979 in time for Oscar nominations. Reviews were almost unanimous: Sellers the comic genius was back. His performance as Chauncey Gardiner was a tour de force as powerful as the "triple crown" of *Dr. Strangelove*.

Being There rejuvenated Sellers. He began to seek out similar material. Some years before, Sellers had found himself in a private jet sitting next to an arms dealer. They struck up a conversation and Sellers found himself fascinated by the incongruity of the man. On one hand, there was the obvious obscenity of a man whose income was based on instruments of death. On the other, there was the fact that the man was well dressed, courteous, and worldly. He was the perennial guest of kings, presidents, and statesmen. He traveled the world in luxury in spite of the fact that his wheeling and dealing helped to create further conflicts, displace the lives of millions, and lead to the death of countless others. Like *Being There*, the idea of a film about the international arms trade percolated for some time. Sellers gathered books and magazine articles on the subject. Now, with Lorimar asking if Sellers and Ashby would like to develop a follow-up project, Sellers contacted a writer who seemed perfect to write about this shadow world of diplomacy, espionage and genocide. Sellers and producer Andrew Braunsberg contacted Southern and made a deal. Terry was in seventh heaven. This was a can't-fail dream deal—Sellers, Ashby, and Southern.

The resulting script, *Grossing Out,* with Ashby attached as director, was steeped in the kind of technical minutiae found in *Jane's Fighting Ships.* Despite its coarse title, *Grossing Out* was a deeply serious script. Like *A Piece of Bloody Cake,* it is a character study of an intelligent, well-intentioned, politically conservative man who realizes he is working for self-interested psychotics. In this case, Bob Larchmont, the auditor at Republic Aviation, an aerospace firm, becomes caught up in a world of Pentagon slush funds, payoffs, and clandestine deals with supposedly enemy nations, terrorism, and covert operations of byzantine complexity. Profoundly cynical about the Western nations' professions of peace and global harmony, *Grossing Out* offers vignette after vignette detailing the selling and trading of arms in far-flung hotel lobbies and dingy cantinas to high-tech trade shows and office towers. In one scene, Bert Murchison, a vice president of a California aerospace firm, gives his chief auditor, Bob Larchmont, a lecture in Kissinger-style realpolitik:

LARCHMONT
Tell me why one of the largest aircraft companies in the world has to pay a million and half dollar *bribe* to sell its planes? Why don't you tell me that?

Murchison stares at him, expressionless for a moment, then sighs heavily.

MURCHISON
(very serious)
All right, Bob, you call it a 'bribe' . . . we call it a 'consultant's fee' . . . the Japanese call it 'brokerage expenses' . . . the French 'entertainment costs' . . . the British call it 'grease' . . . 'grease for the squeaky wheel,' they say—the point is, *they* were all doing it before we were even in business . . . I mean it's their ballgame, and if we don't learn to play by the rules, we're *out of it* —it's as simple as that. While Murchison speaks, Larchmont stares vacantly at the silent

Third World footage: an endless column of Cambodian refugees—
mostly women, children, and old men—walking over a vast expanse
of countryside, belongings in hand and on their backs.

> MURCHISON
> (continuing)
>
> And we *can't afford* to be out of the game, Bob—our economy would
> collapse. (gently) Don't worry, the Pentagon knows all about it—
> you'll be covered.

> LARCHMONT
> (absently, still watching the set)
>
> Yes, well, I guess 'consultant fee' is as good a phrase as any . . .

> MURCHISON
> (sagely)
>
> The phrase-of-choice, Bob, the phrase-of-choice.

> LARCHMONT
> (after a pause)
>
> Just out of curiosity—how *is* the money . . . *transferred* . . . to the
> 'consultant'?

> MURCHISON
> (smiles, knowing he has won him over)
>
> *Gracefully*, Bob, *gracefully*.

Southern began working on the script steadily through the winter and
spring of 1979–80. Restless as always, he couldn't help working on other
projects. Dennis Hopper raised the possibility of an *Easy Rider* sequel.
James Coburn was still trying to get *Extreme Prejudice* together. There
were meetings with Lewis Allen to discuss a musical about the Cotton Club
called *Johnny Blood*. Southern had come up with the idea with two unlikely
collaborators, *New Yorker* writer Brendan Gill, who lived near Southern in
Norfolk, Connecticut, and Harry Nilsson, as the composer.

"He wrote that with Brendan Gill," Lewis Allen recalls. "They talked
about it coming in on the bus from Canaan together. I didn't commission it,
but they gave me the script. I have it around somewhere. It was quite good . . .
it was all set in Harlem and Johnny Blood was kind of the king of black
pimps there and he was protected by the Harlem community and the cops

couldn't get in there, that sort of thing. It was very interesting. But you know a musical is a complicated thing. . . . They brought it to me. Brendan was a good friend of mine, too. Musicals are so hard to do. You've got to get something extraordinary or a star or something like that."

Southern stayed at the Chelsea Hotel on his business trips to New York. For *Grossing Out,* he made occasional trips to Los Angeles to discuss progress on the script. Nile was starting an undergraduate film studies program at UCLA.

"I remember attending a few Hollywood parties that my dad invited me to and let's say they would be at Si Litvinoff's house and Pablo Ferro would come along," recalled Nile. "Pablo was Hal Ashby's creative consultant and helped Hal do some tricky sequences. . . . He did Kubrick's trailers and titles. He still does work for Jonathan Demme and John Carpenter. He's half Cuban and half American Indian and has a very interesting kind of all-consuming, slightly dictatorial style in dealing with producers. He just says, 'Look, I am creating this thing!' At these parties, Haskell Wexler would be there. This guy, I forget his name, but he was called the 'Shrink to the Stars.' He was a psychiatrist. . . . My dad really liked him. My dad would say to him, 'I want you to look inside my son's *head.*' At the time I was having some real problems, so it was pretty funny. It was a great, ironic moment for me when I am kind of at a breaking point and my dad's joke 'look inside my son's head.' Barbi Benton, Richard Benjamin, George Segal . . . all sorts of characters would be at the parties."

On July 24, 1980, Sellers died of a heart attack in a London hospital. His last film, *The Fiendish Plot of Fu Manchu,* overshadowed his performance in *Being There.* Yet another overproduced, underwritten comedy, it was distinguished only by the elaborate disguises Sellers wore and the behind-the-scene battles with the original director, Piers Haggard, who resented being reduced to a traffic warden by the manic actor. Sellers's death left *Grossing Out* in limbo. Lorimar put the project in turnaround. Hal Ashby moved on to more promising projects, which turned out to be a series of dreadful films, including a mediocre concert film, *Let's Spend the Night Together,* and a dire Neil Simon vehicle, *The Slugger's Wife.* Southern tried to shop his script around to the likes of Stanley Kubrick and actor Paul Newman.

Not one to indulge in self-pity, Southern gamely threw himself into another project. Si Litvinoff had purchased the rights to a novel called *Aria* by Brown Meggs. *Aria* was a comic behind-the-scenes look at the world of opera. Litvinoff approached George Segal to star and Ted Kotcheff to direct. Segal and Kotcheff had worked well together on *Fun with Dick and Jane* and *Who Is Killing the Great Chefs of Europe?*, two slick comic entertainments that had enjoyed healthy box office returns. Twentieth Century-Fox was underwriting the development of the project. According to a contract drawn up on August 25, Southern would be paid a $30,000 advance from a total writing fee of $85,000. Unfortunately, the work he turned in seemed to lack energy.

"What killed [*Aria*] was Terry's script," said Litvinoff. "In my estimation it was [intended to be] the *Dr. Strangelove* of the classical world. He didn't do it like *Strangelove*, but like *Easy Rider*, unfortunately."

"[*Aria* dealt with this] Duddy Kravitz–type record producer who wanted to make the ultimate recording of one of his favorite operas," said Kotcheff. "It was a very funny book and I've always been interested in classical music. . . . Si and I thought Terry was the perfect writer [but] he was spreading himself too thin. It was obvious around the time of *Aria* that you felt he had a crushing financial problem. He was not able to work at his best . . . [the] script was really bad structurally, with shades of Southernisms, nuggets here and there. Fox just dismissed it."

The East Canaan farm had been remortgaged at one point to pay off the IRS, and this of course created more obligations. Thirty thousand dollars could disappear quite quickly when one had old debts, college fees, and current expenses to deal with. Gerber and Southern were also fond of fine dining. Shuttling back and forth between upstate Connecticut and New York often required overnight stays at a hotel.

Around this period, Southern took on the job of writing a soft-porn film, *Electric Lady,* directed by Philip Schuman (who later made a documentary about the making of *Yellowbeard,* a rather leaden pirate comedy written by Graham Chapman). The plot, such as it was, concerned a team of sex researchers. Southern's name was proudly displayed in the credits by the producers. On the bright side, no one seemed to notice and the film seemed to circulate mainly in the twilight world of adult cinema.

On December 8, 1980, John Lennon was shot and killed in New York City outside his apartment at the Dakota. Along with the election of Ronald Reagan as the new president of the United States in a landslide victory, Lennon's death was an almost too-perfect confirmation that the dreams of the sixties had died. For Southern, who was as indelibly associated with the counterculture as Lennon and the other Beatles, it was painfully clear that many Americans were retreating into the old Cold War standbys of xenophobia, militarism, and the pursuit of wealth for its own sake. What made this shift to the right more depressing were the number of baby-boomers who embraced these harsh values as avidly as they had embraced sex, drugs, and rock 'n' roll a few years before. Here lay part of the problem. Unlike Southern and other members of the World War II generation who were inspired by the emancipating influences of the sixties—free speech, civil rights, ecology, artistic experimentation, etc.—many of the boomers who weren't politically active merely saw the decade as one long frat party. Now it was time to return the empty beer bottles for the deposit. The eighties would become the decade of the yuppie, where no one batted an eye when Jerry Rubin cut his hair and began to throw "networking" parties for up-and-coming entrepreneurs.

Despite the emerging dog-eat-dog tenor of the new decade, there were still plenty of Southern watchers in the hinterlands who were beginning to despair of ever seeing new Terry Southern stories or books in print. In 1980, an enticing morsel from *The Donkey and the Darling* appeared alongside a nursery rhyme by Norman Mailer and a scary story about a girl who turns into a cat by Paul Bowles in Jonathan Cott's delightful anthology *Wonders*. Those fans who managed to stumble on the oddball squibs in places like *Hustler* or *Oui* were usually more depressed than enchanted. Thus when "Heavy Put Away, a Hustle Not Entirely Devoid of a Certain Grossness Granted" appeared in the twenteith-anniversary edition of the *Paris Review* in the spring of 1981, there was cause for celebration.

Inspired by an anecdote told to Southern by John Calley, "Heavy Put Away" was a classic meditation on innocence versus colder-than-ice cynicism. Framed as a magazine query rejected by a woman's magazine, the story unfolds as Southern's allegedly "verbatim" recording of a con perpetrated by an acquaintance called Art, who was interviewed "on the terrace of the 'Sow 'n' Merkin." Art describes the fateful tragedy of Sally, who agrees to sleep with a charming middle-aged man in exchange for a couple of thousand dollars. Sally needs the money to pay a pile of bills incurred by her stuntman husband's work-related accident. She rationalizes this distasteful pact on the basis that the man is "wonderful, gentle, sweet, attractive, generous" and her family desperately needs cash. On the night of her assignation, she sleeps with the man in a luxury bungalow at the Beverly Hills Hotel. Yet to be paid, Sally is persuaded to give up her wedding ring on the pretext that he wants to buy her a more expensive replica and become a kind of silent benefactor to the woman and her family. The man then disappears and the woman waits for his return. As the hours pass, Sally begins to realize she has been duped. She is forced to call her husband, who is in a partial body cast, to help her sneak out of the hotel. In the process, she is also forced to explain how she ended up at the hotel.

Southern asks Art the point of this elaborate setup that only earned the con men a couple of hundred bucks from the sale of an inexpensive wedding band. Art replies, "You've got a pretty *materialistic* slant on things, don't you?" This is the last sentence in the story.

"Heavy Put Away" is a brutal glimpse into the mind of a narcissistic neohipster motivated only by the art of the con. Where the narrator of "The Blood of a Wig" was searching for the ultimate high as a gateway to greater knowledge, here Art and his conmen acquaintances are engaged solely in a kind of nihilistic endgame. The story is a prescient fable of a decade in which deal-making took precedence over any considerations of right or wrong.

Much later, Ron Rosenbaum wrote an insightful commentary on what is Southern's last great short story, calling "Heavy Put Away" "a slyly disguised parable about Art—not Art the con man, but Art as a cruel con game, a discipline that drives those in its thrall to dark and ugly transgressions for the cold contemplative rewards of the esthete . . . the story isn't *exactly* an excuse for bad behavior . . . in the parable, as I read it, Southern sees himself as both perpetrator and *victim,* both the con man and the woman in the hotel so cruelly deceived by Art. Southern, too, is a victim of Art, robbed of innocence, of stability, by the deranging, impoverishing obsession with its cold con."

Southern's ambivalence toward Art's cold duplicity—which is essentially an act of malice against a defenseless woman and her desperate family—is insightful. Like many shy and sensitive individuals, Terry lived vicariously through the impulsive confidence of acquaintances and friends who can politely be described as less than ethical. As loyal and supportive as friends such as Ted Kotcheff, Jean Stein, or George Plimpton were, Southern was just as easily influenced by charismatic and amoral movie executives and producers whom he encountered in the bistros and hotel lounges of Los Angeles. "Heavy Put Away" is an acknowledgment that Southern understood and perhaps admired their cutthroat ethos. Although in practice, he was too much of a nice guy ever to act on them or employ such techniques to a tactical advantage in his business dealings.

The period 1980–81 was relatively quiet. There were nibbles. Andrew Braunsberg took out a $12,500 eighteen-month option on *Blue Movie.* If the film went into production, Southern would get first crack at the script. Maurice Girodias, who had unsuccessfully transferred Olympia Press to New York in the mid-sixties, approached Southern about updating *Candy*. This time Southern kept his distance and passed.

Meanwhile, another opportunity was developing in the form of some television work. Beginning in 1975, *Saturday Night Live,* the hit late-night comedy show conceived by Lorne Michaels, had successfully sneaked some of Southern's satirical outrage past the homogenizing filters of NBC executives. For its first few years, the show was a refreshing oasis of hip, engaged music and comedy sketches whose subjects and targets roamed freely across such sacred cows as sex, drugs, religion, and politics.

One of the show's founding producer/writers, Michael O'Donoghue, had left the show in the late seventies to work on various film projects. In 1980–81, after the departure of Lorne Michaels, Jean Doumanian, the show's music booker, was promoted to executive producer. Although she was good friends with Woody Allen, her comic instincts were sadly lacking. A new cast and writing staff selected by Doumanian turned out to be disastrous. Doumanian was fired and replaced by Dick Ebersol. He asked O'Donoghue to come back and overhaul the ailing show. It was a strange decision. O'Donoghue had deeply mixed feelings about his *Saturday Night Live* work. He accepted Ebersol's offer only in order to give the show what he called "a decent Viking burial." His opinion of Doumanian's handiwork was even less charitable. Referring to her 1980–81 cast and writing team, he said, "The Angel of Talent had passed over these people."

Over the summer, O'Donoghue began firing much of Doumanian's cast. The revamped cast for the forthcoming 1981–82 season would include Christine Ebersole, Mary Gross, Brian Doyle Murray, Tony Rosato, and a few survivors from Doumanian's reign: Robin Duke, Tim Kazurinsky, Eddie Murphy, and Joe Piscopo. For the writing staff, O'Donoghue assembled Rosie Shuster, who had written for the first seasons of *SNL*, veteran comedy writer Herb Sargent, and Mark O'Donnell. O'Donoghue also decided to hire two close friends whose television series experience was minimal. They were Nelson Lyon and Terry Southern.

Southern had known O'Donoghue on a friendly basis since the latter had contributed a comic strip, *Phoebe Zeitgeist,* to the *Evergreen Review.* The strip began as a spirited homage to *Candy* and then morphed into something sinister and darker . . . like O'Donoghue himself. O'Donoghue had also supported Southern's contributions to *National Lampoon.* To O'Donoghue and Lyon, Southern was a national resource.

NBC's business affairs department drew up a contract that would pay Southern $2,154.55 a week during the show's sixth season (this would go up to $2,692.30 the next season, with the option of increases up to $3,000 over the next three years). However, in return for a steady paycheck, Southern would have to adapt to the physical demands of a television show that taxed the stamina of even the hardiest boob-tube veterans.

While O'Donoghue was often busy juggling network politics with Ebersol and the other NBC suits, Terry increasingly sought out Nelson Lyon as an ally and friend on the show. Although to discerning viewers, the show often resembled the world's longest-running office skit, the behind-the-scenes competition to get sketches on air was strictly *All About Eve* time. Such competition was never Southern's métier.

Lyon describes the routine: "What would happen on *Saturday Night Live,* and I guess it still is the mode, was on Monday you would pitch ideas. Everybody sat around, the cast and the writers, Ebersol and the bosses, and Michael silent. People don't laugh too easily . . . it's a highly competitive, tense atmosphere starting off. Luckily, before I got into writing sketches, I had a piece of film I had put together called *Clams,* so I felt quite at home with film and I knew what to do. I could do a satirical five-minute parody of Alfred Hitchcock and Brian De Palma. I could play around in the editing room with opticals and write and put it together, so I was at home."

But Lyon knew Terry felt defenseless in this snake pit of übercool wits.

"People were pitching these ideas and they were just funny sketch ideas and had a certain snap and there's a routine for sketch comedy, a formula. Then it was Terry's turn and everybody was waiting for the great Terry Southern. Terry, in a voice that could hardly be heard, shyly starts talking about these Tough Tours of the ghetto in a dry voice and really so scared in front of these bunch of kids. Nobody laughs and then he talks about 'Sex with Brookie,' another sketch idea, and nobody laughs."

Southern may have been broke, alcoholic, a little overweight, and shabby looking, but he was no fool. He knew he needed to be protected in this climate where the only aesthetic criterion was which sketches got the easy laughs during read-through.

"About three, four weeks before the opening of the first show," says Lyon, Southern approached him in the bar in the Time-Life Building. "He said, 'Let me pay for the drinks. And put me on your team' and all this stuff. I said, 'I know you can write comedy.' In other words, he needed some ally and help and friends, which is really what collaboration is about. You really have to like [people], be friendly with and have a natural support system. . . .

SNL is actually a protected atmosphere. In Hollywood, it's something else again, so much fear and terror and arrogance and power. If you are writing with somebody, you need somebody who is really good, who you can really work with, and who can defy the others. It's an us-against-them marriage"

Hal Wilner, who worked with the musical acts and coordinated the use of incidental music for the sketches, concurs with Lyon's assessment of Southern's unease with the *SNL* work environment. "I remember one of Terry's first sketches being done in the read-through and I don't think the upper ups got it at all. It was called 'Sex with Brookie.' . . . It's about these two guys and one talks about how he went about fucking Brooke Shields. It was very Lenny Bruce. You could just hear the voice. I think NBC was just a weird kind of atmosphere for Terry. Michael left midway through the season, so Terry didn't have his guy up there. So he just had a few sketches in. He got involved in this *Dr. Strangelove* sketch. You could just tell Terry wasn't very happy with this and he made the most horrifying remark to me: 'I feel like the professor at the end of *The Blue Angel.*' Okaaay. Well, it was a bad year. He didn't get a number of things on that were very memorable."

On the surface, the 1981–82 season was boilerplate *SNL* mixing up the occasionally interesting combination of host and musical act with the more familiar flavor-of-the-moment TV/film star with one-hit-wonder music act. Beneath the surface, one could detect signs of O'Donoghue's take-no-prisoners, snake-in-the-grass, sniper-on-the-rooftop approach to comedy. The appearance of L.A. hard-core punk band Fear almost led to a riot. The following week, Lauren Hutton introduced William Burroughs reading "Twilight's Last Gleaming" behind a desk and in front of surreal black-and-white rear projections.

Then there were the sketches that Southern had a hand in. In addition to "Sex with Brookie," Southern collaborated with O'Donoghue and Lyon on "An Imaginary Conversation with Ron Reagan," "Do Your Darndest," "Donnie and Marie," "Heroic Dog," "Hooker Brides," and "KY Madness in High Places." Not all these sketches made the final cut. Southern was contemplating putting together a collection of censored sketches called *Too Hot for SNL.* Sometimes he just sat in the room and riffed with Lyon or Donoghue and simply looked over such pieces as "Last 10 Days of Silverman's Bunker," the scathing portrait of NBC programming head Fred Silverman, which compared the executive's management style to Adolf Hitler's last mad days in a Berlin bunker. Silverman, a Jew, was naturally shocked and hurt by the comparison. After the assassination of Egyptian president Anwar Sadat, Southern wrote a thoughtful film montage, that shows a janitor cleaning up the bloody podium where the incident took place. Among the debris is a bloody white dove. It was an atypical piece in a season that seemed to draw a line in the sand between the play-it-safe-sophomoric-humor of Ebersol and the scorched-earth nihilism of O'Donoghue.

The show's production routine required the cast and staff to generate new material from scratch every week in the space of two to three days. At the same time, sets were being designed and constructed, props organized, and costumes fashioned, depending on the complexity of the sketch. The ego of that week's host had to be massaged in one form or another. To get through the rigors, many staff members used various stimulants, including cocaine. Southern reacted to the availability of the drug in tones of mock outrage and delight: "Talk about your everlovin' cornucopias of sense-derangement! Wow-ee! Boy-oh-Boy! Bro-ther! Holy Mack! I mean, I've been to some heavy-hitting Hollywood soirees, and on two Rolling Stones tours, and I've seen nose-candy by the carload, toot by the truckful, but I've yet to see anything comparable to the sheer quantity of primo-primo heaped and stacked in the writer's wing of *SNL*!"

According to Lyon, Southern was generally well liked by everybody (no small accomplishment in *SNL*'s fishbowl of dueling egos), but he was doing a lot of cocaine.

"His office was like a whole fucking den, bottles, a cocaine grinder. He would play these little practical jokes on me . . . he would put weird clippings on my desk so the production assistants would see them. He had this little voodoo doll that he had taped to the top of the desk. This [girl] was supposed to give blow jobs and it was a blow-job device. The voodoo doll had little hairs around its mouth. I would find these pranks. He was a prankster in everything he wrote, too."

By mid-January, the growing divide between the Dick Ebersol and Michael O'Donoghue visions of the show was becoming unbridgeable. O'Donoghue seemed to have no respect for the costing infrastructure of the show. The "Last 10 Days of Silverman's Bunker" sketch, if it had been staged, would have taken a hefty $20,000 chunk of that week's budget. Ebersol also railed at O'Donoghue's increasing preference for longer sketches that paid little attention to commercial breaks. When Burroughs appeared on the show, O'Donoghue refused to edit the writer's monologue despite Ebersol's demands. O'Donoghue simply had no respect for Ebersol. The breaking point was Ebersol's refusal to run the "Silverman's Bunker" sketch in its original form. On January 17, 1982, O'Donoghue was fired.

In the midst of these conflicts, Lyon tried to support his hero and friend—Southern—and create enough solo work to prove to O'Donoghue, Ebersol, et al., that he was pulling his weight on the new writing team. While he shared O'Donoghue's desire to push the envelope of *SNL*'s sketch comedy, he felt the contretemps over "Silverman's Bunker" was much ado about nothing.

"[The sketch] just went on and on and on," Lyon recalls. "I never thought it was particularly funny. I mean, who gave a shit about Silverman, but Terry was just too happy to write anything if that was the project. He needed nurturing and protection from Michael. He went on writing his own sketches and fragments for ideas."

Southern's strengths at embellishing upon a premise did gain him some notice on the *42nd Street* sketch. When Bernadette Peters was guest hosting, Lyon came up with the idea of a parody of the classic musical, *42nd Street*. He pitched it to Peters.

"'Let's do *42nd Street,* but do it where a girl comes to the Forty-second Street of today. The world of porno.' Bernadette laughs and says, 'I like that.' Ebersol laughs and so that was my first fucking independent sketch. Terry says I am on my own, let me join you. So I said, 'By all means.' Terry's contributions to the sketch were great.

"I created this porno star by the name of Miles Long, you know the old movie *42nd Street.* The ingenue who saves the show is named Hedda Gabler, that's her stage name, her real name is like 'I'm Ruby Sawyer from all that shit.' Terry had characters coming in and out saying, 'Oh, let's go have a fix.' He had this black dominatrix with two midgets in tutus and black masks on a leash. I mean, just out there.

"Michael O'Donoghue had really disassociated himself from the show at that point. He wasn't even showing up and he was giving the finger to everybody. That was really freaking Terry out because his chief protector is gone.

"[Terry] needed the money really badly and he was getting paid more than anybody. So here he is in this agony position of being so great and having the reputation and being older than everybody, getting paid more than anybody, and really feeling alienated from the show."

Lyon helped Southern shepherd previously rejected sketches like "Sex with Brookie" on air.

"We knew we had this bond, but we could really write these subversive things and we could do that together, so it made it really jolly for us," says Lyon. "Then I did 'The Mild One' [a parody of the Marlon Brando film

The Wild One] . . . that was one I didn't get Terry on. He was cross with me. He wanted to be part of that, but there was just no room for him."

Toward the end of the season, after O'Donoghue's departure, Lyon went out to Los Angeles. He was working on a screenplay with John Belushi, who was living at the Chateau Marmont. A teetotaler when it came to drugs, Lyon made the fateful mistake of joining Belushi and Cathy Smith for a cocktail of a heroin speedball. It was the kind of once-only experiment-for-experiment's-sake that the cosmopolitan Lyon could rationalize. He left the two in their bungalow later that same evening. The next day, he found out that Belushi had overdosed. Lyon would spend much of the next few years tainted by the scandal of being one of the last people to see Belushi alive.

"It wasn't really resolved until 1985 when they had to extradite [Cathy Smith]," he recalled ruefully. "It was just like 'Oh, he was involved, he was one of those druggies.' Belushi's death was the watershed. It was like 'Oh God, drugs, no more drugs.' It was like the only time I had done heroin . . . it was like John and Cathy Smith making cocktails. I had never shot up anything in my life and I had to be very careful about saying that, too because I was the key witness. If they were able to prove that I had ever taken more heroin or if I had shot up anyone, my testimony would have been thoroughly discredited, so I was just telling the truth."

Terry's tour of duty at *SNL* was exhausting. Lyon was taken to dinner at Ma Maison one night by Dick Ebersol, who offered to renew his contract. However, Ebersol, said Lyon, told him "'a lot of your friends aren't coming back,' meaning Terry. He couldn't wait to ax [Terry]. And the thing was, Terry really wasn't writing and at that point it was really 'what's the use?'"

O'Donoghue believes Southern's work was just too subtle and delicate for many in the cast to perform. For O'Donoghue, the only cast members he really felt had an ear for Southern's work were Eddie Murphy and Christine Ebersole, who later starred in Milos Forman's *Amadeus*. "It was hard to get the people to play his stuff. They weren't Peter Sellers. They didn't know how to play the reality. They were always going for the cheap laugh. You can't do that. They would blame the failure on him rather than themselves."

In the years after the disastrous 1981–82 season, O'Donoghue would often refer to *SNL*'s decline into formula as a case of the avant-garde becoming the garde. For Southern, the experience had been draining. "[Working on *SNL*] was the best-paying job, but the worst I've ever had, given the sort of deadlines you have to work to," Southern said. "It was difficult because you had this very strict deadline each week, but it's not the way to go about anything. It's pushing back the theory of art."

It was sadly characteristic of Southern that he confused a television writing gig with the more personal kind of writing that a novel or short story might entail. Of course, Southern was not alone in such confusion. At any rate, the experience injected much-needed cash into Southern's bank account.

12
Various Cowriters

. . . preoccupation with '"style"' is surely the greatest jeopardy (more so than booze or dope) that exists for the serious writer. One must take care, as the English novelist Henry Green so aptly put it, "not to become trapped in one's own clichés."

—Terry Southern, preface to "The Road out of Axotle"

One of the few good things about Southern's tumultuous stint on *Saturday Night Live* was that he had forged a deeper friendship with Nelson Lyon. The striking New Yorker, who bore an uncanny resemblance to Aleister Crowley, became Southern's frequent collaborator in the eighties and (although Lyon would no doubt recoil at the term) something of an artistic conscience. The collapse of *Grossing Out* and Terry's brief sojourn on *Saturday Night Live* were demoralizing. Southern became more reliant on collaboration as a way to weather the emotional ups and downs of screenwriting. Nelson Lyon, who was becoming a pariah because of the Belushi death, enjoyed Southern's company, humor, and ability, when pressed, to come up with the word, line, sequence, or image that elevated mere craft to something approaching genius.

After *Saturday Night Live,* Lyon became involved with *Johnny Blood,* the on-again, off-again Cotton Club project that had been kicking around for the last few years. Lewis Allen and Brendan Gill, recalls Lyon, were still involved in a nebulous capacity. They hoped to turn the musical into a screenplay. Lyon was not impressed with the material so far, but he took a deep breath and began to write. He decided to take the premise of the 1937 French film *Pépé le Moko,* in which Jean Gabin plays a gangster hiding out in the Casbah in Algiers, and transfer it to Harlem in the twenties. Collaborating with Terry on *Johnny Blood* was a tad problematic because Lyon lived in Los Angeles, while Southern stayed in East Canaan, still trying to work with Gill.

"Terry brought in Brendan Gill because we were separated by the coasts," recalls Lyon. "He needed somebody to write with. Then Gill wrote this useless, terrible shit. He just couldn't write. It was the only argument Terry and I had. Why are you bringing this ridiculous, arrogant hack into this project? He can't deliver the goods.' 'No, no, he was wondering about you and I had to defend you.' And I said, 'Terry, how dare you? Get fucking rid of him! He's your responsibility. You brought this shit in. I thought this thing up. Get him the fuck out.' At that point there was some interest in this thing from the Quincy Jones people and shit like that."

There was an attempt by a powerful agent at ICM to package the script with hot stars and actors, but eventually it ran up against a competing project initiated by the formidable team of Robert Evans and Francis Coppola. The Coppola-Evans project was eventually filmed and released in December 1984.

Around the same time, Southern was meeting Peter Beard at the latter's Park Avenue apartment to work on *The End of the Game*. By this stage, the script was an excuse for Beard and Southern to riff off each other for a few hours and then go partying. Despite the informal never-ending story nature of *The End of the Game*, the script that emerged from their sporadic writing sessions had potential. If one can imagine *Born Free* mixed with *Dr. Strangelove* and *Walkabout*, one gets a sense of the script's bizarre tone. Where *The End of the Game* stumbled was in the use of a lazy framing device. The main story, dealing with wildlife mismanagement in contemporary Kenya, turns out to be a rough cut being viewed by jaded and corrupt Hollywood executives. After brief consideration, the execs decide to make an action film called *The Man-Eaters of Tsavo* on the back lot. "It's a cruel cold world," one exec observes, "and our audiences deserve a bit of *entertainment*—not a damnable *sermon*." While the core of the script focusing on well-meaning but deluded conservationists is rich in irony and pathos, the studio prologue and coda are perfunctory to the point of self-parody.

In late September, Southern was contacted via his latest West Coast representative, Ron Mardigian at William Morris, by James B. Harris. Since amicably parting from Kubrick in 1963, Harris had embarked on a directing career. His first film, *The Bedford Incident*, was a realistic study of Cold War brinkmanship closer in spirit to *Fail-Safe* than to *Dr.*

Strangelove. Harris then made *Some Call It Loving* in 1973, starring Richard Pryor as a drunken hipster philosopher in a funky update of *Sleeping Beauty*. When he called Southern, he had just released his third film, *Fast-Walking*, a tense prison drama starring James Woods.

"I had a deal to pick up this book," Harris recalled, "called *The Gold Crew* [by Thomas N. Scortia and Frank Robinson]. It was about an American submarine that used to be out on patrol all the time. There were two crews that would take the boat out. They would have a gold crew and a blue crew. The gold crew would come back and the other crew would take the boat out.

"This book, which was written as a serious piece, dealt with a situation where the captain and the crew went insane and decide that they were going to start World War III and attack. It turned out that the boat was recently painted and that there was some kind of chemical in the paint fumes that makes the men crazy."

Southern and Harris met in New York through the fall and winter of 1982–83 to cowrite a darkly comic adaptation retitled *Floaters*. Harris had no trouble working with Terry on a one-on-one basis. It was when he left Southern alone, says Harris, that things would get a little unpredictable. For example, upon returning from the Rotterdam Film Festival where he was screening *Fast-Walking*, Harris would find a series of notes all high-lighted MAYDAY.

"I guess he used that term because we were doing a navy picture and Mayday is a code for being in terrible trouble," said Harris. "He was having a problem on delivery on the date he said he was going to deliver, and what can you do? Nothing except to encourage him to get on with it. Which he always promised me he would do and eventually he did. I don't know what was going on in his personal life at that time and it was none of my business anyway. All I know is that when we were together he was coherent, easy to work with, and very talented. I thought the script was pretty damn good."

Alas, Harris discovered that the rights to the source novel had become embroiled in a dispute with MGM, which wanted to keep the book and bought Harris out of the project. In 1986, a made-for-TV movie called *The Fifth Missile* starring Sam Waterston, Richard Roundtree, and David Soul was shot in Italy returning to the sober tones of the source material. *Dr. Strangelove* Redux remained elusive.

Part of Terry's problem delivering *Floaters* to Harris was his work on yet another fringe project where friendship and pleasure intermingled with business. Larry Rivers continued to harbor filmmaking aspirations. He and

Joe Loguidice had collaborated on a forty-five-minute short film called "The Gardener," based mainly on improvisations, that was shot in the Hamptons. Rivers wanted to do something in Mexico, where he and Loguidice were partners in a time share.

"Larry wanted to get into more scripted stuff so I starting working on *At Z Beach,* which Terry helped write and I directed," said Loguidice. "It was a film about how artists come to choose a certain subject and we wrote it like a black comedy."

In December, Terry and Nile joined Rivers, Loguidice, and various friends and acquaintances such as William Claxton, Peggy Moffatt, Lauren Hutton, and the cabaret artist Phoebe Legere, in the coastal town of Zihuatanejo, approximately a hundred miles south of Acapulco. *At Z Beach* began shooting on video. Southern and Loguidice conducted interviews with various expatriate Americans. Some were recent arrivals with lots of money. Others were dissolute down-and-outers. Terry would craft scenarios out of their conversations. The yellow script pages that survive of this strange Cassavetes-like enterprise focus, not unsurprisingly, on the sexual tensions among this community. As this excerpt shows, *At Z Beach* was an attempt to document and fictionalize a portrait of Larry Rivers and Friends in a kind of *La Ronde* situation:

                              MARGO
Hey you know I don't think I've ever seen a *landscape* of yours
before.

                               LAR
Well actually it isn't . . .

                              MARGO
Well is it a *seascape*?

                               LAR
                             (laughs)
No, I mean it isn't *mine*—I had someone else paint it for me.

                              MARGO
                            (surprised)
Are you kidding?

LAR

No, it's a new period for me, Margo—I hire someone else to do the actual painting, and then I just *sign* it. Pretty far-out huh?

MARGO
(uncertainly)

Very funny.

The increasing emphasis on sex led to Loguidice falling out with Rivers on the project. Rivers took over the loosely defined director's chair and continued to shoot.

"*At Z Beach* was a misconceived project in my view," recalls Nile, "but what do you expect from a painter wanting to make a movie about himself? I think Larry really wanted a 'direct cinema,' which was made—quite excitingly by Pennebaker or the Maysles—and I knew and worked with both of them at the time—so I kind of wanted that to happen."

Nile also recalled some of the script sessions that dealt with Larry's obsession with children and in particular a twelve-year-old-girl, Chelan, who was a figure of innocence and budding adolescence in the films.

"Terry always kidded Larry about his interest in children—sending him letters and postcards—for instance he'd take a notice about Girl Scouts looking for a 'fun guy' counselor and he'd say, 'Attention, attention Lar E. Rivers,' or another with a 'Tot Finder' fireman decal. Larry, being very self-absorbed and interested in his own psychology, I think was interested in taking on this joke of Terry's and exploring it as an artist."

Under Rivers's direction, the script tried to capture his routine in Mexico and his involvement with an American woman with a daughter fathered by a long-departed Mexican man. Shooting on video was an ordeal for the crew rounded out by Rivers's assistant, John Dike, as cameraman, a model named Diane as production coordinator, and Nile on sound. It was hot and the sun created harsh contrasts on videotape. Nile was bitten by a scorpion. Terry drank a lot.

Nile became friendly with Legere near the end of shooting. Her mix of sexual bravado, intellectual curiosity, and innocence was very Candy-like. The two became partners and lived together for the rest of the eighties. For Terry, the interpersonal ups and downs were all raw material for *At Z Beach*. Apparently an assembly of the video footage was made by Rivers and Dike, but outside of a screening at the Whitney it had little impact on the outside world.

Southern's devotion to what some might call a vanity project when his energies might have been better spent on a legitimate screenplay, or even a novel, was typical of his indifference to any rational sense of career management.

"I never knew Terry not to be working day and night, but his periods of concentration were kind of short. He was also doing three or four different things at one time," Loguidice explains. "The thing was that Terry was driven because of his destitution. He never seemed to have any money. On the one hand, he was constantly taking on these projects in the hope of getting a grand here or two grand there, and so people would say, 'Oh, he's not reliable.' Yet I don't know of any writer who actually worked more all the time, but as far as his financial situation, he was completely undisciplined about money. The IRS, of course, was on his back. He was so deep into the IRS that it was one of those situations that unless you have a windfall it drags on forever."

In April, Southern found himself in the ironic position of being asked to work on *Biker Heaven: Easy Rider 2,* a sequel to a film he, if one heard Fonda and Hopper correctly, allegedly had little to do with. Despite the sheer absurdity of making a follow-up to a film in which all the principal characters were killed, *Biker Heaven*'s coproducers, Bert Schneider and Peter Fonda, felt the idea had possibility. Michael O'Donoghue and Nelson Lyon came up with the black-as-coal concept of having Billy and Captain America come down from heaven to recapture the flag from a postnuke America run by bike gangs, neo-Nazis, and assorted mutants and riffraff. This time, Terry really had little to do with the script. He basically went over the initial drafts put together by O'Donoghue and Lyon, who felt Southern was indifferent to the whole project.

"By this time, Terry really didn't give a shit as long as he had a payday. In fact, I think he felt that writing had betrayed him," argues Lyon. "There was something like 'Oh what's the use of writing for the big bucks and being in that arena and subjecting yourself to torture and betrayals and nobody wants you around anyway.' So although he was always writing little articles and pieces that would appear God knows where, if they were published, he really felt as if his own writing had betrayed him. And also with the porn thing, it had become like—which happens to a writer—these are people who are trapped in their own clichés. That's a little bit of what Terry was trapped in—the clichés and the hip jargon. There was no need to expand or astonish."

When the first draft of *Biker Heaven* was turned in, Fonda apparently balked at the new vision of his Captain America character. Schneider slowly cooled on the project although he did ask for some more rewrites. Ultimately Lyon and O'Donoghue received only a portion of their agreed on writing fee. Lyon believes Southern saw about $20,000 for his work, which was more than he ever made from the first film.

In the summer of 1983, a snapshot of Southern in happier times appeared in a new magazine called *The Movies,* edited by Charles Michener. The column-length piece gave a jokey account of how the term "prevert" originated in *Dr. Strangelove.* All that stood out in the brief piece was the image of Southern and Kubrick sitting in the back of a limo en route to Shepperton Studios talking story. To Southern fans, oblivious to the career follies of the last decade and a half, it was a tantalizing but tiny fragment of what should have been a longer piece.

About the same time the piece appeared, Southern received the long-awaited summons from Stanley Kubrick. For years, Kubrick had held the film rights to the 1926 book *Traumnovelle* (Dream Novel) by Arthur Schnitzler. Attracted by the book's conflict between bourgeois stability and erotic obsession, Kubrick had toyed with the idea of updating the material to contemporary New York. At this stage, Kubrick was envisioning the project (which eventually became his 1999 swan song, *Eyes Wide Shut*) as a vehicle for Steve Martin, whom he loved in *The Jerk,* or for Woody Allen.

Kubrick asked Southern to read the book and send him some sample pages of dialogue. Southern had never heard of the book, but he dispatched Nile to get him a copy. Nile could track down only a library copy, which Southern duly read. He then mailed off some pages to Kubrick.

"What he did was write a letter to Stanley saying, 'Dear Stan, were you serious about one of those protagonists being a gynecologist? How is this for sample dialogue between them?'" recalled Nile. "And the letter goes into three pages of outrageously sexual humor in dialogue form. Of course, Kubrick had no use for it, I'm sure. Terry was implying, 'Let's do that *Strangelove* thing again. I'll be in top form writing the most outrageous lines, just tell me what the basic situation is.'"

The pages concerned the gynecologist's dialogue with a female patient about a medical phenomenon known as "hooded clit." It was the kind of tomfoolery that might have had a place in *Candy* but that sabotaged Southern's chances of getting Kubrick to seriously consider him as a collaborator on this project.

Josh Alan Friedman, an editor at *High Times,* had been trying for years to get Terry to write something for the magazine. The publication had printed an interview by Victor Bockris in which Southern discussed the important, and not entirely negative, role drugs played in Hollywood. In the May 1983 issue, the last of Southern's con stories, "Tito Bandini (If That Indeed Is His Name)," appeared. Friedman had found an unfinished short story by Southern in the *High Times* files and asked Southern to finish it. "Of course, that took him a few months of spit and polish on an old story," says Friedman. The published story dealt with a cocaine deal that goes down during a dog show at Madison Square Garden. Like "Heavy Put Away," it was structured around the conceit that Southern had been told this story verbatim by a reliable source. It was amusing in a shaggy-dog sort of way, but a reader could be forgiven for thinking the whole exercise was beneath Southern's talent. The cocaine world had been more tellingly and amusingly described by Southern in *Easy Rider* and in the book *Snowblind* by Robert Sabbag.

Before coming to *High Times,* Josh had worked as an editor at *Screw.* Because of what Southern felt was Friedman's connection to the adult film industry, he asked him to track down the whereabouts of an actress known as Nancy Suiter, the star of such "classics" as *Wine Me, Dine Me, 69 Me,* and *The Ecstasy Girls.* It was a typical faux-serious lark that Southern used to fuel his letter writing.

"[Suiter] was a young, blond cheerleader type, his favorite," recalls Friedman. "I started to track her down all over the country. Man, what was the outcome of that? I called the agency and the agent said she left the business. . . . It became like a crazed detective thing. I was tracking her down from month to month from one state to another a little bit like *Lolita.* She had married some rich rancher and left the business or something."

In September, Dennis Hopper called Southern and asked him to come out to Los Angeles to work on *The Jim Morrison Story.* Larry Flynt, the notorious founder and publisher of *Hustler,* was underwriting a film about the Doors singer for his wife, Althea Flynt. Hopper was going be the director. A contract was drawn up, paying Southern $25,000 for a first draft and future monies up to $100,000.

Southern and Hopper arrived at Flynt's mansion, "the Pink Palace," in the midst of what looked like a convention of zanies. Acid prophet Timothy Leary and Watergate "plumber" Gordon Liddy were rehearsing for a speaking tour. Native American activist Russell Means, professional atheist Madlyn

Murray, Frank Zappa, and Stokely Carmichael also wandered in and out of the mansion's gaudy halls. Flynt sped about his dream home in a motorized, gold-plated wheelchair wearing a diaper made out of the American flag.

After a few days, Southern discovered that the rights to the Jim Morrison story were controlled by someone else (a Doors film directed by Oliver Stone was eventually released in 1991). He informed Althea and suggested that a film about a fictional character could circumvent this legal problem. Flynt, according to Southern, was preoccupied with a campaign to get various celebrities to "to show gyno-pink" in *Hustler* in exchange for a million dollars. He was also fighting a losing battle with the federal government over tapes he had of automobile magnate John De Lorean, Alfred Bloomingdale (the subject of a heated sex/murder scandal), and the Reagan administration. And last, but not least, Flynt was preparing a presidential campaign.

One morning, Hopper woke up in his guest room to find the Flynt mansion was surrounded by federal agents. They were negotiating with Flynt's bodyguards for access to the mansion. They had a court order authorizing them to seize videotapes of De Lorean in cahoots with drug lords and the FBI, which Flynt claimed to have in his possession. Hopper woke up Southern and they managed to discreetly vacate the mansion before things got out of control. The tapes turned out to be a red herring, but Flynt was still charged with contempt of court, fined, and jailed for a time.

The Jim Morrison/Larry Flynt episode was later reconstructed by Jean Stein in oral history mode for *Grand Street*. As the eighties marched on, in the absence of any new fiction, life often seemed like a Terry Southern novel.

On **May 1, 1984,** Southern turned sixty. *Youngblood,* now known as *South Idyll,* remained on the perpetual back burner. Putnam, who had contracted the novel, was asking for the return of a $20,000 advance. In a special issue of *Esquire* devoted to fiction, Southern was still talking about the book as a work-in-progress. Instead of new fiction, there was a reissue of *Flash and Filigree* by Arbor House with a new introduction by William Burroughs.

Sandy Lieberson, who was working for Twentieth Century-Fox at the time, hired Terry to work on a script called *Intensive Heat,* based on the life of the jewel thief Albie Baker. Southern had known Baker socially in the late fifties and early sixties. Baker was the kind of ex-criminal who goes straight and becomes embraced by the intelligentsia. Baker had turned his exploits into a memoir called *Stolen Suites* and fancied himself as a writer.

"I was just trying to help Terry. I always recommended him for work on scripts and maintained contact with him whenever I would go back to the States," said Lieberson. "Whenever I would go to New York, Terry would come down from Connecticut and we would have dinner or drinks. [*Intensive Heat*] came pretty close to being made because Robert De Niro wanted to do it. . . . De Niro met with Albie a number of times about it. At one point, he even optioned it."

Albie Baker maintained creative control on the film project. He was unhappy with Southern's work. He asked Lyon, Southern's on-again, off-again partner, to salvage things. "Albie said he made such a terrible mess out of the screenplay and failed so abysmally again with this 'ho ho ho' stuff," recalls Lyon. "He wrote Terry this awful letter like, 'Terry, you can't write anymore. You've lost everything da-da-da-duh.'"

Lyon agreed to help Southern out on a rewrite because his friend was once again in difficult, if murky financial straits. Yet it was a demoralizing experience for all concerned.

The few bright spots of this mid-eighties period were Southern's delightful appearance in *Burroughs,* a documentary directed by Howard Brookner, released in 1984, and the Penguin reissues of *The Magic Christian* and *Candy* in trade paperback in 1985. Brookner's well-received documentary had evolved organically in fits and starts between 1978 and 1983. Brookner had initiated the project in film school and had eventually gotten some money from the BBC to finish it. Unlike many of his collaborations, Southern's friendship with Burroughs was relatively uncomplicated by business or work. Toward the end of the documentary, Burroughs and Southern are seen joking around at the kitchen table at the former's Bowery apartment known affectionately as "the Bunker." Burroughs gives Southern a tour of his orgone box, prompting Terry to quip, "It's a bit like California, a nice place to visit, but I wouldn't want to live there." This was the Terry Southern few fans were aware of—a warm, gentle, and funny man with a deep loyalty to old friends.

One old friend reached the end of the line in 1986. On June 1, Mason Hoffenberg died of lung cancer in New York. He was sixty-four. He had remained a heroin addict up until his death.

Southern and Hoffenberg's mutual friend from their Paris and London days, Mordecai Richler, heard the news while eating in a chic restaurant on West Thirty-seventh Street. John Calley, of all people, dropped by his table and said, "Mason's dead."

Richler hadn't seen Mason in any meaningful way since 1966. Back then Richler was living with his wife and kids in London's Kingston Hill financing his novel-writing habit with lucrative screenwriting work. It was the height of the British film boom, when England was flooded by American studios wanting to cash in on "Swinging London." His last meeting with Hoffenberg was a depressing glimpse of an old friend humbled by heroin addiction.

"Mason was in a very bad way and he wanted to kick," recalled Richler. "I had an Irish doctor who was very understanding, and I phoned him. Mason was staying with Marianne Faithfull. So I got him some methadone. I brought him back to our place and put him in the bedroom. He was in there all weekend. Then he came down and said he needed some drugs, so I drove him to Leicester Square, where he could go to an all-night drugstore. I remember guys who had too much pep pills hanging around the tube station. I only saw Mason a few times after that. When I had picked Mason up at Marianne Faithfull's, Mason wanted to shoot up, but he could no longer find a vein. He said, 'You know, you could break my shit with a stick.'"

On another occasion in this period, Richler met Hoffenberg at the White Elephant, a Soho restaurant then favored by film and theater people. Mason was having trouble with a bad needle and was in obvious need of a bath. Sean Connery came by to say hello to Richler and looked askance at Hoffenberg, who then broke into a cold sweat. It was typical of many people's interactions with Mason in the wake of *Candy*.

Hoffenberg spent most of the sixties shuttling between London and Paris. His marriage collapsed. Most of the money Hoffenberg made from the "db" that had briefly made him a household name was from the movie sale. The rest came from his mother. His wife looked after their two kids, Daniel and Juliette.

When Sam Merrill met up with Hoffenberg for the controversial *Playboy* interview, he had been in a methadone maintenance program. He eventually kicked, but became an alcoholic. In Woodstock, New York, he became friendly with Bob Dylan as well as with members of the Band. He seemed to exist by living off friends. What little writing he did was in the form of a long, meandering autobiographical novel.

According to his daughter, Juliette Hoffenberg, Mason began a long romance with Eliza Brownjohn, the estranged wife of the English critic and poet Alan Brownjohn. They lived together in Los Angeles, where Hoffenberg became friendly with the future producer of *The Fly,* Stuart Cornfeld. In L.A., Mason tried to live a relatively stable life, but lack of money and the addiction intervened. He also lived for a year in Majorca. By 1978, he was living with his mother. After her death in the same year, he moved to an apartment on East Seventy-ninth Street, where he lived until his death. Hoffenberg was reconciled with his son and daughter in the intervening years.

One of the last people from the sixties to see Mason was Anita Pallenberg. She was coming to the end of her own torturous journey on heroin and lived a reclusive existence in Long Island.

"One day we went to see the New York Marathon. I don't know for what reason, it was probably drugs," recalls Pallenberg. "We made a few jokes about all these people in the Marathon and us. Once he came out to visit me on Long Island where I was living and by then he was very sick. He already had asthma. He used to say coughing was the only exercise he got and eventually that's what killed him. . . . And he had a prescription we used, too. It was all very drug-related. The next thing I heard was that he died."

By the end of the eighties, Pallenberg had kicked drugs, moved back to London, and enrolled in St. Martin's College of Art to study fashion design. She now works for Vivienne Westwood.

According to Patti Dryden, the illustrator who became his friend in his final New York years, Hoffenberg's influence was steeped in a certain fifties underground way of looking at the world.

"If you're talking about what Mason's claim to fame was, it was not what society thought was valuable," said Dryden. "He once told me he was very proud of the fact he knew Nico, Anita Pallenberg, and Marianne Faithfull and he was responsible for all three of them becoming junkies. He would surround himself with these attractive women. I remember spending an evening with Anita Pallenberg, Marianne Faithfull, and him. They had a great affection for him. I don't know if it's true he turned them on to junk, but I wouldn't put it past him.

"One time I got very depressed over something—and this shows you Mason's introspectiveness—I was crying and he said, 'Let's get together and we'll walk around.' That's nice, I thought. So we got together and I was crying and trying to talk. I think it must have been about romance. He said, 'I've got some junk at home and I think if you start on that it will make you feel better.' That was his solution to everything. 'What are you trying to do, turn me into a fucking junky! I don't want to be like you.' But that was his way of helping. And I can see if you get together with someone who was a little less strong-willed, they might go, 'Well, hmm, maybe that would be a good thing.'"

The copyright wrangles over *Candy* wouldn't be sorted out until long after the book ceased being a bestseller. Southern's comparatively success-ful writing career drove an irreparable wedge between Hoffenberg and his former Left Bank buddy.

Southern did not show up at Hoffenberg's funeral, but they did meet briefly before he died. No one quite remembers the details of the meeting, but it did inspire Terry to pen a short story called "The Refreshing Ambiguity of the Déjà Vu." The story is a slight but elegantly written piece in which a mysterious woman in a limousine stumbles upon Candy Christian putting on a kind of roadside peep show in the Gobi Desert. Her girl-next-door looks are faded, but a brief sparkle of fun can still be dis-cerned. The story was eventually published in *Grand Street* in 1992. In a final salute to a lost friendship, the credit read "written by Mason Hoffenberg and Terry Southern."

13
Hawkeye
(Travels with Harry)

All you have is the power of persuasion," Terry would say again and again to those who asked him about the pitfalls of screenwriting. Screenwriters who wanted to redress the balance had to become producers or writer/directors. Not everyone had the right combination of political instinct, business sense, temperament, ambition, and energy to take a role other than that of hired pen. John Gregory Dunne and Joan Didion viewed screenwriting as a well-paid form of slumming, which bought time to work on novels, nonfiction books, or essays for the *New York Review of Books*. Other writers, like William Goldman, seemed to delight in being the Hollywood equivalent of court advisers. Then there were the script doctors like Robert Towne and Elaine May, who took a surgeon's pride in their ability to save a blockbuster or anonymously polish a comedy. Directing one's own material was no guarantee of success either. Paul Schrader and John Sayles still relied on byzantine layers of international financing, festival acclaim, and solid reviews to sustain their personal films (nor were they above taking on a rewrite or two). Southern was not alone in his frustrations with screenwriting, but unlike other Writers Guild members, he did seem incapable of using the system to his advantage.

On October 23, 1985, Southern made his greatest attempt to change this state of things. Along with a grand good friend, the celebrated singer/songwriter/arranger/producer Harry Nilsson, he joined the executive lineup of Hawkeye. Executive Vice President Nilsson and his company president James Hock conceived Hawkeye as a way to develop and oversee a variety of film and multimedia projects. Cindy Sims was hired as the director and secretary-treasurer of the new company, because of her experience working for Segal and Goldman, a business management firm specializing in entertainment.

Offices were leased at 1130 Ventura Boulevard in Studio City, California. Southern was given his first corporate title, vice president of literary and script development. As a Hawkeye executive, he would receive an annual salary of $40,000 and 400,000 shares in the company. Financing had been arranged by Hock, who had experience working with America's major banks.

Despite expertise at the executive levels of the new company, there was something wrong with this enterprise. By the end of 1990, Hawkeye would collapse like the proverbial house of cards. By Hollywood standards, it would not be a disaster on a par with United Artists and *Heaven's Gate,* but it was certainly a case study in hubris worthy of closer inspection.

Hawkeye was formed out of Southern's strong friendship with Harry Nilsson. Like Randy Newman and Carole King, Nilsson was a songwriter who got his start writing material for others. In the sixties, the Brooklyn native's work was covered by the likes of Herb Alpert, the Monkees, the Byrds, and the Ronettes. The influence of the Beatles and Bob Dylan on Nilsson and other songwriters led to the pursuit of more creative autonomy. In October of 1967, Nilsson released a solo album, *Pandemonium Shadow Show.* The record would have sunk like a stone had it not been for the fact that, out of the blue, the Beatles championed it.

In 1968, Nilsson traveled to London to meet the Fab Four, and was greeted as if he were the fifth Beatle. He wrote "The Puppy Song" for Apple protégée Mary Hopkin, which became a modest hit. He became especially close to John Lennon and Ringo Starr. In 1969, his cover of Fred Neil's "Everybody's Talkin'" from the *Midnight Cowboy* soundtrack helped to put his second album, *Aerial Ballet,* in the top ten. Ironically, the cover elevated Nilsson to the celebrity he had sought. His next hit, the 1972 single "Without You," was also a cover, this time of a Badfinger song.

Still the singles sold very well and raised the sales for Nilsson's solo work up to that time. RCA extended its investment in Nilsson. Through a healthy contract and various recordings of his work by other artists, the money rolled in. By the mid-seventies, Nilsson—who not so long before had managed the evening clearing operations of a bank—was living the rock 'n' roll dream.

Southern recalls meeting Nilsson through Ringo Starr around the time of *The Magic Christian.* Gail Gerber says he knew little of Nilsson's music before then. They were at a gathering arranged by Ringo when Terry heard some music playing. He complained about the singer's voice.

"He was embarrassed," recalls Gerber. "Because then he discovered the guy was in the room. Someone said, 'This is Harry Nilsson, the guy who was just singing.' I mean, I guess he just had to get used to Harry because he really did appreciate him. . . . [Nilsson] was distinctive in the way he would avoid actually ever getting to a note for a long time."

From this inauspicious beginning, a beautiful friendship emerged. Like Southern, Nilsson was a shy and sensitive man with a fragile artistic gift. He was married to a beautiful and loyal Irish woman, Una, and lived for his kids. Nilsson's smooth-as-silk voice was eventually ravaged by drug and alcohol abuse. His delicately evocative solo albums, also like Terry, would eventually shows signs of self-parody. Gerber describes their relationship as "the love of one drunk for another."

During the seventies, whenever the two found themselves together in Los Angeles or New York, they would indulge in some hell-raising. Sometimes it was innocent, like taking Nile to meet Marc Bolan at a recording studio. Other times it involved serious drinking—brandy Alexanders, cognac, whiskey sours, etc.—with the likes of Keith Moon and John Lennon in his "lost weekend of 1974" period. Occasionally Southern and Nilsson would toy with a script, as they did in 1976 with *King Dong,* a rather obvious parody of the classic fantasy film.

"Harry wanted to party and he had enough money to do it," recalls Gerber. "But he couldn't just party, so, under the pretense of partying, he had to pretend it was like work. He wanted to come up with all these projects. I don't think he was ever serious because I think he was too afraid of being judged or exposed. There are a lot of very talented people who are always in rehearsal or always in ballet class because they don't want to get out there on that limb that we all know so well."

By the late seventies, Nilsson began to turn his attention to film projects like animated film *The Point* and the soundtrack to Robert Altman's *Popeye.* He started developing treatments and story ideas for film and television. Because of his song catalog and some astute real estate investments, Nilsson was able to indulge himself. The business reasoning behind Hawkeye was not unsound. In Hollywood, you protected yourself by using the same corporate approach as the big studios and production companies.

After the establishment of Hawkeye, a whole slew of projects were announced. Treatments and scripts were sent to the studios and agencies around town. The two strongest candidates were *Obits* and *The Telephone.*

Obits was originally a screenplay by Roger Watkins. It dealt with a tabloid reporter's investigation into a strange obituary notice. Hawkeye acquired the rights on July 3, 1985. In the fall of that year, Nilsson and Southern rewrote the screenplay.

In the new script, Harry Taylor, a reporter for *News World,* decides to write about the life of Jason Stoat, a Texas oilman who had died several years earlier. His investigation takes him to Crystal City, Texas, the spinach capital of the world. He discovers there were two Jason Stoats, both twins. One is still alive. While searching for the latter, Taylor meets other members of the Stoat family—the incontinent Peirsol; Emily Stoat, who uses a manufactured voice box to communicate and masturbates to a recording of Walter Cronkite's voice; and the obnoxious Vern. The male Stoats try to get Harry to sleep with Emily at a strange dinner. *Obits* continues in this baroque fashion, culminating in a scene set back at the offices of *News World,* where the editor receives a postcard indicating Harry has indeed become a part of the bizarre Stoat family.

A reader's report gives a pretty good sense of the reaction to this script from other production companies: "Apparently the idea here is to create an adult X-rated fantasy featuring a live-action reporter who enters a make-believe world that might even be a world of his deranged fantasies and fears. Whatever the goal is, it is not at all clear from the way the script is written. The opening sequence is intriguing but the rest of the story is vague, puerile, and offensive.

"If one puts aside the many off-color, distasteful scenes long enough to examine the story, it shows itself to be completely lacking in logic and continuity. Unlike *Roger Rabbit,* this fantasy never defines the separate worlds, their origins, or shows under what conditions they might come together. Consequently, everything feels arbitrary and confusing. We don't know if the lead is nutty, if he's happened on a haunted house, or if the make-believe stories he's been writing have actually come into existence."

The reader concluded that the script's lack of commercial appeal was compounded by the "disgusting use of sexual innuendo, masturbation, nudity, and excrement." In a filmmaking climate in which the most popular films were escapist fare like *Back to the Future* and *Mad Max 2,* the mondo-satire of *Obits* was distinctly out of fashion.

Undeterred, Nilsson and Southern continued to shop *Obits* around. However, it was *The Telephone* that managed to attract star power. Written with Robin Williams in mind, *The Telephone* is an O. Henry–type monologue about Roger Wilcox, an unemployed actor coping with mounting debts and possible eviction. As the actor's answering machine fills up with messages from creditors and estranged friends, he launches into a series of impromptu stream-of-consciousness impersonations. His only contact with the outside world consists of neighbors banging on his wall to try to quiet him and a visit by his sleazy agent and bimbo girlfriend. Eventually we discover the telephone connection has been cut off for months and that the actor has clearly gone insane in the interim.

After several attempts to get the script to Williams through his agent, Nilsson and Southern were able to pin the actor down at one of the comedy clubs where he made his impromptu appearances. In the end, Williams passed on *The Telephone.* Then they discovered that Whoopi Goldberg was keen to work on the film. The talented comedienne had made her well-received acting debut as Celie in *The Color Purple,* directed by Steven Spielberg, but subsequent films such as *Jumpin' Jack Flash* and *The Burglar* were indifferently produced. No one seemed to really know how to exploit Goldberg's comic talent.

Goldberg liked *The Telephone* and asked Southern and Nilsson if they would consider rewriting it for her. They agreed and received a letter of intent from Goldberg signaling her commitment to *The Telephone* once a distributor or studio was in place. Over the course of 1986, Hawkeye shopped *The Telephone* around with Goldberg's name attached. Eventually New World Pictures came on board. Rip Torn was hired to direct the film. According to a Hawkeye deal memo, Southern was to be paid $350,000 for his script, but there is little evidence that he ultimately received more than a modest first installment of this sum.

Production began in January 1987, in San Francisco. Goldberg's character was now called Vashti Blue, but the plot remained the same. Elliott Gould played Rodney the agent and Amy Wright was Honey Boxe. John Heard made a brief cameo at the end of the film as an angry representative of the telephone company. Filling out a few minor parts were Severn Darden as a friendly neighbor and Herve Villechaize, whose voice was the only thing that surfaced in the final cut.

It became apparent very quickly as filming began that Goldberg was operating under a different set of rules than Torn, Nilsson, and Southern, regarding the ultimate creative authority on the set. The New World producers had told Goldberg she could improvise as much as she wanted and that she would be allowed to exercise final cut in the editing room.

"One of the producers told Whoopi that she could improvise on their script," recalls Nile. "They told her she was the bread and butter of this production and the script was really not that important. That was, of course a big problem. The other one was that Whoopi put in place her then husband as the cameraman and Rip had gone to great lengths to get John Alonzo [a veteran cinematographer who had shot *Chinatown, The Fortune,* and *Cross Creek*] to shoot. . . . This was a one-set apartment. To make it interesting you could do some really great handheld stuff. Rip ended up saying that this cameraman had dyslexia with the camera. He would shoot what should be a close-up with a wide shot and vice versa, and nothing was working. Rip would say after the end of a few takes with Whoopi doing all her wild improvisations, 'How about one for the author?' and she'd say 'okay' and she would do it like it was written. It was very bad for Rip to have to deal with this scene and he didn't have a good time at all."

"I don't know to this day how she could not appreciate or just be interested [in] . . . two people like Terry and Rip Torn," said Gail Gerber. "I can't understand that. Apparently there was this person who said, 'Really, Whoopi, what we want is for you to wing it.' She would have been wonderful if she had stuck to the script. It was a wonderful monologue. That monologue was so solid that to read it at the kitchen table was wonderful. I had a French friend who read it in her French accent, all the characters. It was just mesmerizing. They could have done it standing on their heads. Anybody could."

The $2 million production wrapped on schedule, but was followed by a yearlong battle between Hawkeye, New World, and Goldberg over final cut. Southern and Torn took a print of their version to Sundance in January 1988. The New World version opened in a few New York and Los Angeles theaters the same month. The reviews were lukewarm and dismissive. New World became embroiled in a lawsuit with Goldberg over whether or not she did have final cut.

In fairness to Goldberg, *The Telephone* was a project that never quite solved the problem of how to make someone going nuts in a room visually interesting. Not unsurprisingly, *The Telephone*'s only success came when two German actresses gained permission to do the script as an intimate theater piece.

In the wake of *The Telephone*'s dismal critical reception and dim commercial prospects, Hawkeye's other projects attracted little attention. Nilsson traveled to London in April 1988, to seek out financing for *Obits* with Pablo Ferro attached as director, but a promising deal fell apart. Those close to Southern felt the Hawkeye management team lacked the discipline and killer instinct to survive in Hollywood's competitive environment.

"I was then managing a lot of artists, a lot of Academy Award– and Grammy-award-winning musicians, writers, actors," said Si Litvinoff, who was briefly attached to the Hawkeye team. "I had a couple of meetings with them to see if we could pull something off. Unfortunately, despite my efforts and a great deal of effort on Terry's part, which managed to get some money in, Harry seemed to change his mind every day. He wouldn't show up for meetings. I saw the ship sinking. When you have some experience with these things you begin to recognize [when] there is something suspect. That was unfortunate because Terry tried and I tried to get [Hawkeye] moving forward, but that was a waste of a lot of money."

For Southern and Gerber, the best thing about Hawkeye was the steady income. The nature of Terry's job at Hawkeye was, Nile believes, too ill-defined for him to be effective.

"Personally I thought the company was not being run terribly well," said Nile. "If he was to be in charge of literary development, he should have a secretary and there should be constant updating of ideas and material. As it was, he and Harry were pretty much riding shotgun and just firing away, but not really making the kinds of business choices you need to make running that kind of company. You shouldn't put energy into one really bizarre script, but you might do a few things and try to make some money, even commission other writers. There were a lot of possibilities. In any case, [Terry] was earning a salary through Hawkeye even though he was living in Connecticut and just wandering around. He would be rewriting these different scripts that Hawkeye was developing. One was about shuffleboard. He was working on these scripts that were in development hell, really."

Hawkeye's other projects included the Saturn Awards for science fiction, horror, and fantasy films released in the previous year. Nile worked with Pablo Ferro on preparing a montage of clips for the broadcast. Nile also worked on a history of the Doobie Brothers documentary. There was also vague talk by Nilsson of commissioning Timothy Leary, William Burroughs, and Southern to develop interactive software. These peripheral projects, along with a dozen or so scripts floating through the offices of agents and producers, did not generate a great deal of heat for the ill-fated company.

"My dad was always based in Connecticut. Harry wanted him to move out and live in L.A. My dad did come out for some meetings and vaguely considered the possibilities of getting a place. It didn't seem like it would happen," said Nile. "At least he was really earning a salary from Hawkeye. It was a godsend and we thank Harry for that, but then the checks started to not come through anymore. The company started to dissolve [and] my dad had to look for another source of income."

Gail remembers a poignant conversation she had with Harry's wife, Una, that sheds some light on one problem with Hawkeye—the relationship between Harry and Terry. "Una said, 'The worst thing that ever happened was Harry meeting Terry.' Well, I told her, 'Well, one of the worst things that happened was Terry meeting Harry,' so that was pretty well both our points of view of their relationship.

"They weren't doing anything really bad. They weren't getting laid or anything. They would hole up in the most expensive hotel in town. Whatever town it was. Fooling around writing things. They were wasting time and other people's time, too. Their own time turned out to be short."

Harry and Terry were their own comedy team and audience. Like Southern, Harry Nilsson came from inauspicious beginnings. His creative gifts—his beautiful voice and joyous songs—were also rare, fragile, and almost too precious for this world. Both men masked their hypersensitivity through gregarious personas. If Southern was the Grand Guy, Nilsson played the fedora-wearing man about town who could hang out with rock 'n' rollers or dine out like a gourmand at the finest restaurants and bars. Both men used drugs and alcohol to mask their insecurities. They were both aware that they were viewed as coasters who had seen much better days. If Southern was the almost forgotten writer of *Dr. Strangelove* and *Easy Rider,* Nilsson had to deal with the public perception of having gotten John Lennon so drunk that he walked into a club with a Kotex on his head.

Despite a penchant for goofing off, Southern continued to work on scripts. The flame that had been ignited by *Dr. Strangelove* still kept his shoulder to the wheel. With Nile's friend Mark Amerika, Southern worked on a treatment for a *Barbarella* sequel. He also toyed with an adaptation of *Modern Baptists,* a critically acclaimed novel by James Wilcox, a young writer with a distinctive satiric voice.

Toward the end of 1989, Hawkeye fell apart. One morning Una and Harry woke up to discover they were virtually bankrupt. Hawkeye's capable secretary-treasurer, Cindy Sims, had stolen from the company. Nilsson was forced to borrow money from friends to sort out the mess. Eventually Sims was charged with embezzlement and served three years in prison.

"Cindy Sims was supposed to be doing the income tax," recalls Gail. "Terry's Hawkeye checks were always late, and his car, which was supposed to be paid [for], was repossessed. She stole Harry's money and went up the river. In the meantime, Terry's lawyer tried to get in touch with

Harry's lawyer, but they wouldn't return the phone calls. . . . Harry just sort of abandoned Terry. Not only did Terry owe $30,000 in income tax, which I paid off, but another $40,000 in penalties."

The brief financial respite provided by Hawkeye went up in smoke. By 1993, Southern would be in another tax mess. Some of it was due to Sims's failure to deduct taxes during Southern's Hawkeye employment. The IRS also decided to tax Southern's residuals from *Easy Rider* and *Dr. Strangelove*. In total, according to Gerber, Southern had to pay back about $70,000 in taxes. This bill was finally settled after his death.

Aside from countless bad reviews for *The Telephone* (which did, however, enjoy a popular afterlife as a video rental), Hawkeye had done nothing to resurrect Terry in the eyes of his fans. Between 1985 and 1990, Southern's published output amounted to the liner notes for Marianne Faithfull's *Strange Weather,* produced by Hal Wilner, and a commentary on Iran-Contra for the *Nation.*

In February 1989, Southern entered Sloan-Kettering to undergo major surgery for stomach cancer. The night after his surgery, Mike Golden, a New York writer and screenwriter, came to visit Terry. Golden had been trying to reach Southern for months for a story he was preparing for *New York Writer* on Maurice Girodias. Out of the blue, he was summoned by Southern to the hospital. Over the next four hours, the two men bonded and Terry got a lot off his chest. Golden couldn't bear to hear the tapes because of their intensity and felt that given Southern's postop manic state it wouldn't be fair to quote him. Eventually Golden rescheduled the interview. Portions of it ran in places like *Reflex* magazine, *Creative Screenwriter,* and the *Paris Review.* Golden represented a generation of writers who had discovered Southern's work as teenagers in the sixties and seventies. Although publishers and editors in New York had consigned Southern to oblivion, the likes of Golden, Bruce Wagner, Mark Leyner, Michael Tolkin, Darius James, and others demonstrated that he was still relevant to a grassroots constituency.

When Southern got out of the hospital, he began collaborating with cartoonist R. O. Blechman on *Billionaire's Ball,* a screenplay inspired by the life of Howard Hughes. He also landed a gig to teach at Sundance's Screenwriters Lab that summer.

Southern in addition began a trip down memory lane by assisting in the preparation and publication of *Blinds and Shutters,* a limited-edition book devoted to the photography of Michael Cooper, who died in 1973 of a heroin overdose. Perry Richardson, an enthusiastic Englishman in his thirties, was the editor. With the assistance of Michael's son Adam, he had assembled and cataloged thousands of Cooper's photos; many of them had never appeared in print before. Each book in the 2,000-copy edition was housed in a salamander-colored box. A sliding blind on the box's cover contained a photograph unique to that copy. The editions were signed by many of Cooper's friends and subjects such as Paul McCartney, Keith Richards, Sandy Lieberson, Allen Ginsberg, and many others. Richardson had also compiled tributes and reminiscences of Cooper and his swinging sixties heyday. Southern helped arrange contacts and wrote a lot of the text for the ambitious project.

Richardson and Southern had met through Nilsson when *Blinds and Shutters* was still in its early stages. Nilsson helped underwrite some of Richardson's initial expenses and introduced him to Genesis/Hedley, a small press that had put out *I Me Mine,* a similar limited-edition project for George Harrison.

"Terry was a constant source of inspiration," says Richardson, "and I don't think the book would have happened without him. It might have happened, but without the degree of quality and detail that we managed. The publishers at one point wanted to just do a book of full-page photographs and we had to argue that it had to be done as a scrapbook, which was the original concept."

During the six years it took Richardson to get *Blinds and Shutters* published, the two men became close friends. Like many of the younger friends Southern made in the later years of his life, Richardson saw Terry as a kind of hip role model.

"Terry never in my experience denigrated anyone," recalls Richardson. "If he had a criticism of anybody it was always made [as a suggestion that the person] could do better. I was so bowled over by the extent of his output . . . the number of scripts that he completed, the number of drafts, the number of outlines, essays—the quantity was astonishing. All of this—even though he wrote every day—was a symptom of his life. . . . One very striking aspect of his situation was that he was not as widely recognized as he should be. I found it extraordinary that although he was commissioned by so many different producers, including characters like Mike Nichols and other substantial figures in Hollywood, not one of his scripts had been produced. *End of the Road* he had a lot to do with himself. Although he managed to hold on to the house which was so big and so wonderful, he was barely making money.

"Harry Nilsson at that time was a real benefit to him. Other people were as well . . . but none of it seemed to bother Terry. It was secondary to what he was doing. What was important was the work he was writing and his life. It was only later that it really started to wear on him."

Richardson believes Southern's terrible reputation as a wild drunk and druggie was based on Southern's occasional public appearances. Terry loved to come into town for a binge, explains Richardson, but few people saw him when he was in East Canaan writing.

"I don't think Terry was trying to take anyone in with the Grand Guy thing," said Richardson. "Obviously it was a role to some extent, but it was also what he was. Of course, he got frustrated, depressed, and angry, but he always knew that was not how he wanted to be. It was certainly secondary to him when set against how great life is and how wonderful people are."

Southern responded to Richardson partly because he was English. Although he hadn't been back to London for some time (Gail had recently gone over to London to attend a summer teaching workshop), he was an unrepentant Anglophile in many ways. One of Southern's favorite films was *Dead of Night,* the anthology film of ghost stories, which became a late-night movie favorite. In the eighties, Southern watched the BBC adaptation of *Brideshead Revisited* every time it reran, and admired Dennis Potter's *Singing Detective* when it aired on PBS. Richardson was also amused by Southern's fondness for *The House of Eliott,* a quaint series about two women who run a dress shop in the twenties.

The work that Southern did on *Blinds and Shutters,* which was launched in the fall of 1989 with a big party organized by Earl McGrath, was sincere and heartfelt. Clearly a part of Southern was still living in the England of the fifties and sixties. However, *Blinds and Shutters* was not without its drawbacks. According to Richardson, Bill Wyman, one of the contributors, blocked plans to publish a trade edition of the expensive book. It became pricey curio priced at $600 a copy (the eternally cash-poor Southern sold his complimentary copy to a book dealer).

Near the end of the eighties, Southern, Burroughs, and Grauerholz heard that David Cronenberg was seriously considering making a film based on *Naked Lunch.* Unlike the others who had tried to tackle the book, Cronenberg was not a marginal figure in the film community. The Toronto-born director had made a series of films—*Scanners, The Dead Zone, The Fly,* and *Dead Ringers*—that successfully incorporated Burroughs's imagery and philosophy. Southern was a particular fan of *Dead Ringers,* a breathtaking tragedy about twin gynecologists in love with the same woman. With this film, Cronenberg had successfully transcended the horror genre that critics and studio heads had tried to pigeonhole him in. Now in collaboration with English producer Jeremy Thomas, the Canadian auteur was seriously developing *Naked Lunch* as his next project.

Grauerholz was not sure of Cronenberg's plans for the adaptation, but he could introduce Terry to the director and see if they made a connection.

"Terry came at his own expense from Connecticut to Toronto for story meetings at the King William, a fancy hotel in Toronto," recalls Grauerholz. "I remember I talked with William, Terry, and David about *Naked Lunch* . . . I did the best I could to try and set Terry up with this job and it just never came to anything after that. I do have an unforgettable memory of the next morning. I remember at the Toronto airport early in the morning, about nine, nine-thirty, Terry stopping at one of the bars at the airport, and really slamming [back] a bunch of drinks. I don't remember if it was Bloody Marys or what. Well before breakfast. He was shaking and he just physically looked very ill and unhappy. I thought to myself, 'My God, he's really turned into a raging alcoholic.' I say nothing to drinking in principle, even heavy drinking, but, my God, if you can't get on a plane at ten in the morning without three, four drinks, something is wrong. I don't know if David perceived this about Terry or what.

"The last time I ever spoke to Terry, I was in Los Angeles at Earl McGrath's place. Terry called to say hi and then he began saying, 'Ah, I was counting on you' (*Naked Lunch* was already out by this point). . . . Terry was remonstrating and rebuking me for not fixing him up with that job. And I was really hurt because I *had* tried to fix him up with the fucking job! It wasn't my fault that David chose to write the script himself, but that was literally the last time we ever spoke."

Grauerholz realized Southern's bitterness was atypical of the Grand Guy. Still, given the last two decades, perhaps Southern could be given some slack for feeling a little abused and neglected.

14

Texas Summer

Dylan Thomas said, "Do not go gentle into that good night . . . rage, rage against the dying of the light." Well, that was easy for him to say. Dead at thirty-nine after drinking himself into an early grave, Thomas had made the big exit just as his celebrity was peaking. By contrast, Southern had survived and paid the price of neglect.

The Hawkeye debacle and the battle with stomach cancer after two decades of critical indifference and energy-draining projects had taken their toll. With his white hair and beard, Southern was looking a lot more like Merlin than the cool and slim hipster of yore. The Grand Guy was becoming all too aware that he was simply another old man.

In late November 1989, Victor Bockris paid Southern a visit. As a fan as well as friend of Southern, Bockris wanted everyone to know about the magic of Terry's art and life. He had pitched Ingrid Sischy at *Interview* magazine on a Southern feature, knowing all too well that any significant media coverage had been almost nonexistent since 1970. Aside from a brief chat in connection with his biography of Keith Richards, Bockris had not seen his friend in a long time. He was touched by the warm hospitality of Southern, who enjoyed playing the gracious host in his country home. Surrounded by fresh snow, the house by Blackberry River looked especially beautiful in the moonlight—a quiet haven between melancholy and calm.

In a kind of baronial splendor, Southern sat across from Bockris in an armchair next to a fire. Bockris could see a typewriter nearby. A freshly opened bottle of red wine sat on the table along with a wooden tray of cheese, bread, and crackers. Books and papers were scattered everywhere. Bockris jumped into the questions right away. What was it like, he asked, to be living in Geneva and working on *Flash and Filigree* and *The Magic Christian*?

"He described his wife and where he was living at the time," said Bockris. "It was great. As he was talking to me all the age melted away from his face. I saw this really beautiful young guy come out and his eyes lit up. He was just telling me this in a really lovely way."

The taping continued for another forty minutes. Then Gail announced dinner was ready. The two men got up and walked into the dining room.

"I was stunned," said Bockris, "because there before me was a picture out of a magazine. The dining room was elegantly furnished with this eighteenth-century table and a feast was laid out very delicately with beautiful plates and glasses. A great roast on the table with bottles of wine. Terry could see that I was completely stunned. He laughed and said, 'Special night for you, Vic, here at Blackberry Manor. Best for Squire.'"

Terry seemed to be in great spirits and so was Bockris, who was admittedly a little light-headed from the wine and a joint he'd shared with Terry upon arriving. They sat down and ate dinner. During dessert and cocktails, Bockris started the interview again.

"About fifteen minutes in, I asked a question along the lines of 'Terry, there are so many people who love your work and really want to know why you haven't published a book in the last twenty years?' Then the atmosphere changed dramatically in a way that was frightening and my stomach sort of went three revolutions. He suddenly got cold and removed and changed and said, 'What is this! An interview with the artist manqué!' and he didn't say it humorously. Gail got really uptight and said something like 'Terry can do what he wants!' or something kind of stupid that didn't really make any sense. It was so extreme. There was a long silence and I thought I had blown the interview and completely turned him off. I felt totally zonked the way you do when you've got yourself in this wonderful state, you're up there because you've smoked all this grass and had a couple of drinks, but you're also vulnerable and fragile."

Bockris did his best to restore the jovial mood. He reassured Terry that he was only asking the question out of a deep sense of love and awe for his friend's work. Like many of the people who would read the interview, Bockris was at pains to emphasize he couldn't get enough of Terry's writing and was just puzzled there wasn't more. Everyone wants to know about all the crazy experiences behind your books and films. In short, Bockris stressed how much Terry Southern had been *missed*.

"I was saying this because it was true and then he sort of melted a bit. We kind of got over that point," says Bockris. "Then he told me that story about crossing the Atlantic in the *QE2* with Peter Sellers. That bridged the gap and the interview went on. We went back into the living room, it now being quite late, and had some more drinks. He and I got into a kind of bantering thing and making jokes. He said some pithy things about people. . . . He was actually praising the people and not putting them down at all."

Bockris delicately tried to get Terry to respond to the kinds of thorny aesthetic questions that writers like Mailer and Vidal would have parlayed with ease. Often, when asked a direct question that touched on feelings of failure, regret, or frustration, Southern retreated into anecdotes. At their best these anecdotes would give glimpses of Terry's worldview via the backdoor. In talking about others, Terry was able to talk about himself.

Bockris stayed the night, but left for New York at 7:00 A.M., leaving a thank-you note for Terry and Gail. Later that day, Terry called Victor to express misgivings about the taping session.

"He was like, 'I don't want to say anything bad about Norman.' I said, 'You didn't say anything bad, and secondly I wouldn't publish anything you said that was.' I put the piece together and took it to the editor of *Interview*, Ingrid Sischy, and she did a brilliant cut on it. All she did was cut out the bit about Peter Sellers, because the rest of the interview was really all about Terry."

Condensed from more than forty pages of transcript to a taut two-page spread with evocative pictures of Terry in the fifties and sixties, Bockris's *Interview* piece gave fans a long-overdue treat and piqued the curiosity of general readers. With the reissue of *Red Dirt Marijuana* and the long-awaited appearance of *Texas Summer* just around the corner, Bockris's *Interview* article promised a major Terry Southern renaissance.

"[The interview dealt with] his whole thing about not wanting to be famous and not courting celebrity. Sischy thought it was a great interview. I got a great response from it. I called Terry up after it came out. He said, 'Well, I thought the pictures were good,' so he was obviously uncomfortable," Bockris recalls, "but I could tell that he wasn't able to see it was a well-crafted piece that actually showed him in a favorable, enlightened, high-minded way. He also answered a few questions people were wondering about. I guess what I did was I kept the hard and harsher stuff. We didn't pursue the biographical line and so I wasn't able to run the stuff about *Flash and Filigree*, because it didn't fit into the overall conversation. The interview became, in a sense, a combat between interviewer and interviewee."

Bockris was right. Southern could not recognize that Victor was paying homage. Southern's first interview in a mass-circulation publication since the sixties contained a superb photo collage that provided a rare celebratory glimpse of Southern in his prime. Southern's discomfort with the interview appeared to stem from the regret, frustration, and disappointment he had experienced since those halcyon days.

By 1990, Southern's work was indeed in limbo. Many of his novels were out of print. New work showed up in odd places—a commentary in the *Nation,* a liner note for a Marianne Faithfull album, or an interview in some obscure Canadian arts magazine. To say that Southern was operating below radar was an understatement. The Quality Lit Game had long ago been supplanted by corporate mergers, synergies, and cost cutting.

Southern was not without resources, however, and usually in the form of friendships. Jean Stein had always been an unabashed fan of all things Southern. She had even considered writing an *Edie*-type book about her friend. When she took over *Grand Street* from Ben Sonnenberg in 1990, she injected an enormous amount of cash into the magazine and revamped it completely in design and format. The modest black-and-white digest was replaced by a glossier format to compete with Bill Buford's *Granta*. Each issue now contained a full-color art portfolio breaking up the prose, poetry, and other belles lettres. Stein set up an editorial board that included the Farrar, Straus & Giroux editor Jonathan Galassi, Edward Said, and English critic and writer Jeremy Treglown.

In the first issue of the revamped *Grand Street,* published in the spring of 1991, Stein ran an excerpt from her long-in-progress Los Angeles book, a cross-cultural, multivoiced secret history of the city. The piece consisted of Southern and Dennis Hopper's *Rashomon*-like reminiscences of hanging out at Larry Flynt's Pink Palace in 1983. The gonzo tale of mischief and misadventure read like classic Southern à la *Blood of a Wig.* Eager to help her friend and stand apart from such competitors as *Granta* and the *Paris Review,* Stein encouraged Southern to contribute on a regular basis to the magazine. He did his best to comply even if his heart wasn't in it. Terry loved Jean. As with many of his friends, he often sent her ribald letters pretending to be the head of the panty-of-the-month club and asking Stein to donate. Jean thought Terry was the closest thing America had to Jonathan Swift. She had helped Terry off and on over the years and was now supplying him with a couple of hundred dollars a month as a retainer. It eased his cash-flow problems. Gail continued to bring in most of the income through her ballet school.

The favorable reaction to Bockris's interview and the *Grand Street* piece demonstrated that there was considerable untapped curiosity about Southern. But Terry's temperament as a writer, complicated by his recent bout with cancer, made him a challenging figure for an agent to market. On movie projects, he dallied with a score of agents including such high-powered names as Arlene Donovan, Michael Carlisle, Rowland Perkins, and Ron Mardigian without settling with anyone. Yet he stayed loyal to his representative in the Quality Lit world, Sterling Lord. Lord had been rewarded with little but broken contracts since *Blue Movie,* but he did arrange for *Red Dirt Marijuana* to be reissued. Citadel Underground, a new imprint specializing in out-of-print counterculture fiction and nonfiction from the sixties, reprinted the collection in 1990 along with Emmet Grogan's *Ringolevio,* Ed Sanders's *Tales of Beatnik Glory,* and Jane Alpert's *Growing Up Underground.*

Nile, Victor Bockris, and others close to Southern felt Lord wasn't pushing him in the same way someone like superagent Andrew Wylie had relaunched the careers of William Burroughs and Allen Ginsberg. Like Burroughs and Ginsberg, Southern had amassed an amazing amount of unpublished work—in the form of stories, letters, screenplays, and treatments—that Nile felt had the potential to be packaged.

Southern's long-in-the-works autobiographical novel, *Texas Summer,* became Nile's pet project in what he hoped would become a Terry Southern renaissance now that Bockris's interview and the *Red Dirt Marijuana* reissue had attracted interest. *Texas Summer* was in many respects a kind of never-ending story for Southern. Richard and Jeanette Seaver, who now ran Arcade Books for Little, Brown, agreed to publish the book. Southern was paid a modest $7,500.

According to Nile, Southern had the novel lying around his office in a binder labeled *Behind the Grassy Knoll.* While helping to renovate a few rooms in the East Canaan house, Nile took it upon himself to organize his father's papers.

"I used to just leave it out for him in a very organized way, hopefully in a way that was enticing him a little bit. Like, 'Oh, what's this? Maybe I should have a look at this.' And I would say, 'Dad, it looks like you've got a lot of that work done. It's like190 pages or something.' So I don't know really what prompted him to take it up again, but something must have clicked. It could just be something as simple as a nostalgia for Texas . . . for instance there wasn't an editor or publisher saying, 'Hey, what about that *Texas Summer*?' It wasn't that kind of situation. I think he had been really out of touch with the literary and publishing scene and I said, 'Look, you really ought to ask my mom what's going on out there. I'm hearing of advances that are really outrageous. There's a lot of money for novels these days.' Of course, it didn't turn out to be really true for *Texas Summer* in his case."

Southern had finished most of what became his last published novel in the early eighties. The ambitious plan to trace the life of his alter ego, Harold, up to the Paris expatriate period of the late forties and fifties was abandoned. Instead *Texas Summer* became an uncharacteristically sentimental journey to a Texas that might have existed only in Southern's imagination. The previously published stories, "Red Dirt Marijuana" and "Razor Fight," were incorporated into a longer narrative dealing with a visit to a county fair where Harold and Big Lawrence kidnap the Monkey Man, Harold's crush on his slightly older cousin, Caddy, and the escape of CK's brother, Big Nail, from prison. Southern shifts the time of the novel to the 1950s instead of the Depression, but the few references to the Elvis decade seem superfluous. *Texas Summer* exists outside conventional notions of time. The real subject of the book is a distillation of distant memories—that point when the blissful confidence and ignorance of youth gives way to a grim awareness of one's limitations and mortality.

With Nile and Richard Seaver's encouragement, Southern dusted off *Texas Summer* and dutifully cleaned up the manuscript. He dedicated the book to Gail and sent it off to Seaver, who scheduled it for publication in the fall of 1991.

In the winter of 1990–91, Southern began writing *The Green Mountain Boys*, a script dealing with Ethan Allen and the American Revolution. James Goldstone, a veteran director of television and film whose credits included the Paul Newman racing flim, *Winning*, and the Mafia spoof *The Gang That Couldn't Shoot Straight*, lived in Vermont, where much of Allen's battles with the British took place. This was a spec project, but Southern threw himself into the work. He joined Goldstone in barnstorming around New England, visiting battle sites and old graveyards to gather research. However, Goldstone couldn't get any studio interest in the film. The disastrous box office of the Al Pacino film *Revolution* still lingered in the memory of Hollywood decision makers.

While Southern was finishing the script for Goldstone, his first cover story in years, a feature on the Texas rock band ZZ Top, appeared in the February 1991 issue of *Spin*. Publisher Bob Guccione Jr. had recently

made Southern a contributing editor along with William Burroughs and
Michael O'Donoghue to add more street credibility to a publication that
seemed to always be in second place to *Rolling Stone*. Presumably
Guccione or someone else at *Spin* thought it would be a good idea to get a
Texan to write about a rock band from Texas. Desperate for work as usual,
Southern wasn't going to argue. He traveled to St. Louis to see the band
play and managed to churn out an unusually long article. With the exception of odd tangents like a description of Rip Torn as Howard Hughes in an
off-Broadway play, the piece was unremarkable. ZZ Top were a fun band,
but they never possessed the influence or emotional impact of the Rolling
Stones at their peak. A lot of the feature was written in overcooked gonzo
mode with overused Southern catchphrases like "damnable wog hemp,"
"hot damn, Vietnam," and even "precious bodily fluids." These were the
clichés of style Green had warned him about years ago. It was nice to see
Southern's name on the cover of a prominent magazine, but readers could
be forgiven wondering where the astonishment had gone.

Southern began another piece for *Spin* about the Gulf War, which had
just started. Now that was a subject Southern should have sunk his satiric
teeth into. When the war ended, a short but eloquent piece on the outburst of
jingoism that had engulfed mainstream culture during the Gulf conflict came
out in the *Nation*'s July 8, 1991, issue. "The Bandwagon Moves On" did
employ familiar Southern imagery of Texas fighter pilots and gung-ho generals, but this time the clichés seemed apt in describing the absurdity of
America's "turkey shoot" in Iraq. Yet ultimately the piece was too little too
late. The American character had become distinctly postmodern. The patri-
otic binge had passed like a twenty-four-hour flu back in February. When
Southern's piece was published, recession-weary American voters were gear-
ing up to toss George Bush out of the White House in the next election.

The *Nation* piece did signal a resurgence of interest in the political
scene. He had regularly taken to watching congressional hearings and
debates on C-SPAN. The petulant self-absorbed rhetoric of a Phil Gramm
or Newt Gingrich would prompt Southern to pick up his yellow notepad
and dash off a terse riposte in the form of a letter to the *Village Voice* or a
squib for the *Nation, Newsday,* or *In These Times*. One such dispatch, an
August 17, 1993, letter to the *Voice,* was a miniature classic. Recollecting the
Clarence Thomas/Anita Hill hearings, Southern described committee
chairman Joe Biden's "inappropriate nightmare grimace of hilarity" and
then added that a psychologist friend had concluded that the senator might
be suffering from a mild form of Tourette's syndrome. What made the short

letter so amusing was the quizzical, deadpan tone, reminiscent of Southern's work from the late fifties and early sixties. It was the kind of effective, quietly detached rage that was missing from recent prose like the ZZ Top piece.

While Terry was steeling himself to complete the final manuscript of *Texas Summer* for Richard Seaver at Arcade, he received a letter from Annette Insdorf, head of Columbia's graduate film department. She wanted to know if Terry was interested in teaching a graduate screenwriting course at Columbia beginning in the fall of 1991. The money wasn't great, but it was a steady gig. He accepted the offer.

The money from the teaching job went to pay the taxman, but it did boost Southern's spirits. While he and Gail hated the weekly two-hour drive into Manhattan, it provided a steady routine until his death in 1995. The M.A. students appreciated Southern's nonformulaic approach to the craft of film writing. Terry was not Syd Field or Robert McKee preaching a beat every ten minutes into the script. If he had a philosophy, it was for students to push their ideas as far as they could.

According to John Emile, who attended the course in 1992–93, Southern would arrive at the weekly afternoon seminar with a satchel bulging with students' screenplays-in-progress. "It seemed unlikely that they would ever be read; but they were always returned well thumbed—ragged, even—and tagged with innumerable yellow Post-its. Terry used three sizes of Post-its: large for extended commentary, medium for annotations involving sentences, and small for suggestions regarding word choice. The small ones were found throughout, in great number. Like every good teacher, he was persistent in trying to show that there was a [higher] level to aspire to. At one point, apparently frustrated by my careless spewing of words, he attached a large Post-it which read: 'There are usually only *one* or *two* words which work in a given instance.'"

Another student, Caroline Marshall, recalls falling out of her chair with laughter when she received these comments: "He crossed out 'bazookas' like any high school teacher grading an essay and wrote in the margin, 'Try hooters, knockers, tits, or bazooms.'" Marshall says Southern urged his students to use description with precision: "Never say just 'red dress.' Be specific: ultra-revealing, micro-mini with fringe."

For the most part, Southern was a silent but encouraging presence at the seminars. Students would read selected pages of dialogue from their scripts and share comments. Southern's comments were usually positive. However, another student, Charles Zigman, who made a film of "Heavy Put Away" as his thesis project, recalled an occasion when Southern lost his cool with a student. A sincere young woman began reading a lengthy excerpt from her script, an interminable feminist rewrite of Joan of Arc. When she completed reading a rambling scene in which Joan confesses her love and devotion to her same-sex lover, she asked Southern what he thought. He gracefully replied, "Why don't they just get stoned and fuck?" The student ran out of the classroom, never to return. The rest of the class took Southern out for a beer.

In addition to his new duties as an instructor, Southern continued to work on screenplays. In February 1992, Southern's old pal from England Joe McGrath asked Terry if he would like to work on a spoof about the Cannes Film Festival. An independent producer, Walter Robin, had raised the development money. McGrath and Southern had stayed friendly since *The Magic Christian* via late-night phone calls and postcards. Whatever misgivings Southern had about McGrath's adaptation of his classic novel did not get in the way of a warm friendship.

McGrath flew out to East Canaan to get the ball rolling. The producer's original title for the film was *Starlets*. McGrath and Southern decided to call it *Festival*, which was clear enough to reassure the money men, but vague enough to allow them to push the premise to the limit. Robin had approached Tony Curtis about the part of Sid Berko, a porn producer selling his wares at the film festival.

"Terry found out [Walter Robin] was a voice-over artist. He had a good voice that sounded like Orson Welles, so Terry called him 'Big Walt.' Curtis and Robin didn't get along. Curtis phoned me and said, 'Never forget this, McGrath, we're both poor boys, we don't need this!' He didn't want to do [the film] so then we met George Segal. George came to London and saw me and said, 'If you guys get it together you can hawk it around with my name on it, too,'" recalls McGrath.

On the surface, *Festival* sounded suspiciously like a retread of *Blue Movie*. McGrath and Southern wanted to emphasize the fact that in Cannes you are never out of camera range. They hoped to convey a slapstick hall of mirrors where narcissistic actors, directors, and producers are followed by camera-wielding television crews and paparazzi. Some of the script's funniest moments are Berko's philosophic exchanges with his secretary, Velocity Storm:

INT. BERKO'S SUITE. ALCOVE.
Berko is sunning himself, lying on a recliner, reflector bib under his chin. Velocity lets herself in quietly. Berko regards her one eye open.

> BERKO

Well, how was the Fassbinder? Same old "Let's hide the knockwurst in the ingenue?" Haw!

> VELOCITY
> (archly)

No, it was really quite charming. The sort of thing that could benefit people like yourself.

> BERKO

What did they do, give out free cocksplints to the audience?

> VELOCITY

And Spanish fly to the starlets. How'd you make out with the toddler?

> BERKO

You won't believe it, Vel. I gave her six big ones. Hey, talk about your ever-loving 'oohs' and 'aahs'! Vel, she came like a *machinegun*! It was scary.
(Pause, gives her a narrow look.)
Any sign of our nemesis?

> VELOCITY

Nope. I really don't think they're crazy enough to try anything in a situation like this.

> BERKO

Oh yeah? Isn't that what people used to say about the grassy knoll.

McGrath joined Walter Robin on a strange location trip to a Baltic resort in Russia that was going to double for Cannes. McGrath gamely tried to see the possibilities in the bleak complex of poorly built hotels. Then, perhaps mercifully, Robin ran out of development money. *Festival* might have worked with a more secure production team. Robert Altman's *The Player* and Garry Shandling's *Larry Sanders Show* would build upon the coarse politics of moviemaking to create some of the funniest and most exciting film and television of the nineties.

A **certain piece** of unfinished business resurfaced while Southern toiled on *Festival*. Peter Fonda and Dennis Hopper, in spite of their mutual antipathy, were still keen to do an *Easy Rider* sequel. One of the latest variations, which was unintentionally funny, was that River Phoenix and Keanu Reeves would play the sons of Captain America and Wyatt, who had been conceived in the commune. In order to get the sequel moving, Fonda tried to get Southern to relinquish any claim to the film in exchange for $30,000. *Easy Rider* had made all the above-the-line players, especially Fonda and Bert Schneider, rich or at least free of money worries. However, all Southern received from the film were residuals—annual checks amounting to $50, maybe $100 a year. That was barely enough to cover his *New York Times* subscription. To his credit, Southern ignored Fonda's offer.

In late 1991, *Texas Summer* was published, but it seemed to take months for the book to catch the attention of reviewers. Arcade/Little, Brown hadn't done much in the way of publicity. David Streitfield of the *Washington Post* went out to East Canaan to find out what had happened to Southern between *Blue Movie* and the new novel. His article, which ran in the *Post*'s style section, gave the impression Southern was an addled burnout case. The reviews of *Texas Summer* that began trickling in did little to suggest otherwise. The *New York Times*'s Brad Tyer wrote, "From his vantage point as a literary hipster, Mr. Southern used to cast a good-natured sneer at what he called the 'quality lit game,' even as his work redefined what literature could include. One is left wishing he had re-entered the game on a more fertile field." Sadly, this was not a minority opinion.

The publication of Southern's first novel since *Blue Movie* should have been the kind of media event heralded by *Vanity Fair* profiles and similar coverage. Instead the book seemed to be released in a vacuum.

"I think *Texas Summer* is a fine piece of work," said Richard Seaver, "but he had been gone from the scene so long that every reviewer said, 'Here's Terry Southern twenty years later, but this is not the Terry Southern we knew.' Of course it isn't, it's a totally other voice. It is not sarcastic. It is not him being acerbic, flippant, acid, funny, or satirical. People weren't ready for this other voice, but I think the book would have been better had he done a little more with it."

Perhaps Southern's legacy might have been better served if he had turned in another Texas-inspired tale called *Whut?*, a script that grew out of a series of running jokes between the painter Neil Welliver and Terry about hillbilly hicks making "A-Dult Movies." Written in the late eighties just when Southern was beginning to resurrect his Texas novel, it might have satisfied the craving for one more satiric romp on the order of *Blue Movie* or *Candy*.

In spite of *Texas Summer*'s indifferent reception Terry did what he always did in these circumstances, which was to keep busy. He began helping Perry Richardson with *The Early Stones*, a new book using unpublished photos by Michael Cooper for Hyperion. It was a way for Richardson to make some money out of *Blinds and Shutters*. When the limited-edition book was published, the publishers had diminished Richardson's involvement and he received only a small credit.

For *The Early Stones*, Southern supplied an amusing but all too short preface about meeting Brian Jones and Anita Pallenberg for the first time. A rambling Q-and-A banter between Southern and Richards formed the book's accompanying text, but the pictures tended to explain themselves. Whereas *Blinds and Shutters* was a mesmerizing and exhaustive visual and oral history, *The Early Stones* seemed sketchy and provisional. It was a frustrating book for Southern fans, who admittedly would have bought his collected laundry lists at this stage, and even more so for the casual reader. In the final analysis, it was just another book about the Stones and not in the same league as Robert Greenfield's *STP*, Stanley Booth's *Sympathy for the Devil*, or Roy Carr's *The Rolling Stones: An Illustrated Record*.

The book allowed Richardson to establish A Publishing Company, which he ran from his home in Devon in partnership with Julio Santo Domingo, a mysterious Guy Grand–like Spanish businessman. Richardson and Southern tried to get Domingo to invest in a film project about the rock musician Lenny Kravitz. The idea never seemed to get past the riffing stage. Southern had the half-serious notion of getting Woody Allen and Spike Lee to codirect a film with the general theme of race relations.

In the same summer that *The Early Stones* arrived in bookstores, Terry and Gail traveled to a post-wedding party held at Carol Southern's Long Island place. Nile had been married a few weeks earlier in Boulder to a Greek-born beauty, Theodosia, whom he met in Athens on a cultural exchange. Terry was happy to see his only child get married. He had always striven to provide his son with the necessities and often expressed concern to friends that Nile would make the same mistakes he had in navigating the tricky waters of art and commerce. Nile had spent much of his twenties working as a film editor for small production companies and had begun writing his own fiction, which owed more to William Burroughs and cyber-punk than to the work of his father.

More occasional pieces came out of Southern's typewriter in the summer and fall of 1992. He wrote liner notes for a promotional copy of the Black Crowes' second album. Chris Robinson, the lead singer of the band, whose music owed a great deal to the Faces and the Rolling Stones in their *Sticky Fingers/Exile on Main Street* phase, was a big fan of *The Magic Christian*. For *Newsday,* Southern wrote "Putting America to Work for Something Besides Killing" just as the 1992 U.S. election campaign was going into high gear. When asked whom he was going to vote for, Southern would say "Frank Zappa" or "Jerry Brown." He even phoned Brown's campaign office to lend support and was delighted to find out that the secretary on the other end of the call was familiar with his work. Brown even returned Terry's call.

When Bill Clinton was elected the new president of the United States that November, Southern vocally supported him. Like many liberals, Southern wanted to share in the optimism of the first one hundred days. At least Clinton wasn't George Bush. Ironically a few years before Southern had written a short teleplay on spec called "The Brightest and the Best" about a Clinton-like president who has an affair. The script contained much discussion of semen samples in test tubes. In the summer of 1998, when Clinton's Oval Office dalliance with Monica Lewinsky turned into a real-life sideshow, many of Southern's friends remembered how they thought Terry's teleplay was too wacky and coarse for its own good.

The commute to teach at Columbia was grueling for Terry and Gail. Gail did most of the driving while Southern looked over students' scripts. They tried to shape the new routine around a dinner, visit with friends, an opening, a book launch, or a similar event.

In November, Terry began feeling dizzy in class. His vision was blurred. Gail took him to the doctor. He had had a mild stroke. Southern was very lucky. The attack made it difficult for him to walk without a cane, but he was still able to function as before. However, the stroke was an unsubtle reminder that he was no longer invincible. The martinis, the Dexamyl, the wine, and the dope smoking would have to stop . . . or at least, their use must be dramatically reduced. Aside from a couple of rescheduled classes, the stroke did not affect his ability to teach. Gail hoped that if Southern listened to his doctor and took his medication, he could live and play for a few more years.

Before the year ended, "The Refreshing Ambiguity of the Déjà Vu," the *Candy*-inspired sketch, appeared in *Grand Street*. It was barely a short story, but somehow the seductive style kicked in. Fans wondered if Terry and Mason really wrote it together. In some ways the story was the literary equivalent of the Beatles' "Free As a Bird" single. The piece was meant as a lark, but the effect was elegiac. Its publication raised a question no one wanted to ask or answer—why weren't there more Terry Southern novels and short stories?

If Southern sensed that the snows of yesteryear were now (to push a literary allusion further) being washed away by the torrents of spring, he did not let on to those who saw him. Despite the cane and white beard, he surprised friends and visitors with his energy and curiosity.

In late February 1993, Southern and Gail flew out to Dallas for a long-overdue salute to a prodigal son. Josh Alan Friedman had moved to Dallas in the mid-eighties to pursue a musical career. He enterprisingly organized a series of screenings and a reading at the Dallas Museum of Art. The afternoon of the reading, Friedman took Gail and Terry out to nearby Alvarado for what would be the writer's final visit to his birthplace.

That evening, after *Dr. Strangelove* was screened, Southern read from *The Magic Christian*. Despite his frail appearance, Southern recited his classic with unusual vigor and enthusiasm. The spontaneous laughter of the audience almost made Southern lose his cool repose as he recited the adventures of Guy Grand.

"If he had in the four days that he was here been acting feeble and frail," recalled Friedman, "he was not during that one hour. It was if he had reserved all his energy for that reading. It was Terry in his prime reading from *The Magic Christian*. He was wonderful and the audience cracked up. The day afterward, there were fifty people lined up outside with Terry at a table. This is a big museum and a big recital hall. Terry was sitting at a table and he didn't bring any copies of *Texas Summer* down, which had just come out. I told him you should get a box from the publisher because everybody is going to want one directly from you. But he didn't know about stuff like that. Novelists today sell their own books. Musicians sell their own CDs. He was from the old school and he was too dignified to do that. But people were lined up with records, like the soundtrack to *Easy Rider* or *Barbarella,* old copies of books and paperbacks and any other type of memorabilia. Again he didn't show a lick of emotion as he sat there just smiling and signing any book or record that people wanted signed. Later Gail said it really meant a lot to him. He had never once done a bookstore signing like that or had a line of people. Nobody had ever bothered to set that up for him except that particular thing."

When Southern returned to East Canaan, he began work on the text for another photo book, *From a Dead Man's Wallet.* Peter Beard had been asked by a Japanese publisher to put together a book of images from his famous diary collages. Beard had described his journal as the project that never ends. In addition to the coffee-table-book text, Beard also got Terry to write captions for a series of photo spreads in *Esquire*'s revamped *Gentlemen's Quarterly.* The latter assignment represented a new low in Southern's postsixties career. Beard was only trying to help, but the sight of Southern dashing off two- to three-sentence captions for an unmemorable fashion layout was a major comedown from the days when he was part of Harold Hayes's all-star team along with Mailer, Talese, and Wolfe.

Meanwhile Hal Wilner, whom Southern had befriended during *Saturday Night Live,* had developed a lucrative sideline as a record producer. He achieved considerable critical acclaim and respectable sales by creating a series of tribute albums. The records paid homage to composers like Thelonious Monk, Nino Rota, and Kurt Weill by getting artists as varied as Todd Rundgren, Lou Reed, and Marianne Faithful to record intriguing interpretations of the work of these masters. Wilner's model would become widely imitated in the nineties, but often without the same care and passion. In 1990, in collaboration with Nelson Lyon and Michael O'Donoghue, Wilner had assembled *Dead City Radio* featuring William Burroughs reading his work to a vocal and musical accompaniment provided by the likes of Donald Fagen and John Cale. Wilner, O'Donoghue, and Lyon felt Southern could benefit from a similar project.

Setting up the recording sessions was easier said than done. Wilner had become increasingly involved with lucrative film work, such as Robert Altman's *Short Cuts,* in addition to his *SNL* duties. Recording didn't begin until 1994 and then proceeded in erratic fashion.

"It was like the impossible record," Lyon recalls, "because Terry was often gasping. He was like on his last legs. I was pushing him to the point where he nearly fainted. He was only doing it finally out of a friendship thing and enduring the pain of take after take after take, which I would insist on because I knew there were problems in the editing."

In order to take some of the pressure off Southern, Lyon commissioned a troupe of players including Sandra Bernhard, Jonathan Winters, and Marianne Faithfull. Wilner came up with the conceit of a cabaret to frame the various readings. The recording begins with an answering machine message by Terry and then segues into a section of *The Loved One* with Southern playing the roles of a funeral director and a client. The record, which Lyon described as "the most carefully fucking designed thing I've ever done," remains tragically unreleased.

Through 1993 and 1994, Southern's health ebbed and flowed. Sometimes he seemed in boyish high spirits. At other times, he was barely able to walk. In June, he and Gail flew to Greece for a second wedding ceremony thrown by Nile's Greek in-laws. Southern enjoyed the festivities, but the flight to and from was exhausting. He stayed in his chair during most of the reception and made full use of the wheelchair service provided by the airline.

In January 1994, Harry Nilsson, who had spent his remaining years fighting a legal battle to restore financial stability for his family after the collapse of Hawkeye, died from a heart attack. Then, in November of the same year, Michael O'Donoghue died suddenly of a cerebral hemorrhage. Both men were only in their fifties.

Southern's encroaching sense of mortality, coupled with his weakening health, must have made his latest foray into Quality Lit challenging. Little, Brown had commissioned Terry to write a memoir on the basis of a proposal put together by Nile. Only two chapters would emerge, "Flashing on Gid" and "Strangelove Outtake," dealing with Maurice Girodias and the making of *Dr. Strangelove* respectively. Both appeared in *Grand Street*.

The memoir excerpts nicely balanced Southern's penchant for abbreviated nicknames and mock-heroic exaggeration with more sober insights into the creative process. In general, the tone was warm, reflective, and witty. Little, Brown's Fredrica Friedman expected something different: "On the basis of the pages now, I would suggest that two areas need work. First, the material should be funnier, wilder, more *antic*. It also needs *context* for the reader: who are you, what do/did you do, what are you known for? And what is the *point* of telling these stories?"

One can imagine Southern reading this memo, which in fairness was intended to help him with a form not close to his heart, and asking, "And *just* who are *you*, Ms. Friedman, if that is indeed your name?" Gradually Southern's interest in the memoir dwindled and the project lapsed.

In September 1994, Southern received a Gotham award for Lifetime Achievement by the Independent Film Producers. The lavish dinner and ceremony were held at Roseland. Sigourney Weaver and the Coen brothers also received awards. The Gotham was a long-overdue recognition that Southern did matter and had made a difference to film culture. If he had been healthier and more career savvy, perhaps he would have been working with some of the young turks in the audience. Certainly the Coen brothers, Jim Jarmusch, Steven Soderbergh, and other independent filmmakers owed Southern a few aesthetic debts. Quentin Tarantino's just-released *Pulp Fiction* had flashes of Southern-like weirdness, but the hot young director, who might have benefited from Southern's depth, seemed more infatuated by the neo-noir of Elmore Leonard and the so-bad-it's-good trash of countless exploitation films.

Earlier in the year, on May 31, Dennis Hopper appeared on *The Tonight Show*. Hopper made some flippant remarks about Rip Torn's non-appearance in *Easy Rider*. When Jay Leno asked why Rip passed on the George Hanson role that went to Jack Nicholson, Hopper said they had a problem.

LENO: What kind of problem?

HOPPER: Well, at dinner he pulled a knife on me. He thought I was— I was cutting him out of the picture, as he put it—uh, before, we were just writing the script, and he decided the script wasn't really correct.

LENO: Now, is that the best way to settle an argument with a director? If he's cutting, I mean if he cut you out of the picture before— somehow knifing the director seems like it would pretty much end your—

HOPPER: Yeah, well, it was, uh, it was, uh, it was one way for me to say we're not working together. That was pretty easy.

Hopper's ill-advised late-night joking triggered a lawsuit by Torn, who initially asked for a public retraction. Hopper refused. Before the case came to an end in March 1997, Torn's lawyer compiled a series of eyewitness accounts of what happened back in 1968 when *Easy Rider* was still in pre-production. Because Terry agreed to testify on Torn's behalf, he had a falling-out with Jean Stein, who was Hopper's friend as well as Southern's. During a dinner, she told Southern she wouldn't give him an allowance anymore if he was going to gang up on a friend. Stein had stood by Hopper's side when he was a drug casualty in the hospital in the early eighties and she wasn't letting her money go, even very indirectly, to anyone planning to sue her good friend. The dinner ended abruptly, and soon after, the checks stopped coming.

Stein and Southern never spoke again. On the bright side, Southern's drafts for *Easy Rider* were entered into evidence when the lawsuit between

Torn and Hopper came to court. Their appearance sucker-punched Hopper, who claimed he had written the screenplay himself. As of this writing, Hopper's draft remains missing.

Like so many new years, 1995, Southern's last on earth, was filled with uncertainty. After almost thirty years with Sterling Lord, Southern changed agents. Jimmy Vines, in his late twenties, took over Southern's representation and arranged a reissue deal with Grove. *Flash and Filigree, Candy, The Magic Christian,* and *Blue Movie* were reissued in handsome trade paperback volumes by Grove in the summer of 1996. Vines was also going to explore the possibility of publishing Southern's drafts of *Dr. Strangelove, Barbarella,* and *Easy Rider* in book form. This was a great idea that quickly became bogged down in the old issues of authorship and copyright. While it was clear that Southern had made emphatic and valuable contributions to these and other films, it wasn't as easy to conclude that he was the sole creator. Unlike Paddy Chayefsky, William Goldman, or Harold Pinter, Southern had never had the foresight to spell out his creative control in contractual terms. Even at the peak of his screenwriting career, Southern had depended on the good graces of his friendly auteurs.

Southern grew weaker and more fragile over the spring and summer. His hair looked ghostly white. On windy days, it seemed as if his beard were trailing behind like a small cloud. Still he agreed to run a screenwriting workshop at the Whiteheart, a restaurant up the road from his house. There were plenty of weekenders who would pay good money to sit at the feet of a film legend.

On May 1, Southern turned seventy-one. The year before, Stein had thrown a birthday party for him at Elaine's. Darius James, author of *Negrophobia,* recalled Mick Jagger making an appearance at that bash. The Stones's singer ignored everyone else, but spent a long time talking to Southern. It had been quite a night, but now, a year later, Stein and the Southerns were no longer speaking.

Southern's final project during 1994–95 was his text for Virgin. Perry Richardson had won the contract to write a history of Richard Branson's record company. He been given a rare degree of creative autonomy considering the corporate PR nature of the commission. The conceit behind the Virgin book was to make fun of the whole idea of rock 'n' roll history. Richardson promptly hired Terry.

"Terry was so precise with language even when we were doing the

Virgin book," said Richardson. "A classic example for me was when we were describing some wild-eyed musician. I had come up with the phrase 'rabid glee' and Terry said, 'I think that's too garish.' So we kicked around ideas for about half an hour and finally Terry said, 'I got it! How about "grim relish"!' What we were doing was just playing with the English language."

Southern dutifully finished his work by the spring. In the summer, he made a muted appearance at the Yale Summer Writing Program. Jeff McGregor, a humorist who attended Southern's lecture, thought he looked like the Anti-Santa. When asked how he wanted his work to be remembered, Southern stumbled over his words, but eventually delivered a considered and serious reply:

"Well, the work I like, art of all kinds, is work that has a multilevel appeal and interpretation. One musicologist I was reading was talking about some passages from Bach, where you analyze all you cared but you couldn't decide whether it was celebrating joy or sorrow. You were unable to make a convincing distinction between the two. . . . I like to think I aspire to that often and hopefully sometimes manage it."

In October, a BBC film crew arrived at George Plimpton's apartment to interview the *Paris Review* editor, Richard Seaver, and Southern for a documentary on Alexander Trocchi. Seaver, Southern, and Plimpton gathered in the kitchen to reminisce. The hot lights almost seemed to melt Southern away. His comments were very brief. Another BBC crew wanted to meet with Southern in a few weeks to talk about *Easy Rider* for a special documentary to be aired during the Christmas break.

The last week of October turned out to be very busy. In addition to the *Easy Rider* documentary, Richardson had generously arranged through ace publicist Bobby Zarem to hype Southern's role in the Virgin book. Drinking Bombay Sapphires at the Algonquin, Southern answered the usual questions about *Dr. Strangelove, Easy Rider,* and *Candy* for various journalists. The publicity for the book would culminate in two launch parties, one in London and another a week later at Elaine's, in early November. Southern arranged to get his passport updated for the visit to London.

On Wednesday, October 25, at approximately 2:00 P.M., on his way to teach another class at Columbia, Southern collapsed on the steps of Dodge Hall. He was having severe difficulty breathing. An ambulance took him to nearby St. Luke's Hospital. His condition stabilized. He was taken into emergency, Gail recalls, where he spent what seemed an eternity lying on a gurney. Gail was told that Southern would be given a bed as soon as one became available. She spent the night at Amy Wright's apartment near Washington Square.

Early the next morning, Gail went in to visit Terry and his mood lightened. He made jokes about how good the oxygen made him feel. Some of his students came to visit, including Caroline Marshall, who brought him some magazines.

On Friday, with Southern's condition appearing to stabilize, Gail felt hopeful. She almost went back to Connecticut, but the doctors told her that the next forty-eight hours were crucial. She called Carol and told her things were bad and asked her to come. Carol arrived and Nile booked a flight from Boulder to see his father for what could be the last time. After Southern was moved to intensive care, his condition deteriorated.

Gail and Carol were shown X rays of Terry's lungs. "They were absolutely white," Gail said. "The doctor took Carol and me into the room and asked 'Did Terry ever work in a coal mine?' 'Coal mine?' I looked at Carol and she looked at me. Then [the doctor] said, 'Well, has he ever been a farmer?' 'Yeah, but it was an organic farm.' It turned out that Terry's lungs had calcified."

Gail told the doctor about Terry's pathological hatred of flies. In the summer, he would spray them with huge cans of Raid. The doctor dismissed the Raid as a possible cause of the calcification.

"But I don't think the doctor understood how pathological he was. Every time I found a can of Raid, I would stash it. I had about fifty cans of Raid under the sink," said Gail.

Given many of Terry's struggles to complete one promising script after another in the last twenty-five years of his life and the plague of money problems, he might as well have been working in a coal mine. The seemingly insignificant stroke in 1992 had sapped his strength in the last three years of his life. There were, as it turned out, some limits.

At one point, Southern asked for his oxygen mask to be removed so he could talk. He stiffened and said, "Something's happening." "What?" asked Gail. "I don't know. . . . I feel like an icon." She asked why. "Because they are doing so much." Gail told Terry that there was more attention being paid to the patient next to him. These words seemed to give Terry a great sense of relief.

All day Saturday, with Carol and Gail in attendance, Southern drifted in and out of consciousness. One young doctor came in and said, "I loved *The Magic Christian*." It was like something you would hear at one of Plimpton's parties. Another doctor, a beautiful blond woman not unlike a young Candice Bergen, came in. And yet another doctor asked, "Mr. Southern, Mr. Southern, do you know that you are dying?" Gail admonished him, "If you talk to him like that, he's going to tear this room apart." The voices seemed like a distant parade of the routine, surreal and banal.

Saturday afternoon, Nile arrived at St. Luke's directly from the airport. Gail had left for the day to check on the house in Connecticut. In the last seven hours he spent with his father while he was still conscious, Nile heard Terry ask, "What's the delay?" Nile watched his father pitch forward in bed upright as if preparing to leave the hospital. "I'm out of here. . . ." Terry said. "Got to GET OUT!" Then he fell back into the pillows and sheets with sudden resignation. "All right, let's go. . . . I'm ready for the next step . . . I've had enough of this. . . ."

Nile asked Terry if he could sleep.

"Yes . . . yes . . . time for a bit of shut-eye . . . *bedways is rightways now.*"

Southern was pronounced dead at 11:30 A.M., October 29.

Carol and Nile made arrangements for Terry to be cremated. His ashes were strewn over the pond on the grounds of the East Canaan home. Texas might have occupied a big part of his imaginative landscape, but he was, in the end, an Easterner.

As the news of his death traveled, the tributes began. The original Grand Guy was gone forever, but his voice remained clear and distinct in print, on-screen, and in memory. Where there was darkness, there was laughter.

The majority of the obituaries and tributes for Terry Southern that appeared in newspapers, wire stories, and magazines around the world foregrounded this quote from the 1964 *Life* profile by Jean Howard: "The important thing in writing is the capacity to astonish. Not shock— shock is a worn-out word—but astonish. The world has no grounds whatever for complacency. The *Titanic* couldn't sink, but it did. Where you find smugness, you find something worth blasting. I want to blast it."

Terry Southern's work on *Dr. Strangelove* topped the list of astonishing works, along with *Candy, Easy Rider,* and *The Magic Christian,* most often cited in the news stories and tributes published in publications as varied as the *New York Times, People, New Musical Express,* the *Guardian,* and the *International Herald Tribune.* These achievements tended to be contextualized as the work of a writer who had peaked in the mid-sixties when the counterculture was in full swing. The London *Times* said Southern

"never really recovered the creative edge he possessed in the Fifties."
Variety, the trade paper of an industry Southern gave too many of his best
years to, mercifully made no such judgments in a brief obit that dutifully
listed his on-screen credits. Henry Allen, a staff writer at the *Washington
Post* and a fan of Southern's work, rose above the predictable cookie-cutter
copy with a concise and insightful essay. "Southern," Allen wrote, "was
either way ahead of his time or way behind it, it's hard to tell. In any case,
nobody astonishes now in this Decade of the Dead, and nobody seems to
have any of the fun Southern had."

As simplistic as it sounds, the idea of *fun* ran through all of Southern's
writing. *What if? Wouldn't it be cool? Why don't we just follow this crazy
idea and see how far it goes, eh? Nothing wrong with that. It will be grand.*

Southern was serious about having fun with his writing. He didn't
think it was possible, or even helpful, for a writer to separate the joy of writing from the labor and routine of sitting at a desk and putting pen to paper
hour after hour, day after day. He wasn't a writer given to agonizing over the
fickleness of his muse. Nor was he a clock-watcher—putting in so many
hours, churning out the exact same number of words each day. He liked to
write when the mood hit him, whether that mood was anger or delight. His
best collaborations, *Candy,* with Mason Hoffenberg, and *Dr. Strangelove,*
with Stanley Kubrick, succeeded because they shared Southern's desire to
communicate the wonder of pushing a crazy idea to the limit.

The success of *Candy* and *Dr. Strangelove* in 1964—that year when so
many lives were changed forever—turned Terry into a "professional." It was
a status he and so many of his generation of writers strove to avoid in the
Hipster fifties. But it would be trite to argue that Southern "sold out."
Instead, the mainstream was briefly taken over by the underground values
of Hip in the form of the counterculture. For a brief period, 1964–1970,
Southern was in perfect sync with the times. When his day in the sun was
over, "selling out" became increasingly meaningless as a way to define one's
beliefs and values. When the glory days of the sixties ended, Southern
remained a writer with a sensitive and precise gift for pitch-perfect dialogue
and outlandish situations and characters that seemed to stand outside time.

Buck Henry, a contemporary who managed to navigate the vagaries of
success and fashion more adeptly than Southern, believed Southern's gift
was unique: "He invented his own idiom out of the 50s and 60s, his own
language; García Márquez meets Eisenhower. I think because his work is
very specific and noncopyable, he had no influence on us at all. It was a
whole new chapter in black comedy, in farce."

One can certainly find traces of Southern's influence, but few writers have attained what Henry Allen described as "a style of spectacular grace, clarity and modulation" in recent years. Certainly the generation that grew up with *Saturday Night Live, National Lampoon,* and *Monty Python's Flying Circus* in the seventies can see their connections with the joyful subversion of *The Magic Christian, Candy,* and *Dr. Strangelove.* However, the eighties and nineties beat the daylights out of any profound notions of "hip" or "cool" making it harder for the fragile ironic precision of these books and films to resonate meaningfully. "Hip" and "cool" began and continue to be aligned with the things one buys and consumes as opposed to what one believes. Thus Tom Cruise wearing Ray-Bans in *Risky Business* became cool. Huey Lewis sang "It's Hip to Be Square," and for a time, he was cool.

By the end of the twentieth century, the mass media, thanks to the unending wave of the Internet, was flooded with all kinds of seemingly cutting-edge information that tended to emphasize diversion rather than enlightenment. Much of this information is conveyed through a brand of irony that reassures the consumer with the following mantra: "Yeah, we know that you know you are being sold a bill of goods, but hey it looks cool and you don't really care anyway." Indifference, apathy, smugness, and snobbery have increasingly taken the place of the commitment, openness, activism, community, and love that the truly hip aspired to in the fifties and sixties. This is not to say that these selfless qualities do not exist today, but they are certainly not encouraged or valued by the culture at large.

Intriguingly Southern's last great satire, *Blue Movie,* may be having the most palpable influence on some of the more interesting films and television of recent years. Cable, video, DVDs, and the Internet have made all manner of erotica (or "smut," "porn," "sleaze," name your poison) available to even the most isolated, naive, or repressed citizen. Although some directors have made the kinds of "blue movies" Southern and Kubrick once dreamed of—the quirky list might include Nicolas Roeg's *Bad Timing,* Michelangelo Antonioni's *Identification of a Woman,* Ken Russell's *Crimes of Passion,* and Paul Verhoeven's *Basic Instinct*—that goal is less important in an era where the revelatory shock of seeing two beautiful stars fuck on screen is an all too frequent and predictable exercise in diminishing returns.

Southern's 1970 novel, however, remains a template for media satire. Since the countercultural assumptions of right and left, us versus them, and old against young have been rendered meaningless by the rise of the media culture of the last twenty years, the media culture itself has become the focus of some of the best satire in recent years. *Blue Movie*'s scathing portrait of a universe where everyone has their price and any experience, no matter how personal, can be packaged for immediate consumption in the form of a film, bestseller, hit record, or celebrity has surfaced in Robert Altman's *The Player*, and in *The Larry Sanders Show, Bulworth, The Truman Show, There's Something about Mary, Bowfinger, American Beauty,* and *The Fight Club*. These films share *Blue Movie*'s cynicism about an age when our true responses to the world seem diluted by the virtual experiences provided by the media culture. None of these works is Southernesque in a specific sense, but they all possess the qualities of defiance, outrage, razor-sharp wit, off-the-wall speculation, whimsy, and awe that the writer aspired to in his writing.

Southern's influence on the current generation of novelists and short story writers is harder to define. Thanks to the proliferation of superbookstores and phenomena like Oprah's Book Club, Quality Lit seems to be everywhere, but the notion of the writer as a kind of visionary outlaw or deflater of bourgeois pretension and hypocrisy has also fallen victim to the coopting influence of the media culture. Kerouac's image was used in ads for The Gap and William Burroughs even appeared in a commercial and several rock videos before he died.

When attention is given to writers at the best of times, it is not for their ability to alter the way we see ourselves and the world (and thereby challenge the assumptions of the status quo and the received ideas that lead to complacency) but for "life lessons." Novels and short stories are reduced to the level of self-help manuals. Memoirs are no longer valued for the evocative style or language of, say, Nabokov's *Speak, Memory,* but for the narrator's triumph over adversity, abuse, or addiction.

In a climate where simplistic answers are king, perhaps it is just as well that Southern's literary legacy is not that dissimilar from Henry Green's. To be a writer's writer is not such a bad thing. It means that those who care about the kinds of books they write are responding to work that cuts through the silence of reading and reawakens the senses. Michael O'Donoghue, Darius James, Bruce Wagner, and Mark Leyner are a few of the disparate writers who have been liberated by Southern's non-naturalistic approach to the novel and short story. Many of the writers interviewed for this book told me again and again how *Candy, The Magic Christian,* or the enigmatic stories and articles in *Red Dirt Marijuana* expanded their notions of what writing could be.

But beyond this quiet but enduring influence, the books—which Grove Press and Bloomsbury have reissued in the years since Southern's death—

are being read. Southern is one of those writers who keep being discovered by readers at just the right time—usually, if this writer's informal poll is of any value, when they are in their teens or early twenties. As homogeneous and deadening as the media culture of today seems, Southern's targets—violence, ignorance, hypocrisy, and pretension—remain as important to attack as they did during the Cold War conformity of the fifties. Just as readers have rediscovered the seemingly "dated" work of Mark Twain, Dorothy Parker, F. Scott Fitzgerald, George Orwell, Henry Miller, Paul Bowles, Kurt Vonnegut Jr., Ken Kesey, Hunter Thompson, and others, so will they find Terry Southern. Good writing is always hip.

To the extent that this wildly inventive writer had a single theme, it was in his poignant exploration of innocence, naïveté, and idealism on the one hand, and worldliness, cynicism, and materialism on the other. In his greatest novel, *The Magic Christian,* Southern created an alter ego, Guy Grand, who embodied all these qualities and contradictions. The book is more than just a satire about money and greed, it is also a fable about making one's dreams a reality and the importance of giving for its own sake. Southern manifested this level of generosity, kindness, and humor in his life as well as his art.

Acknowledgments

Biographies are labor-intensive and this book presented its own unique challenges. My work on Terry Southern's life and art felt like a high-wire act at times, but the journey was turned into a grand adventure by the many people ("a veritable cast of thousands!") who helped me since this project's modest beginnings in 1990. I am extremely grateful to Nile and Carol Southern, and to Gail Gerber for their warm and open cooperation during all stages of my research. As executor of the Terry Southern estate, Nile was especially helpful in providing me with complete and unmediated access to his father's papers.

I am also grateful for the assistance of the following individuals who either allowed themselves to be interviewed, answered queries, or assisted with research: Ellen Adler, Lewis Allen, Mark Amerika, David Amram, Diana Athill, George and Alexandra Avakian, Peter Beard, Richard Benjamin, Victor Bockris, Peta Button, David Cammell, William Claxton, Stuart Cornfeld, Andre Deutsch, Bettina Drew, Patti Dryden, Roger Ebert, Harlan Ellison, James Goldstone, Jonathan Gill, Bruce Jay Friedman, Josh Alan Friedman, Anthony Frewin, Jack Gelber, Mike Golden, James Grauerholz, James Harris, Buck Henry, Helene Hladum, Juliette Hoffenberg, Darius James, Nick Jones, Arthur Kopit, Paul Krassner, Ted Kotcheff, Christiane Kubrick, Sandy Lieberson, Si Litvinoff, Joe Loguidice, Nelson Lyon, Norman Mailer, Gerard Malanga, John Marquand Jr., Susan Martin, Peter Matthiessen, Harry Matthews, Joseph McGrath, Barry Miles, Jonathan Miller, Laura Mulvey and Mike Allen at the British Film Institute, David Newman, Michael O'Donoghue, Maggie Paley, Anita Pallenberg, Charles Pike, George Plimpton, Perry and Ellie

Richardson, Mordecai Richler, Nicolas Roeg, Barney Rosset, Ovid Santoro, Richard and Jeanette Seaver, Jerry Schatzberg, Mark Singer of the *New Yorker*, Jean Stein, Jeremy Treglown, Dorothy Tristan, David Tully, Kathleen Tynan, Gore Vidal, Jimmy Vines, and Hal Wilner.

This book was written in New York City, London, England, and Calgary, Alberta, Canada, and I wish to acknowledge the assistance of the staffs of the Columbia University Rare Book Room, the British Film Institute, the British Library, the University of London libraries, the University of Calgary, and the Calgary Public Library system in making my research easier.

For advice, counsel, hospitality, friendship, and in some cases much needed freelance work: John Baxter, Victor Bockris, the Calgary Society of Independent Filmmakers, Paul Cremin, Phil Coombs, Elaine's Restaurant, Sean French, David Godwin, Stephen and Colin Gilmour, Matthew Hamilton at Bloomsbury Publishing, Jean, Leonie, and Piers Hartard, Warren Kinsella, Maria and Gabriella Licudi, David Locke, Patrick McGilligan, Tom McSorley, Kirk Miles, Martin Morrow, Scot Morison of the sadly defunct Alberta Foundation for the Arts, Dan Nearing, Leslie Needham, Annie Nocenti at *Scenario,* Dennis Perrin, Sandra Sawatzky, Mathew Schneck, Nick Stevens, David Tully, Eamonn and Jean Whelan, Damon Wise, the music of the Beatles, John Barry, Burt Bacharach, Stereolab, Miles Davis, and the Rolling Stones, and the inimitable Andre Zelli at *Vox.*

I would like to extend a special thanks to my editors, Tom Dupree and Yung Kim, and their colleagues at Spike/Avon and HarperCollins for their support, faith, enthusiasm, and patience. I am also grateful to my agent, Kim Witherspoon, and her staff at Witherspoon and Associates, New York City, for making the business of writing easier.

And last and certainly not least to Terry Southern, the original Grand Guy, who allowed me to become his "Boz."

Sources

Legend for sources: TS = Terry Southern, CS = Carol Southern, NS = Nile Southern, GG = Gail Gerber, LH = Lee Hill.

Prologue   For Love, Art, and a Lot of Money

General background on this period from *The Log Book of The Loved One* (New York: Random House, 1965) by Terry Southern and William Claxton and "A Creative Capacity to Astonish," by Jean Howard, *Life*, August 21, 1964.

"Greek tragedy rewritten by . . ." "Christian's Pilgrimage," *Newsweek*, May 18, 1964, p. 108.

"I'm treating the script . . ." "Son of Strangelove," *Newsweek*, August 31, 1964, p. 73.

TS phone call to Barney Rosset, Rosset to LH, January 14, 1999.

"Well, I'll say this . . ." TS on the Caspar Citron radio show, New York, June 1964. Tape courtesy of the Terry Southern Estate.

1   Youngblood

"The pond was like an oasis . . ." *Texas Summer* by TS (New York: Arcade/Little, Brown, 1991) p. 14.

"I love Texas . . ." "Beyond the Myth, Beneath the Haze: Digging into Terry Southern's Buried Texas Roots," by Robert Wilonsky, *Dallas Observer*, April 2, 1992, p. 13.

"Growing Up in Texas . . ." "The Vox Interview with Terry Southern," by Lee Hill, *Vox* (Canada), September 1990, p. 16.

"It was like *The Last Picture Show* . . ." Gail Gerber to LH, April 1997.

". . . in order to understand Terry . . ." Carol Southern to LH, March 1993.

Background on Alvarado, Texas Handbook, Texas State Historical Association, 1999.

Southern family information taken from Southern's birth certificate. Terry Southern archives.

Background on Depression, Texas Handbook, Texas State Historical Association, 1999.

"His father was . . ." Gail Gerber to LH, April 1997. Southern Sr.'s alcoholism also corroborated by Carol Southern and coroner's report in Terry Southern archives.

TS's pets, "A Creative Capacity to Astonish," by Jane Howard, *Life*, August 21, 1964, p. 40.

Background on TS's deerhunting, father's drinking, and legacy of, GG to LH, April 1997.

TS's Grade 3 report card. Terry Southern archives.

"[Poe] an extraordinary turn-on . . ." *Vox* Interview with TS, September 1990, p. 16.

"They never seemed to me . . ." Profile of Terry Southern by Francis Wyndham, *London Life*, 1965, p. 27.

TS and Tijuana Bibles, Interview with TS by Lee Server, *Puritan*, Issue 11, 1986, p. 25.

Information on Central Tracks area of Dallas, Texas Handbook, Texas State Historical Association, 1999.

Origins of CK in "Red Dirt Marijuana," "Beyond the Beat, Beneath the Haze," *Dallas Observer*, April 2, 1992, p. 17.

Information on Ku Klux Klan in Texas, Texas Handbook, Texas Historical Association, 1999.

"He got very embarrassed . . ." TS speaking on "Don't Look Back," WFMV, 1973 radio interview with George Cook.

TS's high school background, "Beyond the Beat, Beneath the Haze," *Dallas Observer*, April 2, 1992, p. 13.

TS hitchhikes to L.A. and Chicago, "Ten Minutes with Terry Southern: On Elvis, Strangelove, Barbecue, and Barbarella," by Richard Blackburn, *The Catalog of Cool*, edited by Gene Sculatti (New York: Warner Books, 1983), p. 82.

Accidental death mystery, CS to LH, April 2000.

Death of A. B. Ord, *Dallas Observer*, April 2, 1993, p. 15–16. Near-drowning incident, GG to LH, April 1997.

Information on Southern Methodist University and Lon Tinkle, Texas Handbook, Texas Historical Association.

"It was very inhuman . . ." "No Limits," *Newsweek*, June 22, 1964 pp. 80-81.

TS's military service from discharge papers. Terry Southern archives.

"I want to save it for my fiction . . ." TS to LH, March 1993.

"The main effect of war . . ." TS to LH, *Vox,* September 1990, p. 16.

TS in Battle of the Bulge, GG to LH, April 1997.

German Lüger in drawer, Arthur Kopit to LH, April 15, 1997.

TS on meeting Jews, Ellen Adler to LH, April 22, 1999.

Hanging out with Big Herb, *Dallas Observer,* April 2, 1993.

". . . anybody with any sensitivity . . ." CS to LH, May 4, 2000.

TS at University of Chicago, TS to LH, *Vox,* September 1990, p. 16.

and TS to LH, March 1993.

Larry Rivers on GI Bill, *What Did I Do?: The Unauthorized Biography of Larry Rivers* by Larry Rivers and Arnold Weinstein, (New York: HarperCollins, 1992) p. 75.

2 You're Too Hip, Baby

General background on expatriates in Paris during the late forties and early fifties: *Paris Interzone* by James Campbell; the *Paris Review Reader* edited by George Plimpton (New York: Viking, 1990); the *Continual Pilgrimage* by Christopher Sawyer-Laucanno; "Looking for Hemingway," by Gay Talese, *Esquire,* July 1962; various back issues of the *Paris Review* (est. 1953), especially no. 79, 1981, *Paris Review Sketchbook,* 25th Anniversary Double Issue, pp. 308–420 and no. 150, 45th Anniversary Issue.

"Those were halcyon days . . ." TS to LH, *Vox,* September 1990, p.15.

"From '48 to '52, the cafes . . ." "Now Dig This," by Mike Golden, *Reflex,* No. 27, August 1992, p. 49.

TS's Sorbonne program, TS to LH, *Vox,* September 1990, p.15.

John Marquand Jr. on TS, *Paris Review Sketchbook,* 20th Anniversary issue, *The Paris Review,* 1980 p. 348.

Southern student ID cards show registration at the Sorbonne for 1948 through 1952.

"I had to depend . . ." Profile of Terry Southern by Francis Wyndham, *London Life,* October 30/November 11, 1965, p. 27.

TS's exposure to jazz and foreign films, TS to LH, *Vox,* September 1990, p. 16.

"I'm of the existentialist persuasion . . ." TS to Nona Cleland, "The Drinking Writer," *Publishers Weekly,* September 1978, p.

"On a trip . . ." "Weill and Brecht: The Original Glimmer Twins," by TS, liner notes to *Lost in the Stars* (A&M Records,1985).

TS discarded three novels, Francis Wyndham's *London Life* profile, 1965, p.27.

According to a Deposition of May 3, 1969, Southern says he met Hoffenberg in '49–'50. Further Hoffenberg b.g. from Patti Dryden to LH, October 29, 1993, correspondence with Juliette Hoffenberg, *Literary Outlaw* by Ted Morgan (New York: Avon, 1988) and *The Olympia Reader* edited by Maurice Girodias (New York: Grove Press, 1965).

"Mason was a poet . . ." TS to LH, October 1993.

"I thought Terry was very witty . . ." Mordecai Richler to LH, December 1998.

Background on James Baldwin in *Artist on Fire* by W. J. Wetherby (New York: Donald I.Fine), 1989.

New-Story and *Janus* background from *The Continual Pilgrimage* by Christopher Sawyer-Laucanno. According to Sawyer-Laucanno, *Janus* published dreadful poetry.

"Those who know . . ." TS's reply to a questionnaire from the editors of *Contemporary Authors,* c. 1964. This motto also appears in Alexander Trocchi's *Cain's Book* and *Candy.*

"It was sort of an embarrassment . . ." TS to LH, March 1993.

TS's Dexamyl use verified by Carol and Nile Southern.

"It would be nice . . ." "A Sense of the Ridiculous," *Shoveling Trouble* by Mordecai Richler (Toronto: McClelland and Stewart, 1972), p. 28.

"Mason always tried to . . ." Patti Dryden to LH, October 29, 1993.

Meeting Aram Avakian, TS to LH, March 1993.

"I don't know how to . . ." TS to Robert Wilonsky, *Dallas Observer*, April 2, 1992.

TS and Allen Eager in Amsterdam, TS to Victor Bockris, November 1989.

TS's embellishment of brothel visits in his story "Trib to Von," *Evergreen Review* no. 98, 1984.

Various rejection slips found in Terry Southern archives.

"Doc" Humes's background, "Alen Cheuse on Doc Humes," *Rediscoveries II,* edited by David Madden and Peggy Bach (New York: Carroll and Graf, 1988), pp. 53–59 and Gay Talese's "Looking for Hemingway."

Peter Matthiessen on TS, letter to LH, March 12, 1997.

"I didn't have a lot to do . . ." Mordecai Richler to LH, December 2,1998.

TS "a silent inscrutable presence . . ." John Marquand Jr., *Paris Review,* 20th Anniversary issue, 1981.

"There's this policeman . . ." George Plimpton to LH, October 1993.

"Terry from the start . . ." Richard Seaver to LH, January 14, 1999.

Background on Pud Gadiot taken from interviews with CS and GG.

3 Flash and Filigree

Special thanks to Jeremy Treglown for sharing information from his forthcoming biography of Henry Green.

"Greenwich Village . . ." Fred and Gloria McDarrah. *Beat Generation: Glory Days in Greenwich Village* (New York: Schirmer Books/Simon and Schuster, 1996), p. II.

TS and Gadiot in the Village, CS to LH, May 4, 2000.

Background on Aram Avakian, *Movie People* edited by Fred Baker and Ross Firestone (New York: A Lancer Contempera Book, 1973).

"to con his soul . . ." John Marquand Jr., *Paris Review,* 20th Anniversary issue, 1981.

"Terry fancied himself . . ." David Amram to LH, June 16, 1998.

George Avakian to LH, April 16, 1997.

TS and company's McCarthy protest, TS to LH March 1993.

"[Toynbee's] piece about Henry Green . . ." TS to LH, March 1993. "The Novels of Henry Green" by Philip Toynbee, *Partisan Review,* XVI (May 1949), pp. 487-97.

Additional Green b.g. from "Trapped: The Story of Henry Green" produced by Roger Thompson and aired on BBC in 1992.

"The Double Life of Henry Green," *Life,* XXXIII (August 4, 1952), pp. 83–94.

Terry writes to Green, according to Jeremy Treglown, from New York.

"Since college days . . ." TS to LH, March 1993.

TS on *As I Lay Dying* in the *Nation,* April 23, 1960, p. 348.

Joseph Blotner's biography says William Faulkner was in and out of NY between September 1953 and February 1954.

"Everybody was dazzled . . ." Ellen Adler to LH, April 22, 1999.

"[Terry] was one of the few people . . ." Jean Stein to LH, October 24, 1993.

Art of Fiction Interview with William Faulkner, *Paris Review* no. 12, Spring 1956.

"David and I . . ." TS to LH, October 1993.

"At one point, he described [Gadiot] . . ." CS to LH, May 4, 2000.

"I actually went at one point . . ." TS to Victor Bockris, November 1989.

Amram and TS in Paris, David Amram to LH, June 16, 1998, and his memoir, *Vibrations,* p. 205.

Nelson Algren's Art of Fiction interview, *Writers at Work,* vol. 1, edited by George Plimpton (New York: Viking, New York, 1958).

Various rejection slips, Terry Southern archives.

Meeting Carol Southern, CS to LH, March 1993.

TS on Charlie Parker, "Terry Southern: The Last of the Catdaddy Hipsters" by Darius James, *New York Press Books and Publishing,* February 12–18, 1987, p. 11.

"We were barge captains," Mike Golden, "Now Dig This," *Reflex* no. 27, August 1992, pp. 22–23, p. 49, p. 80. Life on barge, CS to LH, March 1993.

4 Candy Christian Meets Guy Grand

Transatlantic crossing to Europe, CS to LH, May 4, 2000.

". . . not unlike a situation in a Kafka novel . . ." TS to LH, *Vox,* September 1990, p. 16.

Swiss garbage disposal incident, TS to Paul Krassner, *Realist,* 1965.

Candy outline, *Olympia Reader* edited by Maurice Girodias (New York: Ballantine Press edition, 1967) p. 361.

"Terry just adored him . . ." CS to LH, May 9, 1999.

Meetings with London literati, TS to LH, *Vox,* September 1990, p. 16.

"[Green] was a very urbane amusing . . ." CS to LH, May 9, 1999.

Correspondence re: Southern Sr.'s death including coroner's report. Terry Southern archives.

In various letters to TS through January and February 1957, Richler kept Southern posted of opportunities in London and progress of Southern's *Flash and Filigree* manscript as Andre Deustch considered publishing the book. Plans were also made for a reunion in France with Hoffenberg for spring or summer. January 17, 1957.

Andre Deutsch background, *Guardian* obituary, April 12, 2000, and Andre Deustch to LH, November 1993.

Letter from Mordecai Richer to TS, January 1957: keeping TS posted on Andre Deutsch decision about *Flash.* Richler was then living at 5 Winchester Road "no visitors after 2 pm."). Mentions work he and Stanley Mann recently did for TV for £100 each. In letters to TS dated February 15 and February 24, 1957, Richler wrote that Deutsch thought the book was excellent. Plans were discussed about a possible reunion in Tourettes Sur Loup. Correspondence in Terry Southern archives.

According to Jeremy Treglown, Green's biographer, Green arrived in Geneva, April 2, 1957 for a seven-day visit.

"I wired back . . ." TS to LH, March 1993.

Letter to TS from Green, April 21, 1957: Note at top: "Saw [Terrence?] Kilmartin, literary editor of the Sunday paper, Observer. Didn't half say your praises!" Correspondence from Terry Southern archives.

May 13, 1957, letter from Mordecai Richler to TS re: two TV scripts TS had forwarded to Richler, suggests plays were called *Grave* and *Panthers.*

Planning vacation in Spain, Henry Green to TS, April 29, 1957. Letter from Green to TS, June 4, 1957. Looking forward to TS coming to visit at the villa in July which Carol has encouraged. Twenty kilometers north of Barcelona. Mentions he has been offered a commission to write about the Blitz: "I got an idea that this will suit me very well as I can't seem to do novels any more. Also there is a lot of money in it, or appears to be sending a draft of a play to Terry under separate cover."

More observations on Spanish holiday found in *Girlitude* by Emma Tennant (London: Jonathan Cape, 1999).

Green on Art of Fiction interview, Henry Green to TS, September 23, 1957.

Art of Fiction Interview with Henry Green, *Paris Review* no. 19, Summer, pp. 60-77.

"I think the idea amused him . . ." CS to LH, May 4, 2000.

Rejection slips from *Harper's Bazaar* and other journals in Terry Southern archives.

Comments on "The Road out of Axotle," letter from Rust Hills to TS, November 21, 1957: "The ending of ['Axotle'], I think, the sort of postscript or epilogue, is what threw us off the most." Terry Southern archives.

"My idea of pure sloth . . ." November 57, letter from TS to Hoffenberg. Also talks about work on *The Magic Christian*.

"I already knew Kotcheff. . ." TS to LH, October 1993.

Background on *Armchair Theatre* and broadcast of *The Emperor Jones*: Ted Kotcheff to LH, December 17, 1998, correspondence from Kotcheff in Southern archives, *The Armchair Theatre: How to Write, Write, Direct, Design, Act and Enjoy Plays* (London: Weidenfeld and Nicholson, 1959), published to celebrate the first three seasons, and a pristine viewing copy of the broadcast in the British Film Institute archives.

Canadian Sidney Newman, who is credited for much of *The Armchair Theatre*'s success, actually didn't come on board until March 1958, when he took over from Vance, who wished to return to TV directing. Newman went on to green-light such shows as *The Avengers* at ABC and *Dr. Who* at the BBC.

Review of *Emperor Jones* broadcast, *Variety*, April 23, 1958.

On publishing Southern's first two novels, letters to LH from Diana Athill, July 5 and July 19, 1999.

Review of *Flash and Filigree* by Anthony Quinton in *London Magazine*, September 1958, vol. 5, no. 9, p. 65.

New Yorker's rejection of "Janus," Ben Yagoda's *About Town* by Ben Yagoda, (New York: Scribner, 2000) p. 275.

"We were staying in fourth-class hotels . . ." CS to LH, May 4, 2000.

" . . . I consider it an honor . . ." letter from Hoffenberg to TS, May 1, 1958. Hoffenberg signed off as "David Selznick."

"Titles it seems to me . . ." TS to LH, *Vox*, September 1990, p. 16.

Reservations about *On the Road*, letter from TS to Allen Ginsberg, September 20, 1958.

Problems with *Flash and Filigree*, Letter to TS from Allen Ginsberg, October 1, 1958.

"I think it's a first novel . . ." *Recent Novels* radio broadcast, BBC's Third Programme, June 20, 1958.

"Although I feel it is too short . . ." undated 1959 letter by Green to TS not long after *Magic Christian* publication

The other novels mentioned in Anthony Quinton's review of *The Magic Christian* were *Memento Mori* by Muriel Spark, *A Guest and His Going* by P. H. Newby, *Broadstrop Season* by Robert Kee, and *A Net for Venus* by David Garnett.

Correspondence from Coward-McCann and other publishers re: *Christian* in Terry Southern archives November 24, 1959 letter from J. Stewart Johnson,

Coward-McCann Inc., via Andre Deutsch complaining that *Magic Christian* is too short for U.S. publication. Joseph Fox at Random House acquired the book for U.S. publication. December 28, 1959—TS receives a rejection letter from a U.S. publisher regarding *Christian*: "Maybe America isn't up to satire and *Mad*-type humor in $3.50 form yet."

"While we were in Geneva . . ." CS to LH, May 4, 2000.

5 The Quality Lit Game

"She said' when you come back . . ." CS to LH, May 4, 2000.

"[Shaw] was looking for a house . . ." CS to LH, May 9, 1999.

"There was CIA and anti-CIA . . ." Barney Rosset to LH, January 14, 1999.

"The Quality Lit Game . . ." John Marquand Jr. to LH, March 1993.

"I always felt . . ." "Everybody was so young . . ." and "Boris had two friends . . ." all CS to LH, May 4, 2000.

Southerns at Edgewater, letter from Gore Vidal to LH, May 1993.

Possible Tom Ewell biography, letter to TS, March 18, 1959, from Peter Israel. Possible TV work, Letter to TS from Harold Franklin, June 18, 1959. Both from Terry Southern archives.

"[The Tynans] were marvelous . . ." CS to LH, May 4, 2000.

Review of *Flash and Filigree,* "Danse Macabre in Los Angeles," by Martin Levin, *New York Times Book Review,* September 28, 1958, p. 44.

Meeting Jack Gelber and Si Litvinoff, Jack Gelber to LH, January 1999 and Si Litvinoff to LH, January 28, 1998.

"Dark Laughter in the Towers," *Nation,* April 23, 1960, pp. 348–350.

"After the Bomb, Dad Came Up with Ice," Southern's review of *Cat's Cradle* by Kurt Vonnegut Jr., *New York Times Book Review,* June 2, 1963.

"Trocchi got a job . . ." Richard Seaver to LH, January 14, 1999.

Applying for Guggenheim grant, reference letter by Richard Seaver, December 5, 1961. Terry Southern archives.

"Parts of the story . . ." letter from Rust Hills to TS, March 14, 1962. Terry Southern archives.

"I thought I could get this guy . . ." and "He was wearing a dark blue suit . . ." David Newman to LH, December 16, 1995.

Background on "Road out of Axotle," CS to LH, May 4, 2000.

On TS's awareness of Kubrick, Jack Gelber to LH, January 1999. TS's unpublished interview with Kubrick for *Esquire.* Terry Southern archives.

TS "an Ariel-like figure," Jonathan Miller to LH, December 1993.

Kubrick telegram to TS, November 2, 1962. Terry Southern archives.

6 Dr. Strangelove (or How I Learned to Stop Worrying and Love Hollywood)

"Dark London winter mornings . . ." "Memories of Dr. Strangelove," *Movies*, July 1983, pp. 29–30.

"When Film Gets Good," the *Nation*, November 17, 1962, p. 330.

Idea for *Red Alert,* Peter George to Olga Franklin, the *Daily Mail*, February 1964.

"He was like many such people . . ." Christiane Kubrick to LH, July 7, 2000.

"After we finished *Lolita* . . ." and "Stanley told me he . . ." James Harris to LH, July 1, 1999.

Meeting and interviewing Stanley Kubrick, TS to LH, March 1993.

"Since we had absolutely no money . . ." CS to LH, March 1993.

"too weird to treat in an ordinary way . . ." TS to LH, March 1993.

Official period of production according to liner notes on Columbia's laser-disc release of *Dr. Strangelove*. A February 11, 1962, shooting script that includes revisions made January 25, indicating Terry was on the set longer than the official period. Terry Southern archives.

"We were together a great deal . . ." Christiane Kubrick to LH, July 7, 2000.

CS's observations of production, CS to LH, May 9, 1999.

Shift to black comedy, TS to LH, March 1993.

"He's got a weird metabolism," TS quoted in *Newsweek*, February 3, 1964.

Terry Southern to LH, March 1993.

"Terry would drink whiskey . . ." Christiane Kubrick to LH, July 7, 2000.

"We shared the vision," TS to LH, April 1990.

Origins of Dr. Strangelove character, TS to Victor Bockris, November 1989.

"The financing of the film . . ." TS to LH, March 1993.

"Sellers would get a distinct high . . ." Christiane Kubrick to LH, July 7, 2000.

"I don't know if . . ." CS to LH, May 9, 1999.

"After a few days, the studio . . ." Christiane Kubrick to LH, July 7, 2000.

"What was happening in the pie fight . . ." TS to LH, March 1993.

"I know that at least . . ." *Bull's Eyes: The Selected Memoirs of Peter Bull*, edited by Sheridan Morley (London: Robin Clark, 1985).

"Nile and I went to Italy . . ." CS to LH, April 1999.

"One night somebody brought . . ." TS to LH, March 1993.

"We would have dinner . . ." CS to LH, March 1993.

TS's *Queen* contributions: article on "The Theater," January 30 and review of John Fowles's *The Collector,* May 8, 1963, editions of *Queen*.

"At the time of the initial release . . ." TS to LH, March 1993.

Bosley Crowther review, "Dr. Strangelove: Kubrick Film Presents Sellers in 3 Roles," the *New York Times*, January 30, 1964.

"There was a lot of publicity . . ." CS to LH, March 1993.

Upset about TS's getting too much credit, letter by Peter George, *Life*, September 18, 1964, p. 32.

"Needless to say . . ." James Harris to LH, July 1999.

"There was gossip written . . ." Christiane Kubrick to LH, July 7, 2000.

"Stanley's obsession . . ." TS to LH, March 1993.

Stanley Kubrick to Diane Johnson on TS, *New York Review of Books*, April 22, 1999.

"Terry and Stanley were good friends . . ." Christiane Kubrick to LH, July 7, 2000.

"[Stanley] had the highest regard . . ." James Harris to LH, July 1, 1999.

Candy sales figures, *80 Years of Best-Sellers: 1895–1975* by Alice Payne Hackett and James Henry Burke (New York: R.R. Bowker Company, 1977), pp. 193–94.

"I think by now [*Strangelove*] is iconographic . . ." Norman Mailer to LH, July 2, 1999.

7 Making It Hot for Them

"I quit before the shooting began . . ." TS to LH, March 1993.

"It was very disruptive . . ." CS to LH, May 9, 1999.

"First, he invited me . . ." Gail Gerber to LH, April 1–6, 1997.

"We spoke . . ." and "During most of our marriage . . ." CS to LH, May 9, 1999.

"He was writing the script . . ." GG to LH, April 1–6, 1997

"[He] is another writer . . ." Peter Bart on *The Loved One*, *New York Times*, August 6, 1964.

Joyboy episode from *Loved One* script, July 21, 1964, pp. 91–92, TS archives.

"[Paddy] Chayefsky . . ." Martin Ransohoff, American Film Institute Seminar transcript March 19, 1975.

TS working with Norman Jewison, GG to LH, April 1–6, 1997.

"Artie Shaw thought Terry . . ." John Marquand Jr. to LH, March 11, 1993.

"A film about love . . ." TS to Alexander Walker, *Evening Standard*, July 1965.

"The only excuse for writing . . ." and "As for my 'outlook' . . ." TS to Maggie Paley from a 39-p. transcript c. 1965. Courtesy of Maggie Paley.

"I received a call from . . ." and "I was staying at the Dorchester . . ." TS to LH, October 1993.

"I think pop artists . . ." "A Creative Capacity to Astonish" by Jane Howard, *Life*, August 21, 1964.

"I'd never seen people . . ." GG to LH, April 1–6, 1997.

"I knew about Robert Fraser's gallery . . ." TS to LH, October 1993.

Michael Cooper's record player, TS in *Blinds and Shutters* (London: Genesis/Hedley, 1989).

"It was really a meeting place . . ." Sandy Lieberson to LH, November 16, 1993.

"He was just very open . . ." Anita Pallenberg to LH, December 9, 1993.

Cannes b.g. Gerard Malanga to LH, April 1999, and Kathleen Tynan to LH, January 1994.

Letter to TS from Godard's Anouchka Films re: *A Certain French Girl*, April 29, 1966. Terry Southern archives.

Candy film info. Southern to LH, October 1993. Southern's 136 pp. first draft can be found in the British Film Institute archives.

John De St. Jorres's *The Good Ship Venus* (London: Hutchinson, 1994) has an exhaustive account of the *Candy* legal mire.

A Clockwork Orange b.g. from LH interviews with Sandy Lieberson, November 16, 1993, TS, October 1993, and Ted Kotcheff December 17, 1999.

Don't Make Waves b.g., TS to LH, March 1993.

"I think the producer was . . ." Bruce Jay Friedman to LH, October 28, 1993.

"I started going to Elaine's . . ." David Newman to LH, December 16, 1995.

"Jack Richardson had a play . . ." Bruce Jay Friedman to LH, October 28, 1993.

"Edie Sedgwick would always . . ." TS to LH, October 1993.

"We were going from L.A. . . ." GG to LH, April 1-7, 1997.

"I think this is a golden age . . ." TS quoted in "No Limits," *Newsweek*, June 22, 1964.

"Terry created the enigmatic . . ." Arthur Kopit to LH, April 15, 1997.

Andy Warhol sits in on TV taping, Ted Kotcheff to LH, December 17, 1998.

"I had to go pick up Edie . . ." Lewis Allen to LH, January 15, 1999.

"'Frank Dell at the Palladium' . . ." Bruce Jay Friedman to LH, October 28, 1993.

Seeing father after long absence, Nile Southern to LH, March 23, 1993.

"I said I'm happy . . ." CS to LH, May 9, 1999.

8 An Easy Rider at the End of the Road

Barbarella background, Jean-Claude Forest obit, the *Guardian*, January 5, 1999. TS's draft, Interview, CS to LH, May 4, 2000. Charles Griffith discusses his *Barbarella* work in *Backstory 3: Interviews with Screenwriters of the 60s* (Berkeley: University of California Press, 1997).

"The strain was with Dino De Laurentiis," TS to LH, October 1993.

"The fact that Terry was writing . . ." Anita Pallenberg to LH, December 9, 1993.

"Ah by my troth . . ." TS quoted in *Faithfull* by Marianne Faithfull and David Dalton (New York: Little, Brown, 1994), pp. 128–129.

"Blood of a Wig" b.g., Paul Krassner to LH, July 1999.

"Terry was certainly doing more . . ." Peter Fonda in his memoir, *Don't Tell Dad* (New York: Hyperion, 1998) p. 245.

"The first notion was that . . ." TS to LH, October 1993.

This writer has seen two drafts of the script. One version can be found in the archives of the British Film Instiute. Another draft, which is remarkably similar and is covered in Southern's handwriting, is in the Terry Southern archives and was used as an exhibit in the lawsuit between Rip Torn and Dennis Hopper over the latter's comments on *The Tonight Show*. A suit which Hopper lost.

Dennis Hopper on Adamski, BBC2 documentary, "Born to Be Wild," broadcast on December 19, 1995. George Adamski's book *Inside the Spaceships* (a.k.a. *Inside the Flying Saucers*) was published in 1955 and became popular with UFO aficionados.

"I didn't know anything about Terry's screenplay . . ." Buck Henry in letter to LH, January 23, 1997.

Ringo's scenes in *Candy* were shot December 7–16 at Incom Film Studios. The 119-minute film was released on December 17, 1968, in New York and February 20, 1969 in London. Additional Candy information in *Brando* by Peter Manso (New York: Hyperion, 1994).

Richard Corliss on TS in *Talking Pictures* (New York: Penguin, 1975).

"When money came in . . ." Si Litvinoff to LH, January 28, 1998.

"I remember bursting into tears . . ." CS to LH, May 9, 1999. CS adds "Then Terry did the same thing over again [1993] but not on such a large scale and that's when the house was remortgaged. He couldn't get a mortgage so I got a mortgage for him. Then he died." Additional IRS background, Nile Southern E-mail to LH, May 26, 2000.

Easy Rider location trip described in Paul Lewis letter, *Dallas Observer*, March 4, 1999. Lewis says TS opted out of profit participation during the writing because he felt he didn't contribute enough to merit credit and that Fonda got those points.

Laszlo Kovacs on TS's script, quoted in my *Easy Rider* book. Kovac refers to TS's role in the BBC2 documentary as well as "Shaking the Cage," a documentary featured on the 1999 DVD release of *Easy Rider*.

"The idea of meeting a kind of a straight guy . . ." TS to LH, October 1993.

Fonda's "dumb-bell dialogue," Letter from TS to Peter Fonda, April 24, 1968, Terry Southern archives.

"Going there wasn't our idea . . ." TS to LH, March 1993.

Chicago Democratic Convention b.g. from *Genet* by Edmund White (New York: Alfred A. Knopf, 1993) and *It Wasn't Pretty, Folks, but Didn't We Have Fun?: Esquire in the Sixties* by Carol Polsgrove (New York: W.W Norton & Company, 1995).

"Burroughs on my right . . ." Allen Ginsberg in *Blinds and Shutters* (London: Genesis/Hedley, 1989).

"Groovin in Chi," by TS, *Esquire,* November 1968, pp. 83–86.

"During the writing of it . . ." Dorothy Tristan to LH, March 16, 1997.

Stacy Keach on *End of the Road, Actors Talk: Profiles and Stories from the Acting Trade* (New York: Proscenium Publishers, Inc., 1999), pp. 14–15.

"There was this seven-page rave . . ." Dorothy Tristan to LH, March 16, 1997.

"We tried to give . . ." TS to LH, October 1993.

John Cleese on *The Magic Christian, Life (Before and After) Monty Python* by Kim "Howard" Johnson (New York: St. Martin's Press, 1993), p. 42.

"I always remember John Cleese . . ." Joseph McGrath to LH, November 11, 1993.

The Magic Christian production dates from *The Complete Beatles Chronicle* by Mark Lewisohn (New York: Harmony Books, 1992), pp. 314–15. A letter from Joe McGrath to TS, January 23, 1969 confirms Southern's lodgings during the shoot.

"Working with Sellers . . ." TS to LH, October 1993.

"There's a sequence . . ." Joseph McGrath to LH, November 11, 1993.

A March 18, 1969, letter from Ted Ashley's Famous Agency re: plans for Terry and Joseph McGrath to do *The Last Days of Dutch Schultz* in spring 1970.

"My wife and I . . ." McGrath to LH, November 11, 1993.

On *Christian* cameos, GG to LH, April 1–6, 1997.

"So we all went on this fantastic crossing . . ." TS to LH, October 1993.

Blue Movie review by David Dempsey, *New York Times Book Review,* September 13, 1970.

Blue Movie review by Michael Wood, *New York Review of Books,* March 11, 1971, pp. 43–44.

"I remember I was told . . ." George Plimpton to LH, October 25, 1993.

"Terry made a tremendous amount . . ." CS to LH, May 9, 1999

"I am aware . . ." letter to Dennis Hopper from TS, December 5, 1970. Terry Southern archives.

9 From Green to Amber

"If a writer is sensitive . . ." TS in *Movie People* edited by Fred Baker with Ross Firestone (New Yorker: Lancer, 1973), pp. 95–96.

"Terry didn't know how to . . ." and "There was this embourgeoisement . . ." Ellen Adler to LH, April 22, 1999.

Background on *DJ,* Dick Fontaine to LH, December 1998. *Double Pisces* viewed at British Film Institute.

God Is Love outline, dated September 10, 1971. Terry Southern archives.

Background on Kubrick and Southern relationship: "Re: your note—of course I would like to work with you again—any ideas?" Letter from Kubrick to Southern, July 10, 1971.

"With each new film . . ." Christiane Kubrick to LH, July 7, 2000.

Dennis Hopper and TS outside Chelsea Hotel photographed by Fred McDarrah of the *Village Voice,* September 30, 1970.

Jay Cocks on *A Clockwork Orange, Time,* December 20, 1971, p. 53.

"We started to make . . ." NS to LH, March 22, 1993.

"I think Chuck Barris . . ." Grauerholz to LH, May 29, 1999.

"Nathanael West was one of my favorites . . ." Jerry Schatzberg to LH, April 23, 1999.

TS on Peter and Stones's 1972 Tour, TS to LH, March 1993.

"He really looked like a lunatic . . ." Josh Alan Friedman to LH, May 18, 1999.

Southern's boss at New York University was David Oppenheim, the dean of the School of Fine Arts. TS left the job in 1974 because he claimed it was taking too much time away from writing.

"We're getting into a golden age . . ." *Screw,* no. 86, October 26, 1970, reprinted in *Escapade* May/August, 1971, p. 82.

Background on "Foreplay," "How to Cast a Porno Film and Not Get Too Nervous," *Playboy,* December 1974, pp. 187–190, pp. 324–334.

Double Date script pages and outline c. 1973 found in Terry Southern archives.

"Have no concern about . . ." Letter to TS from Stanley Kubrick, August 29, 1973, in response to TS letter of July 14, 1973. Inquiry about *Blue Movie* points, September 17, 1973—TS to Kubrick.

Deposition in TS's suit against *Playboy* and Mason Hoffenberg was filed April 30, 1975. The suit was later dropped.

"As soon as I had this news . . ." TS to LH, October 1993.

"It is really too grotesquely . . ." Letter to Calley from TS, April 16, 1975. Terry Southern archives.

"I wish I were able to give you . . ." *Blue Movie* draft by Southern, c. winter 1975.

Blue Movie documentation: In a letter from Ringo to TS, June 7, 1974, mentions awaiting clearance from Kubrick on *Blue Movie* option. On June 19, 1974, Ringo's lawyer, Bruce V. Grakal, writes to TS confirming an advance of $1,000 for *Blue Movie* work. *Blue Movie,* the book and film, was jointly owned by TS and Kubrick (a 60/40 split). The book was optioned by Ringo between 1974 and 1977.

"[Calley] had the idea . . ." TS to LH, October 1993.

A December 23, 1974, contract in TS archives for *Hunters of Karin Hall* by (Nya Svenska Nordish Tonefilm), based on novel by Carl-Henning Wijkmark, to be directed by Ingmar Ejve. TS's fee was $10,000 payable in four installments and $5,000 payable on the second draft. He was also given 2.5 percent of the net.

Hunters of Karin Hall c. 1975, excerpt, courtesy of Terry Southern estate.

"Actually I was in the middle of . . ." David Newman to LH, December 18, 1995.

"*A Piece of Bloody Cake* was . . ." Ted Kotcheff to LH, December 17, 1998.

Kubrick on *Bloody Cake,* handwritten note to TS, August 2, 1974.

Visit to Nicolas Roeg set, NS to LH, March 23, 1993.

TS running off with car, David Cammell to LH, January 1994.

10   Junky

"Good writers have . . ." "Drugs and the Writer," Unpublished, mid-seventies, Terry Southern archives.

"With reference to the pornographic library . . ." FBI memorandum, New Haven, February 26, 1965, Terry Southern archives.

"It was kind of vague . . ." Gerard Malanga to LH, April 20, 1999.

Dennis Hopper's arrival from *Apocalypse Now* set, James Grauerholz to LH, May 29, 1999.

"Stern was trained . . ." TS to LH, March 1993.

"Étonnez-moi" joking, tape recording, c. 1977, Terry Southern archives.

"I remember one time . . ." James Grauerholz to LH, May 29, 1999.

"I think that Burroughs . . ." Victor Bockris to LH, October 1993.

Notes by Grauerholz on *Junky* meetings, William Burroughs archives: April 29, 1977, meeting at Gramercy Park Hotel, Hopper, Southern, Burroughs, Joe Bianco, and assistants in attendance. April 30, 1977, meeting—Grauerholz meets with TS, then Hopper and Mimi, Joe Bianco meets with Grauerholz, Hopper, Mimi, and Southern. Bianco at this stage confirmed that West German financing through Paul Hoffman, Johnny Brasha, and Rita Jennings, of Abracadabra had collapsed.

Grauerholz notes describing an 11:00 A.M. phone call by Stern to Burroughs.

The May 10, 1977, meeting is described by Grauerholz in a letter to Peter Matson, Burroughs's agent, dated May 15, 1977. Gathering at Hopper's apartment, where TS and GG, Mimi, Hopper's secretary, and "one Michael Green" are present.

"I have never known . . ." memo to Grauerholz and Burroughs, dated May 11, 1977, from Joe Bianco.

May 11, 1977, a memo from Jacques Stern re: *Creation of Adam,* an idea of Stern's, which appears to have overlapped with *Junky* and created confusion as to what film they were making.

Background on James Jones's funeral, Ellen Adler to LH, April 22, 1999.

Junky first draft by TS, May 25, 1977, Terry Southern archives.

May 29, 1977, Grauerholz notes: Terry and Hopper met with François de Menil and passed on copies of *Junky* with the hope that de Menil would cover costs of development such as securing Paul Lewis's partcipation. Grauerholz phone conversation with TS suggests that "wildcat independent" financing be found utilizing various contacts or approaching est. producers. Lewis Allen, a friend of Terry's, is mentioned.

"It turns out that . . ." TS to LH, March 1993.

"The whole thing was really a . . ." James Grauerholz to LH, May 29, 1999.

Hopper, TS, and *Junky* mentioned in *Time*, p. 44, June 20, 1977.

"The first scene of [Southern's draft] . . ." TS to LH, March 1993.

Excerpt from *The Donkey and the Darling*, 1968–1977, courtesy of Terry Southern Estate.

Junky in limbo, background from: Grauerholz meeting notes, June 25, 1977: Joe Bianco asks Julian Neal to take over exec. producer role. Burroughs was in Paris for most of June. Option on *Junky* was expiring, but terms of renewal did not mean Burroughs was entitled to more money [a request for $5,000]. Hopper out of project by this stage. Grauerholz notes, June 29, 1977: As attempts to salvage the mess of *Junky* continued, mainly on Grauerholz part, he jotted down names of directors: Scorsese, Spielberg, Nick Roeg, Sydney Pollack, Terry Malick, John Milius, John Schlesinger, and Milos Forman. Joe Bianco was eager to keep project together. Hopper was considering waiving directorial role for $5,000 a month for four months. Letter from Grauerholz to Rudy Wurlitzer, August 4, 1977, states option on *Junky* would expire March 1978. Grauerholz mentions that he has written his own draft.

"What it *means* Bill . . ." letter from Grauerholz to Burroughs in Boulder, Colorado, August 10, 1977.

Grauerholz notes: August 23, 1977. Joe Bianco approching Eisner at Paramount, who is also considering *Fear and Loathing*. September 2, 1977, Grauerholz writes to Hopper and forwards a copy of *Bill Lee* to him. Explains Southern is now out of project. By 1979–80, the project was dead despite Grauerholz's efforts including a feeler to Wim Wenders via his producing partner, Chris Sievernich.

"You've got this prostitution factor . . ." James Grauerholz to LH, May 29, 1999.

With Extreme Prejudice (February 5, 1978) with Ugo Pirro financed by Artiofilm, c/o Gee and Durbridge, 81 Piccadilly, London SW1. Set against the backdrop of the Aldo Moro kidnapping and the political strife of Italy in the seventies.

June 4, 1978, date of screen outline of *Most Dangerous Game* based on the short story by Hamilton Graves. Terry Southern archives.

Extract from "Haven Can Wait" by TS with Joe Loguidice and others, Terry Southern archives, courtesy of Terry Southern Estate.

Not the New York Times parody reported in Time, October 23, 1978, p. 44.

11 Grossing Out

Excerpt from *Grossing Out* draft, c. 1979–80. Terry Southern archives, courtesy of Terry Southern Estate.

"He wrote that with Brendan Gill . . ." Lewis Allen to LH, January 22, 1999.

"I remember attending . . ." NS to LH, March 23, 1993.

Contract by Twentieth Century-Fox drawn up for Terry to adapt novel *Aria* by Brown Meggs mentions total fee of $85,000 with a $30,000 advance. Terry Southern archives.

"What killed [*Aria*] . . ." Si Litvinoff to LH, January 28, 1998.

"[*Aria* dealt with this] . . ." Ted Kotcheff to LH, December 17, 1998.

Ron Rosenbaum on "Heavy Put Away," from his column, "The Edgy Enthusiast," *New York Observer*, December 18, 1995.

"The Angel of Talent . . ." Michael O'Donoghue quoted in *Saturday Night: A Backstage History of Saturday Night Live* by Doug Hill and Jeff Weingrad (New York: Beech Tree Books/William Morrow, 1986), p. 448.

TS's *SNL* salary, memo from NBC to TS. Terry Southern archives.

"What would happen on . . ." Nelson Lyon to LH, May 1999.

"I remember one of Terry's . . ." Hal Wilner to LH, March 1993.

"Talk about your everlovin' cornucopias . . ." Hill and Weingrad, p. 450.

"His office was like . . ." Nelson Lyon to LH, May 1999.

According to O'Donoghue, he was fired by Dick Ebersol via the former's manager, Barry Secunda, on January 17, 1982, Hill and Weingrad, p. 457.

"[The sketch] just went on . . ." Nelson Lyon to LH, May 1999.

"It was hard to get people . . ." Michael O'Donoghue to LH, March 1993.

"[Working on *SNL*] was . . ." TS to LH, April 1990.

12 Various Cowriters

"Terry brought in Brendan Gill . . ." Nelson Lyon to LH, 1999: "I thought of this as a fucking Broadway show. Lewis Allen was involved and Lewis Allen took it to his agent. At that time they were making *The Cotton Club* and there was this huge agent at ICM, monstro agent, but they couldn't do it because of the fucking *Cotton Club*." *Johnny Blood* was registered with the Writers Guild of America on August 27, 1982.

"It's a cruel world . . ." *The End of the Game* screenplay by Peter Beard and Terry Southern, c. 1982, Terry Southern archives.

"I had a deal to pick up . . ." James Harris to LH, July 1, 1999.

"Larry wanted to get . . ." Joe Loguidice to LH, June 21, 2000.

Excerpt from *At Z Beach* handwritten dialogue, c. 1982–83, Terry Southern archives courtesy of Terry Southern Estate.

"*At Z Beach* was a misconceived project . . ." NS to LH, March 19, 2000.

"I never knew Terry not . . ." Joe Loguidice to LH, June 21, 1999.

"By this time, Terry . . ." Nelson Lyon to LH, May 1999.

NS on TS's pages for early version of *Eyes Wide Shut, Denver Post,* July 11, 1999. Three pages of dialogue exist in Terry Southern archives.

"Of course, that took him a . . ." Josh Alan Friedman to LH, May 18, 1999.

Larry Flynt and Doors project, "Larry Flynt at Home," oral history with Dennis Hopper and TS, edited by Jean Stein, *Grand Street* no. 36, Spring 1990.

July 2, 1984, letter from Putnam's lawyer, Barry Preiss, to TS asking for return of $20,000 advance re: *Texas Summer* (then known as *South Idyll*), Terry Southern archives.

"I was just trying to help Terry . . ." Sandy Lieberson to LH, November 16, 1993.

"Albie said . . ." Nelson Lyon to LH, May 1999.

"Mason was in a very bad way . . ." Mordecai Richler to LH, December 2, 1998.

Additional Mason Hoffenberg background provided by Juliette Hoffenberg to LH, May 2000.

"One day we went to see . . ." Anita Pallenberg to LH, December 9, 1993.

"If you're talking about . . ." Patti Dryden to LH, October 29, 1993.

"The Refreshing Ambiguity of the Déjà Vu," by TS and Mason Hoffenberg in 1985, was finally published in *Grand Street*, Fall 1992.

13 Hawkeye (Travels with Harry)

"All you have is the power of persuasion . . ." repeated by TS in various interviews including my first conversation with TS in April 1990.

When Hawkeye's formation was announced, the executive lineup included: James Hock as president, Nilsson as executive vice president, Richard Riccio as vice president of music development and marketing. Hawkeye offices were located at 1130 Ventura Boulevard, Studio CI130 Ventura Boulevard, Studio City, California 91604.

Harry Nilsson background taken from Nilsson Web site Jadebox, liner notes to *Personal Best: The Harry Nilsson Anthology* (US, BMG/RCA, 1995), and obituaries from the London *Times* and *Independent*.

"He was embarrassed . . ." and "Harry wanted to party . . ." GG to LH, April 1997.

Anonymous reader's report on *Obits,* c. 1986, posted on Harry Nilsson Web site, Jadebox.

January 21, 1986, letter of intent from Whoopi Goldberg re: *Telephone*. Terry Southern archives.

TS's agent for *The Telephone* was CAA's Rowland Perkins. TS's fee for the film was $350,000. For the ten-page treatment he was paid $10,000. Contract in Terry Southern archives.

"One of the producers . . ." NS to LH, March 23, 1993.

"I don't know to this day . . ." GG to LH, April 1997.

"I was then managing . . ." Si Litvinoff to LH, January 28, 1998.

"Personally I thought the company . . ." and "My dad . . ." NS to LH, January 1994.

"Oona said, "The worst . . ." and "Cindy Sims was supposed to be . . ." GG to LH, April 1997.

Mike Golden visits TS in hospital, Golden to LH, January 1999.

"Terry was a constant source of inspiration . . ." and other Perry Richardson quotes for this chapter, Richardson to LH, April 1999. Readers may be interested to know that *Blinds and Shutters* is in the British Library.

"Terry came at his own expense . . ." James Grauerholz to LH, May 29, 1999.

14 Texas Summer

Victor Bockris made a copy of the full transcript of his November 1989 interview available to the author.

"He described his wife . . ." and other details of 1989 interview, Victor Bockris to LH, October 23, 1993.

TS closest thing America had to Jonathan Swift, Jean Stein to LH, October 1993. Allowance from Stein confirmed by GG and NS.

December 4, 1990 Little, Brown contract for *Texas Summer* cites an advance of $7,500. Terry Southern archives.

"I used to leave it out for him . . ." NS to LH, March 23, 1993.

Green Mountain Boys draft by TS and James Goldstone completed February 25, 1991. According to GG, TS wrote the script on spec.

Invitation to teach at Columbia, letter to TS from Annette Insdorf, November 5, 1990. Southern archives.

"It seemed unlikely . . ." "Give Back" by John Emile, unpublished memoir on TS's Columbia screenwriting class, c. 1995.

"He crossed out *bazookas* . . ." "Remembrance" by Caroline Marshall, *Paris Review* no. 138, Spring 1996, p. 239.

TS losing cool with student, "Adventures of an Ultra-Fab Prof" by Charles Zigman, posted on terrysouthern.com, 1999.

"Terry found out . . ." Joe McGrath to LH, October 10, 1998.

Excerpt from *Festival* draft, c. 1992, Terry Southern archives, courtesy of Terry Southern Estate.

June 3, 1992, fax from Hopper asking TS to relinquish any claim to *Easy Rider*. According to Darius James's article (*New York Press,* February 18, 1997), Fonda offered TS $30,000 to relinquish credit on *Easy Rider*.

Review of *Texas Summer* by Brad Tyer, *New York Times Book Review,* February 16, 1992, p. 18.

"I think *Texas Summer* . . ." Richard Seaver to LH, January 14, 1999.

TS phoning Jerry Brown's campaign office, Robert Wilonsky, "Beyond the Myth, Beneath the Haze: Digging into Terry Southern's Buried Texas Roots," *Dallas Observer*, April 2, 1992.

The Brightest and the Best, c. 1990. Terry Southern archives.

"If he had in the four days . . ." Josh Alan Friedman to LH, May 18, 1999.

"It was like the impossible record . . ." Nelson Lyon to LH, May 1999.

"On the basis of the pages now . . ." letter from Fredrica S. Friedman, Little, Brown VP, executive editor and associate publisher, to TS, September 3, 1993.

Dennis Hopper on *Tonight Show*, quoted in "Whose Movie Is This?" by Mark Singer, *New Yorker*, June 22 and 29, 1998, pp. 117–18.

Stein's fallout with TS, GG to LH, April 1997.

Mick Jagger at TS's birthday party, Darius James to LH, June 2000.

"Terry was so precise with language . . ." Perry Richardson to LH, April 1999.

"Well, the work I like . . ." TS quoted in "The Hot Day Terry Southern, Cool and Fatalistic, Strode In," by Jeff McGregor, the *New York Times*, November 12, 1995, p. 24.

Details of TS's last days, GG to LH, April 1997, and "Envoi" by Nile Southern, *Paris Review*, Spring 1996, p. 241.

"He invented his own idiom . . ." Buck Henry quoted in the *New York Times*, November 12, 1995, p. 24.

Bibliography

The following is a list in order of publication of Terry Southern's output, including most recent editions:

Flash and Filigree. London: Andre Deutsch, 1958. Reissued in 1996 by Grove Press and Bloomsbury in 1997.

The Magic Christian. London: Andre Deustch, 1959. Reissued in 1996 by Grove Press and Bloomsbury in 1997.

Candy with Mason Hoffenberg. Paris: Olympia Press, 1958 (a.k.a. *Lollipop)* under psuedonym Maxwell Kenton. First published in the U.S. by Putnam in 1964. Reissued in 1996 by Grove Press and Bloomsbury in 1997.

Writers in Revolt, edited with Richard Seaver and Alexander Trocchi. New York: Frederick Fell, 1962. Currently out of print.

The Log Book of The Loved One. Photographs by William Claxton. New York: Random House, 1965. Currently out of print.

Red Dirt Marijuana and Other Tastes. New York: New World Publishing, 1967. Reissued in 1996 by Grove Press and Bloomsbury in 1997.

Blue Movie. New York: New World Publishing, 1970. Reissued in 1996 by Grove Press and Bloomsbury in 1997.

The Rolling Stones on Tour: A Log Book. Photographs by Annie Leibowitz. Paris/London: Dragon's Dream, 1978. Out of print.

Texas Summer. New York: Arcade/Little, Brown & Co., 1992. Out of print.

The Early Stones: Legendary Photographs of a Band in the Making 1963-1973, with Perry Richardson. Photographs by Michael Cooper. New York: A Publishing Company/ Hyperion, 1992.

Virgin with Perry Richardson. London: A Publishing Company, 1995.

Now Dig This!: The Quality Lit of Terry Southern, edited by Nile Southern and Josh Alan Friedman. Forthcoming from Grove Press and Bloomsbury in 2001.

The following selected list indicates published materials which also provided information on Southern's work, life, and times:

Amram, David. *Vibrations: The Adventures and Musical Times of David Amram.* New York: Macmillan Co., 1968.

The Armchair Theatre: How to Write, Write, Direct, Design, Act and Enjoy Plays. London: Weidenfeld and Nicholson, 1959.

Baker, Fred, and Ross Firestone, eds. *Movie People: At Work in the Business of Film.* New York: A Lancer Contempora Book, 1973.

Baxter, John. *Stanley Kubrick: A Biography.* London: HarperCollins, 1997.

Biskind, Peter. *Easy Riders, Raging Bulls: How the Sex-Drugs-and-Rock-n'roll Generation Saved Hollywood.* New York: Simon and Schuster, 1998.

Blotner, Joseph. *Faulkner: A Biography.* New York: Random House, revised edition, 1984.

Bockris, Victor. *On Wiiliam Burroughs.* New York: Richard Seaver Books, 1991.

———. *Keith Richards: The Biography.* New York: Hyperion, 1992.

———. Original sixty-page interview transcript with Terry Southern for *Interview* magazine. East Canaan, Connecticut: November 1989. Courtesy of Victor Bockris.

Bowermaster, Jon. *The Adventures and Misadventures of Peter Beard in Africa.* New York: Bulfinch Press/Little, Brown & Co., 1993.

Brookner, Howard, director. *Burroughs.* 1985 feature length documentary on William Burroughs featuring Terry Southern and others. 90 min. Available from Mystic Fire video.

Burroughs, William. *Junky.* Introduction by Allen Ginsberg. New York: Penguin Books, 1977 edition.

———. *Naked Lunch.* New York: Grove Press, 1964 edition.

Campbell, James. *Paris Interzone: Richard Wright, Lolita, Boris Vian and Others on the Left Bank, 1946–1960.* London: Secker and Warburg, 1994.

———. *This Is the Beat Generation: New York—San Francisco—Paris.* London: Secker and Warburg, 1999.

Carroll, Jim. *The Downtown Diaries: 1971–1973.* New York: Penguin, 1987.

Ciment, Michel. *Kubrick.* Translated by Gilbert Adair. New York: Holt, Rinehart and Winston, 1982.

Connolly, Ray. *Stardust Memories: Talking About My Generation.* London: Pavilion Books/Michael Joseph Ltd., 1983.

Cooper, Michael. *Blinds and Shutters.* England: Genesis/Hedley, limited edition, 1989.

Corliss, Richard. *Talking Pictures: Screenwriters in the American Cinema.* New York: Penguin, 1975.

Drew, Bettina. *Nelson Algren: A Life on the Wild Side.* New York: G.P. Putnam and Sons, 1989.

Faithfull, Marianne, with David Dalton. *Faithfull: An Autobiography.* New York: Little, Brown & Co., 1994.

Fonda, Peter. *Don't Tell Dad: A Memoir.* New York: Hyperion, 1998.

Gelber, Jack. *The Connection: A Play.* New York: Grove Press, 1960.

Gitlin, Todd. *The Sixties: Years of Hope, Days of Rage.* New York: Bantam, Revised edition, 1993.

Gooch, Brad. *City Poet: The Life and Times of Frank O'Hara.* New York: Alfred A. Knopf, 1993.

Gold, Herbert. Review of *Candy*, the *Nation*, May 18, 1964.

Golden, Mike. "Now Dig This: Interview With Terry Southern," *Reflex* magazine, September 1992.

Goldman, Albert, with Lawrence Schiller. *Ladies and Gentleman, Lenny Bruce.* New York: Random House, 1974.

Green, Henry. *Surviving: The Uncollected Writing of Henry Green,* ed. Mathew Yorke. New York: Viking, 1992.

Green, Jonathan. *Days in the Life: Voices from the English Underground 1961–1971.* London: William Heinemann, Ltd., 1988.

Greenfield, Robert. *STP: A Journey Through America with the Rolling Stones.* New York: Saturday Review Press/E. P. Dutton, 1974.

Gruen, John. *The Party's Over.* New York: Viking, 1972.

Hamilton, Ian. *Writers in Hollywood: 1915–1951.* New York: Harper and Row, 1990.

———. Review of *Candy, Punch,* September 18, 1964.

Harris, Oliver, editor, *The Letters of William Burroughs: 1945–1959.* New York: Viking. 1993.

Hayes, Harold, ed. *Smiling Through the Apocalypse: Esquire's History of the Sixties.* New York: Esquire Press/Crown Publishing, 1987.

Hendra, Tony. *Going Too Far: The Rise and Demise of Sick, Gross, Black, Sophomoric, Weirdo, Pinko, Anarchist, Underground, Anti-Establishment Humor.* New York: Dolphin/ Doubleday, 1987.

Henke, James, with Parke Puterbaugh, eds. *I Want to Take You Higher: The Psychedelic Era 1965–1969.* With essays by Charles Perry and Barry Miles. San Francisco: Chronicle Books, 1997.

Herr, Michael. *Kubrick.* New York: Grove Press, 2000.

Hill, Doug, and Jeff Weingrad. *Saturday Night: A Backstage History of Saturday Night Live.* New York: Birch Tree Books/William Morrow, 1986.

Hill, Lee. *Easy Rider: A BFI Modern Classic.* London: BFI Publishing, 1996.

———. "The Vox Interview with Terry Southern," *Vox* magazine, September 1990.

Howard, James. *Stanley Kubrick Companion*. London: B. T. Batsford Ltd., 1999.

Howard, Jane. "A Creative Capacity to Astonish." *Life*, August 21, 1964.

Jones, Nick, director/producer. *Born to Be Wild: The Making of Easy Rider*. Half-hour documentary, BBC 2. First broadcast, December 19, 1995.

Kemp, Philip. *Lethal Innocence: The Films of Alexander Mackendrick*. London: Methuen, 1991.

Krassner, Paul. *Impolite Interviews*. New York: Seven Stories Press, 1999.

Lewisohn, Mark. *The Complete Beatles Chronicle*. New York: Harmony Books, 1992.

Lobrutto, Vincent. *Stanley Kubrick: A Biography*. New York: Donald I. Fine, 1997.

MacDonald, Ian. *Revolution in the Head: The Beatles' Records & the Sixties*. London: Fourth Estate, 1994. Fully updated edition, 1997.

Manso, Peter. *Brando: A Biography*. New York: Hyperion, 1994.

Marwick, Arthur. *The Sixties: Cultural Revolution in Britain, France, Italy and The United States, c. 1958–1974*. Oxford: Oxford University Press, 1998.

McDarrah, Fred W., and Gloria S. McDarrah. *Beat Generation: Glory Days in Greenwich Village*. New York: Schirmer Books/ Simon and Schuster, 1996.

McGilligan, Patrick. *Jack's Life: A Biography of Jack Nicholson*. New York: W. W. Norton & Company 1994.

McGilligan, Patrick. *Backstory 3: Interviews with Screenwriters of the Sixties*. Berkeley and Los Angeles: University of California Press, 1997.

Merrill, Sam. "Mason Hoffenberg Gets a Few Licks," *Playboy*, November 1973.

Miles, Barry. *The Beat Hotel*. New York: Grove Press, 2000.

Miles, Barry. *Ginsberg*. New York: Viking, 1990.

———. *William Burroughs: El Hombre Invisible*. London: Virgin Books, 1992.

Mitford, Jessica. "Something to Offend Everyone," *Show*, December 1964.

Morgan, Ted. *Literary Outlaw: The Life and Times of William S. Burroughs*. New York: Henry Holt and Company 1988.

Morris, Willie. *New York Days*. New York: Little, Brown and Co., 1993.

Neaverson, Bob. *The Beatles Movies*. London: Cassell, 1997.

Nelson, Thomas Allen. *Kubrick: Inside a Film Artist's Maze*. Bloomington, Indiana: Indiana University Press, 2000.

Norman, Philip. *The Stones*. London: Hamish Hamilton, 1984. Revised edition, 1993.

Obst, Lynda Rosen, editor. *The Sixties: The Decade Remembered Now, by the People Who Lived It Then*. New York: A Rolling Stone Press/Random House Book, 1977.

Perrin, Dennis. *Mr. Mike: The Life and Work of Michael O'Donoghue*. New York: Avon Books, 1998.

Polsgrove, Carol. *It Wasn't Pretty, Folks, but Didn't We Have Fun?: Esquire in the Sixties.* New York: W. W. Norton & Company, 1995.

Raphael, Frederic. *Eyes Wide Open: A Memoir of Stanley Kubrick.* New York: Ballantine, 1999.

Rodriguez, Elena. *Dennis Hopper: A Madness to His Method.* New York: St. Martin's Press, 1988.

Paley, Maggie. Unpublished twenty-page interview with Terry Southern on screenwriting, New York, 1966. Courtesy of Maggie Paley.

Plimpton, George, editor. *The Paris Review Anthology.* New York: W. W. Norton & Company, 1990.

———. series editor. *The Paris Review Interviews,* volumes 1–8. New York: Penguin.

Richardson, Tony. *Long Distance Runner: A Memoir.* New York: William Morrow, 1993.

Rivers, Larry, with Arnold Weinstein. *What Did I Do?: An Autobiography.* New York: Harper Collins Perennial, 1992.

Robins, Natalie. *Alien Ink: The FBI's War on Freedom of Expression.* New York: William Morrow, 1992.

De St. Jorres, John. *The Good Ship Venus: The Erotic Voyage of the Olympia Press.* London: Hutchinson, 1994.

Sanchez, Tony. *Up and Down with the Rolling Stones.* New York: William Morrow, 1979.

Sargeant, Jack. *Naked Lens: An Illustrated History of Beat Cinema.* London: Creation Books, 1997.

Sawyer-Laucanno, Christopher. *The Continual Pilgrimage: American Writers in Paris, 1944–1960.* New York: Grove Press, 1992.

Scott, Andrew Murray. *Alexander Trocchi: The Making of the Monster.* Edinburgh: Polygon, 1991.

———. *Insurrection of a Million Minds: A Trocchi Reader.* Edinburgh: Polygon, 1991.

Singer, Mark. "Who Wrote This Movie?", the *New Yorker,* June 22 & 29, 1998.

Stein, Jean. edited with George Plimpton. *Edie.* New York: Alfred A. Knopf, 1982.

Sterrit, David. *Mad to Be Saved: The Beats, the 50s and Film.* Carbondale and Edwardsville, Illinois: Southern Illinois University Press, 1998.

Talese, Gay. "Looking for Hemingway," *Esquire,* July 1962.

Trow, George W. S. *Within the Context of No Context.* Boston: Little, Brown & Co., 1981.

Tennant, Emma. *Girlitude: A Portrait of the 50s and 60s.* London: Jonathan Cape, 1999.

Tynan, Kathleen. *Kenneth Tynan: A Life*. New York: William Morrow, 1987.

———. editor. *Kenneth Tynan: Letters*. London: Weidenfeld and Nicholson, 1994.

Wakefield, Dan. *New York in the 50s*. New York: St. Martin's Press, 1992.

White, Ray Lewis. *Index to Best American Short Stories and O. Henry Prize Stories*. Boston: G. K. Hall and Co., 1988.

Wilonsky, Robert. "Beyond the Myth, Beneath the Haze," the *Dallas Observer*, April 2, 1992, pp. 12–14, 16–17.

Woodward, Bob. *Wired: The Short and Fast Times of John Belushi*. New York: Simon and Schuster, 1984.

Vyner, Harriet. *Groovy Bob: The Life and Times of Robert Fraser*. London: Faber and Faber, 1999.

White, Edmund. *Genet: A Biography*. New York: Alfred A. Knopf, 1993.

Wilmut, Roger. *From Fringe to Flying Circus: Celebrating a Unique Generation of Comedy 1960–1980*. London: Methuen, 1980.

Wolfe, Tom, and A. W. Johnson, editors. *New Journalism*. London: Picador, 1973.

Yagoda, Ben. *About Town: The New Yorker and the World It Made*. New York: Scribner, 2000.

Index

About the Author

Lee Hill has written about film, literature, music, and popular culture for the *Guardian, Scenario,* and *Neon, Cameo, Vox,* and other U.S., Canadian, and English publications. He is also the author of *Easy Rider,* a part of the British Film Institute's ongoing Modern Classic Series. This biography grew out of a series of conversations and interviews with Terry Southern that began in 1990 and lasted until the writer's death in 1995.